1 477062

INLAND WATERWAYS OF
FRANCE

Paris. River Seine

INLAND WATERWAYS

OF

FRANCE

Written and Compiled by

E. E. BENEST

IMRAY LAURIE NORIE AND WILSON LTD

SAINT IVES HUNTINGDON

1971

Published by

IMRAY, LAURIE, NORIE AND WILSON LTD

WYCH HOUSE, ST IVES, HUNTINGDON

©

IMRAY, LAURIE, NORIE AND WILSON LTD

1971

While every care has been taken to ensure accuracy, neither the Publishers nor the Author will hold themselves responsible for errors, omissions or alterations in this publication. They will at all times be grateful to receive information which tends to the improvement of the work.

1st Edition   1956
2nd   ,,   1963
3rd   ,,   1971

I.S.B.N. 0 85288   006   5

Printed in Great Britain by
W. Heffer & Sons Ltd, Cambridge, England

'Heureux qui, comme Ulysse, a
'fait un beau voyage
'Et puis est retourné, plein
'd'usage et raison

JOACHIM DU BELLAY
(1522-1560)

FOREWORD

BY HIS EXCELLENCY MONSIEUR GEOFFROY DE COURCEL, G.C.V.O., M.C.

AMBASSADOR EXTRAORDINARY AND PLENIPOTENTIARY AT THE COURT OF ST JAMES

Cruising on canals in England has always been a popular pastime, so the extension of that interest to the canals of France is a perfectly logical step.

Every year many thousands of British visitors enjoy the pleasures of sailing their boats along the canals of France and it is especially apt that this guide to the Inland Waterways should be published.

France has over 10,000 miles of navigable waterways that run through the countryside across from the Alps to the warmth of the Mediterranean, from the green fields of Normandy to the vineyards of Bordeaux and Burgundy. Here too is the true France far away from the bustling cities or crowded roads, where there is a relaxed atmosphere and many pleasant country inns to be enjoyed.

AMBASSADE DE FRANCE
LONDRES
November 1969

CONTENTS

CONTENTS

APPENDIX

*A general map of the navigable waterways
will be found at the end of the book.*

PLATES

ACKNOWLEDGEMENTS

Certain information in Part II of this work has been taken from the official French publication *Guide de la Navigation Intérieure* with the kind permission of the publishers, Messrs. Berger-Levrault, Paris.

Plates are reproduced from photographs kindly loaned by the French Government Tourist Office.

PART I

OFFICIAL FORMALITIES FOR ENTERING THE INLAND WATERWAYS

GENERAL

It is a curious circumstance that the Inland Waterways of France are not more used by British yacht owners. It would hardly be wrong to state that the average yachtsman thinks only of them as a way of taking a pleasure vessel to the South of France thus finding a short and sheltered passage to la Côte d'Azur. That an entire holiday, indeed many holidays, could be spent touring the French inland waterways has never entered his head. This is remarkable and also regrettable, as possibly it is fair to say that no other country in Western Europe provides so large a choice of routes each of which affords a wide variety of magnificent scenery. The owner of a shallow draught power vessel—especially now that a comparatively large cruiser can be towed along the roads on a trailer—could explore the rivers and canals of France for many years and always continue to find something new to see or some interesting custom to investigate.

Having complied with the Immigration and Customs requirements for entering French territorial waters the yachtsman, whether under sail or power, is then at liberty to enjoy the small harbours and creeks of a delightful littoral. But it is perhaps not so generally known that this freedom also extends to the waters of the rivers which run inland from the coast. No further papers or formalities are necessary in order to run upstream from their mouths to the point where the navigation is considered to be no longer 'marine'. A good example of this is La Garonne which is adjudged to be a marine navigation from la Pointe-de-Grave, where it enters the sea, as far up as Bordeaux—a distance of about 100 kilometres. Again, La Seine from Le Havre to Rouen—a distance which is even greater being about 120 kilometres—is classed as la Seine-Maritime.

But before any vessel is allowed to enter the canalized rivers or the canals of France there are, officially, two documents which must be produced on demand. It must be remembered that the French inland waterways carry quite a considerable proportion of the national internal tonnage of transported goods. Unlike the British inland waterways which have been systematically neglected since the dawn of the Railway Age, the French Government has, through good times and bad, steadily spent money improving and renovating the very large system which has been built up from the beginning of the seventeenth century. As a consequence the authorities impose certain regulations designed to ensure that there is not interference with this vital regular traffic. The documents required are:

(1) Permis de Circulation

(2) Certificat Spéciale de Capacité

I

As these documents take time to obtain it is most advisable to start making application for them well in advance of the proposed date of departure. If not less than a month is allowed for the purpose no anxiety need be felt that they will not have been collected in time and that the start of the proposed voyage will have to be postponed.

(1) PERMIS DE CIRCULATION

This document represents another of the valuable concessions made to foreign yachtsmen, as its possession allows a yacht to pass through nearly all locks free of dues. There are a few exceptions where dues have to be paid, notably for the use of a few privately owned canals. Some payment has also to be made for towing through certain tunnels and also for passing over certain *pont-canaux*, but these cases are so few and the dues demanded so nominal that to all intents and purposes the use of the rivers and canals may be considered to be free. This comes as a welcome relief to the amateur sailor who has had to meet the heavy fees which are levied for the use of some of the British inland waterways. The Permis de Circulation is issued free of charge by le Directeur de la Navigation Intérieure, and application for it may be made through the French Government Tourist Office, 178 Piccadilly, London, W.1. If in France, application may be made through the Touring Club de France, 65 avenue de la Grande-Armée, Paris 16e; also through the Automobile Club de France, 6-8 Place de la Concorde, Paris 8e. It is also possible when in Paris to apply directly to le Ministère des Travaux Public, des Transports et du Tourisme (Direction des Voies Navigable, Service Central), 244 boulevard Saint-Germain, Paris 7e, or to le Bureau National de la Navigation, 2 boulevard de Latour-Maubourg, Paris 7e.

In making application for le Permis de Circulation it is most important to state clearly the route to be followed as no deviation from the itinerary shown on the approved document is permitted without making a fresh application to cover the revision and, as this often entails considerable delay, it is as well to avoid it. It may be mentioned that no harm is done if it turns out that the actual journey does not extend as far as was anticipated: it is often found that a tour planned at home cannot be carried out in the time available owing to various delays caused by sight-seeing, weather and the like.

It must be noted that NO PERMIS de CIRCULATION is required for the following rivers:

La SEINE: from Rouen to Montereau—that is about 100 km. *upstream* from Paris.
L'OISE: from Conflans-Sainte-Honorine to Compiègne.
L'AISNE: from Compiègne to Soissons.
La MARNE: from Charenton to Epernay.

(2) CERTIFICAT SPÉCIALE de CAPACITÉ

This document may or may not be required, but in general it can now be said that it will not be necessary. It will only be insisted upon for

(*a*) vessels exceeding 20 tons.

(*b*) places where the navigation is of exceptional difficulty.

This in practice as far as 'places of exceptional difficulty' are concerned reduces to the navigation of the river Rhône from Lyon to the sea. As the majority of foreign yachtsmen employ a certified pilot from Lyon for the passage downstream and he then accepts full responsibility, in such case the necessity for a Certificat Spéciale de Capacité does not arise.

However, when application is made for the Permis de Circulation it might be as well to enquire at the same time as to whether a Certificat Spéciale de Capacité would be needed for any of the waterways mentioned in the application. Should the reply be that such a Certificat *is* necessary for one of the waterways then the easiest and best solution is either to employ a pilot or to change the proposed route so as to avoid the waterway which carries the restriction.

The 'Permis de Circulation' and the 'Certificat Spéciale de Capacité' (if required) are probably best obtained in this country through the Delegate for Great Britain, Touring Club de France, 178 Piccadilly, London, W.1, or, if in France, from the Touring Club de France, 65 avenue de la Grande-Armée, Paris 16ᵉ. Membership of the Touring Club de France should certainly be considered as a necessity by all yachtsmen visiting France because of the many benefits such membership confers. Full particulars concerning the Club will be sent by the Delegate (whose London address is given above) to those who apply to him.

The foreign owner who wishes to use his yacht in French waters all the year round must be prepared to comply with the French import regulations and pay the import duty if the yacht was not built in France. This is because no foreign yacht may be left in France for more than six months in any twelve; if that period is exceeded then the owner must pay the import duty. But a ruling of great importance to foreign yacht owners has been given by le Directeur Général des Douanes. By this ruling it is possible for an owner to make the outward journey during one holiday at the end of which he can get the yacht 'immobilised' officially during his absence in another country. The owner's absence in another country will not be counted as part of the permitted six months mentioned above. The 'immobilisa-tion' can usually be effected by surrendering to the Customs Authorities the *Passeport du Navaire Etranger* which was obtained when entering French Territorial waters. The French Authorities have recognised the plea that to return to England at the end of a holiday often occasions a great loss of time and, in the case of power vessels, expenditure of fuel. There is also the possibility with a small ship of having to wait for suitable weather in which to make the crossing. So that for those who wish to take another holiday in France during the succeeding season this arrangement is, obviously, a great help. Suitable winter storage for a moderate sized yacht in a yard belonging to a local barge builder usually presents little difficulty so that it is seldom necessary to travel to a coastal port if it is more convenient to lay up on inland waters. If, while in France, any difficulty is experienced an appeal to the Touring Club de France will not go unheeded.

NAVIGATIONAL NOTES

RIVER AND CANAL CHARGES

The ordinary commercial vessel has to pay dues for the use of the State-owned waterways, but the visiting yachtsman who has been granted a Permis de Circulation is exempt from all charges except in very few cases. Where charges are made they are usually quite nominal costing but a few francs. Certain private canals levy dues from pleasure craft. Enquiries should be made locally regarding these payments and full particulars obtained before arranging to use them.

All locks and sluices are worked by regular lock-keepers who are Government employees, and there is no arrangement whereby boatmen let themselves through the locks; in fact such action is strictly prohibited and should on no account be attempted. The system found on some British waterways which is known as 'buying a handle' has no counterpart in France.

PILOTAGE

There are four rivers on which pilotage might be thought necessary, and certainly is desirable, for vessels exceeding about 10 tons register. They are La Garonne and La Gironde, Le Rhône, La Saône and La Seine.

(1) La Garonne and La Gironde. A somewhat confusing thing about this river is that it has two names. This can be made clear by remembering that the river is called La Garonne from its source to Bec d'Ambes, a point that is situated about 25 kilometres below Bordeaux. From Bec d'Ambes to the sea the name of the river is La Gironde.

For practical purposes the river is considered to be an inland waterway from Bordeaux (at le Pont de pierre) upwards. Motor yachts of light draught can navigate above Bordeaux without the absolute necessity of employing a pilot if they observe the usual precautions necessary when using tidal river waters. But for any other than light draught craft the assistance of a river pilot is desirable and is recommended. It is customary to engage the pilot for the run up the river from Bordeaux to Castets where the canal latéral à la Garonne joins the river. The river is subject to a tidal bore *(le mascaret)* at certain seasons.

(2) Le Rhône. Le Rhône has its source in Switzerland, crosses Lake Lèman and enters France at Pougny-Chancy. It has a number of tributaries, the most important of which is La Saône which joins the right bank of Le Rhône at La Mulatière in the city of Lyon. Below Lyon at Fourques—just above Arles—the river divides into two branches, le Petit

Rhône on the right and le Grand Rhône on the left: these branches then form a delta which discharges into the Mediterranean sea. Le Haut Rhône is fed almost entirely by glaciers, consequently the greatest flow of water is to be found in the early summer at the time of *la fonte des neiges*. On the other hand la Saône, fed from the rains which run off from its catchment area, carries the major volume of its water during the late autumn and in the winter. The result is to equalise the flow of water in that part of le Rhône which lies below the confluence of the two rivers at Lyon.

Although le Rhône is classified as navigable from the Franco-Suisse frontier to the Mediterranean it has in fact been entirely abandoned by the navigation except for the section which lies between Lyon and the sea; this section is usually referred to as the Lower Rhône *(le Rhône aval* or *Bas-Rhône)*. Until the end of the 1939-45 war the lower Rhône remained very nearly in its natural state with strong eddying currents and shifting sand-banks. Even during the normal flow of the river the current attained a speed of seven kilometres an hour, and during floods it frequently exceeded ten kilometres an hour. That part of the river which lies between Serves and Pont-St.-Esprit, where the current was particularly violent, was known as *le région des rapides*.

From about the year 1885 records show that certain works designed to improve conditions at the worst places were carried out, but in fact little good resulted and the river remained a 'free river' with *le courant libre*.

During the last two decades, however, great changes have taken place and a plan, long considered, was approved and is now being carried out. This plan was to make the Lower Rhône a part of a navigable waterway stretching from the Mediterranean to the North Sea which would comply with the European Standard for Inland Waterway vessels: this standard allows self-propelled barges of 1,500 tons and 'pusher-trains' of 3,000 tons. The plan called for twelve canalised sections between Lyon and the sea. Each section has to contain a hydro-electric power station and a navigation lock. To feed the power station and lock a 'deviation' canal has to be cut just upstream of a barrage built across the river. On the downstream side of the power station and lock a 'restitution' canal *(un canal de fuite)* returns the water to the river. At present (1969) six of these canalised sections are in service, namely, Pierre-Bénite, Bourg-lès-Valence, Beauchastel, Baix-le-Logis-Neuf, Montélimar, and Donzère-Mondragon. The remaining six sections, with the year during which they are expected to be put into service, are:

Vallabregues	1970
Saint-Vallier	1972
Avignon	1973
Peage-de-Roussillon	1975
Vaugris	1976
Orange	1976

It will be seen that the work of canalisation between Lyon and the sea will not be completed until 1976.

Whatever may be the case in the future at present the services of a qualified pilot are considered to be indispensable. Moreover, it must not be forgotten that if it is proposed to make the passage without a qualified pilot a *Certificat speciale de Capacité* might be

B

demanded by the authorities and if such certificate could not be produced this could lead to delay and vexation.

(3) La Saône. There are no difficulties that a small or light-draught yacht need fear in the navigation of this beautiful river. But it is advised that every pleasure vessel should carry a copy of the large scale (1/40,000) map of the river particulars of which are given elsewhere*. It must, however, be pointed out that the sandbanks and shoals are apt to shift slightly. Further there exist here and there the remains of old broken-down jetties and wharves, though these latter, as they are well clear of the fairway, are not really much of a menace to navigation. There are now red and white beacons to mark the starboard side of the channel all the way from Chalon to Lyon. All things considered it is recommended that a pilot should be employed by medium and large yachts (for example those whose draught exceeds 4 ft. (1.22 metres)) especially during periods of flood. In a few places heavy growths of rushes rather restrict the waterway as far as landing is concerned (the main channel is always free) but practically throughout its length the banks are low and pastures extend along the river side. A notable feature of this river is that the water nearly always appears extraordinarily pellucid and clear which makes it very inviting during the hot days of high summer.

(4) La Seine. From Le Havre to Rouen is considered as a marine navigation and no remarks are made concerning it because reference should be made to the various sailing directions and Pilots. The river above Rouen as far as Paris presents no difficulties to any yacht which does not exceed 6 or 7 ft. draught. But as this draught implies a considerable size in a power craft it may be better to give a further indication. Say, then, that a small yacht carrying about four or five persons and one which is easily manoeuvred can safely find her own way up to Paris without a pilot. With a vessel of greater size and value it might be considered advisable to employ a pilot for other reasons than those of actual navigation; this question must be left for each particular owner to decide. Above Paris draught is more restricted but the actual pilotage is, perhaps, simpler and the traffic is less. In any case the use of the two excellent large scale (1/40,000) charts referred to under Charts and Publications, will greatly assist in making the passage safe and enjoyable and it is recommended that they should be at hand.

SPEED LIMITS

Although the following are the official speed limits (which if a vessel exceeds renders the owner liable to prosecution) it is most earnestly recommended to the owners of power yachts to be particularly careful never by excessive speed to cause annoyance to other users of the waterways:

(1) Le Rhône *For vessels over 20 tons*

    Not to exceed ... ... 25 km./hr.
    When meeting other vessels ... ... 15 km./hr.

* See p. 7.

(2) La Seine   *For vessels over 10 tons*

Upstream	15 km./hr.
Downstream	18 km./hr.
Downstream at times of high water	20 km./hr.
Within the limits of Paris and Rouen, also in narrow passages	8 km./hr.

For vessels below 10 tons

In general, except where otherwise stated in the T.C.F. *Guide de la Basse-Seine*	60 km./hr.

(3) On other Rivers.

by day	10 km./hr.
by night (where permitted)	6 km./hr.

(4) On Canals and between Locks on Rivers.

by day	6 km./hr.
by night (where permitted)	4 km./hr.

CHARTS AND PUBLICATIONS

Of charts, those published by La Societe d'Editions Maritimes et d'Outre Mer, 17 Rue Jacob, Paris 6e are useful. They are all to a scale of 1/40,000:

(*a*) Carte de la Basse-Seine

(*b*) Carte de la Haute-Seine

(*c*) Carte de la Saône, de Lyon à St.-Jean-de-Losne

(*d*) Carte de la Saône, de St.-Jean-de-Losne à Corre

(*e*) Carte de la Marne

(*f*) Carte de l'Yonne, de Montereaux à Auxerre

The Touring Club de France issue booklets giving many valuable particulars of the region described, such as places of interest, situations of yachting clubs, hotels and restaurants, repair yards, etc. The booklets are:

(*a*) Guide de la Basse-Seine, de Paris à Rouen

(*b*) La Haute-Seine, de Paris à Montereau

(*c*) La Marne et Canal latéral, du Confluent à Vitry-le-Francois

A general map of the waterways of France and the more important waterways of Belgium and the Netherlands, scale 1/1,500,000, paper folded in a cover is published by Imray Laurie Norie and Wilson, this is useful for the planning of tours and for giving a comprehensive view of the major waterways in the three countries. It is obtainable from bookshops and yacht suppliers.

A series of small charts of La Saône is available from R. Salagnac, 142 Cours Lafayette, Lyon, France, at a cost of about 35 fr., and by the same author, Le Rhône, de Lyon à Port-St.-Louis du Rhône.

Yachtsmen who propose to visit the canals of Brittany should make sure to have on board a copy of the excellent guide: *The Canals of Brittany* (1966), in English; obtainable from the Touring Club de France, 178 Piccadilly, London, W.1.

Those seriously interested in the Inland Waterways of France should not fail to obtain that most comprehensive work in two volumes *Le Guide de la Navigation intérieure* which is published by la Librairie Berger-Levrault, 5 rue Auguste-Comte, Paris 6e, under the auspices of l'Office National de la Navigation. The first of these volumes gives all the essential navigational particulars of the waterways. The second which is called *the Atlas* gives, in strip map form, particulars of all navigable waterways with their locks, bridges, ports, etc., to scales of 1/100,000, 1/50,000 and even some at 1/25,000.

The well-known Michelin series of maps covering all France to a scale of 1/200,000 are very useful for details of the country through which the selected route passes and, as they are very reasonable in price and always up-to-date, it is suggested that they form part of the ship's library.

As for books, their name is legion, but these must be left to the individual to choose only stating that the familiar *Guide Michelin* for the current year should always be carried as it is quite without a substitute. Le Guide and the Maps are both published by Services de Tourisme du Pneu Michelin, 97 boulevard Peréire, Paris 17e.

A number of these publications may be obtained in London from Captain O. M. Watts Ltd., 49 Albemarle Street, W.1., or Sifton Praed & Co. Ltd., 67 St. James's Street, S.W.1. Otherwise it is recommended that they be ordered direct from the addresses given. The leading retailers of nautical publications in France are Editions Maritimes et d'Outre Mer at 17 Rue Jacob, Paris 6e. If the visiting yachtsman has become a member of the Touring Club de France he should take the opportunity when in Paris to visit the library at the Club's headquarters, 65 avenue de la Grande-Armée, where he will find a very informing and interesting collection of volumes.

DIMENSIONS OF WATERWAYS

All particulars which concern yachtsmen are given in detail elsewhere in this work, but summarised information for several of the main routes is here noted for quick and ready reference. The standard dimensions of the locks and the headroom under bridges vary slightly on the different canalised river and canal systems but, basically, they are:

Length	38 m. 50
Width	5 m. 20
Depth (minimum)	1 m. 80
Headroom (above normal level) ...	3 m. 50

The following are the dimensions of the locks and the minimum headroom from normal water level under bridges.

(1) **La Seine**: Amfreville-Poses to Ry. Bridge, Argenteuil

Length	141 m. 25
Width	11 m. 60
Depth	3 m. 00
Headroom	6 m. 00

8

(2) **La Seine:** Ry. Bridge, Argenteuil to Corbeil

Length	...	...	...	...	140 m. 50
Width	...	...	...	...	11 m. 60
Depth	...	...	...	...	3 m. 00
Headroom	...	...	...	...	6 m. 00

(3) **Le Seine:** Corbeil to Montereau

Length	...	...	...	...	172 m. 00
Width	...	...	...	...	11 m. 80
Depth	...	...	...	...	2 m. 00
Headroom	...	...	...	...	5 m 08

(4) **L'Oise:** Conflans-Ste-Honorine to Janville (Compiègne)

Length	...	...	...	...	125 m 00
Width	...	...	...	...	12 m 00
Depth	...	...	...	...	2 m. 50
Headroom	...	...	...	...	6 m. 00

(5) **L'Aisne:** Compiègne to Celles

Length	...	...	...	...	46 m. 00
Width	...	...	...	...	7 m. 95
Depth	...	...	...	...	2 m. 10
Headroom	...	...	...	...	4 m. 70

(6) **La Marne:** Charenton to Epernay

Length	...	...	...	...	45 m. 00
Width	...	...	...	...	7 m. 80
Depth	...	...	...	...	2 m. 20
Headroom	...	...	...	...	4 m. 80

MAIN ROUTES

(1) **Paris to Northern France**

Length	...	...	...	...	38 m. 50
Width	...	...	...	...	5 m. 08
Depth	...	...	...	...	2 m. 20
Headroom	...	...	...	...	3 m. 60

(2) **Paris to Belgium via L'Escaut**

Length	...	...	...	...	38 m. 50
Width	...	...	...	...	5 m. 18
Depth	...	...	...	...	2 m. 50
Headroom	...	...	...	...	3 m. 70

(3) **Paris to Belgium via La Sambre**

Length	...	...	...	...	38 m. 50
Width	...	...	...	...	5 m. 20
Depth	...	...	...	...	2 m. 20
Headroom	...	...	...	...	3 m. 70

(4) Paris to Strasbourg

Length	38 m. 50
Width	5 m. 13
Depth	2 m. 20
Headroom	3 m. 70

(5) Paris to Lyon via Burgundy

Length	39 m. 00
Width	5 m. 20
Depth	2 m. 00
Headroom	3 m. 40

(6) Paris to Lyon via Le Bourbonnais

Length	39 m. 00
Width	5 m. 12
Depth	2 m. 00
Headroom	3 m. 50

(7) Paris to Lyon via La Marne

Length	38 m. 30
Width	5 m. 10
Depth	2 m. 00
Headroom	3 m. 50

(8) Calais to Lyon via Reims

Length	38 m. 30
Width	5 m. 08
Depth	2 m. 00
Headroom	3 m. 48

(9) Lyon to Strasbourg

Length	38 m. 70
Width	5 m. 10
Depth	2 m. 00
Headroom	3 m. 55

(10) St. Malo to Nantes via Redon

Length	26 m. 50
Width	4 m. 65
Depth	1 m. 60
Headroom at centre	2 m. 50
Headroom at sides	2 m. 30

(11) Bordeaux to Étang de Thau (Sète)

Length	30 m. 00
Width	5 m. 50
Depth	1 m. 80
Headroom at centre	3 m. 40
Headroom at sides	2 m. 50

(12) **Étang de Thau** (Sète) **to Beaucaire** (Le Rhône)

Length	..	..	..	..	80 m. 00
Width	..	..	..	..	12 m. 00
Depth	..	..	..	..	2 m. 00
Headroom	..	..	..	..	4 m. 32

THE TIME OF YEAR

As far as the spring and summer months are concerned, that is to say from late April to the end of August, none can be considered as 'the best', for good weather may be enjoyed at any time during that period. It must be recognised that, as a general rule, the weather in France, being of the continental type, tends to be more settled than that of the British Isles, and that long periods of high temperature are by no means infrequent. If the cruise takes place much before the end of April (except if it be in the south of France) the nights may well prove to be cold, and the days may be equally so if overcast and rainy. Moreover, it is always colder on the water than on the land and, owing to the higher humidity, it feels colder apart from the probability of the vessel not having really adequate heating arrangements. Some of the finest weather often occurs during September and October, and at that time of the year the scenery is usually particularly beautiful owing to the autumnal colouring; but some early frosts must certainly be expected.

About the middle of May the waterway authorities start their annual repair and cleaning programme (*chômage*) which has the effect of delaying, or even holding up, traffic at certain places. These annual programmes which extend into September will seldom interfere with a tour as it is essential to plan the route well ahead of the proposed date of departure. Early planning enables enquiry to be made as to the incidence of *chômage* over the selected route; there would then be time enough left to vary the itinerary, if thought desirable, to avoid any lock or length of canal which would cause undue delay. Thus it is opportune when applying for the *Permis de Circulation** to ask for information with respect to any repair works which may be in hand at the probable date of passage along the proposed route. However, the work is usually carried out in such sequence that alternative detours are available. The Touring Club de France issue a useful map 'Carte des Chomages'. In the late autumn and during the winter months (which are not the usual ones for touring) the intrepid voyager must be prepared for floods (November to March) and also for icing (December to February); for it must be remembered that some of the canals rise to a considerable height above sea level and with the increase of elevation the fall of temperature will be accentuated. Such severe conditions will not, however, usually extend beyond the month of March.

HOURS OF NAVIGATION

It is as well when planning a tour to realise that for all practical purposes there is no navigation after dark or, during the lighter months of the year after 1930 hours. The locks are not normally operated except between the hours of 0630 hours and 1930 hours. Lock-keepers usually have a lunch-hour break between noon and 1300 hours. These figures are

* See p. 2.

11

those obtaining during high summer and the working hours progressively shorten as the nights close in. While it is possible to run between locks during the dark hours (the proper navigation lights being shown and the regulation reduction in speed being observed) it is unusual for pleasure craft to do so. Except in an emergency few tourists will wish to move at night, when, apart from the difficulty of navigation, the scenery and surrounding country cannot be seen and enjoyed. It need hardly be mentioned that the hours given above are 'clock' hours and are not affected by Summer Time. On Sundays and public holidays it is as well not to arrive at a lock before 0900 hours though this is a matter of custom rather than of regulation. Of course if it is seen that a commercial vessel or a tug with a string of lighters is entering before that hour the opportunity of following in behind them should not be neglected.

RULE OF THE ROAD

There is no fixed rule of the road; that is to say there is no invariable rule such as 'always keep to the right'. The course to be followed is dictated by circumstance. Generally it may be stated that as far as self-propelled yachts are concerned the following directions will meet most situations:

(*Note:* By 'motor vessel' is meant a self-propelled vessel.)

(1) Meeting *(Croisement)*. If a motor vessel meets a vessel which is being towed from a bank, the motor vessel must keep towards the bank opposite to the tow-path.

If two motor vessels meet each other, each must keep to the bank which is on her right side. But on some reaches this rule does not hold and when meeting both vessels hold to the left bank. This is frequently the case on la Saône. The large-scale strip maps mentioned before give notes and details about this matter and should certainly be at hand to consult.

If a motor vessel when meeting another motor vessel is unable to keep to the right (owing to special circumstances, depth of water, etc.) she will signify her intention in ample time by giving a long and a short blast to pass on the right, a long and two short blasts to pass on the left on whistle or horn, and at the same time moderate her speed. The other motor vessel must then reply by giving one short blast for being passed on right, two short blasts for being passed on left, on whistle or horn.

Where there is insufficient width to allow two vessels to pass abreast notices to that effect are placed on notice posts showing the limits between which meeting is prohibited. It is the duty of all vessels not to attempt the passage until the master is satisfied that the channel is not occupied. (These places are rather uncommon but if it is found necessary to wait in such circumstances always moor up against the bank opposite to the tow-path so that the oncoming vessel may have a clear way if being towed from the bank; if the oncoming vessel is under her own power then keep to the right bank as usual.)

If in a channel which has a current two motor vessels are about to meet the vessel which is going downstream has the right of way, and the other vessel must keep clear.

If in a channel without current two motor vessels are about to meet on a bend or curve in such a manner as to cause risk of collision, the vessel which has the *outside of the bend or curve on her right hand* shall have the right of way, and the other vessel must wait until the bend or curve is clear.

(2) Overtaking *(Trématage)*. Any vessel which by reason of her *normal* speed overtakes another has the right to pass, no matter how the overtaken vessel is propelled.

No vessel should accelerate momentarily for the *exclusive* purpose of passing another.

Notice posts are often to be seen marked *Limite de Trématage* about 500 metres from locks, but if no such posts are observed it is still obligatory not to attempt to overtake another vessel within a distance of at least 500 metres from a lock. No yachtsman should ever 'cut in' and steal a commercial vessel's turn at a lock; this indefensible action causes much bitterness and gives the visiting craft a very bad name.

Vessels travelling in the same direction should not attempt to overtake when passing round bends or curves, or when passing under bridges and similar works which may restrict the normal width of the waterway.

No motor vessel should attempt to overtake another, unless there is ample room, until the *overtaking vessel* has given a *prolonged blast* on whistle or horn (to warn the *overtaken vessel* of the intention to pass) followed by *one short blast* to pass on the *right* or *two short blasts* to pass on the *left*. The *overtaken vessel* when ready to be overtaken must hold as close to her proper bank and moderate her speed, giving at the same time *one short blast* if she is to be passed on the *right* and *two short blasts* if she is to be passed on the *left*.

If the overtaken vessel is of opinion that it is not practicable for the other vessel to pass she must give *four short blasts* on whistle or horn.

(3) Turning *(Virement)*. When a vessel, going with the current, wishes to turn to head upstream, notice of the intention must be given by *two prolonged blasts* of the whistle or horn followed by *(a) one short blast* if the swing is to the right, *(b) two short blasts* if the swing is to the left. Vessels which are coming upstream will stop and vessels which are going with the stream will ease up until the turning vessel is no longer an obstruction.

When a vessel wishes to turn in a waterway which has no current, notice to other vessels in the neighbourhood must be given by signals similar to those described in the paragraph above.

(*Note:* All these signals are to be heard and so it is as well to know of them, but most of the time they are not used. However, be ready for them, especially the one for making a turn.)

LOCKS—ENTERING AND LEAVING

On approaching a lock it is usual to warn the lock-keeper by giving *one prolonged blast* on the whistle or horn. If other traffic is moored up waiting to enter, there is, obviously, no need to warn the lock-keeper, and in such cases it is best to moor to the bank remote from the tow-path and, of course, at the end of the queue of waiting vessels. If there are no other vessels waiting their turn it is in any case advisable to make a complete stop at a distance of not less than 50 metres from the lock entrance and to remain about there until the lock-keeper signals permission to enter. While waiting, if it is thought not necessary to moor up to the bank, care should be taken not to obstruct the passage of any vessel which may emerge from the lock when the gates are opened; it is not always easy to see what is in the lock if it is a high one and the vessel inside is already partially down.

After having entered the lock, which should be done at a very moderate speed (usually the slower the better), arrange matters so as to stop near one of the vertical ladders let into the lock wall; it will then be easy for the crew to land to attend to the warps. It is not part of the lock-keeper's duty to attend to mooring ropes, either to make them fast or to let them go, though some of them are very obliging in this respect. Some of the old locks, particularly on la Seine, have sloping sides and this makes extra care very necessary, especially when descending. A good way is to bear off with two quants or two long boat-hooks, one forward and one aft. But better still is to make fast to another vessel and this can usually be done as these large locks generally take several vessels at a time in order to save water.

The lock-keeper has authority to determine the precedence of entry into the lock, but this will usually be in accordance with the order of arrival. However, the lock-keeper may instruct a small vessel to enter out of turn so as to ensure that the lock chamber is filled to the best advantage. Although according to the regulations a yacht can claim priority over most classes of commercial vessels this privilege should never be used, always remembering that pleasure vessels are using the waterways on sufferance and should avoid in any way impeding the ordinary working traffic. It will frequently happen that the lock-keeper will call a small yacht forward out of her turn if he sees that there is room in the lock.

No vessel may remain in the lock chamber for a length of time greater than is necessary to manoeuvre and clear the gates.

Whenever possible if it is necessary to enter a lock with other vessels, do so last. This is generally easy to arrange and it avoids being in the way as the other vessels berth in the lock; also it saves being caught up in the rush when the forward gates are opened.

However, when in a lock with large self-propelled barges and moored behind them, be particularly on the alert when they start up their engines to pass out of the lock, as the disturbance caused by their propellers may be very considerable and a small vessel may even be drawn into them.

Always when in a lock with other vessels ask permission to make fast to the most convenient. This will, of course, save attention to the mooring ropes as the water level changes. Barge crews are nearly always both helpful and kindly in this respect and will make fast and let go warps readily if asked to do so.

If alone in a lock choose to be rather nearer to the back of the lock chamber than towards the front. When locking up this will avoid the rush of water at the further gates and make control of the vessel easier, especially so if the lock is a deep one.

GENERAL INFORMATION

It is unnecessary to 'tip' the lock-keepers as they are but doing the duty for which they are paid by the State. Of course, if they assist with the mooring lines—which, as mentioned before, is no part of their duty—that no doubt changes the position. Lock-keepers are very often disabled war veterans; they are a civil and obliging body of men who are usually willing to give advice upon matters concerning the waterways, and this is extremely useful to a stranger.

It is worth remarking that frequently the lock-keeper's wife is able and willing to supply garden produce at very reasonable rates which is both handy and convenient. A pot or tin of jam for the children is usually appreciated.

On any given route it is the number of locks which will determine the time taken to cover it. But do not on that account hurry along and attempt to work through a large number of locks in a day. Take it easy and look around for you may not have the chance to pass that way again and by taking your time much that is of interest will be seen that otherwise would have been missed.

Do not forget that on a bend the shoal water is usually on the inside of the curve, therefore do not cut corners.

Do not hesitate to sound the whistle or horn in order to warn other traffic of your approach. Be particularly cautious at narrow sections, around curves, at blind bends and in all similar situations.

Always give way to commercial vessels. Remember that time is money to them and that they pay the tolls and dues which maintain the waterways that yachts enjoy free of charge.

When passing through towns, around bends, through narrow sections, in front of wharves, past quays and near construction works the speed of the vessel must be reduced to the extent necessary to avoid all danger of causing damage. Should such damage occur the owner of the yacht is held responsible and this may lead to unpleasantness, delays and costs.

To which it must be added that it is at least courteous to ease up when passing fishermen in light punts and also when passing washerwomen washing clothes at the water's edge.

Finally, it is shyly suggested that good manners pay excellent dividends, and also that it is salutary to remember that you are 'the foreigner' when you are abroad.

SOME THROUGH ROUTES

PARIS TO LYON (via La Bourgogne)

This route is the shortest, but has a large number of locks. It passes through some very beautiful country and close to the celebrated wine district of Burgundy. The traffic is usually slight and no delays at locks need be anticipated.

Waterway	Town	kilom.	lock
La Seine	PARIS	0	0
	Charenton (confluence La Marne)	6	0
	Corbeil	35	3
	Melun	60	5
	Saint-Mammès	88	8
	Montereau	101	9
L'Yonne	Sens	141	17
	Villeneuve-sur-Yonne	158	21
	Laroche-St-Cydroine	185	26
Canal de Bourgogne	Saint-Florentin	204	33
	Tonnerre	229	44
	Montbard	287	76
	Pouilly-en-Auxois	340	139
	Dijon	397	193
	Saint-Jean-de-Losne	427	215
La Saône	Chalon-sur-Saône	496	220
	Mâcon	560	221
	LYON (La Mulatière)	640	223

PARIS TO LYON (via Le Bourbonnais)

This route is a little longer than La Bourgogne but has considerably fewer locks. It passes through pleasant agricultural country though at a few places it has been industrialised and there is a mining section in one part. In these places the barge traffic is inclined to be rather heavy and some delay may at times occur at locks.

Waterway	Town	kilom.	lock
La Seine	PARIS	0	0
	Charenton (confluence La Marne)	6	0
	Corbeil	35	3
	Melun	60	5
	Saint-Mammès	88	8

16

Waterway	Town	kilom.	lock
Canal du Loing	Nemours	107	17
	Souppes	118	20
	Buges	137	28
Canal de Briare	Montargis	140	30
	Châtillon-Coligny	166	40
	Briare	191	60
Canal latéral à la Loire ...	Pont-canal de Briare...	194	60
	Saint-Satur	235	65
	Branch to Nevers	294	77
	Branch to Decize	326	82
	Digoin...	390	97
Canal du Centre	Paray-le-Monial	403	100
	Montceau-les-Mines	440	117
	Chalon-sur-Saône	502	158
La Saône	Mâcon	566	159
	LYON (La Mulatière)	646	161

PARIS TO LYON (via La Marne)

This route is longer than either of the other two already given, but on the other hand it has the least number of locks. It runs through an agreeable countryside and the traffic is, as a rule, quite light.

Waterway	Town	kilom.	lock
La Seine	PARIS	0	0
	Charenton (confluence La Marne)	6	0
La Marne	Meaux (Pont des Saints-Pères) ...	51	6
	Château-Thierry	128	13
	Dizy (d'Hautvillers)	179	18
Canal latéral à la Marne ...	Châlons-sur-Marne	214	24
	Vitry-le-François	246	33
Canal de Marne au Rhin ...	Vitry-le-François	247	33
Canal de la Marne à la Saône	Saint-Dizier	277	46
	Joinville	310	60
	Chaumont	356	80
	Langres	395	102
	Heuilley-sur-Saône	471	147
La Saône	Auxonne	491	149
	Chalon-sur-Saône	578	155
	Mâcon	642	156
	LYON (La Mulatière)	721	158

CALAIS TO LYON

This is the most direct route from Calais to Lyon. It joins the Marne route from Paris at Condé-sur-Marne. For those who take the short Channel crossing and who do not wish to visit Paris by the waterways this is a useful alternative.

Waterway	Town	kilom.	lock
Canal de Calais	CALAIS	0	0
	Le West	30	1
L'Aa	Saint-Omer	43	—
Canal de Neuffossé	Aire	63	2
Canal d'Aire	Bauvin	103	3
Canal de la Deûle	Courrières	116	—
	Flers-en-Escrebieux	127	3
Dérivation de la Scarpe autour de Douai	Corbehem	135	5
Canal de la Sensée	Etrun	159	6
L'Escaut	Cambrai	171	11
Canal de Saint-Quentin	Saint-Quentin	221	—
	Chauny	263	46
Canal latéral à l'Oise	Abbécourt	266	—
Canal de l'Oise à l'Aisne	Bourg-et-Comin	313	59
Canal latéral à l'Aisne	Berry-au-Bac	333	60
Canal de l'Aisne à la Marne	Reims	356	—
	Condé-sur-Marne	391	84
Canal latéral à la Marne	Châlons-sur-Marne	410	—
	Vitry-le-François	440	—
Canal de la Marne au Rhin	Vitry-le-François	441	97
Canal de la Marne à la Saône	Saint-Dizier	471	111
	Joinville	504	125
	Chaumont	550	144
	Langres	590	166
	Heuilley-sur-Saône	665	211
La Saône	Auxonne	685	213
	Chalon-sur-Saône	772	219
	Mâcon	836	220
	LYON (La Mulatière)	915	222

LYON TO LA MEDITERRANEE (via Saint-Louis-de-Rhône)

This route is a continuation of the previous routes which were carried as far as Lyon. It makes communication between that City and the Mediterranean Sea in the Golfe de Fos. On account of the hydro-electric installations now being built along the whole length, this part of le Rhône is undergoing extensive modification. Up-to-date information should always be obtained and the services of a pilot is recommended, for an attempt to run the river without a pilot may result in the authorities demanding a *Certificat de Capacité*.

Waterway	*Town*				*kilom.*	*lock*
Le Rhône	LYON (La Mulatière) ...	...	...		0	0
	Pierre-Bénite	...	...	...	4	1
	Givors ...	...	...	...	18	—
	Vienne... ...	...	...	...	29	—
	Bourg-lès-Valence	...	...	...	106	2
	Beauchastel ...	...	...	...	124	3
	Baix-Logis-Neuf	...	...	...	143	4
	Montélimar ...	...	...	...	164	5
	Donzère-Mondragon	...	...	...	187	6
	Orange ...	...	...	...	218	—
	Avignon ...	...	...	...	234	—
	Arles ...	...	...	...	282	—
	PORT-SAINT-LOUIS	...	...	...	323	—
Canal St-Louis et Golfe de Fos	Port-Saint-Louis ...	...	...		323	7
	Discharge into La Méditerraneanée					
	Golfe de Fos	...	...	...	326	—
	Lighthouse at end of jetty	...	...		328	—

CALAIS TO PARIS (via Canal du Nord)

A decree passed in December 1903 authorised the construction of a Canal du Nord, but two major wars prevented the realisation of the project. A section of this new canal was provisionally opened to traffic from Pont l'Evêque to la Somme in October 1964 and a couple of years later the whole length from Pont le Evêque to Arleux became available for navigation. The Canal du Nord by-passes a part of the canal latéral à l'Oise, the whole of the Canal de Saint-Quentin, a length of the river Escaut and about two-thirds of the Canal de la Sensée. From Arleux to Pont l'Evêque via Saint-Quentin it is about 140 kilometres, with two tunnels and 42 locks; by the new route it is only 95 kilometres with two tunnels and 18 locks. The traffic through the tunnels is regulated by traffic lights.

Waterway	*Town*				*kilom.*	*lock*
Canal de Calais	CALAIS ...	...	...	...	0	0
	Le West ...	...	...	...	30	1
L'Aa	Saint-Omer ...	...	...	...	43	—
Canal de Neuffossé	Aire	...	...	...	63	3
Canal d'Aire	Bauvin ...	...	...	...	103	4
Canal de la Deule ...	Flers-en-Escrebieux ...	...	...		126	—
La dérivation de la Scarpe autour de Douai	Corbehem ...	...	...	...	134	6
Canal de la Sensée	Arleux ...	...	...	...	144	—

19

Waterway	*Town*	*kilom.*	*lock*
Canal du Nord	Souterrain de Ruyaulcourt ...	169	—
	Clery-sur-Somme	189	18
	Béthencourt-sur-Somme	209	20
	Souterrain de la Panneterie...	222	—
	Pont l'Evêque	239	25
Canal latéral à l'Oise	Janville	254	27
L'Oise ...	Compiègne	261	—
	Creil ...	300	—
	Pontoise	346	—
	Conflans-Ste-Honorine	358	34
La Seine	Le Pecq (Saint-Germain)	379	—
	Bougival	383	—
	Argenteuil	395	—
	Suresnes	415	—
	PARIS (Pont de la Tournelle)	432	36

CALAIS TO PARIS (via Canal-de-Saint-Quentin)

While the scenery along this route cannot be described as beautiful, at least until l'Oise is reached, the waterways run through good farming land and a pleasant countryside. The route passes through many places whose names are familiar from having been the scene of much bitter fighting during the 1914-18 and 1939-45 wars. The lower reaches of l'Oise are very picturesque and agreeable. The traffic on the whole is rather heavy, especially in the neighbourhood of both Douai and Chauny.

Waterway	*Town*	*kilom.*	*lock*
Canal de Calais	CALAIS	0	0
	Le West	30	1
L'Aa ...	Saint-Omer ...	43	—
Canal de Neuffossé ...	Aire ...	63	3
Canal d'Aire ...	Bauvin	103	4
Canal de la Deule ...	Flers-en-Escrebieux ...	126	—
La dérivation de la Scarpe autour de Douai ...	Corbehem	134	6
Canal de la Sensée ...	Bouchain	159	7
L'Escaut ...	Cambrai	171	12
Canal de Saint-Quentin ...	Chauny	263	47
Canal latéral à l'Oise ...	Janville	297	51
L'Oise ...	Compiègne	304	—
	Creil ...	343	—
	Pontoise	389	—
	Conflans-Sainte-Honorine ...	401	58
La Seine ...	Le Pecq (Saint-Germain)	422	—
	Bougival	426	—
	Argenteuil	438	—

Waterway	Town	kilom.	lock
	Suresnes	458	—
	PARIS (Pont de la Tournelle) ...	475	60

PARIS TO STRASBOURG

This is the direct route from Paris to the Rhine, which is reached at Strasbourg. The scenery throughout is not very impressive, the land being given over chiefly to agriculture. The wine-growing district around Epernay is of interest and the slopes of the vine-covered hills are charming in their colouring, especially in the early autumn. As a rule the traffic is not very heavy and congestion at locks is not usual.

Waterway	Town	kilom.	lock
La Seine	PARIS	0	0
	Charenton	6	0
La Marne	Meaux...	53	7
	Château-Thierry	134	13
	Dizy-Magenta	185	18
Canal láteral à la Marne ...	Chalons-sur-Marne	220	25
	Vitry-le-François	252	33
Canal de la Marne au Rhin ...	Bar-le-Duc	297	64
	Demange-aux-Eaux	337	103
	Toul	381	128
	Nancy	415	132
	Arzviller	504	153
	STRASBOURG	565	204*

LYON TO STRASBOURG

From the south of France this route provides the most direct way by water to Germany and thence to Holland. It also forms a useful route from the Côte d'Azur to England if the passage across the North Sea is no objection. Both la Saône and the Canal du Rhône au Rhin pass through some splendid country, and both are easy of navigation except during periods of flood. The valley of le Doubs, along which the Canal du Rhône au Rhin takes its course, is very picturesque especially in the neighbourhood of the town of Besançon. The traffic throughout the route is not heavy excepting for the part which lies between Mulhouse and Strasbourg.

Waterway	Town	kilom.	lock
La Saône	LYON	0	0
	Mâcon	79	3
	Chalon-sur-Saône	143	4
	Saint-Jean-de-Losne	213	8
Canal du Rhône au Rhin ...	Saint-Symphorien	217	8
	Dôle	236	17
	Besançon	291	38

* If the Inclined Plane at Arzviller is used, deduct 17 locks.

Waterway	Town				kilom.	lock
	Baume-les-Dames	...	...	...	326	49
	L'Isle-sur-Doubs	...	...	...	358	62
	Montbéliard ...	...	...	...	381	75
	Montreux-Vieux	...	...	...	404	87
	Mulhouse	...	...	...	435	125
	Ile Napoléon ...	...	...	...	440	126
Embranchement de Kembs-Niffer	Niffer ...	...	...	...	453	127
Grand Canal d'Alsace	Ecluse d'Ottmarsheim	...	...	462	128
	Ecluse de Fressenheim	...	...	478	129
	Ecluse de Vogelgrün	...	...	493	130
Le Rhin Canalisé	Ecluse de Marckolsheim	...	...	508	131
	Ecluse de Rhinau-Sundhouse	...	525	132
	Ecluse de Gerstheim	...	...	541	133
	Ecluse de Strasbourg	...	...	556	134
	STRASBOURG (Avant-port sud) ...			559	

DINARD (SAINT-MALO) TO THE BAY OF BISCAY

From the English Channel it is possible for vessels of shoal draught to take a useful short cut through Brittany to the west coast of France thus avoiding a long open sea passage and the strong tides around the iron-bound coast of Ushant. From the estuary of La Rance maritime the Canal d'Ille-et-Rance may be entered through the Le Châtelier lock near Dinan. The canal runs southwards to the city of Rennes where it makes junction with La Vilaine canalisée. That river (also running south) passes through the town of Redon before finally discharging into the Bay of Biscay. At Redon, La Vilaine crosses the Canal de Nantes à Brest but is not passable owing to a barrage in the river just below the crossing.* Downstream of the barrage the river is called La Vilaine maritime and is tidal. From Redon there are now three possible routes by which the sea may be reached. The first, and also the shortest, is into La Vilaine maritime via l'écluse des Bellions (No. 17) which is reached from le Canal de Nantes à Brest. The second, and the most usual one, is from Redon to Nantes using the south-eastern part of the Canal de Nantes à Brest. The third possibility is to turn north-west along the Canal de Nantes à Brest at the crossing of La Vilaine and carry on to Pontivy. There one finds le Canal du Blavet on the port hand and descending the canal to Hennebont the sea is reached by le Blavet maritime.

Waterway	Town				kilom.	lock
La Rance maritime	DINARD	...	...	...	...	0	0
	Barrage (Mariémotrice)	...	...	4	1
Canal d'Ille-et-Rance	Le Châtelier ...	...	...	...	23	2
	Dinan ...	...	...	...	...	29	—
	Tinténiac	...	...	...	...	60	—
	La Plousière ...	...	...	...	72	29

* But see p. 272.

Waterway	Town	kilom.	lock
	St-Germain-sur-Ille	84	—
	RENNES	108	49
La Vilaine	Malon	159	—
	REDON	196	61

(A) Redon to Trehiguier (Mouth of La Vilaine)

Canal de Nantes à Brest ...	Redon	0	0
Canal de Nantes à Brest ...	Ecluse d'Isac	0	1
La Vilaine maritime	Ecluse des Bellions	6	2
	La Roche Bernard	33	—
	Trehiguier	47	—
	Mouth of La Vilaine maritime ...	48	—

(B) Redon to Nantes

Canal de Nantes à Brest ...	Redon	0	0
	Ecluse d'Isac	0	1
	St-Clair-Guenrouet	22	—
	Blain	45	6
	Quiheix	73	16
	NANTES	95	17

(C) Redon to Hennebont (mouth of Le Blavet maritime)

Canal de Nantes à Brest ...	Redon	0	0
	Ecluse d'Oust...	0	1
	Gueslin	23	—
	Roc-St-André	46	11
	Josselin	62	18
	Rohan...	87	34
	Pontivy	111	89
Canal du Blavet	Ecluse des Recollets	111	90
	St-Nicholas-des-Eaux	129	—
	Hennebont	171	117

BORDEAUX TO SÈTE

This route joins the Atlantic Ocean to the Mediterranean Sea. The Canal du Midi, which forms the eastern half of the route begins at *le bassin octogonal* in Toulouse and ends in l'Étang de Thau. The Port of Séte stands at the eastern end of l'Étang. The Canal du Midi is of ancient origin having been cut by the engineer Riquet in 1681. Although it is thus nearly 300 years old it still retains its original trace and its original sources of feed water. Moreover the lock which connects the canal to the Garonne at Toulouse may yet be seen leading out of *le bassin octogonal*. The river from Bordeaux to Toulouse constituted the first part of the journey for about 150 years but the upper reaches becoming silted and the traffic becoming heavier and more impatient of delays, another canal—the canal latéral à la Garonne—was dug and opened to the navigation in 1838, its eastern end joining with the Canal du Midi in *le bassin octogonal*. The western end of the new canal fell into the Garonne at Castets-en-Dorthe, about 200 kilometres downstream from Toulouse. This arrangement still exists today, and the river continues to play a part in completing the route between the Atlantic and the Mediterranean.

Waterway	Town	kilom.	lock
La Garonne	BORDEAUX (Pont de Pierre) ...	0	0
Canal latéral à la Garonne ...	Castets	54	0
	Pont-des-Sables (Marmande) ...	83	9
	Tonneins	99	11
	Agen	137	20
	Valence-d'Agen	166	23
	Castelsarrasin	191	35
	Toulouse	247	53
Canal du Midi	Castelnaudary	312	85
	Carcassonne	352	109
	Homps (Olonzac)	392	130
	Capestang	435	137
	Béziers	455	146
	Agde (Écluse Ronde)	478	151
	Les Onglous	486	154
Etang de Thau	SÈTE	504	—

LE RHÔNE TO SÈTE (Bassin de Thau)

At present the entrance to the Canal du Rhône à Sète is through a narrow channel at Beaucaire, but it is probable that, as the canalisation of le Rhône continues, the entrance will be shifted to Saint-Gilles at a point where le Petit Rhône approaches very near to the canal. Le Petit Rhône leaves the main stream about a kilometre upstream of Arles-Trinquetaille; it can easily be dredged to the required depth. This route passes through the low-lying country of the Rhône delta and through the interesting district of La Camargue. The walled town of Aigues-Mortes is of considerable historical interest and well repays a detailed visit. The passage through *les étangs* (which are salt water lakes) is very pleasant if the weather is fine. But take precautions against the mosquitoes which at some seasons are very troublesome at night. The coastal fringe is now being 'developed' into summer *plages*, sun-bathing resorts and marinas.

Waterway	Town	kilom.	lock
Le Rhône	BEAUCAIRE	0	0
Canal du Rhône à Sète ...	Beaucaire	0	1
	Bellegarde	13	2
	Saint-Gilles	24	—
	Beauvoisin	35	—
	Aigues-Mortes	51	—
	Le Lez...	75	—
	Frontignan	92	—
	La Peyrade	96	—
	SÈTE (Bassin de Thau)	98	—

Canal de l'Est
(*Northern Section*)

1   *Near Revin*

2   *At Monthermé*

3 *Le Rhin et Grand Canal d'Alsace at Ottmarsneim*

4 *La Meuse at Givet*

5 *Canal de Briare.*
Le Pont-canal de
Briare

6   *Canal de la*
Marne au Rhin
near Bar-le-Duc

8 *Canal de la Marne
à la Saône near Langres*

PART II

LIST OF RIVERS AND CANALS

The name of the town given in brackets after the name of a River or Canal indicates the place in which the Chief Engineer resides who has charge of the waterway. Requests for information concerning conditions of navigation, *chômage*, etc., should be addressed: Monsieur l'Ingénieur en Chef, Ponts et Chaussées, Direction des Voies Navigables, (name of town).

The rising cost of maintaining the tow-paths and the roving bridges taken together with the fact that self-propelled barges now greatly outnumber those which depend upon being towed, has led the French Government to decide to reduce and subsequently to abolish the subsidies hitherto paid to the towing companies. It is therefore probable that the tow-paths and roving bridges will fall into disuse.

As a general rule if the width of a bridge exceeds 5 m. oo the width dimension is not noted in the Distance Tables.

DISTANCE TABLES

AA

General

That part of the river Aa which is canalised begins in Saint-Omer, where it makes junction with the old Canal d'Arques à Saint-Omer, and ends at the North Sea port of Gravelines a few miles eastward of Calais. The river also communicates with the Canal de Calais, the Canal de Bourbourg, and the Canal de la Colme. Two kilometres downstream from the head of the canalised river it joins the Canal de Neuffossé thus linking up the important industrial areas of Lille and Valenciennes with the port of Dunkerque. From its junction with the Canal de Neuffossé to the town of Watten the river has been deepened and the bridges raised as that section forms part of the improved route known as *La liaison Dunkerque-Valenciennes.* Also at Watten a new canal has been cut—la dérivation de Watten— to join the river to the improved length of the Canal de la Colme.

Length

From Saint-Omer to Gravelines the canalised river has a length of 29 kilometres.

Locks

Officially there is but one lock over the entire length and thus the sea lock at Gravelines is not counted. However, both locks have a useful length of 38 m. 85 with a width of 5 m. 10. The first lock is situated about a kilometre below Saint-Omer while the sea lock is reached shortly after the railway bridge at Gravelines has been passed.

Depth

From the junction with the Canal de Neuffossé to the junction with la dérivation de Watten, 3 m. 50. Over the remainder of its length there is, normally, a depth of 3 m. 00, but at times of exceptional drought there may be less: during such periods local information should always be sought.

Bridges

In the improved section all bridges have a headroom of 5 m. 25 above highest navigable water level: over the rest of the length there is a headroom of 4 m. 50 above normal water level except the Pont de Mathurin which has but 3 m. 80. As it is not necessary to pass under this bridge (the deviation *autour de Saint-Omer* usually being taken) this restriction of height can be ignored for through traffic.

Tow-path	There is a good tow-path throughout at first along the right bank changing to the left bank at le Guindal.

Distance Table

		kilom.	lock	kilom.
*Saint-Omer**	*Junction with the Canal de Neuffossé by the old Canal d'Arques a Saint-Omer.* Railway bridge (de Mathurin). Lift bridge (Pont-Vert)	0.0	—	29.0
	Swing bridge (Pont-Rouge). Lock (du Haut-Pont)	1.0	I	28.0
	Junction with Canal de Neuffossé by la dérivation autour de Saint-Omer	2.0	—	27.0
Saint-Momelin	Bridge (de Saint-Momelin)...	4.0	—	25.0
Watten	Bridge (de Watten). Port (de Watten). *Junction with la dérivation de Watten.* (Liaison Dunkerque-Valenciennes) ...	9.0	—	20.0
Ruminghem	Bridge (du Ruth)	11.0	—	18.0
Saint-Mariekerque	Le West. *Junction with Canal de Calais (at K.o)*	15.0	—	14.0
	Lift bridge (de la Bistade)	17.0	—	12.0
Bourbourg	Lift bridge (de Saint-Nicolas)	20.0	—	9.0
Saint-Folquin	Le Guindal. *Junction with Canal de Bourbourg (at K.o)*	23.0	—	6.0
	Lift bridge (de Saint-Folquin)	24.0	—	5.0
Gravelines	Railway bridge	28.0	—	1.0
	Lock (No. 63 bis). Quay and Port (de Gravelines)	29.0	—	0.0

Dérivation de Watten

Watten	Bridge (Pont de Watten)	0.0	—	0.9
	Beginning of dérivation de Watten (at K.9)	0.1	—	0.8
	End of dérivation de Watten. *Junction with Canal de la Colme (at K.0.0)*	0.9	—	0.0

ADOUR

General	The river Adour is navigable only from the Port de Pouy to the sea where it debouches into the Gulfe de Gascogne and is the boundary of the départements des Basses-Pyrenees and des Landes. Formerly it was navigable as far upstream as Saint-Sever at 133 kilometres from the sea, but now that part which lies above the port of Puoy (which is situated 6 kilometres above the town of Dax) is much

* See Plan No. 18.

encumbered by sandbanks over which the depth of water is small. From Port de Pouy to the confluence with le Luy de France the depth is somewhat greater but great care is necessary to avoid the numerous training groins which are set out from the banks. From le Luy to Bec du Gave (confluence with les Gaves Réunis) not so much difficulty should be encountered especially if the precaution is taken to follow the outsides of the curves as, in certain places, the waterway on the inside of the bends is obstructed by shoals. From Bec du Gave to Bayonne there are no obstructions. A large part of this navigation is tidal as the spring tides make themselves felt as high up as Dax. The passage between Bayonne and Dax will be made much easier if the tidal stream is properly worked. It is best to leave Bayonne about two hours after low water, but local advice should be sought. That part of the river which lies between Bayonne and the sea will not be detailed here as it is purely marine, but it may be remarked that the estuary of l'Adour is a maze of shifting banks and is of a very dangerous character.

Length	From Port de Pouy to Bayonne is a distance of 66 kilometres; from Bayonne to the sea, 7 kilometres.
Locks	None.
Depth	From Dax to the confluence with le Luy de France, normally the depth is about 1 m. 00. From le Luy de France to Bec du Gave it is about 1 m. 50 but this is dependant upon the tides; from Bec du Gave to Bayonne it is about 2 m. 00, but also dependant upon the tides.
Bridges	A clear headroom of 6 m. 50 is normal.
Tow-path	A tow-path exists along certain parts, but is not continuous; for all practical purposes towing from the bank has ceased.

Distance Table

		kilom.	lock	kilom.
Port de Pouy	Port	0.0	—	66.0
Dax	Port. Bridge. *Drinking water*	6.0	—	66.0
	Railway bridge	7.0	—	59.0
Meés	Port (de Meés)	13.0	—	53.0
Vimport	Port (de Vimport). Bridge. *Drinking water*	16.0	—	50.0
Siest	Confluence with le Luy, not navigable ...	18.0	—	48.0
Saubusse	Port (de Carrère). *Drinking water*	20.0	—	46.0
Josse	Port (de Lamarquèze). Bridge. *Drinking water*	26.0	—	40.0
Saint-Jean-de-Marsacq	Port (de Gelez)	30.0	—	36.0

Distance Table   *kilom.*   *lock*   *kilom.*

		kilom.	lock	kilom.
Saint-Etienne-d'Orthe	Port (de Rasport). *Drinking water*... ...	33.0	—	33.0
Lanne	Port (de Lanne). *Drinking water*	36.0	—	30.0
	Bridge	38.0	—	28.0
Sames	Bec du Gave. Confluence with les Gaves Réunis *(at K.9)*	40.0	—	26.0
Sames	Bec de la Bidouze	42.0	—	24.0
	Confluence with la Bidouze	43.0	—	23.0
Saint-Laurent-de-Gosse	Port (de Saint-Marie-de-Gosse)	44.0	—	22.0
d'Urt	Port (de Saint-Laurent-de-Gosse)	49.0	—	17.0
	Confluence de l'Aran. Bridge Port (d'Urt)	50.0	—	16.0
	Port (des Salines d'Urt)	51.0	—	15.0
Saint-Barthélemy	Port (de Saint-Barthélemy)...	52.0	—	14.0
	Confluence with l'Ardanavy	55.0	—	11.0
	Port (d'Urcuit)	56.0	—	10.0
Lahonce	Port (de Lahonce)	58.0	—	8.0
Mougerre	Port (de Mougerre)...	63.0	—	3.0
Bayonne	Railway bridge. Bridge (Pont Saint-Esprit). Port. *Confluence with la Nive (at K.57)* ...	66.0	—	0.0

CANAL D'AIRE

General

The Canal d'Aire branches off from the Canal de la Deûle at Bauvin and joins both the Canal de Neuffossé and la Lys at the town of Aire. This canal thus provides a direct route from the River Escaut to the sea ports of Calais and Dunkerque, and is now improved as part of the new Valenciennes-Dunkerque route *(Liaison Dunkerque-Valenciennes)*. In places, however, the canal has sections which are narrow. There are two branch canals; the one being the Canal de Beuvry which is a cul-de-sac leading to a colliery close to Béthune and of which no further mention will be made; the other branch is the old canal *traversant Béthune* by which anyone wishing to visit that town may do so if the draught of the vessel does not exceed 2 m. 20 (see below). The distance by *l'ancien canal traversant Béthune* is about 2 kilometres longer than by the direct route.

Length

From Bauvin to the junction with the Canal de Neuffossé is a distance of 40 kilometres.

Locks

There is one lock, which has a length of 144 m. 60 with a width of 12 m. 00.

Depth		There is a depth of water of 3 m. 50 throughout. But in the *l'ancien canal traversant Béthune* the depth is only 2 m. 60.		
Bridges		Those bridges which are fixed have a clear headroom of not less than 5 m. 25 above the normal water level.		
Tow-path		There is a metalled tow-path throughout along the right bank.		

Distance Table

		kilom.	lock	kilom.
Bauvin	*Junction with le Canal de la Deule (at K.23)*	0.0	—	40.0
Billy-Berclau	Bridge	0.0	—	40.0
	Bridge	1.0	—	39.0
Douvrin	Ferry	3.0	—	37.0
	Rivage public (de Douvrin)	4.0	—	36.0
La Bassée	Railway bridge. Port (de la Bassée) ...	6.0	—	34.0
	Bridge (de l'avenue de la Gare). Narrow channel	6.0	—	34.0
Haisnes	Bridge	6.0	—	34.0
Givenchy	Bridge (de Crêtes)	9.0	—	31.0
Cuinchy	Lock (de Cuinchy)	10.0	I	30.0
	Bridge (de Cuinchy). *Narrow channel* ...	10.0	—	30.0
	Rivage public (de Cuinchy)	11.0	—	29.0
Beuvry	Beginning of narrow channel	13.0	—	27.0
	End of narrow channel	14.0	—	26.0
	Bridge (de Gorre)	15.0	—	25.0
	Upstream junction with l'ancien canal traversant Béthune	15.0	—	25.0
	Ferry	16.0	—	24.0
Essars	Bridge	17.0	—	23.0
Annezin	Bridge (du Long Cornet)	19.0	—	21.0
	Downstream junction with l'ancien canal traversant Béthune	19.0	—	21.0
	Bridge (d'Avelettes)	20.0	—	20.0
Hinges	Bridge (d'Hingettes)	21.0	—	19.0
	Bridge (d'Hinges)	22.0	—	18.0
Mont-Bernenchon	Footbridge	24.0	—	16.0
	Bridge (de Suppli)	25.0	—	15.0
	Bridge (de Saint-Venant)	26.0	—	14.0
	Rivage Robecq public (de Robecq) ...	27.0	—	13.0
	Bridge (de l'Eclemme)	27.0	—	13.0
	Bridge (de la Biette)	29.0	—	11.0
Guarbecque	Railway bridge	31.0	—	9.0
	Rivage public (de Guarbecque)	32.0	—	8.0
	Lift bridge (de Guarbecque)	33.0	—	7.0
Isbergues	Railway bridge	35.0	—	5.0
	Bridge (d'Isbergues)	36.0	—	4.0

Distance Table

			kilom.	lock	kilom.
Aire-sur-la-Lys	Bridge (de la Lacque)	37.0	—	3.0
	Bridge (d'Aire). *Narrow channel*	39.0	—	1.0
	Junction with Canal de Neuffossé and la Lys			
	canalisée (at K.o)	40.0	—	0.0

Old Canal passing through Béthune

				kilom.	lock	kilom.
Beuvry	*Junction with Canal d'Aire (at K.15)*	...	0.0	—	5.0
Essars	Swing bridge (d'Essars)	1.0	—	4.0
	Lift bridge (d'Essars)	1.0	—	4.0
Béthune	Bridge (du Rivage)	2.0	—	3.0
	Port (de Béthune). Bridge (de la Gare) ...	3.0	—	2.0
	Bridge (de Catorive)	3.0	—	2.0
	Junction with Canal d'Aire (at K.19) ...	5.0	—	0.0

AISNE

General

L'Aisne can be considered only to be navigable from Celles (which is situated some 15 kilometres east of Soissons) to its confluence with l'Oise at Bouche-d'Aisne not far from Compiègne. Over this length the river has been entirely canalised; the remainder still continues in its natural state and has been abandoned as far as navigation is concerned. Several short deviations have been cut to rectify the river, the most important of which is close to the lock of Villeneuve-Saint-Germain. This deviation *(dérivation de Bucy)* cuts off a bend in the river which is accessible from downstream but barred at the upstream end. *No Permis de Circulation is necessary for the navigation of this river between Compiègne and Soissons.*

Length

The canalised length is 57 kilometres.

Locks

There are 7 locks. These have a length of 46 m. 00 with a width of 7 m. 95.

Depth

The canalised part of the river is maintained at a depth of 2 m. 30 at normal water level. There are two shelves of sandstone towards the left bank of the river at K.47 and K.47.5, the first called *La Pierre Marion* and the second *La Pierre du Lorrain;* care should be taken to hug the right bank to avoid these dangers.

Bridges

All fixed bridges show a headroom of 3 m. 70 above the highest navigable water level, and normally there is 4 m. 70.

Tow-path

There is a tow-path throughout with a good metalled surface.

Distance Table   *kilom.*   *lock*   *kilom.*

Celles-s-Aisne	Downstream side of lock (de Celles). *Junction with canal latéral a l'Aisne (at K.51)*...	0.0	—	57.0
Condé-s-Aisne	Port and Bridge (de Condé)	1.0	—	56.0
Missy-s-Aisne	Port and Bridge (de Missy)...	4.0	—	53.0
Venizel	Bridge (de Venizel)	7.0	—	50.0
Villeneuve				
Saint-Germain	Beginning of deviation (de Bucy)	12.0	—	45.0
	Lock (de Villeneuve-s-Germain)	13.0	I	44.0
Soissons	Railway bridge	14.0	—	43.0
	Bridge (de Cambetta)	15.0	—	42.0
	Foot bridge, Port (de Soissons)	16.0	—	41.0
	Bridge (du Mail)	16.0	—	41.0
	Lock (de Vauxrot)	17.0	—	40.0
Pasly	Bridge (de Pasly)	18.0	—	39.0
Pommiers	Bridge and Port (de Pommiers)	22.0	—	35.0
Pernant	Port (de Pernant)	24.0	—	33.0
Osly-Courtil	Port (d'Osly-Courtil)	26.0	—	31.0
Fontenoy	Lock (de Fontenoy)	28.0	3	29.0
	Bridge and Port (de Fontenoy)	30.0	—	27.0
Vic-s-Aisne	Bridge and Port (de Vic-s-Aisne)	34.0	—	23.0
	Lock (de Vic-s-Aisne)	35.0	4	22.0
	Railway bridge	36.0	—	21.0
Attichy	Bridge and Port (d'Attichy)	40.0	—	17.0
Couloisy	Lock (de Couloisy)	41.0	5	16.0
Berneuil-s-Aisne	Bridge (de Berneuil)	43.0	—	14.0
Rethondes	Lock (d'Herant)	47.0	6	10.0
	La Pierre Marion. *(Shoal near left bank)* ...	47.0	—	10.0
	La Pierre du Lorrain. *(Shoal near left bank)*	47.0	—	10.0
	Bridge (de Rethondes)	48.0	—	9.0
Choisy-au-Bac	Bridge (du Francport)	52.0	—	5.0
	Lock (du Carandeau)	54.0	7	3.0
	Bridge (de Choisy-au-Bac). Port	55.0	—	2.0
Compiègne	*Confluence with left bank l'Oise (at K.38)*...	57.0	—	0.0

CANAL LATERAL A L'AISNE

General   The canal latéral à l'Aisne connects the canalised river Aisne with the Canal des Ardennes. It also communicates with the Canal de l'Aisne à la Marne and the Canal de l'Oise à l'Aisne; it thus forms a link between these two canals. It begins at Vieux-lès-Asfeld at the downstream side of the lock No. 14 of the Canal des Ardennes, and ends by falling into the River Aisne at Celles-sur-Aisne.

Length	From Vieux-lès-Asfeld to Celles-sur-Aisne is a distance by canal of 51 kilometres.
Locks	There are 8 locks with a length of 38 m. 50 and a width of 5 m. 20, all of which fall towards Celles. The last two locks are staircase locks.
Depth	Normally there is a depth of 2 m. 20.
Bridges	All the fixed bridges have a clear headroom of at least 3 m. 70 above the normal water level.
Tow-path	There is a tow-path throughout. Towing is along the left bank from Vieux-lès-Asfeld to Berry-au-Bac. The tow-path then runs along the right bank. From Bourg-et-Comin the towing is again from the left bank employing diesel power.

Distance Table

		kilom.	lock	kilom.
Vieux-lès-Asfeld	*Junction with Canal des Ardennes (at K.88)*	0.0	—	51.0
Neufchâtel	Port (de Neufchâtel)	5.0	—	46.0
	Bridge (de Neufchâtel)	6.0	—	45.0
Pignicourt	Lock (de Pignecourt. Port	7.0	I	44.0
Variscourt	Bridge and Port (de Variscourt)	11.0	—	40.0
	Railway bridge	13.0	—	38.0
Condé-sur-Suippe	Port and Bridge (de Guignicourt)	13.0	—	38.0
	Lock (de Condé-s-Suippe)	14.0	2	37.0
Berry-au-Bac	*Junction with Canal de l'Aisne à la Marne*			
	(at K.0)	18.0	—	33.0
	Port and turning basin	18.0	—	33.0
	Lock (de Berry-au-Bac). Bridge	18.0	3	33.0
	Turning basin	19.0	—	32.0
Gernicourt	Bridge and Port (de Gernicourt)	21.0	—	30.0
	Bridge (des Cauries)	23.0	—	28.0
Pontavert	Bridge and Port (de Pontavert)	24.0	—	27.0
Concevreux	Bridge (des Canards)	26.0	—	25.0
	Port and Bridge (de Concevreux)	28.0	—	23.0
Maizy	Port and Bridge (de Maizy)	33.0	—	18.0
	Bridge (de l'Adventure)	34.0	—	17.0
	Port (de Villers-en-Prayères). Wet dock ...	35.0	—	16.0
	Port (d'Oeuilly). Bridge (de Villers) ...	36.0	—	15.0
Villers-en-Prayères	Bridge (du Moulin de Villers)	37.0	—	14.0
	Bridge and basin (de Bourg)	38.0	—	13.0
*Bourg-et-Comin**	*Junction with Canal de l'Oise a l'Aisne*			
	(at K.48). Port Lock (de la Cendrière) ...	39.0	4	12.0
	Public quay (de Viel-Arcy)	39.0	—	12.0

* See Plan No. I.

Distance Table		*kilom.*	*lock*	*kilom.*
Pont-Arcy	Bridge and Port (de Pont-Arcy)	41.0	—	10.0
Saint-Mard	Port and Bridge (de Saint-Mard)	43.0	—	8.0
Cys	Port and Lock (de Cys)	44.0	5	7.0
Presles-et-Boves	Port and Bridge (de Presles)	45.0	—	6.0
	Lock (de Saint-Audebert)	47.0	6	4.0
Vailly	Bridge and Port (de Vailly)	49.0	—	2.0
	Bridge (de Chassemy)	50.0	—	1.0
Celles-s-Aisne	Locks (de Celles). *Junction with l'Aisne canalisée* (*at K.0)*	51.0	7 & 8	0.0

CANAL DE L'AISNE A LA MARNE

General

The Canal de l'Aisne à la Marne leaves the canal latéral à l'Aisne at Berry-au-Bac and joins the canal latéral à la Marne at Condé-sur-Marne. There is a summit level on this canal which passes through a tunnel. The summit level is not less than 95.7 metres above sea level. The tunnel, which is at Mont-de-Billy, has a length of 2,300 metres. Vessels with a draught of 2 m. 20 and a beam of 5 m. 00 can pass through the tunnel if the superstructure does not exceed 3 m. 70. Towage is compulsory for all vessels (whether self-propelled or not) and convoys are made up at unspecified times according to the incidence of traffic in each direction. The actual times of departure must, therefore, be ascertained locally. But yachts are allowed to go through under their own power at their own risk.

Length

From Berry-au-Bac to Condé-sur-Marne by canal is 58 kilometres.

Locks

The water level of the canal is controlled by 24 locks, 16 of which fall towards l'Aisne and the remaining 8 towards la Marne. All the locks have a useful length of 38 m. 50 with a width of 5 m. 20.

Depth

The normal depth of water is 2 m. 20.

Bridges

Nearly all the bridges over the canal are fixed, except for two swing bridges in the City of Reims. They all have a clear headroom of 3 m. 70, *except* the bridge over the downstream end of the lock at Condé-sur-Marne which has only a headroom of 3 m. 53 at normal water level.

Tow-path

There is a tow-path throughout. From Berry-au-Bac to Reims it runs along the left bank; from Reims to Pont de Vrilly (K.27) it is on the right bank, where it again returns to the left bank and so continues to Condé-sur-Marne. There is, however, a short length near the tunnel (K.44 to K.51) which is on the right bank.

Tunnel du Mont de Billy

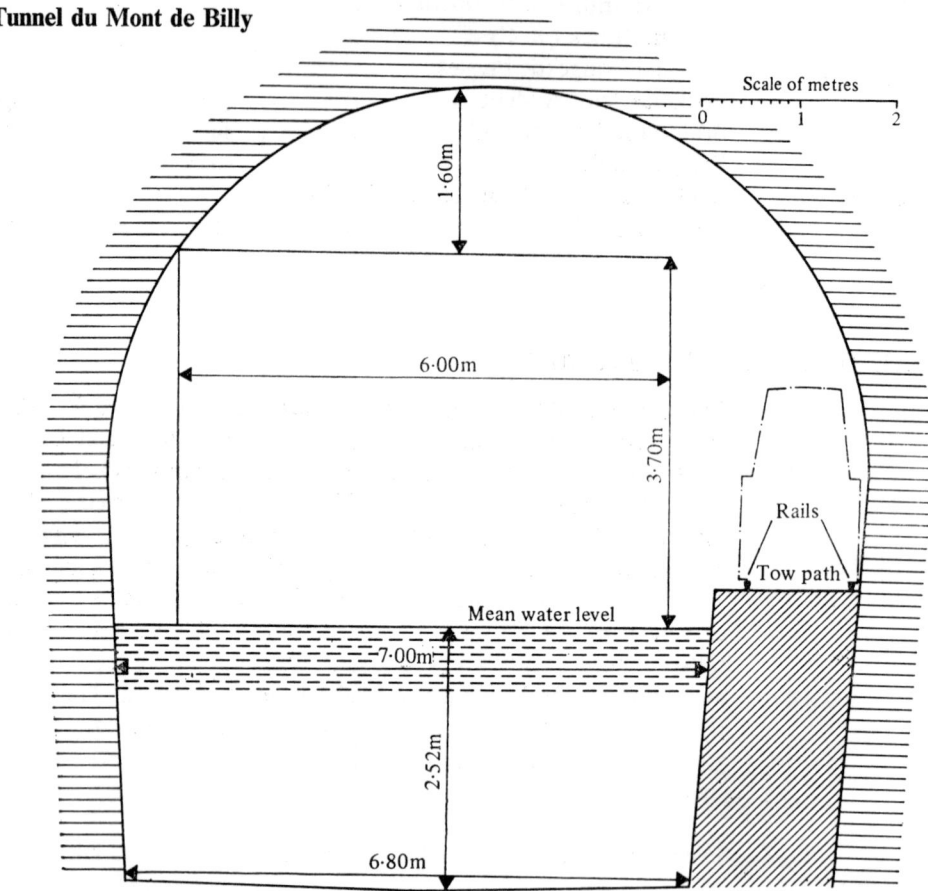

CAUTION. *The tunnel is lit by electric light and live electric wires run throughout its length.*

Distance Table

		kilom.	lock	kilom.
Berry-au-Bac	Junction with canal latéral a l'Aisne (at K.18). Bridge and Railway bridge. Lock (de Berry-au-Bac)	0.0	1	58.0
Cormicy	Lock (du Moulin de Sapigneul)	1.0	2	57.0
	Lock (de Sapigneul)	2.0	3	56.0
	Bridge and Port (de Neuville)	4.0	—	54.0
	Lock (d'Alger)	5.0	4	53.0
Cauroy-lès-Hermonville	Lock (du Gaudart)	6.0	5	52.0
Loivre	Lock (de Loivre). Port (de Loivre)... ...	9.0	6	49.0
	Lock (des Fontaines)	10.0	7	48.0
	Lock (de la Noue-Gouzaine)	11.0	8	47.0

Distance Table *kilom.* *lock* *kilom.*

		kilom.	*lock*	*kilom.*
Courcy	Lock (de Courcy)	12.0	9	46.0
	Bridge (de Brimont). Port (de Courcy) ...	13.0	—	45.0
La Neuvillette	Port and Bridge (de La Neuvillette) ...	17.0	—	41.0
Saint-Brice-Courcelles	Bridge (de Saint-Thierry)	19.0	—	39.0
	Bridge (de Courcelles). Entrance to Port Colbert de Reims	20.0	—	38.0
Reims	Bridge (de Saint-Brice)	21.0	—	37.0
	Two Railway bridges	22.0	—	36.0
	Bridge (de Vesle). Foot bridge (Libergier) Old Port de Reims	23.0	—	35.0
	Bridge (de Venise). Lock (de Fléchambault)	24.0	10	34.0
	Lock (du Château)	25.0	11	33.0
	Lock (d'Huon)	26.0	12	32.0
	Bridge (de Vrilly)	27.0	—	31.0
	Bridge (de Saint-Léonard)	29.0	—	29.0
Puisieux	Bridge (de Couraux)	32.0	—	26.0
Sillery	Lock (de Sillery). Pont-canal over la Vesle	33.0	13	25.0
	Bridge (de Petit-Sillery). Port (de Sillery). Bridge (du Moulin de Sillery)	34.0	—	24.0
Verzenay	Lock (de l'Espérance)	36.0	14	22.0
	Bridge (de Prunay)	36.0	—	22.0
Beaumont-s-Vesle	Lock (de Beaumont-s-Vesle). Port... ...	38.0	15	20.0
Courmelois	Lock (de Wez). Beginning of summit level	39.0	16	19.0
	Bridge and Port (de Courmelois)	41.0	—	17.0
Sept-Saulx	Port and Bridge (de Sept-Saulx)	43.0	—	15.0
	Bridge (d'Issus). Upstream end of tunnel of Mont de Billy (2,300 m.) Tariff Office ...	46.0	—	12.0
Billy-le-Grand	Downstream end of tunnel of Mont de Billy	49.0	—	9.0
Vaudemange	Bridge and Port (de Vaudemange)... ...	50.0	—	8.0
	Lock (de Vaudemange)	51.0	17	7.0
Isse	Lock (du Champ Bon-Garçon)	52.0	18	6.0
	Lock (des Longues-Raies)	52.0	19	6.0
	Lock (de Saint-Martin)	53.0	20	5.0
	Lock (de la Fosse-Rodé)	54.0	21	4.0
	Lock (d'Isse)	54.0	22	4.0
	Bridge (d'Isse)	55.0	—	3.0
*Condé-sur-Marne**	Lock (de Coupé)	56.0	23	2.0
	Lock (de Condé-s-Marne). Port	58.0	24	0.0
	Junction with canal latéral à la Marne (at K.48)	58.0	—	0.0

* See Plan No. 3.

CANAL DES ARDENNES

General

The Canal des Ardennes (really at this point the canalised river la Meuse) branches off from the Canal de l'Est (Northern Section) at Pont-à-Bar which is some 14 kilometres south-eastward of Mézières and close to Dom-le-Mesnil. It ends at Vieux-lès-Asfeld where it is joined to the beginning of the canal latéral à l'Aisne. Officially the canal is divided into two lengths, that is from Pont-à-Bar to Semuy and from Vouziers to Vieux-lès-Asfeld, the junction of the two being at Semuy. Each has its separate *kilométrage*, but it is thought more convenient here to carry the distance through from one end to the other. The distance from Vouziers to Semuy is 12 kilometres and is here treated as a branch. The conditions of navigation are similar throughout. At Saint-Aignan there is a tunnel which is 197 metres in length and which allows only of one-way traffic. All vessels must carry the usual lights when passing through. The order in which they pass is that of their arrival at the basin at the downstream end of the tunnel, or at the stopping posts placed at the upstream end, at which places they may only halt pending their entry into the tunnel. When a vessel has entered the downstream basin no up going vessel may pass the lock which is sited immediately below the basin. If, in spite of these regulations, two vessels meet each other in the tunnel they must refer the matter to the lock-keeper in charge of Lock No. 4 who will then rule which one is to go back. There is a summit level between Sauville and Le Chesne, the height of which is over 500 ft. above sea level. The Canal des Ardennes was opened to traffic in the year 1833.

Length

From the junction with the Canal de l'Est at Pont-à-Bar to where it meets the canal latéral à l'Aisne at Vieux-lès-Asfeld is a distance of 88 kilometres.

Locks

There are in all 44 locks between Pont-à-Bar and Vieux-lès-Asfeld of which 7 fall towards la Meuse and the remaining 37 towards l'Aisne. In addition there are 4 locks on the Vouziers branch whose dimensions are the same as those on the main canal. All have a length of 38 m. 50 with a width of 5 m. 20.

Depth

The normal depth of water is 2 m. 20 in both the main and branch canals.

Bridges

There is a large number of fixed bridges (between 50 and 70) all of which have a clear headroom of 3 m. 50 above the normal water level.

Tow-path

The tow-path, which continues throughout the length of the canal, is metalled for the whole distance.

Tunnel de St. Aignan

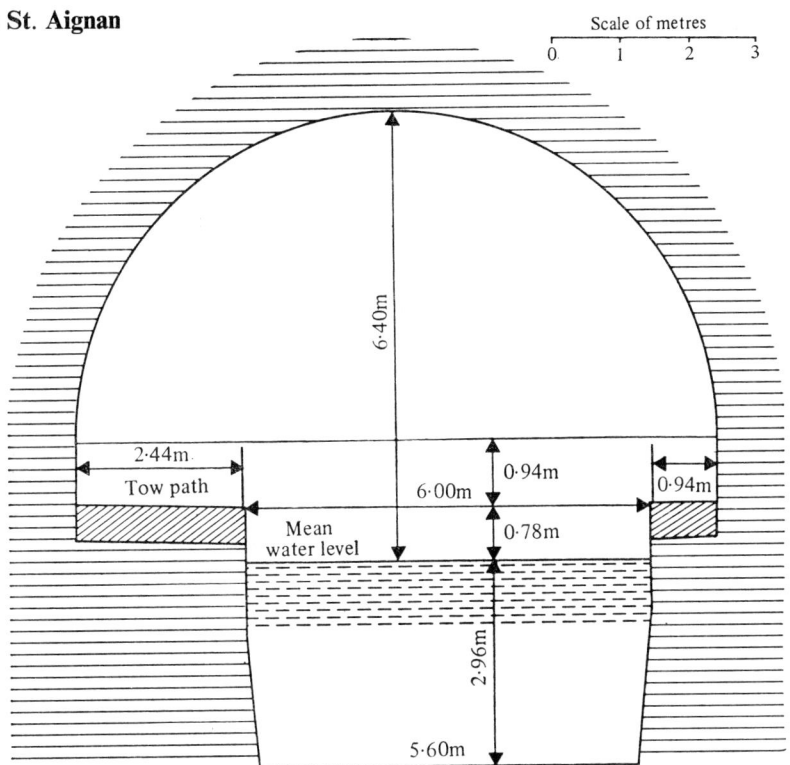

CAUTION. *Live electric wires may be established throughout the length of this tunnel.*

Distance Table		*kilom.*	*lock*	*kilom.*
*Dom-le-Mesnil**	Pont-à-Bar. *Junction with Canal de l'Est (at K.96).* Lock (No. 7 de Meuse)... ...	0.0	I	88.0
	Lock (No. 6 de Pont-à-Bar). Ports. Bridge (de Pont-à-Bar)	1.0	2	87.0
Hannogne-Saint-	Bridge (de Saint-Martin)	2.0	—	86.0
Martin	Bridge (de Saint-Martin)	3.0	—	85.0
Saint-Aignan	Lock (No. 5). Turning basin	6.0	3	88.0
	Lock (No. 4 de Saint-Aignan). Tunnel de Saint-Aignan (197 m.)	6.0	4	88.0
d'Omicourt	Port. Bridge (d'Omicourt)	8.0	—	80.0
Malmy	Lock (No. 3 de Malmy). Port (de Malmy)	12.0	5	76.0
	Turning basin	13.0	—	75.0
Vendresse	Bridge (de la Morteau). Port (de Ambly) ...	15.0	—	73.0
	Bridge (de Ambly-s-Bar)	16.0	—	72.0
La Cassine	Lock (No. 2 de la Cassine)	17.0	6	71.0
Sauville	Lock (No. 1 de Sauville). Beginning of summit level	20.0	7	68.0
	Port (d'Armageat)	21.0	—	67.0

* See Plan No. 11.

43

Distance Table

		kilom.	lock	kilom.
Tannay	Bridge (de Tannay)	23.0	—	65.0
	Port (de Pont-Bar). Bridge (de Pont-Bar)...	25.0	—	63.0
Chesne	Port (du Chesne). Bridges (Le Chesne)			
	Turning basin. Port (Le Chesne)	28.0	—	60.0
	Turning basin. Port (Le Chesne)	29.0	—	59.0
	Lock (No. 1 du Chesne). End of summit level	30.0	8	58.0
	Lock (No. 2 du Chesne). Turning basin ...	30.0	9	58.0
	Lock (No. 3 du Chesne)	30.0	10	58.0
	Lock (No. 4 du Chesne)	31.0	11	57.0
Montgon	Lock (No. 5 de Montgon)	31.0	12	57.0
	Lock (No. 6 de Montgon)	31.0	13	57.0
	Lock (No. 7 de Montgon)	31.0	14	57.0
	Lock (No. 8 de Montgon)	32.0	15	56.0
	Lock (No. 9 de Montgon)	32.0	16	56.0
	Lock (No. 10 de Montgon)	32.0	17	56.0
	Lock (No. 11 de Montgon)	33.0	18	55.0
	Lock (No. 12 de Montgon)	33.0	19	55.0
	Lock (No. 13 de Montgon)	33.0	20	55.0
	Lock (No. 14 de Montgon)	33.0	21	55.0
	Lock (No. 15 de Montgon)	34.0	22	54.0
	Lock (No. 16 de Montgon)	34.0	23	54.0
Neuville-Day	Lock (No. 17 de Neuville-Day)	34.0	24	54.0
	Lock (No. 18 de Neuville-Day)	35.0	25	53.0
	Lock (No. 19 de Neuville-Day) Port ...	35.0	26	53.0
	Lock (No. 20 de Neuville-Day)	35.0	27	53.0
	Lock (No. 21 de Neuville-Day)	36.0	28	52.0
	Lock (No. 22 de Neuville-Day)	36.0	29	52.0
Semuy	Lock (No. 23 de Semuy)	37.0	30	51.0
	Lock (No. 24 de Semuy)	37.0	31	51.0
	Lock (No 25 de Semuy) Bridge (de Semuy)	38.0	32	50.0
	Lock (No. 26 de Semuy). *Junction with the branch to Vouziers*	39.0	33	49.0
Rilly-s-Aisne	Lock (No. 27 or No. 4 de Rilly)	39.0	34	49.0
	Official kilométrage 12 from Vouziers.			
	Railway bridge. Bridge (de Rilly) ...	40.0	—	48.0
	Bridge (de Forest)	42.0	—	46.0
d'Attigny	Lock (No. 5 d'Attigny)	44.0	35	44.0
	Bridge (d'Attigny)	45.0	—	43.0
Givry	Lock (No. 6 de Givry)	47.0	36	41.0
	Bridge. Port (de Givry)	48.0	—	40.0
	Bridge (de Montmarin)	49.0	—	39.0
d'Ambly	Bridge (de Fleury)	52.0	—	36.0
	Bridge (d'Ambly). Port (d'Ambly) ...	53.0	—	35.0

Distance Table		*kilom.*	*lock*	*kilom.*
Seuil	Lock (No. 7 de Seuil)	55.0	37	33.0
Thugny	Bridge (de Thugny)...	57.0	—	31.0
	Lock (No. 8 de Thugny). Port (de Thugny)	58.0	38	30.0
Biermes	Lock (No. 9 de Biermes). Port (de Biermes)	60.0	39	28.0
Rethel	Two Railway bridges. Port (de Rethel)		
	Bridge. Turning basin	63.0	—	25.0
	Lock (No. 10 de Romance)	65.0	40	23.0
Nanteuil	Lock (No. 11 de Nanteuil) Port	67.0	41	21.0
Taizy	Railway bridge	72.0	—	16.0
Château-Porcein	Bridge (de Château-Porcein). Port ...	73.0	—	15.0
	Lock (No. 12 de Pargny)	75.0	42	13.0
Blanzy	Bridge (de Blanzy)	78.0	—	10.0
	Port (de Balham)	79.0	—	9.0
	Bridge (de Balham)...	80.0	—	8.0
d'Asfeld	Lock (No. 13 d'Asfeld)	83.0	43	5.0
	Railway bridge	84.0	—	4.0
	Bridge (d'Asfeld). Port	85.0	—	3.0
Vieux-lès-Asfeld	Port (Vieux-lès-Asfeld)	86.0	—	2.0
	Bridge (de Vieux-lès-Asfeld)	87.0	—	1.0
	Lock (No. 14 de Vieux-lès-Asfeld). *Junction with the canal latèral a l'Aisne (at K.0)* ...	88.0	44	0.0

Branch Canal to Vouziers

 | | | |
---|---|---|---|---
Vouziers | *Beginning of branch canal.* **Bridge. Ports** ... | 0.0 | 0 | 12.0
 | Lock (de Vouziers) ... ... | 1.0 | 1 | 11.0
Conde-lès-Vouziers | Bridge (de Conde-lès-Vouziers). Port ... | 2.0 | — | 10.0
Vrizy | Port. Bridge (de Vrizy). Port ... ... | 3.0 | — | 9.0
 | Lock (No. 2 de Vrizy) ... ... | 5.0 | 2 | 7.0
 | Bridge (d'Echarson) ... ... | 6.0 | — | 6.0
Voncq | Lock (de Voncq) ... ... | 8.0 | 3 | 4.0
Rilly-s.-Aisne | Bridge (de Rilly). Port ... ... | 11.0 | — | 1.0
 | Lock (de Rilly). *Junction with the main canal (at K.39)* ... ... | 12.0 | 4 | 0.0

CANAL D'ARLES A BOUC

General

The Canal d'Arles à Bouc branches off from le Rhône at Arles and finishes at the end of la tranchée de Bouc, which same falls into the marine Canal de Port-de-Bouc à Martigues. Port de Bouc is situated on the eastern side of the Golfe de Fos and is connected, as mentioned above, by the marine canal which runs between the Golfe de Fos and the town of Martigues. This latter lies at the entrance de l'Etang de Berre and has been called *la Venise provençale.*

The passage along the canal d'Arles à Bouc being in still water saves both time and fuel over the route via Port Saint Louis, and also the necessity of an open sea passage. The run from Port Saint Louis to Arles is some 40 kilometres against the stream of le Rhône. Incidentally it is useful to know that if a vessel cannot make that 40 kilometre run in two hours or less then there is small hope of her being able to stem the stream on the higher reaches. Reverting to the Canal d'Arles à Bouc it is important to note that during periods of low water in le Rhône there may be less than 2 m. oo over the sill of the lock at Arles, and also that the influence of the sea running up from Port-de-Bouc makes itself felt as far as l'Etourneau; so it is very necessary to obtain local advice before attempting the passage.

Length

The distance from Arles to Port-de-Bouc is 47 kilometres.

Locks

There are 4 locks, but that at Fos is frequently found open as it is used as a guard lock dependant upon the levels in the other pounds. The length of the locks is 33 m. oo with a width of 8 m. oo.

Depth

The normal depth of water is 2 m. oo but this may fall to 1 m. 60 or even less during times of low water. See also the remarks about the water over the sill of the lock at Arles.

Bridges

All the bridges have a clear headroom of 3 m. 70 above the normal water level.

Tow-path

There is no regular tow-path as the canal is used only by self-propelled vessels, or vessels towed by tugs.

Distance Table

		kilom.	lock	kilom.
Arles	*Junction with le Rhône.* Lock (d'Arles) Port (du canal). Bridge (Réginel)	0.0	I	47.0
	Railway bridge	1.0	—	46.0
	Lock (de Montcalde)	3.0	2	44.0
	Bridge (d'Allen)	5.0	—	42.0
	Bridge (de la Ville)	7.0	—	40.0
	Bridge (de Mollégès)	9.0	—	38.0
	Bridge (de Beyne)	14.0	—	33.0
	Bridge (de Mas-Thibert)	18.0	—	29.0
	Lock (de l'Etourneau)	21.0	3	26.0
Fos	Salt-pans (du Relai)	31.0	—	16.0
	Lock (de Fos)	36.0	4	11.0
	Bridge. Salt-pans (des Salins du Midi) ...	42.0	—	5.0
	Beginning of la tranchée du Port-de-Bouc	45.0	—	2.0
	Railway bridge	46.0	—	1.0

Distance Table		*kilom.*	*lock*	*kilom.*
Port-de-Bouc	Railway bridge. Bridge. End of la tranchée du Port-de-Bouc. *Entrance to canal maritime de Port-de-Bouc à Martigues*	47.0	—	0.0

CANAL DE LA VIEILLE AUTISE

General   The Canal de la Vieille-Autise is navigable from Courdault to its confluence with la Sèvre-Niortaise at Damvix (K.32). This waterway is really the canalised River l'Autise but it is always referred to as *le canal de la Vieille-Autise*. The conditions of navigation are the same as those obtaining on la Sèvre-Niortaise.

Length   From the head of the navigation at Courdault to the point where it falls into la Sèvre-Niortaise the canal has a length of nearly 10 kilometres.

Locks   There is only one lock and this has a length of 31 m. 50 with a width of 5 m. 20.

Depth   The normal depth of water is 1 m. 20, but drops to 0 m. 80 during times of low water.

Bridges   The fixed bridges have a clear headroom of 3 m. 05 above the normal water level.

Tow-path   Of natural earth throughout.

Distance Table		*kilom.*	*lock*	*kilom.*
Bouille-Courdault	*Head of the navigation.* Port (de Courdault)	0.0	—	10.0
Saint-Sigismond	Bridge (de Saint-Sigismond)	3.0	—	7.0
Saint-Arnault	Lock (de Saint-Arnault)	6.0	1	4.0
	Bridge	7.0	—	3.0
	Bridge. La Bernegoue	8.0	—	2.0
Damvix	L'Ouillette. Foot bridge. *Confluence with la Sèvre-Niortaise (at K.32)*	10.0	—	0.0

AUTISE (Jeune)

General   The river Jeune-Autise is made up of a part of l'Autise together with an artificial channel *(une dérivation)* fed from la Vieille-Autise; however, it is considered to be a separate river. The navigable course extends from the Port de Souil to the confluence from la Sèvre-Niortaise in the loop of that river called *le contour de*

Maillé. The traffic consists almost entirely of local agricultural produce and timber.

Length
From the Port to the confluence with la Sèvre-Niortaise the distance is nearly 9 kilometres.

Locks
There is only one lock, and that is situated at Maillé. It has a length of 7 m. 00 with a width of 3 m. 00. Unfortunately the sill depth at normal water level is only 0 m. 60. This is an obstruction to the navigation as the usual depth of the river both upstream and downstream is considerably greater.

Depth
The normal depth in the channel between Port de Souil and the lock at Maillé is 2 m. 20; below the lock to the confluence with la Sèvre-Niortaise the depth is 2 m. 50. But during times of low water these depths may fall to 1 m. 70 and 2 m. 00 respectively.

Bridges
There are three bridges, all fixed. The least headroom at normal water level is 2 m. 40.

Distance Table

		kilom.	lock	kilom.
St. Pierre-le-Vieux	Port de Souil	0.0	—	8.9
	Bridge	1.8	—	7.1
Maillezais	Bridge (de Maillezais)	3.3	—	5.6
Maillé	Pont Aqueduc (de Maillé). Lock	7.5	I	1.4
	Bridge (St. Nicholas)	8.0	—	0.9
	Confluence with la Sèvre-Niortaise in 'le contour de Maillé'	8.9	—	0.0

BAISE

General
La Baïse is canalised and was formerly navigable from Condom. It is a tributary on the left bank of la Garonne and falls into that river at Saint-Léger-Monplaisir. Most of it is now abandoned as far as navigation is concerned, only a short length from Buzet to the confluence now being practicable. The river is connected with the canal latéral à la Garonne at Buzet by a branch called *Descente en Baïse.*

Length
The navigable length is now 6 kilometres.

Locks
There are 2 locks, both of which have a length of 31 m. 40 with a width of 5 m. 20.

Depth
From Buzet to the confluence with la Garonne the depth of water is normally maintained at 1 m. 80.

Bridges	The bridges, all fixed, have a minimum headroom of 5 m. 50 above the normal water level.		
Tow-path	The tow-path is of natural earth, except for about 10 kilometres which has been metalled. It runs along the right bank from Bordes to Buzet, but from there to the confluence it is on the left bank.		

Distance Table

		kilom.	lock	kilom.
Buzet	Junction with canal latéral a la Garonne by			
	the Descente en Baise	0.0	—	6.0
	Bridge (de Buzet). Port	0.3	—	5.7
	Lock (No. 14 de Buzet)	0.4	1	5.6
Saint-Léger-	Lock (No. 15 de Monplaisir). *Confluence*			
Monplaisir	*with la Garonne*	6.0	2	0.0

CANAL DE BERGUES

General	The Canal de Bergues branches off from the Canal de la Colme at the town of Bergues and connects with the port of Dunkerque at the marine canal called *canal de Jonction*. The first 400 metres of the Canal de Bergues is common with the Canal de la Colme. It is one of the more ancient canals its course being already shown on the map of the IXth century.
Length	From the lock in Bergues (Ecluse Neuve) to its junction with the canal de Jonction at Dunkerque the distance is 8 kilometres.
Locks	There are no locks.
Depth	The normal depth of water is 2 m. 50.
Bridges	All the fixed bridges have at least a headroom of 3 m. 70 above the normal water level.
Tow-path	There is a good tow-path throughout.

Distance Table

		kilom.	lock	kilom.
Bergues	Junction with Canal de la Colme (at K.24)			
	Port (de Bergues)	0.0	—	8.0
Coudekerque	Bridge (des Sept-Planetes)	5.0	—	3.0
	Bridge (Pont Saint-Georges). Railway			
	Bridge	7.0	—	
Dunkerque	Bridge (Pont Rouge). *Junction with marine*			
	canal (called 'de Jonction')	8.0	—	0.0

CANAL DU BLAVET

General	The Canal du Blavet joins the Canal de Nantes à Brest at Pontivy and runs to the seaport of Hennebont. The canal is really the River Blavet which has been canalised, and below the last lock at Polhuern the river is tidal.
Length	The length of the canal between the junction at Pontivy and the bridge at Hennebont is 60 kilometres.
Locks	There are 28 locks, each of which has a length of 26 m. 30 with a width of 4 m. 70.
Depth	The normal depth of water is 1 m. 60.
Bridges	Of the 20 or so fixed bridges which span the canal the lowest has a headroom of 2 m. 60 above the normal water level, but this headroom may be reduced to 2 m. 00 at times of highest navigable water level.
Tow-path	There is now no tow-path which is practicable, and the vessels which use the canal are now all motor vessels.

Distance Table

		kilom.	*lock*	*kilom.*
Pontivy	*Junction with Canal de Nantes a Brest (at K.205)* Basin (du Champ de Foire), Lock (des Récollets). Bridges	0.0	I	60.0
	Bridge (Pont de l'Hôpital)	0.0	—	60.0
	Bridge (de la Caserne). Bridge (Pont Neuf)	1.0	—	59.0
Sourn	Railway bridge. Lock (de Lestitut) ...	2.0	2	58.0
	Railway bridge	3.0	—	57.0
	Lock (de Signan or Saint-Michel)	4.0	3	56.0
Saint-Thuriau	Lock (du Roch)	7.0	4	53.0
Bieuzy-les-Eaux	Lock (du Dividit)	9.0	5	51.0
	Lock (de Rimaison). Bridge	12.0	6	48.0
	Lock (de Kerblesquer)	14.0	7	46.0
	Lock (de Guern)	16.0	8	44.0
	Railway bridge	16.0	—	44.0
	Railway bridge	17.0	—	43.0
	Lock (St.-Nicolas-des-Eaux). Port. Bridge	18.0	9	42.0
	Lock (de La Couarde)	19.0	10	41.0
	Railway bridge	20.0	—	40.0
	Lock (de Camblen)	21.0	11	39.0
Melrand	Lock (de Moulin-Neuf)	23.0	12	37.0
	Lock (de Boterneau). Port...	25.0	13	35.0
Saint-Barthélémy	Bridge	25.0	—	35.0

Distance Table					*kilom.*	*lock*	*kilom.*
Quistinic	Lock (de Tréblavet)	...	...	...	27.0	14	33.0
	Lock (de Talgouet)	...	...	...	28.0	15	32.0
	Bridge. Railway bridge	...	...	...	30.0	—	30.0
Baud	Lock (de Saint-Adrien). Port	...	...	31.0	16	29.0
	Lock (de Trémorin). Railway bridge	...	34.0	17	26.0
	Lock (de Saint-Barbe)	...	...	...	36.0	18	24.0
	Bridge (de Pont-Augan). Port	...	...	37.0	—	23.0
Languidic	Lock (de Minazen)	...	...	...	39.0	19	21.0
d'Inzinzac	Lock (de Maneruen)	...	...	...	45.0	20	15.0
	Bridge. Port	...	...	...	46.0	—	14.0
	Lock (de Rudet)	...	...	...	47.0	21	13.0
	Lock (de Trebihan)...	...	...	...	49.0	22	11.0
	Lock (de Kerousse)	...	...	...	51.0	23	9.0
	Lock (de Quellenec)	...	...	...	52.0	24	8.0
Hennebont	Lock (de Lochrist). Port. Landing stage ...			55.0	25	5.0
	Lock (du Grand Barrage) ...	...	...	56.0	26	4.0
	Lock (de Gorets)	...	...	...	56.0	27	4.0
	Lock (de Polhuern)...	...	...	...	57.0	28	3.0
	Junction with le Blavet Maritime	...	...	60.0	—	0.0

CANAL DE BOURBOURG

General

The Canal de Bourbourg joins the River Aa to the marine canal called the *canal de jonction* at Dunkerque. It was formerly a part of the route connecting the port of Dunkerque with Paris and also with the industrial region of Lille and Valenciennes. But recently, owing to the great increase of water-borne freight, a major improvement work was put in hand and is now complete. This work, known as *la liaison Dunkerque-Valenciennes*, has used a short length of the ancient canal—to which has been added *la dérivation Ouest vers le port de Dunkerque:* this *dérivation* leads directly into one of the marine basins in Dunkerque harbour.

For more particulars of the improved route see *la liaison Dunkerque Valenciennes.**

Length

The length of the canal is 21 kilometres.

Locks

There are 3 locks. Two of these have a length of 40 m. 30 with a width of 5 m. 20. The final lock at the junction with the marine canal has a length of 110 m. 25 with a width of 12 m. 00.

Depth

Except for the short length of about a kilometre lying between the junction of la dérivation de la Colme and la dérivation Ouest vers le port de Dunkerque along which the depth is 3 m. 50, the normal

* P. 74.

51

depth of water in the canal is 2 m. 50, but may be slightly less during times of exceptional drought.

Bridges From the River Aa to the junction with la dérivation de la Colme the minimum headroom under bridges is 3 m. 50; from that point to the end of the canal the headroom is not less than 4 m. 70.

Tow-path There is a tow-path throughout.

Distance Table

		kilom.	lock	kilom.
Bourbourg	Le Guindal. *Junction with l'Aa (at K.23).*			
	Lock and Bridge (du Guindal)	0.0	I	21.0
	Railway bridge	2.0	—	19.0
	Lift bridge (called 'de Maisonneuve') ...	3.0	—	18.0
	Lift bridge (Pont Louis Magniez). Port ...	3.0	—	18.0
	Lock (de Bourbourg)	3.0	2	18.0
Craywick	Quay (de Coppenaxfort). Bridge	8.0	—	13.0
Loon-Plage	Junction with la dérivation de la Colme (at K.8)	9.0	—	12.0
	Beginning of la dérivation Ouest vers la port de Dunkerque	10.0	—	11.0
Spycker	Lift bridge (de Spycker)	12.0	—	9.0
	Port and Bridge (de Spycker)	13.0	—	8.0
Petite-Synthe	Quay (de Petite-Synthe)	15.0	—	6.0
	Bridge (de Petite-Synthe)	16.0	—	5.0
	Railway bridge. Quay (de Petite-Synthe) ...	19.0	—	2.0
	Port (de Petite-Synthe)	19.0	—	2.0
Dunkerque	Lock (du Jeu de Mail). Public staithe ...	20.0	3	1.0
	Bridge. *Junction with marine canal (called 'de Jonction')*	21.0	—	0.0

Dérivation Ouest vers le port de Dunkerque

Distance Table

		kilom.	lock	kilom.
Canal de Bourbourg	Beginning of la dérivation Ouest vers le port de Dunkerque *(at K.10)*	0.0	—	10.6
	Lock (écluse de Mardyck)	7.6	I	3.0
Dunkerque	End of la dérivation. Ouest vers le port de Dunkerque. Port de Dunkerque	10.6	—	0.0

CANAL DE BOURGOGNE

General The Canal de Bourgogne forms a connection between Paris and Lyon by way of the River Yonne and the River Saône. It thus provides one of the main routes between the Mediterranean and the estuary of la Seine. The canal, which rises to a height of 378 metres above the sea, contains a summit level. It is on this level that the tunnel of Pouilly-en-Auxois is situated. This tunnel is 3,350 metres in length and is preceded by a double cutting of the same name. There are several other double cuttings the most notable of which is that called *du Creuzot* which has a length of over a 1,000 metres. There is no tow-path through the tunnel and over the whole length of the summit level a system of compulsory towage is in force *for all vessels*, a distance of about $5\frac{1}{2}$ kilometres. Yachts having a special permit from the Chief Engineer may pass, at their own risk, under power by themselves. Tows leave Pouilly every day at 0715 hours and 1345 hours; the times from Escommes is variable depending upon the time taken in the other direction (usually from 1 to $2\frac{3}{4}$ hours). Local enquiries must be made.

Tunnel de Pouilly-en-Auxois

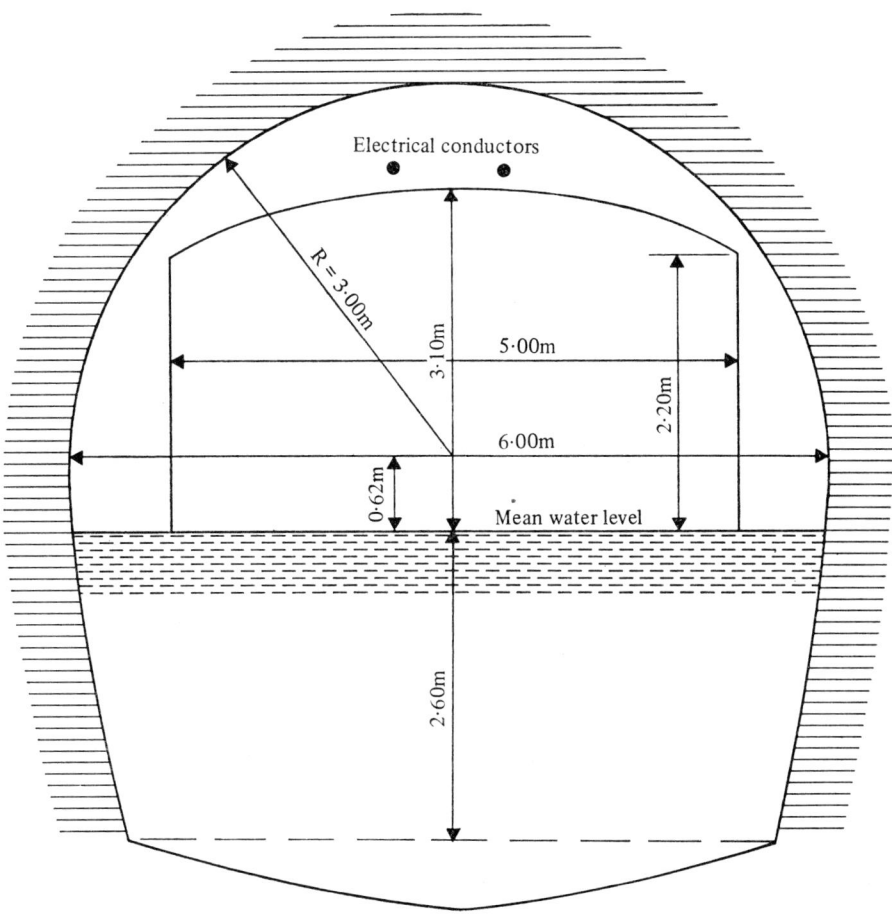

CAUTION. Live electric wires may be established throughout the length of this tunnel.

53   E

Length	The total length of the canal from L'Yonne at Laroche to la Saône at St. Jean-de-Losne is 242 kilometres.

Locks	There are 189 locks; of these 113 fall towards l'Yonne and 76 fall toward la Saône. All the locks have a length of 39 m. 00 with a width of 5 m. 20.

Depth	The normal depth of the canal is 2 m. 20.

Bridges	There is a large number of fixed bridges, about half of which are sited at locks. They all have a clear headroom of 3 m. 40 above the normal water level.

Tow-path	There is a good tow-path throughout except along the summit level and through the tunnel.

Distance Table

		kilom.	lock	kilom.
*Laroche**	*Junction with l'Yonne (at K.22).* Bridge. Locks (Nos. 115-114.Y de Laroche)†			
	Basin and Port (de Laroche)	0.0	I	242.0
Cheny	Port (de Cheny) Lock (No. 113.Y de Cheny)	2.0	2	240.0
Esnon	Port and Bridge (d'Esnon)	6.0	—	236.0
Brienon	Lock (No. 112.Y du Moulin-Neuf). Basin			
	Port	8.0	3	234.0
	Lock (No. 111.Y du Boitoir). Pont-canal	10.0	4	232.0
D'Avrolles	Bridge and Port (de Crécy)	13.0	—	229.0
	Port (de Frécambault)	14.0	—	228.0
	Lock (No. 110.Y de Duchy)	15.0	5	227.0
Vergigny	Lock (No. 109.Y de la Maladrerie) ...	17.0	6	225.0
Saint-Florentin	Lock (No. 108.Y de Saint-Florentin) ...	18.0	7	224.0
	Pont-canal. Basin. Bridge (de St. Florentin). Railway bridge	19.0	—	223.0
Germigny	Port (de Germigny)	20.0	—	222.0
	Locks (Nos. 107-106.Y de Germigny)† ...	22.0	8	220.0
	Lock (No. 105.Y d'Egrevin)	23.0	9	219.0
Butteaux	Bridge. Port (de Butteaux)	25.0	—	217.0
Percey	Lock (No. 104.Y de Percey). Port	27.0	10	215.0
	Lock (No. 103.Y de Chailley)	28.0	11	214.0
Flogny	Lock (No. 102.Y de Villiers-Vineux) ...	29.0	12	213.0
	Lock (No. 101.Y de Flogny)	30.0	13	212.0
	Lock (No. 100.Y de Flogny). Port. Bridge	31.0	14	211.0
La Chapelle-Vieille-Foret	Port and Bridge (de la Chapelle)	33.0	—	209.0

* See Plan No. 15.
† Now one lock (1962).

Distance Table

		kilom.	*lock*	*kilom.*
Marolles	Lock (No. 99.Y de Charrey)	35.0	15	207.0
Cheney	Lock (No. 98.Y de Cheney)	39.0	16	203.0
Dannemoine	Port and Lock (No. 97.Y de Dannemoine)	40.0	17	202.0
Tonnerre	Lock (No. 96.Y de Tonnerre). Basin ...	44.0	18	198.0
	Lock (No. 95.Y de Tonnerre)	45.0	19	197.0
	Lock (No. 94.Y d'Arcot)	46.0	20	196.0
Saint-Martin	Lock (No. 93.Y d'Arthe). Bridge	49.0	21	193.0
	Lock (No. 92.Y de Saint-Martin)	50.0	22	192.0
Commissey	Lock (No. 91.Y de Commissey). Bridge ...	51.0	23	191.0
Tanlay	Lock (No. 90.Y de Tanlay). Basin. Port. Bridge	53.0	24	189.0
Saint-Vinnemer	Lock (No. 89.Y de Moulin St. Vinnemer). Bridge	55.0	25	187.0
	Basin and Lock (No. 88.Y de St. Vinnemer)	56.0	26	186.0
d'Argentenay	Lock (No. 87.Y d'Argentenay)	60.0	27	182.0
Ancy-le-Libre	Lock (No. 86.Y d'Ancy-le-Libre)	61.0	28	181.0
Lezinnes	Railway bridge	63.0	—	179.0
	Lock (No. 85.Y de Lezinnes). Basin, Port	63.0	29	179.0
	Lock (No. 84.Y de Batilley)	65.0	30	177.0
	Port (de Saint-Quentin)	65.0	—	177.0
Pacy	Lock (No. 83.Y de Pacy)	66.0	31	176.0
	Port (de Pacy-Varennes). Bridge (de Pacy)	67.0	—	175.0
Argenteuil	Lock (No. 82.Y d'Argenteuil)	69.0	32	173.0
	Railway bridge	70.0	—	172.0
	Lock (No. 81.Y de la Rapille)	71.0	33	171.0
Ancy-le-Franc	Bridge, basin, and Port (d'Ancy-le-Franc)	73.0	—	169.0
	Lock (No. 80.Y d'Ancy-le-Franc) ...	74.0	34	168.0
Chassignelles	Lock (No. 79.Y de Chassignelles)	75.0	35	167.0
	Bridge (de Fulvy)	77.0	—	165.0
	Lock (No. 78.Y de Fulvy)	78.0	36	164.0
	Lock (No. 77.Y de la Papeterie) ...	80.0	37	162.0
Ravières	Lock (No. 76.Y de l'Huilerie) ...	82.0	38	160.0
	Railway bridge. Bridge (de Ravières) ...	82.0	—	160.0
	Bridge (Pont de Nuits)	83.0	—	159.0
	Lock (No. 75.Y de Nuits)	84.0	39	158.0
Cry	Lock (No. 74.Y d'Arlot)	86.0	40	156.0
	Lock (No. 73.Y de Cry)	87.0	41	155.0
Perrigny	Lock (No. 72.Y de Perrigny) ...	89.0	42	153 0
Rougement	Lock (No. 71.Y de la Forge d'Aisy) ...	91.0	43	151.0
	Bridge (d'Aisy)	92.0	—	150.0
	Port and Bridge (de Rougement)	93.0	—	149.0
	Lock (No. 70.Y de Rougement)	94.0	44	148.0
Buffon	Lock (No. 69.Y de Buffon)	95.0	45	147.0
	Bridge (de la Grande-Forge). Port (de Buffon)	95.0	—	147.0

55

Distance Table

		kilom.	lock	kilom.
	Bridge (de Buffon)	96.0	—	146.0
	Lock (No. 68.Y de Buffon)	97.0	46	145.0
Saint-Rémy	Bridge and Port (de Saint-Rémy)	98.0	—	144.0
	Lock (No. 67.Y de Saint-Rémy)	99.0	47	143.0
Montbard	Lock (No. 66.Y de Fontenay)	100.0	48	142.0
	Lock (No. 65.Y de Montbard)	101.0	49	141.0
	Pont-canal (over la Brenne)	101.0	—	141.0
	Lock (No. 64.Y de Montbard)	102.0	50	140.0
	Railway bridge	103.0	—	139.0
Nogent	Lock (No. 63.Y de Nogent)	105.0	51	137.0
	Port and Bridge (de Nogent)	106.0	—	136.0
	Lock (No. 62.Y du Moulin de Nogent) ...	106.0	52	136.0
Courcelles	Lock (No. 61.Y de Courcelles). Port ...	108.0	53	134.0
Benoisey	Lock (No. 60.Y de Benoisey)	109.0	54	133.0
	Bridge (de Benoisey)	110.0	—	132.0
Grignon	Lock (No. 59.Y de Seigny). Bridge ...	111.0	55	131.0
	Lock (No. 58.Y de Grignon)	112.0	56	130.0
	Lock (No. 57.Y des Granges). Bridge ...	113.0	57	129.0
Venarey	Lock (No. 56.Y de Venarey). Bridge. Port	115.0	58	127.0
	Lock (No. 55.Y de Venarey). Bridge ...	116.0	59	126.0
	Lock (No. 54.Y de Venarey)	116.0	60	126.0
Mussy-le-Fosse	Lock (No. 53.Y de Mussy)	117.0	61	125.0
	Lock (No. 52.Y de Mussy)	117.0	62	125.0
Pouillenay	Lock (No. 51.Y de Pouillenay)	118.0	63	124.0
	Lock (No. 50.Y de Pouillenay)	118.0	64	124.0
	Lock (No. 49.Y de Pouillenay)	118.0	65	124.0
	Basin (Bassin Rond)	118.0	—	124.0
	Lock (No. 48.Y de Pouillenay)	119.0	66	123.0
	Lock (No. 47.Y de Pouillenay)	119.0	67	123.0
	Lock (No. 46.Y de Pouillenay)	119.0	68	123.0
	Bridge and Port (de Pouillenay)	119.0	—	123.0
	Lock (No. 45.Y de Pouillenay)	119.0	69	123.0
	Lock (No. 44.Y de Pouillenay)	120.0	70	122.0
	Lock (No. 43.Y de Pouillenay)	120.0	71	122.0
	Lock (No. 42.Y de Pouillenay)	120.0	72	122.0
	Lock (No. 41.Y de Pouillenay)	120.0	73	122.0
	Lock (No. 40.Y de Pouillenay)	121.0	74	121.0
	Lock (No. 39.Y de Pouillenay)	121.0	75	121.0
	Lock (No. 38.Y de Pouillenay)	121.0	76	121.0
	Lock (No. 37.Y de Pouillenay)	122.0	77	120.0
Chassey	Lock (No. 36.Y de Chassey)	122.0	78	120.0
	Lock (No. 35.Y de Chassey)	122.0	79	120.0
	Lock (No. 34.Y de Chassey)	122.0	80	120.0
	Lock (No. 33.Y de Chassey). Bridge ...	123.0	81	119.0
	Lock (No. 32.Y de Chassey). Port ...	123.0	82	119.0

Distance Table

		kilom.	lock	kilom.
	Railway bridge	123.0	—	119.0
	Lock (No. 31.Y de Chassey)	123.0	83	119.0
Marigny	Lock (No. 30.Y de Marigny ...	124.0	84	118.0
	Lock (No. 29.Y de Marigny) ...	124.0	85	118.0
	Lock (No. 28.Y de Marigny) ...	125.0	86	117.0
	Lock (No. 27.Y de Marigny) ...	125.0	87	117.0
	Lock (No. 26.Y de Marigny) ...	125.0	88	117.0
	Lock (No. 25.Y de Marigny). Basin ...	126.0	89	116.0
	Lock (No. 24.Y de Marigny) ...	126.0	90	116.0
	Lock (No. 23.Y de Marigny) ...	126.0	91	116.0
	Lock (No. 22.Y de Marigny) ...	127.0	92	115.0
	Lock (No. 21.Y de Marigny) ...	127.0	93	115.0
	Lock (No. 20.Y de Marigny) ...	128.0	94	114.0
	Lock (No. 19.Y de Marigny) ...	128.0	95	114.0
	Lock (No. 18.Y de Marigny) ...	129.0	96	113.0
Charigny	Lock (No. 17.Y de Charigny) ...	129.0	97	113.0
	Lock (No. 16.Y de Charigny) ...	129.0	98	113.0
Villeneuve-sur-Charigny	Bridge	131.0	—	111.0
Braux	Lock (No. 15.Y de Braux) ...	132.0	99	110.0
	Cutting (tranchée de la Croisée) 470 m. ...	132.0	—	110.0
	Basin and Bridge (de Braux) ...	134.0	—	108.0
	Bridge (de Pierre-My)	134.0	—	108.0
	Lock (No. 14.Y de Braux) ...	135.0	100	107.0
	Cutting (tranchée de Saucy). 280 m. ...	135.0	—	107.0
Clamerey	Bridge (de Saucy)	136.0	—	106.0
	Basin and Bridge (de Pont-Royal) ...	137.0	—	105.0
	Lock (No. 13.Y de Pont-Royal) ...	137.0	101	105.0
Saint-Thibault	Cutting (tranchée de Creuzot. 1130 m. Bridge	138.0	—	104.0
	Bridge (de St. Thibault). Basin ...	140.0	—	102.0
	Cutting (de Saint-Thibault) 145 m. ...	140.0	—	102.0
	Bridge	141.0	—	101.0
Beurizot	Bridge	142.0	—	100.0
	Basin (de Beurizot). Bridge... ...	143.0	—	99.0
Gissey-le-Vieil	Basin and Bridge	145.0	—	97.0
	Bridge	146.0	—	96.0
	Lock (No. 12.Y de Gizzey-le-Vieil) ...	148.0	102	94.0
	Bridge (Pont Garreau)	148.0	—	94.0
	Bridge (Pont d'Eguilly)	149.0	—	93.0
	Lock (No. 11.Y d'Eguilly) ...	149.0	103	93.0
	Lock (No. 10.Y de la Croix-Rouge) ...	150.0	104	92.0
Bellenot	Lock (No. 9.Y des Morons) ...	151.0	105	91.0
	Lock (No. 8.Y des Carrons) ...	151.0	106	91.0
	Lock (No. 7.Y de Chailly) ...	152.0	107	90.0

Distance Table

			kilom.	lock	kilom.
Thoisy-le-Désert	Lock (No. 6.Y de l'Argilas)	... ...	153.0	108	89.0
	Lock (No. 5.Y de Pelleson)	... ...	153.0	109	89.0
	Lock (No. 4.Y de Cercey)	... ...	153.0	110	89.0
	Lock (No. 3.Y de Champ-Roger) ...	...	153.0	111	89.0
Pouilly-en-Auxois	Lock (No. 2.Y de La Lochère)	...	154.0	112	88.0
	Lock (No. 1.Y de Pouilly). Beginning of summit level. Basin and Dry Dock	...	154.0	113	88.0
	Railway bridge. Cutting (tranchée de Pouilly)	...	155.0	—	87.0
	Northern entrance to tunnel (de Pouilly) ...		156.0	—	86.0
Créancey	Southern entrance to tunnel (de Pouilly) ...		159.0	—	83.0
	Bridge (de La Lochère). Cutting (tranchée de Creancey)	...	160.0	—	82.0
Maconge	Basin (d'Escommes). End of summit level.				
	Lock (No. 1.S d'Escommes)	... ...	160.0	114	82.0
	Lock (No. 2.S de Sermaize)	... ...	161.0	115	81.0
	Lock (No. 3.S de Rambourg)	... ...	161.0	116	81.0
Vandenesse	Lock (No. 4.S du Grand-Pré)	... ...	161.0	117	81.0
	Lock (No. 5.S de la Chevrotte)	... ...	162.0	118	80.0
	Lock (No. 6.S de la Chaume)	... ...	162.0	119	80.0
	Lock (No. 7.S de Vachey)	... ...	162.0	120	80.0
	Lock (No. 8.S de Vandenesse). Port	...	163.0	121	79.0
	Lock (No. 9.S du Fourneau)	... ...	163.0	122	79.0
	Lock (No. 10.S de la Mine)	... ...	163.0	123	79.0
	Bridge (de Châteauneuf). Lock (No. 11.S de la Rêpe)	...	164.0	124	78.0
	Lock (No. 12.S de Revin)	...	165.0	125	77.0
Saint-Sabine	Lock (No. 13.S de Saint-Sabine) ...	...	165.0	126	77.0
	Bridge (de Saint-Sabine). Port (du Pont de Bois)	...	166.0	—	76.0
Bouhey	Lock (No. 14.S de Bouhey)	... ...	167.0	127	75.0
Crugey	Lock (No. 15.S de Fontenis)	... ...	168.0	128	74.0
	Lock (No. 16.S de Crugey). Bridge. Basin		169.0	129	73.0
	Lock (No. 17.S du Rempart)	... ...	170.0	130	72.0
	Lock (No. 18.S de la Roche-aux-Fées)	...	171.0	131	71.0
	Lock (No. 19.S de la Sarrée)	... ...	171.0	132	71.0
	Bridge (de Froideville)	...	172.0	—	70.0
	Basin (du pont d'Ouche). (Pont-canal over l'Ouche)	...	172.0	—	70.0
Aubaine	Lock (No. 20.S du pont d'Ouche) ...	...	172.0	133	69.0
Veuvey	Lock (No. 21.S de Baugey)	... ...	173.0	134	69.0
	Lock (No. 22.S de Veuvey). Port (de Veuvey-sur-Ouche). Bridge	...	175.0	135	67.0
	Lock (No. 23.S d'Antheuil)	... ...	176.0	136	66.0
	Lock (No. 24.S des Angles)	... ...	177.0	137	65.0

Distance Table		*kilom.*	*lock*	*kilom.*
Labussière	Lock (No. 25.S de la Forge). Port 179.0	179.0	138	63.0
	Lock (No. 26.S Labussière) 179.0	179.0	139	63.0
Saint-Victor	Lock (No. 27.S de Bochot) 180.0	180.0	140	62.0
	Lock (No. 28.S de la Chaume) 181.0	181.0	141	61.0
	Lock (No. 29.S de Saint-Victor) 182.0	182.0	142	60.0
Barbirey	Lock (No. 30.S de Dennevy). Bridge ... 184.0	184.0	143	58.0
	Lock (No. 31.S de Barbirey) 185.0	185.0	144	57.0
Gissey-sur-Ouche	Lock (No. 32.S de Gissey-s-Ouche). Port 186.0	186.0	145	56.0
	Bridge (de Gissey-s-Ouche) 186.0	186.0	—	56.0
	Lock (No. 33.S de Saint-Eau) 187 0	187 0	146	55.0
	Lock (No. 34.S du Moulin Banet) ... 188.0	188.0	147	54.0
Saint-Marie	Lock (No. 35.S de Champagne) 189.0	189.0	148	53.0
	Lock (No. 36.S de Saint-Marie) 190.0	190.0	149	52.0
	Lock (No. 37.S de Roche-Canot) 192.0	192.0	150	50.0
Fleurey	Lock (No. 38.S de Pont-de-Pany). Basin ... 193.0	193.0	151	49.0
	Lock (No. 39.S de la Chassagne) 194.0	194.0	152	48.0
	Lock (No. 40.S de Morcoeuil) 195.0	195.0	153	47.0
	Lock (No. 41.S du Potet). Port (de Fleurey) 196.0	196.0	154	46.0
	Bridge. Lock (No. 42.S de Fleurey) ... 197.0	197.0	155	45.0
	Railway bridge 198.0	198.0	—	44.0
	Lock (No. 43.S du Creux-Suzon) 199.0	199.0	156	43.0
Velars	Lock (No. 44.S de la Combe-de-Fain) ... 200.0	200.0	157	42 0
	Lock (No. 45.S de Velars). Port 201.0	201.0	158	41.0
	Lock (No. 46.S de la Verrerie) 202.0	202.0	159	40.0
	Lock (No. 47.S du Crucifix) 203.0	203.0	160	9.03
Plombières	Lock (No. 48.S de Neuvon) 204.0	204.0	161	38.0
	Lock (No. 49.S de la Craie) 205.0	205.0	162	37.0
	Port and Basin (de Plombières) 206.0	206.0	—	36.0
	Lock (No. 50.S de Plombières) 207.0	207.0	163	35.0
	Lock (No. 51.S de Bruant) 208.0	208.0	164	34.0
*Dijon**	Lock (No. 52.S des Carrières Blanches) ... 210.0	210.0	165	32.0
	Lock (No. 53.S des Marcs-d'Or) 210.0	210.0	166	32.0
	Lock (No. 54.S de Larrey) 211.0	211.0	167	31.0
	Bridge (Pont Eiffel). Port and Basin (de Dijon) 212.0	212.0	—	30.0
	Lock (No. 55.S de Dijon) 212.0	212.0	168	30.0
	Railway bridge 213.0	213.0	—	29.0
	Lock (No. 56.S de la Colombière) ... 214.0	214.0	169	28.0
	Railway bridge 215.0	215.0	—	27.0
	Lock (No. 57.S de Romelet) 215.0	215.0	170	27.0
	Bridge (Pont de Longvic) 216.0	216.0	—	26.0
	Lock (No. 58.S de Longvic) 216.0	216.0	171	26.0
Ouges	Lock (No. 59.S de Beauregard). Port (de Longvic) 217.0	217.0	172	25.0

* See Plan No. 5.

Distance Table

		kilom.	lock	kilom.
	Lock (No. 60.S de Préville)	218.0	173	24.0
	Lock (No. 61.S du Grand-Ouges). Port ...	219.0	174	23.0
	Lock (No. 62.S du Petit-Ouges) ...	220.0	175	22.0
	Lock (No. 63.S du Vernois) ...	221.0	176	21.0
Bretenières	Lock (No. 64.S d'Epoisses) ...	222.0	177	20.0
	Lock (No. 65.S de Bretenières) ...	223.0	178	19.0
Thorey-en-Plaine	Lock (No. 66.S de Rouvres) ...	225.0	179	17.0
Rouvres-en-Plaine	Lock (No. 67.S de Thorey) ...	226.0	180	16.0
Longecourt	Lock (No. 68.S de la Combe) ...	227.0	181	15.0
	Lock (No. 69.S de Longecourt). Basin ...	228.0	182	14.0
	Lock (No. 70.S de Potangey) ...	229.0	183	13.0
Aiserey	Bridge (de Potangey)	230.0	—	12.0
	Lock (No. 71.S d'Aiserey) ...	231.0	184	11.0
	Lock (No. 72.S de la Bièttre) ...	233.0	185	9.0
Brazey	Lock (No. 73.S de Pont-Hémery). Port ...	235.0	186	7.0
	Bridge (de la Chapelle)	236.0	—	6.0
	Lock (No. 74.S de Brazey) ...	236.0	187	6.0
	Bridge (de Montot). Basin (de Brazey) ...	237.0	—	5.0
	Lock (No. 75.S de Viranne) ...	239.0	188	3.0
Saint-Usage	Railway bridge	240.0	—	2.0
	Bridge (de Saint-Usage). Basin ...	241.0	—	1.0
*Saint-Jean-de-Losne**	Lock (No. 76.S de Saint-Jean-de-Losne) ...	242.0	189	0.0
	Junction with la Saône (at K.163) ...	242.0	—	0.0

CANAL DE BRIARE

General

The Canal de Briare commences on la Loire at the town of Briare and ends in the village of Buges which is some 5 kilometres north of Montargis. It joins the canal latéral à la Loire to the Canal du Loing. The junction with the canal latéral à la Loire is now made, since the construction of le pont-canal de Briare, at La Cognardière which is 3 kilometres from the town of Briare. The effect of this was that the portion of the Canal de Briare which lay between la Loire and La Cognardière was not used by through traffic and was, in short, but a backwater leading from the main route to the town and (by l'écluse du Baraban) to the River Loire; it has now been abandoned. The main part of the canal contains a summit level at Rondeau (165 metres above sea level) from which it falls one way towards la Loire by 12 locks, and the other way towards la Seine by 24 locks. It is interesting to know that this canal was the first in Europe to be constructed containing a summit level and was completed in 1642.

* See Plan No. 17.

Length	The total length of the canal is 57 kilometres but 3 kilometres of this is not on the main through route, as explained before, but lies between La Cognardière and la Loire. The official *kilométrage* is taken from l'écluse du Baraban but here it is taken from the junction with the canal latéral à la Loire which makes the computation of a through route easier.	
Locks	There are in all 36 locks; all have a length of 39 m. 00 with a width of 5 m. 20.	
Depth	The canal has a depth of 2 m. 20.	
Bridges	All the bridges have a minimum headroom of 3 m. 70 above the normal water level.	
Tow-path	There is a metalled tow-path throughout and towing is by diesel tractors generally, although a few vessels are still drawn by horses and mules. In the latter case the animals usually have their stabling on board.	

Distance Table

		kilom.	lock	kilom
La Cognardière	*Junction with the canal latéral à la Loire (at K.200)* (close to Lock No. 4 de la Cognardière)	0.0	0	54.0
	Port (du Petit Moulin)	2.0	—	52.0
Ouzouër-s-Trézée	Lock (No. 5 de Venon)	2.0	1	52.0
	Port (de Courenvaux)	3.0	—	51.0
	Lock (No. 6 de Courenvaux). Lift bridge ...	3.0	2	51.0
	Lock (No. 7 d'Ouzouer-s-Trézée)	5.0	3	49.0
	Lock (No. 8 du Moulin-Neuf). Lift bridge	7.0	4	47.0
	Lock (No. 9 des Fées). Port	8.0	5	46.0
	Lock (No. 10 Notre-Dame). Railway bridge	8.0	6	46.0
	Lock (No. 11 du Petit-Chaloy)	8.0	7	46.0
	Lock (No. 12 de la Gazonne). Beginning of summit level	9.0	8	45.0
	Port (du Rondeau). Bridge (de Rondeau)...	12.0	—	42.0
Rogny	Bridge (de La Noue)	13.0	—	41.0
	Lock (No. 13 de La Javacière). *End of summit level*	14.0	9	40.0
	Lock (No. 14 de Racault)	14.0	10	40.0
	Lock (No. 15 Saint-Joseph)	14.0	11	40.0
	Lock (No. 16 de Chantepinot)	15.0	12	39.0
	Lock (No. 17 de Rogny)	15.0	13	39.0
	Lock (No. 18 Saint-Barbe)	16.0	14	38.0
	Port (de Rogny). Bridge (of the village of Rogny)	16.0	—	38.0

Distance Table

		kilom.	lock	kilom.
Dammarie-s-Loing	Bridge (de Bruxelles)	19.0	—	35.0
	Port and Bridge (de Dammarie-s-Loing) ...	20.0	—	34.0
	Lock (No. 19 de Dammarie-s-Loing) ...	20.0	15	34.0
	Lock (No. 20 de la Picardie)	21.0	16	33.0
	Lock (No. 21 de Moulin-Brûle). Bridge ...	21.0	17	33.0
Châtillon-Coligny	Lock (No. 22 de Briquemault) ...	24.0	18	30.0
	Lock (No. 23 du Gazon)	25.0	19	29.0
	Lock (No. 24 de Châtillon). Port	25.0	20	29.0
	Bridge (du Puirault)	26.0	—	28.0
	Lock (No. 25 de Lépinoy)	29.0	21	25.0
Montbouy	Bridge (des Brangers)	30.0	—	24.0
	Lock (No. 26 de Montbouy). Bridge. Port	31.0	22	23.0
	Bridge	33.0	—	21.0
	Bridge and Port (des Salles)	34.0	—	20.0
Montcresson	Turning basin	35.0	—	19.0
	Port and Bridge (de Montcresson)... ...	37.0	—	17.0
	Lock (No. 27 de Montambert)	40.0	23	14.0
	Lock (No. 28 du Chesnoy)	40.0	24	14.0
	Lock (No. 29 du Moulin de Tours) ...	41.0	25	13.0
	Lock (No. 30 de Souffe-Douleur) ...	41.0	26	13.0
Conflans	Lock (No. 31 de La Sablonnière) ...	43.0	27	11.0
Amilly	Lock (No. 32 de la Tuilerie)	45.0	28	9.0
	Bridge and Port (de la Tuilerie)	45.0	—	9.0
	Railway bridge	46.0	—	8.0
	Bridge (du Moulin Bardin)	47.0	—	7.0
	Bridge (Saint-Roch)	49.0	—	5.0
Montargis	Bridge (de Saint-Roch). Port	49.0	—	5.0
	Lock (No. 33 de la Marolle)	49.0	29	5.0
	Lock (No. 34 de la Reinette)	49.0	30	5.0
	Bridge (de la Reinette). Bridge (du Loing)	50.0	—	4.0
	Bridge (des Pâtis)	50.0	—	4.0
Chalette	Bridge (a l'Ane)	52.0	—	2.0
	Lock (No. 35 de Langlée)	53.0	31	1.0
Buges	Lock (No. 36 de Buges). *Junction with canal du Loing (at K.o)*	54.0	32	0.0

CANAL DE CALAIS

General The Canal de Calais joins the River Aa to the Port of Calais. It has three branches, namely, to Audruicq, to Ardres and to Guines; these are not much used except by local craft.

Length The length of the canal from its beginning on the River Aa at Le West to the bridge Mollien (where it joins the Bassin Carnot in the maritime port of Calais) is 30 kilometres. The branches to Audruicq, Ardres and Guines are 2, 5 and 6 kilometres in length respectively.

Locks   There is only one lock, sited at Hénuin, which has a fall of only about 1 metre. The length of the lock is 38 m. 78 and its width is 5 m. 20.

Depth   The normal depth of the canal is 2 m. 40. The branch canals have somewhat less at 2 m. 20. The very beginning of the Guines branch is silted up for a length of nearly 250 metres.

Bridges   All the bridges over the main canal have a headroom of at least 3 m. 60 above the normal water level. On the Audruicq branch the headroom is 3 m. 70, and the Guines branch has at least the same. The Ardres branch is restricted to 3 m. 10. It must also be noted that vessels which exceed 28 metres in length cannot use the branch to Ardres on account of the difficulty in turning at the bridge of Sans-Pareil which lies close to the junction with the main canal.

Tow-path   There is a metalled tow-path throughout and towing is by diesel tractors and, sometimes, by horses.

Distance Table

		kilom.	lock	kilom.
Le West	*Junction with l'Aa (at K.15).* Swing bridge	0.0	o	30.0
Ruminghem	Ferry	2.0	—	28.0
	Ferry (de la 'Grise-Pierre')	3.0	—	27.0
Ste-Mariekerque	Lock (d'Hénuin). Lift bridge. Port ...	6.0	I	24.0
Vieille-Eglise	Le Rebus. *Junction with Canal d'Audruicq*	8.0	—	22.0
Nouvelle-Eglise	Bridge (du Fort-Bâtard)	11.0	—	19.0
Attaques	Bridge (Pont Sans-Pareil). *Junction with Canal d'Ardres*	18.0	—	12.0
	Lift bridge (Les Attaques)	21.0	—	9.0
Coulogne	Bridge (called 'pont de Briques')	24.0	—	6.0
	Junction with Canal de Guines	25.0	—	5.0
	Lift bridge (de Coulogne)	26.0	—	4.0
Calais	Railway bridge. Lift bridge	27.0	—	3.0
	Bridge (de Saint-Pierre)	28.0	—	2.0
	Swing bridge (de Vic)	29.0	—	1.0
	Calais. Port. Bridge (Pont Mollien). *Junction with the marine docks and basins* ...	30.0	—	0.0

Branch canal to Audruicq

		kilom.	lock	kilom.
Audruicq	Audruicq. Port (150 m.)	0.0	—	2.0
	Bridge (called 'Pont Rouge')	1.0	—	1.0
	Le Rébus. *Junction with Canal de Calais (at K.8)*	2.0	—	0.0

Distance Table

		kilom.	lock	kilom.

Branch canal to Ardres

		kilom.	lock	kilom.
Ardres	Ardres. Quay (150 m.)	0.0	—	5.0
Bremes	Turning foot bridge (de Bremes) ...	1.0	—	4.0
Attaques	Bridge. Railway bridge. *Junction with Canal de Calais (at K.18)*	5.0	—	0.0

Branch canal to Guines

Guines	Guînes. Port (200 m.)	0.0	—	6.0
	Turning foot bridge (de Guînes)	1.0	—	5.0
Hames-Boucres	Lift bridge	2.0	—	4.0
Coulogne	Lift bridge (de l'écluse Carrée)	4.0	—	2.0
	Lift bridge (de la Planche-Tournoire) ...	5.0	—	1.0
	Railway bridge. *Junction with Canal de Calais (at K.25)*	6.0	—	0.0

CANAL DU CENTRE

General

The Canal du Centre joins la Saône to the canal latéral à la Loire. It begins at Chalon-sur-Saône and ends at Digoin. It contains a summit level which is nearly a 1,000 feet above sea level. The canal was opened to navigation in the year 1790.

Length

The total length of the canal is 112 kilometres. In former times the junction of le canal du Centre with la Saône was made at le Port de Chambre de Commerce de Chalon-sur-Saône at K.232 on the river. But now the junction has been moved upstream by a new cut to reach la Saône at K.230. This new cut leaves the old route at the old *kilométrage* K.5.8; it has a length of 3.8 km. to reach la Saône. In order not to upset the *kilométrage* throughout by this shortening of the canal the new junction is officially assumed to start at K.2 instead of K.0. But in our Distance Table the actual length has been tabulated.

Locks

There are 61 locks on the canal of which 35 fall towards Chalon-s-Saône and 26 towards Digoin. These locks all have a length of 39 m. 00 with a width of 5 m. 20, excepting the lock (No. 35.M) on the new pound at the Port Fluvial, Chalon-s-Saône, which has a length of 40 m. 00 with a width of 6 m. 00. The fall at this lock between the two pounds at normal water level is 10 m. 76. Some of these locks are now operated electrically and are automatic; others are being converted. At the lock side a steel pillar carries two cords, one blue and the other red. The blue cord is the one to use; the red cord is only to be used in an emergency.

Depth	The normal depth of water in the canal throughout its length is 2 m. 00.
Bridges	Over the main route there are numerous bridges all of which have a headroom of 3 m. 70.
Tow-path	There is a metalled tow-path throughout. From Saint-Léger-sur-Dheune to Digoin the tow-path runs alongside the *route nationale No. 74* for nearly the whole distance.

Distance Table

		kilom.	*lock*	*kilom.*
Chalon-s-Saône*	*Junction with la Saône (at K.230)*	0.0	—	112.0
	Port Fluvial (de Chalon-s-Saône)	0.0	—	112.0
	Lock (No. 35.M). Bridge	1.0	I	111.0
	Railway bridge. Bridge	2.0	—	110.0
	Bridge	3.0	—	109.0
Champforgeuil	*Junction with old reach of canal†*	3.0	—	109.0
Franges	Port (de Franges)	5.0	—	107.0
	Lock (No. 34.M)	6.0	2	106.0
La Loyère	Lock (No. 33.M). Turning basin	8.0	3	104.0
Fontaines	Bridge (du Gauchard). Lock (No. 32.M) ...	9.0	4	103.0
	Port and Bridge (de Fontaines)	11.0	—	101.0
	Lock (No. 31.M)	12.0	5	100.0
Rully	Lock (No. 30.M)	12.0	6	100.0
	Lock (No. 29.M)	13.0	7	99.0
	Lock (No. 28.M)	14.0	8	98.0
	Lock (No. 27.M). Port (de Rully)	14.0	9	98.0
	Lock (No. 26.M)	15.0	10	97.0
Chagny	Lock (No. 25.M)	15.0	11	97.0
	Lock (No. 24.M). Port and Bridge (de Chagny)	17.0	12	95.0
	Bridge (de Bouzeron)	18.0	—	94.0
Remigny	Bridge and Port (de Remigny)	20.0	—	92.0
Chassey	Bridge (de la Fontaine Beaunoise)... ...	21.0	—	91.0
Santenay	Port (de Santenay). Bridge (de Corchanu)	23.0	—	89.0
Cheilly	Port and Bridge (de Cheilly)	24.0	—	88.0
Saint-Gilles	Port and Bridge (de Saint-Gilles)	26.0	—	86.0
	Lock (No. 23.M)	27.0	13	85.0
Dennevy	Lock (No. 22.M)	27.0	14	85.0
	Bridge and Port (de Dennevy)	28.0	—	84.0
	Lock (No. 21.M). Bridge (de Planche-Tapois)	29.0	15	83.0

* See Plan No. 2.
† Dead-end.

Distance Table

		kilom.	lock	kilom.
Saint-Léger	Lock (No. 20.M)	30.0	16	82.0
	Bridge and Port (de Saint Léger)	31.0	—	81.0
Saint-Bérain	Lock (No. 19.M). Bridge (des Lochères) ...	32.0	17	80.0
	Lock (No. 18.M)	34.0	18	78.0
	Lock (No. 17.M). Port (de Saint-Bérain) ...	35.0	19	77.0
	Lock (No. 16.M). Lock (No. 15.M) ...	36.0	21	76.0
Morey	Port (de Perreuil)	37.0	—	75.0
	Lock (No. 14.M)	37.0	22	75.0
	Lock (No. 13.M)	38.0	23	74.0
	Lock (No. 12.M)	39 0	24	73.0
St-Julien-s-Dheune	Lock (No. 11.M de Villeneuve)	40.0	25	72.0
	Bridge (de Rousselet)	41.0	—	71.0
	Lock (No. 10.M de chez le Roi)	41.0	26	71.0
	Lock (No. 9.M du Moulin de St-Julien) ...	42.0	27	70.0
	Port and Bridge (de St-Julien)	42 0	—	70 0
	Lock (No. 8.M de l'Abbaye)	43.0	28	69.0
	Lock (No. 7.M du Rocher)	43.0	29	69.0
Ecuisses	Lock (No. 6.M de la Motte)	44.0	30	68.0
	Bridge and Lock (No. 5.M de la Forge) ...	45.0	31	67.0
	Bridge (de la Motte). Lock (No. 4.M de Revin)	45.0	32	67.0
	Lock (No. 3.M du Fourneau)	45.0	33	67.0
	Lock (No. 2.M du Charmois)	46.0	34	66.0
	Port (de Longpendu). Lock (No. 1.M). Beginning of summit level	46.0	35	66.0
	Railway bridge	47.0	—	65.0
	Bridge (Jeanne-Rose)	48.0	—	64.0
Montchanin	Bridge (du Creusot)	49.0	—	63.0
	Lock (No. 1.O). *End of summit level* ...	50.0	36	62.0
Saint-Eusebe	Lock (No. 2.O des Brenots)	51.0	37	61.0
	Port (de la Grue). Turning basin	52.0	—	60.0
	Lock (No. 3.O de la Favée)	52.0	38	60.0
	Lock (No. 4.O de Parizenot). Bridge ...	53.0	39.0	59.0
Blanzy	Lock (No. 5.O de la Planche-Calard) ...	55.0	40	57.0
	Lock (No. 6.O de Brûlard)	56.0	41	56.0
	Lock (No. 7.O de la Roche). Bridge (St-Gelin)	57.0	42	55.0
	Railway bridge	58.0	—	54.0
	Port and Bridge (de Blanzy)	59.0	—	53.0
	Lock (No. 8.O des Mireaux)	60.0	43	52.0
Montceau-les-Mines	Lock (No. 9.O de Montceau). Port. Bridges	62.0	44	50.0
	Railway bridge	63.0	—	49.0
	Bridge and Port (de Lucie)	64.0	—	48.0
	Railway bridge	64.0	—	48.0
Saint-Vallier	Bridge and Lock (No. 10.O des Chavannes)	65.0	45	47.0

Distance Table

		kilom.	lock	kilom.
	Lock (No. 11.O des Vernois)	65.0	46	47.0
	Railway bridge	66.0	—	46.0
	Bridge (de Galuzot)	67.0	—	45.0
	Bridge (de Maison Morin)	68.0	—	44.0
Pouillox	Bridge (des Vernes)...	69.0	—	43.0
	Lock (No. 12.O du Four). Bridge (du Four)	69.0	47	43.0
Ciry-le-Noble	Lock (No. 13.O d'Azy)	72.0	48	40.0
	Bridge and Port (de Ciry)	73.0	—	39.0
	Lock (No. 14.O de Ciry)	73.0	49	39.0
	Port (des Touillards)	74.0	—	38.0
Génelard	Lock (No. 15.O de Civry)	77.0	50	35.0
	Port (de Vernizy). (Bridge de la Tranchée de Génelard)	78.0	—	34.0
	Lock (No. 16.O de Génelard). Bridge and Port	79.0	51	33.0
Palinges	Lock (No. 17.O de Montet)	80.0	52	32.0
	Bridge and Port (du Montet)	81.0	—	31.0
	Port and Bridge (de Palinges)	83.0	—	29.0
	Bridge (de Corbary)	84.0	—	28.0
	Lock (No. 18.O du Thiellay)	85.0	53	27.0
	Lock (No. 19.O de Digoine). Bridge, Port	86.0	54	26.0
Saint-Aubin	Bridge (du Montceau)	87.0	—	25.0
	Port and Bridge (de la Gravoine)	89.0	—	23.0
	Lock (No. 20.O de la Gravoine)	89.0	55	23.0
Volesvres	Lock (No. 21.O des Haillers)	92.0	56	20.0
	Bridge and Lock (No. 22.O de Volesvres)...	94.0	57	18.0
Hauteford	Bridge and Port (de Bord). Turning basin	96.0	—	16.0
	Port (de Corneloup, called 'Port de Bord')	97.0	—	15.0
	Railway bridge. Bridge (de Romay) ...	97.0	—	15.0
Paray-le-Monial	Lock (No. 23.O de l'Hyron). Port	99.0	58	13.0
	Turning basin. Bridge (de Faubourg) ...	99.0	—	13.0
	Bridge (des Quatre Chemins)	100.0	—	12.0
	Bridge (des Quarrés)	101.0	—	11.0
Vitry-en-Charollais	Lock (No. 24.O des Quarrés)	101.0	59	11.0
	Lock (No. 25.O du Mont)	102.0	60	10.0
	Bridge (de Colayot)	103.0	—	9.0
	Lock (No. 26.O des Bessons)	105.0	61	7.0
	Port and Bridge (du Paradis)	108.0	—	4.0
*Digoin**	Bridge (des Blattiers)	110.0	—	2.0
	Railway bridge	111.0	—	1.0
	Port (de Digoin). Turning basin. Graving dock. *Junction with canal latèral à la Loire (at K.o)*	112.0	—	0.0

* See Plan No. 4.

CANAL DE LA COLME

General

Quite close to the Pont de Watten a new canal—*la dérivation de Watten*—leaves the River Aa. La dérivation de Watten runs west-north-west for about a kilometre to join with the beginning of the Canal de la Colme. La dérivation de Watten together with 6 kilometres of la Haute-Colme and la dérivation de la Colme is part of the improved waterway known as *la liaison Dunkerque-Valenciennes*. Beyond the junction with la dérivation de la Colme, the Canal de la Colme continues northward and, passing the French frontier, ends at Furnes in Belgium. Having crossed the French frontier it changes its name and is called *Canal de Furnes**. That part of the canal which lies between Watten and Bergues is known as the *Canal de la Haute-Colme*, while the part lying between Bergues and the frontier is called the *Canal de la Basse-Colme*. The Canal de la Basse-Colme is but a second class canal, shallow and not suitable for the standard size barge of 38 m. 50. As mentioned there is a *dérivation* leading off from the Canal de la Haute-Colme which joins the Canal de Bourbourg. The Canal de la Haute-Colme also makes connection with the Canal de Bergues, in fact the last 400 metres, that is to say from Lock No. 3 (de Bierne) the trace is common to both canals. In Bergues there is a basin containing 3 locks which is called *l'écluse triangulaire*. The upstream one of these locks is l'Ecluse Neuve, and the downstream one is Lock No. 4; both these locks lie on that part of the canal known as la Basse-Colme. The remaining lock of the 3 is of little interest as it controls only a feeder canal and is not used by vessels. The canal de la Basse-Colme has one short branch which leads to Hondschoote; it has the same characteristics as La Basse-Colme.

Length

From the junction with la dérivation de Watten to Bergues is 23 kilometres, and from Bergues to the frontier is 12 kilometres, thus making 35 kilometres in all.

Locks

There are 5 locks. Of these, the Lock (de Watten) has a length of 144 m. 60 with a width of 12 m. 00. The other two on la Haute-Colme, have a length of 38 m. 50 with a width of 5 m. 20. The lock called l'Ecluse Neuve and Lock No. 4 (de Furnes) have a length of 45 m. 00 with a width of 4 m. 70.

Depth

From la dérivation de Watten to la dérivation de la Colme there is a depth of 3 m. 50. From Lock No. 2 (Lynck) to the junction with the Canal de Bergues the depth is 2 m. 20. In la Basse-Colme and its branch (to Hondschoote) there is a depth of 0 m. 80.

* See *Inland Waterways of Belgium*, Imray Laurie Norie & Wilson.

			kilom.	lock	kilom.

Bridges — From the dérivation de Watten to la dérivation de la Colme the bridges have a headroom of 5 m. 25. From that point to Bergues the headroom is 3 m. 82 at normal water level, while on la Basse-Colme and its branch only 2 m. 97 is available.

Tow-path — There is a tow-path throughout.

Distance Table			kilom.	lock	kilom.
La Haute—Colme					
Watten	Junction with la dérivation de Watten ...		0.0	—	35.0
	Lock (de Watten)		0.0	1	35.0
Millam	Port (de Millam)		3.0	—	32.0
Cappellebrouck	Port (de Cappellebrouck)		4.0	—	31.0
Merckeghem	Bridge (de l'Abbesse)		5.0	—	30.0
Cappellebrouck	Junction with la dérivation de la Colme ...		6.0	—	29.0
	Public quay (de Lynck). Lift bridge. Lock (No. 2 de Lynck)		6.0	2	29.0
Looberghe	Lift bridge (de Looberghe). *Public quay* ...		9.0	—	26.0
Brouckerque	Lift bridge (de Stalenbrugghe). Port ...		4.0	—	21.0
Spycker	Ferry (de Vlamvynck-Strate)		6.0	—	19.0
Steene	Lift bridge and Port (de Grand-Millebrugghe)		17.0	—	18.0
Bierne	Lift bridge (de Petit-Millebrugghe) ...		21.0	—	14.0
	Lock (No. 3 de Bierne). Lift bridge. Railway bridge		22.0	3	13.0
Bergues	Bridge. *Junction with Canal de Bergues (at K.0)*		23.0	—	12.0
La Basse-Colme					
Bergues	Lock (Ecluse Neuve)		23.0	4	12.0
	Lock (No. 4 de Furnes). Bridge (de la demi-lune)		23.0	5	12.0
	Bridge (des Glacis)		24.0	—	11.0
Hoymille	Port and Lift bridge (d'Hoymille)		25.0	—	10.0
	Lift bridge (de Benties-Meulen)		26.0	—	9.0
Warhem	Lift bridge (à moutons)		27.0	—	8.0
	Port and Lift bridge (de Millebrugghe) ...		29.0	—	6.0
	Lift bridge (de Pauwkenswerf)		30.0	—	5.0
Hondschoote	Junction with la Becque d'Hondschoote ...		32.0	—	3.0
	Bridge (du Cerf)		33.0	—	2.0
	Frontier *(Franco-Belge)*		35.0	—	0.0
Dérivation de la Colme					
Cappellebrouck	Junction with la Haute-Colme (at K.6) ...		0.0	—	8.0
Looberghe	Bridge		3.0	—	5.0

Distance Table   *kilom.*   *lock*   *kilom.*

Brouckerque   Bridge (Pont de Dieppe-Straete) ...   ...   6.0   —   2.0

                       Junction with le Canal de Bourbourg (at K.9)   8.0   —   0.0

Branch canal from Becque d'Hondschoote

Hondschoote   Junction with Canal de la Basse-Colme.

                       Swing bridge (La Croix) ...   .   0.0   —   2.0

                       Port (d'Hondschoote). Bridge (de la

                       brasserie) ...   .   2.0   —   0.0

CANAL DE LA DEÛLE

General*   The Canal de la Deûle begins at the town of Douai and ends at Deulément, thus joining the River Scarpe to the River Lys. For the greater part of its length the canal is really the canalised River la Deûle. Between Douai and K.23 (near Bauvin) it forms part of the newly improved route *liaison Dunkerque-Valenciennes*. During its course it communicates with

                      (a) Canal de Lens

                      (b) Canal d'Aire

                      (c) Canal de Roubaix

                      The canal has also four branches of which only the branch to Seclin is likely to be of interest to yachtsmen, and which is briefly noted here. The branch has no locks and is 4 kilometres in length with the conditions of navigation the same as in the main canal. The first 3 kilometres of the Canal de la Deûle are now no longer · open to through traffic and are used as a kind of garage. A somewhat complicated system of waterways joins the Canal de la Deûle to la Scarpe Supérieure and to la Scarpe Inférieure. It is thus possible to pass from either of these two parts of la Scarpe into the Canal de la Deûle when going towards or coming from Lille†.

Length   Omitting the first 3 kilometres for the reason given above, and reckoning the distances from the junction with la Dérivation de la Scarpe autour de Douai the navigable length of the canal is 59 kilometres to its junction with la Lys at Deulémont.

Locks   There are 5 locks. Their dimensions are as under:

                      Ecluse de Don   80 m. 00 × 12 m. 00

                                                 38 m. 50 × 5 m. 08

                      Ecluse de la Barre   38 m. 75 × 5 m. 08

* See also *la Dérivation de la Scarpe autour de Douai* p. 238.
† See Plan No. 7.

Ecluse de Ste-Hélène ...	38 m. 50 ×	5 m. 20
Ecluse de Wambrechies ...	38 m. 60 ×	5 m. 21
Ecluse de Deulémont	85 m. 00 ×	8 m. 00

Depth   From the junction with la dérivation de la Scarpe autour de Douai to the junction with le canal d'Aire the depth is not less than 3 m. 50. From the junction with le canal d'Aire to l'écluse de Wambrechies the depth is 2 m. 30; from that point it is slightly less (2 m. 20). The branch to Seclin has a depth of 2 m. 00.

Bridges   From the junction with la dérivation de la Scarpe autour de Douai to the junction with le canal d'Aire the headroom under bridges is now 5 m. 25; over the remaining length the bridges have a minimum headroom of 3 m. 70 above normal water level. The same on the branch to Seclin.

Tow-path   There is a metalled tow-path throughout.

Distance Table

		kilom.	lock	kilom.
*Flers-en-Escrebieux**	*Junction with 'la dérivation de la Scarpe de Douai' (at K.7)*	0.0	—	59.0
Auby	Quay and Bridge (d'Auby)	1.0	—	58.0
Evin-Malmaison	Bridge (de Courcelles)	4.0	—	55.0
Noyelles-Godault	Railway bridge (des Houillères)	5.0	—	54.0
Dourges	Railway bridge. Quay (de Dourges) ...	6.0	—	53.0
	Bridge (Pont-à-Sault)	7.0	—	52.0
Oignies	Bridge (de la batterie d'Oignies)	10.0	—	49.0
	Railway bridge (des Houillères)	11.0	—	48.0
Courrières	*Junction with Canal de Lens (at K.11)* ...	12.0	—	47.0
	Railway bridge	12.0	—	47.0
	Bridge and Quay (de Courrières)	13.0	—	46.0
Harnes	Quay (d'Harnes)	14.0	—	45.0
	Railway bridge (des Houilléres)	16.0	—	43.0
Vendin-le-Vieil	Bridge (Pont-à-Vendin). Railway bridge ...	17.0	—	42.0
Meurchin	Bridge and Quay (de Meurchin)	20.0	—	39.0
	Railway bridge (des Houillères)	20.0	—	39.0
Bauvin	Bridge and Quay (de Bauvin)	22.0	—	37.0
	Junction with Canal d'Aire (at K.0) ...	23.0	—	36.0
Sainghin-en-Weppes	Railway bridge. Beginning of dérivation de Don	25.0	—	34.0
	Lock (Nouvelle écluse de Don). Bridge ...	26.0	I	33.0
	Bridge	27.0	—	32.0

* See Plan No. 7.

Distance Table

		kilom.	lock	kilom.
Allennes-les-Marais	End of dérivation de Don. Bridge (des Ansereuilles)	28.0	—	31.0
Hérin	Port (d'Hérin)	29.0	—	30.0
Gondecourt	Bridge (de Wavrin)	30.0	—	29.0
Santes	*Junction with branch de Seclin*	31.0	—	28.0
	Port and Bridge (d'Houplin)	32.0	—	27.0
Haubourdin	Footbridge (de l'Allumette)	33.0	—	26.0
	Junction with old canal	34.0	—	25.0
	Bridge (Pont de Santes)	34.0	—	52.0
	Railway bridge. Port (d'Haubourdin) ...	35.0	—	24.0
	Junction with old canal	35.0	—	24.0
	Bridge (d'Haubourdin)	36.0	—	23.0
	Bridge (de l'Abbaye de Loos)	37.0	—	22.0
Loos-lez-Lille	Foot bridge (de Sequedin). Entrance to Port de Lille	39.0	—	20.0
	Lift bridge (de Sequedin)	39.0	—	20.0
	Foot bridge (des Bois Blancs)	40.0	—	19.0
Lille	Bridge (de Canteleu)	40.0	—	19.0
	Bridge (de l'Hippodrome)	41.0	—	18.0
	Port (Port Vauban). Lock (de la Barre) ...	42.0	2	17.0
	Bridge (de la Citadelle)	42.0	—	17.0
	Lift bridge (du Ramponneau)	42.0	—	17.0
	Lift bridge (du Petit-Paradis)	43.0	—	16.0
Saint-André	Bridge (Pont Royal)	44.0	—	15.0
	Lock (Saint-Hélène)	44.0	3	15.0
	Railway bridge	45.0	—	14.0
Marquette	Bridge (de l'Abbaye). Port	46.0	—	13.0
	Junction with Canal de Roubaix (at K.0) ...	47.0	—	12.0
	Bridge (de Marquette)	47.0	—	12.0
Wambrechies	Port and Lift bridge (de Wambrechies) ...	49.0	—	10.0
	Lock (de Wambrechies)	49.0	4	10.0
Quesnoy-s-Deûle	Bridge	54.0	—	5.0
	Port (de Quesnoy). Railway bridge ...	54.0	—	5.0
Démont	Lock (de Deulément). Lift bridge ...	59.0	5	0.0
	Port (de Deulement). Bridge	59.0	—	0.0
	Junction with la Lys (at K.48)	59.0	—	0.0

Branch canal to Seclin

Santes	*Junction with main canal (K.31)*	0.0	—	4.0
	Bridge (du Bac à Aucoisne)	0.0	—	4.0
Houplin	Bridge (du Marais)	1.0	—	3.0
	Bridge (village of Houplin)	2.0	—	2.0
Seclin	Bridge (des Postes)	3.0	—	1.0
	Port (de Seclin). *End of navigation* ...	4.0	—	0.0

DORDOGNE

General   La Dordogne was formerly navigable from the barrage de Bergerac to its confluence with la Garonne at Bec d'Ambès. Of late years, however, navigation has become impossible for a distance of about 14 kilometres below the barrage de Bergerac and now ends at Saint-Pierre-d'Eyraud. Although the official *kilométrage* still counts from the barrage de Bergerac, we have here taken 14 kilometres downstream of the barrage for the zero of the Distance Table. Nearly the whole length of the navigable part of the river is subject to tidal influence; that is to say, as far upstream as Pessac-sur-Dordogne, and consequently attention must be paid to this influence.

Length   The navigable length of the river from St-Piere-d'Eyraud to Bec d'Ambès is 117 kilometres.

Locks   There are no locks.

Depth   The depth of water to be found in the river is variable. Upstream of Branne the depth may fall to 0 m. 30 during times of drought and it is then only possible to make a passage from half-tide. Below Branne there is usually 1 m. 25 at low water neaps with as much as 4 m. 80 at high water during the same period. Local advice must, therefore, always be sought.

Bridges   Above Libourne at normal high water no fixed bridge has a less headroom than 5 m. 90. Below that town there are but two bridges and at least 2 m. 80 may be counted upon at normal times.

Tow-path   The tow-path has fallen into disuse as most of the vessels using the waterway are self-propelled.

Distance Table

		kilom.	*lock*	*kilom.*
Saint-Pierre-d'Eyraud	Head of navigation	0.0	—	117.0
St-Nazaire-du-Moiron	... ...	1.0	—	116.0
Fleix	Bridge and Port (de Fleix)	7.0	—	110.0
Sainte-Foy-la-Grande	Port and Bridge (de Port-Sainte-Foy) ...	12.0	—	105.0
Pineuilh	Railway bridge	13.0	—	104.0
	Port (du Chantier)	15.0	—	102.0
Eynesse	Port (d'Eynesse)	18.0	—	99.0
	Port (de Sainte-Aulaye)	20.0	—	97.0
St-Avit-de-Soulège	Port	22.0	—	95.0
Pessac-s-Dordogne	Port (de Pessac-s-Dordogne). Port. Suspension bridge	27.0	—	90.0
Flaujagues	Port (de Flaujagues)	30.0	—	87.0
Lamothe-Montravel	Port (de Lamothe-Montravel)	33.0	—	84.0

Distance Table

				kilom.	lock	kilom.
Castillon	Confluence with la Lidoire	...	...	38.0	—	79.0
	Port (de Castillon). Bridge	...	...	39.0	—	78.0
Saint-Magne	Bridge	...	...	40.0	—	77.0
Civrac	Port (de Civrac) ...	...	...	43.0	—	74.0
St-Jean-de-Blaignac	Port (de Sainte-Terre) ...	...	...	45.0	—	72.0
	Port Crespin	...	...	47.0	—	70.0
	Port (de St-Jean-de-Blaignac). Bridge	...	48.0	—	69.0
Cabara	Port (de Cabara) ...	...	...	50.0	—	67.0
Vignonet	Port (de Vignonet)	...	...	52.0	—	65.0
Branne	Port and Bridge (de Branne)	...	...	56.0	—	61.0
Moulon	Port (de Moulon) ...	...	...	59.0	—	58.0
	Boat yard. Slipway	...	...	64.0	—	53.0
Génissac	Port (de Génissac) ...	...	...	69.0	—	48.0
Arveyres	Railway bridge ...	...	...	73.0	—	44.0
Libourne	Bridge and Port (de Libourne)	...	...	74.0	—	43.0
	Confluence with L'Isle ...	...	...	75·0	—	42·0
Fronsac	Port (de Fronsac) ...	...	...	77.0	—	40.0
	Port (d'Arveyres) ...	...	...	82.0	—	35.0
Vayres	Port (de Vayres) ...	...	...	83.0	—	34.0
St-Michel-de-Fronsac	Port (de Saint-Pardon)	...	...	85.0	—	32.0
Lugon	Port (de Petit-Chartron) ...	...	...	90.0	—	27.0
	Port (d'Izon) ...	...	...	91.0	—	26.0
Asques	Port (d'Asques) ...	...	...	95.0	—	22.0
	Port (de Cavernes) ...	...	...	98.0	—	19.0
Cubzac	Bridge. Port (de St-Vincent-de-Paul)	...	101.0	—	16.0
	Port (de Cubzac) ...	...	...	102.0	—	15.0
St-André-de-Cubzac	Port (de Plagne) ...	...	...	105.0	—	12.0
Saint-Gervais	Port (Port Neuf) ...	...	...	106.0	—	11.0
Prignac et Gazelles	Port Despeau ...	...	...	107.0	—	10.0
Ambès	Port (de La Chapelle-d'Ambès) ...	...	110.0	—	7.0
Bourg-s-Gironde	Port (de Bourg) ...	...	...	113.0	—	4.0
	Port Lopès	...	...	114.0	—	3.0
Bayon	Bec d'Ambes. *Confluence with la Gironde*				
	(Marine)	...	...	117.0	—	0.0

DUNKERQUE—VALENCIENNES (La LIAISON)

General

In France during the last 20 years, several major works of improvement have been carried out to bring a number of the inland waterways to a standard commensurate with the growth of water-borne traffic. La Seine between Paris and the sea, la Moselle between Metz and Coblence, le Rhône between Lyon and Arles, and le Rhin between Niffer (Basle) and Strasbourg are notable examples. All these works have received a good deal of publicity, but, probably because it is not so well known, the modernisation of the waterway joining the port of Dunkerque with the coalfields of Le Nord, the industrial area of Lille and Valenciennes, and the iron and steel works in the basin of l'Escaut has hardly been mentioned. La Liaison Dunkerque-Valenciennes, as the renovated waterway is called, has entirely altered the conditions of navigation along the route for a distance of nearly 200 kilometres. Formerly, the old locks with their dimensions of 38 m. 50 by 5m. 20 were only capable of allowing *péniches flamandes* with a maximum load of 250 to 300 tons to pass through. Moreover, because of the ever-increasing volume of traffic, severe congestion occurred at certain points, particularly near Douai and along the valley of l'Escaut. The new locks have a length of 144 m. 60 with a width of 12 m. 00 and the depth has been increased to 3 m. 50 throughout, thus permitting the passage of 'pusher-trains' of 3,000 tons. Also, all fixed bridges now have a headroom of 5 m. 25 at the highest navigable water-level. A summary of the waterway is given below; full details can be found by reference to the individual canals and rivers.

Waterway		kilom.	lock	kilom.
Dunkerque	Junction with le Port maritime	0.0	—	184.0
La dérivation Ouest				
vers le port de				
Dunkerque	Junction with Canal de Bourgbourg ...	10.0	1	174.0
Canal de Bourbourg	Junction with la dérivation de la Colme ...	11.0	—	173.0
La dérivation				
de la Colme	Junction with la Haute-Colme	19.0	—	165.0
La Haute-Colme	Junction with la dérivation de Watten ...	26.0	2	158.0
La dérivation				
de Watten	Junction with l'Aa	27.0	—	157.0
L'Aa	Junction with Canal de Neuffossé ...	37.0	—	147.0
Canal de Neuffossé	Junction with Canal d'Aire	56.0	4	128.0
Canal d'Aire	Junction with Canal de la Deûle	95.0	5	89.0
Canal de la Deule	Junction with la dérivation autour de Douai	118.0	—	66.0
La dérivation autour				
de Douai	Junction with Canal de la Sensée ...	126.0	7	58.0
Canal de la Sensée	Junction with l'Escaut	150.0	8	34.0
L'Escaut	Junction with Canal de Mons à Condé ...	184.0	14	0.0

ERDRE

General

L'Erdre has been canalised from Nort to Nantes, where it falls into la Loire. The part lying between the lock at Quiheix and la Loire has been thrown into the Canal de Nantes à Brest and has thus lost its individuality to a great extent. The length between the lock at

Quiheix and Nort shows similar conditions as regards navigation to those obtaining on the Nantes à Brest canal.

Length   From Nort to the lock at Quiheix is 6 kilometres.

Locks   There are no locks.

Depth   A depth of 2 m. oo is normally found.

Bridges   There are no bridges.

Tow-path   There is no tow-path.

Distance Table

		kilom.	lock	kilom.
Nort	Nort. Port. *Beginning of navigation* ...	0.0	—	6.0
	Port-Mulon. Port	1.0	—	5.0
Petit-Mars	Quiheix. *Junction with Canal de Nantes*			
	a Brest (at K.21)	6.0	—	0.0

ESCAUT

General   The canalised part of the River l'Escaut begins at Cambrai, where it leaves the canal de Saint-Quentin, and, crossing the French-Belgian frontier at Mortagne, passes through Gand and Anvers, to discharge into the North Sea. In general, the traffic is heavy on this river; it consists chiefly of large barges *(Automoteurs)* and even of 'pusher-trains'. It is part of the main waterway which joins Paris, and the eastern regions with the north and with Belgium. It has for a tributary the river Scarpe and also it makes junction with the Canal de Saint-Quentin, the Canal de la Sensée and with the Canal de Mons à Condé. The present route has been deepened and rectified in many places, so much so that the original trace is now becoming known as le Vieil-Escaut. The waterway is divided into three sections:

(1st) runs from the junction with the Canal de Saint-Quentin to the Pont du Bassin-Rond at Bouchain.

(2nd) extends from the Pont du Bassin-Rond to the junction with the Canal de Mons à Condé. This section forms part of the improved waterway known as *Liaison Dunkerque-Valenciennes*.

(3rd) begins at the junction with the Canal de Mons à Condé and ends at the French-Belgian frontier.

Length   From the junction with the Canal de Saint-Quentin at Cambrai to the French-Belgian frontier, the river has a length of 61 kilometres.

Locks   There are in all 13 locks. Those in the first section are 5 in number, each with twin chambers; the chambers each have a length of

40 m. 50 with a width of 6 m. 00. In the second section (Pont du Bassin-Rond to the Canal de Mons à Condé) there are 7 locks. Of these, the lock at Pont Malin has been rebuilt with a single chamber 144 m. 60 in length and 12 m. 00 in width. The lock at Denain, also rebuilt, has a single chamber 144 m. 60 in length and 12 m. 00 in width. The locks at Trith-Saint-Léger, Valenciennes (Folien) and Bruay-s-Escaut (La Folie) are all being brought up to the same standard as l'écluse de Denain. The locks at Neuville and d'Haulchin have been taken out of service. In the third section there is only one lock; this has a single chamber 38 m. 50 long and 5 m. 18 in width.

Depth

In the first section the normal depth of water is 2 m. 60. In the second section, from the junction with the Canal de la Sensée to the junction with the Canal de Mons à Condé, the depth is increased to 4 m. 00 to allow 'pusher-trains' of 3,000 tons to use the waterway. The depth in the third section is 2 m. 50 at normal water-level.

Bridges

In the first section the headroom under fixed bridges is 3 m. 90 at the normal water-level. Throughout the second section the headroom under the fixed bridges is being raised to 5 m. 25 at the highest navigable water-level. In the third section the normal headroom is 4 m. 10 under fixed bridges.

Distance Table

		kilom.	lock	kilom.
Cambrai	Junction with Canal de St-Quentin (at K.o).			
	Railway bridge. Lock (No. 1 de Cantimpré).			
	Bridge	0.0	1	61.0
	Lock (No. 2 de Selles). Bridges. Railway bridge	1.0	2	60.0
Ramillies	Lock (No. 3 d'Erre). Bridge	3.0	3	58.0
Escaudoeuvres	Quay (d'Escaudoeuvres)	4.0	—	57.0
	Quay (de Ramillies)	5.0	—	56.0
Eswars	Bridge. Quay (d'Eswars)	6.0	—	55.0
Thun-l'Eveque	Lock (No. 4 de Thun-l'Evêque). Bridge ...	7.0	4	54.0
	Port (de Thun-l'Evêque)	8.0	—	53.0
	Quay (d'Iwuy)	9.0	—	52.0
	Lock (No. 5 d'Iwuy)	10.0	5	51 0
Etrun	Quay (d'Etrun). Bridge	11.0	—	50.0
	Junction with Canal de la Sensée (at K.o).			
	Bridge (de Bassin-Rond). *Junction with the canal de jonction Escaut-Sensée (at K.o.7)**	12.0†	—	49.0
Bouchain	Lock (No. 6 de Pont-Malin)	14.0	6	47.0
	Bridge (de Bouchain). Port	15.0	—	46.0
	Railway bridge	18 0	—	43.0

* See Plan No. 8.
† See also under Canal de la Sensée.

Distance Table

		kilom.	lock	kilom.
Lourches	... ...	19.0	—	42.0
	Bridge (de Lourches)	20.0	—	41.0
	Railway bridge	21 0	—	40.0
Denain	Lock (No. 8 de Denain)	22.0	7	39.0
	Bridge (Pont de l'Enclos)	23.0	—	38.0
	Bridge (de l'Abattoir). Port (de Denain) ...	24.0	—	37.0
Rouvignies	Railway bridge	25.0	—	36.0
Haulchin	Bridge (de Rouvignies)	25.0	—	36.0
Prouvy	Railway bridge	27.0	—	34.0
Trith-St-Léger	Lock (No. 10 de Trith-St-Léger). Bridge	29.0	8	32.0
	Bridge (Pont de la Concorde)	31.0	—	30.0
Valenciennes	Railway bridge	32.0	—	29.0
	Lock (No. 11 Notre-Dame)	33.0	9	28.0
	Bridge (Notre-Dame)	34.0	—	27.0
	Port (de la Citadelle). Bridge (de St-Waast)	34.0	—	27.0
	Bridge (Pont Jacob)	35.0	—	26.0
	Lock (No. 12 Folien)	36.0	10	25.0
Anzin	Railway bridge (de la Bleuse-Borne) ...	36.0	—	25.0
Bruay	Railway bridge	38.0	—	23.0
	Bridge (Pont des Vaches)	39.0	—	22.0
	Lock (No. 13 de la Folie)	40.0	11	21.0
Escautpont	Bridge (Pont de Thiers)	41.0	—	20.0
Fresnes	Railway bridge	43.0	—	18.0
	Bridge (Pont Bellevue)	44.0	—	17.0
	Lock (No. 14 de Fresnes)	44.0	12	17.0
Condé-sur-Escaut	*Junction with Canal de Mons a Condé (at K.o)*	46.0	—	15.0
	Bridge (de la Renaissance)	46.0	—	15.0
Fresnes	Bridge (Pont du Sarteau)	48.0	—	13.0
Bruille-St-Amand	Bridge (de Hergnies)	52.0	—	9.0
	Ferry	53.0	—	8.0
Rodignies	Lock (No. 16 de Rodignies)	57.0	13	4.0
Mortagne	Lift bridge (de Mortagne)	59.0	—	2.0
	Confluence with la Scarpe (K.66) ...	59.0	—	2.0
	Frontier (*Franco-Belge*)	61.0	—	0.0

CANAL DE L'EST

General   The canal de l'Est joins the canalised river la Meuse to la Moselle and to la Saône. It is divided into two parts, viz.:

    (a) **Northern Section** (Givet to Troussey).

    (b) **Southern Section** (Toul to Corre).

The Northern Section, which is really the canalised River la Meuse, begins at the Franco-Belge frontier near Givet and continues southward to join with the Canal de la Marne au Rhin at Troussey : the Southern Section leaves the same canal (de la Marne au Rhin) at Toul and, still running southward, joins la Saône at Corre. The Canal de la Marne au Rhin thus forms a link between the two sections of the Canal de l'Est; the length of the link is 20 kilometres.

Tunnel de Verdun et des Koeurs

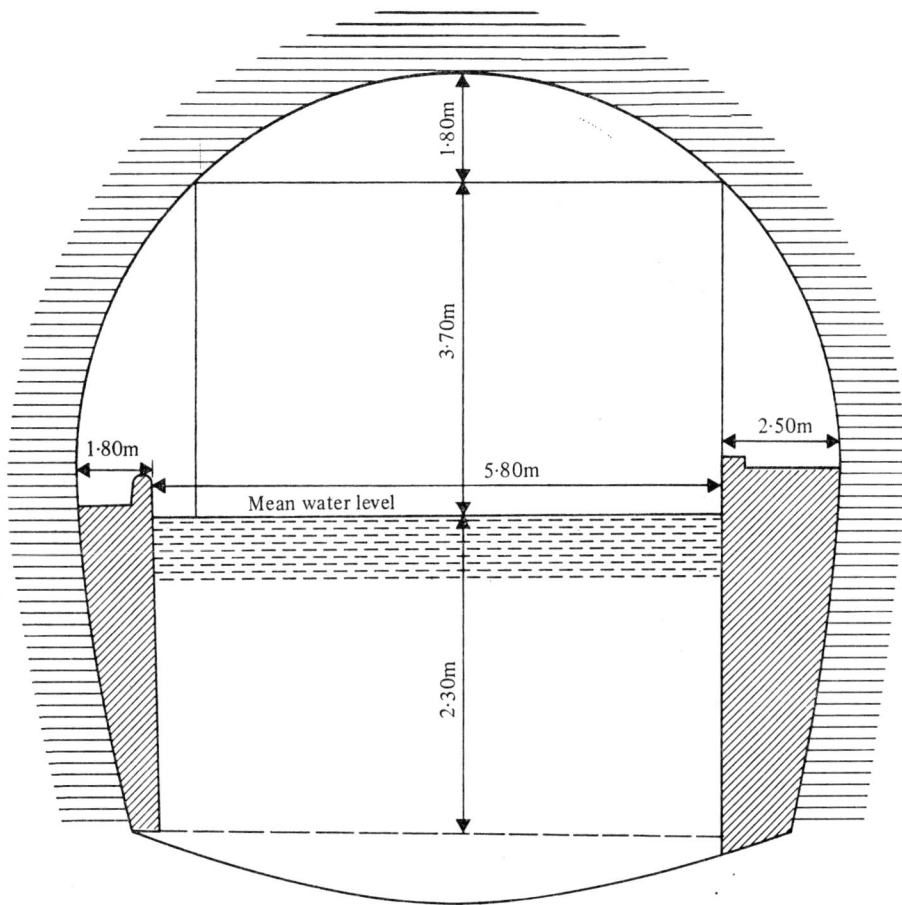

CAUTION. Live electric wires may be established throughout the length of this tunnel.

Northern Section

Length

The length from the Belgian frontier near Givet to the junction with the Canal de la Marne au Rhin at Troussey is 272 kilometres.

Locks

The total rise of this section is nearly 150 metres, and this is regulated by 59 locks. The first of these locks (close to the Belgian frontier) has a length of 100 m. 00 with a width of 12 m. 00. From that point as far as Verdun all the locks, to the number of 39, have a length of

79

48 m. 30 with a width of 5 m. 70. Above Verdun, the remaining 19 locks have a length of 38 m. 50 with a width of 5 m. 20.

Depth The depth is maintained at not less than 2 m. 20 throughout.

Bridges All the bridges have at least a headroom of 3 m. 70 above the normal water level.

Tow-path There is a tow-path throughout and towing is by diesel tractors.

Tunnels There are four tunnels, namely, at Ham, Revin, Verdun and Koeurs. Particulars are as follows:

	HAM (K.7)	REVIN (K.39)
Length	565 m. 00	224 m. 00
Width	5 m. 80	5 m. 95
Depth	2 m. 20	2 m. 20
Headroom ...	3 m. 60	3 m. 60
	No tow-path	Tow-path

	VERDUN (K.204)	KOEURS (K.249)
Length	45 m. 00	50 m. 00
Width	5 m. 80	5 m. 80
Depth	2 m. 20	2 m. 20
Headroom ...	3 m. 70	3 m. 70
	Tow-path	Tow-path

As all the tunnels only allow of one vessel making a passage at a time, Masters are allowed to proceed, under the instruction of the Agents of the Navigation, alternatively in each direction.

Northern Section
Distance Table

			kilom.	lock	kilom.
Givet	Frontier *(Franco-Belge)*.				
	Beginning of Canal de l'Est		0.0	—	272.0
	Lock (No. 59 des Quatre Cheminées) ...		1.0	I	271.0
	Port and Bridge (de Givet)		4.0	—	268.0
Chooz	Bridge (des Trois-Fontaines)		7.0	—	265.0
	Lock (No. 58 des Trois-Fontaines). Port		7.0	2	265.0
	Tunnel (de Ham) (565 m.)		7.0	—	265.0
Ham	Lock (No. 57 de Ham)		8.0	3	264.0
Vireux	Lock (No. 56 de Mouyon)		13.0	4	259.0
	Bridge and Port (de Vireux)		14.0	—	258.0
Montigny	Lock (No. 55 de Montigny)		17.0	5	255.0
	Ferry and Port (de Ridoux)		20.0	—	252.0
Fépin	Lock (No. 54 de Fépin). Bridge		22.0	6	250.0
Haybes	Bridge and Port (de Haybes)		24.0	—	248.0
	Lock (No. 53 de Vanne-Alcorps) ...		25.0	7	247.0

Distance Table

		kilom.	lock	kilom.
Fumay	Bridge and Port (de Fumay)	27.0	—	245.0
	Lock (No. 52 de l'Uf)	30.0	8	242.0
	Railway bridge	32.0	—	240.0
	Lock (No. 51 de Saint-Joseph) ...	33.0	9	239.0
Revin	Lock (No. 50 de Revin)	39.0	10	233.0
	Tunnel (de Revin) (224 m.)	39.0	—	233.0
	Lock (No. 49 d'Orzy)	40.0	11	232.0
Anchamps	Port (d'Anchamps)	44.0	—	228.0
	Railway bridge	45.0	—	227.0
	Lock (No. 48 des Dames de Meuse) ...	45.0	12	227.0
Laifour	Railway bridge	48.0	—	224.0
	Lock (No. 47 de la Commune)	50.0	13	222.0
	Port (de Laifour)	50.0	—	222.0
Deville	Ferry. Port (de Deville)	53.0	—	219.0
	Lock (No. 46 de Deville)	54.0	14	218.0
Monthermé	Bridge (de Monthermé)	58.0	—	214.0
	Port (Saint-Remy)	59.0	—	213.0
Château-Regnault	Railway bridge	61.0	—	211.0
	Bridge (de Château-Regnault)	62.0	—	210.0
Lévrezy	Lock (No. 45 de Lévrezy)	63.0	15	209.0
Braux	Port (de Braux). Bridge (de Braux) ...	65.0	—	207.0
Joigny	Port and Bridge (de Joigny)	69.0	—	203.0
	Lock (No. 44 de Joigny)	70.0	16	202.0
Nouzonville	Port and Bridge (de Nouzonville) ...	72.0	—	200.0
Montcy-Notre-Dame	Lock (No. 43 de Montcy). Railway bridge	79.0	17	193.0
Mézières	Railway bridge. Port. Railway bridge ...	81.0	—	191.0
Saint-Laurent	Port and Lock (No. 41 de Romery) ...	84.0	18	188.0
	Bridge	85.0	—	187.0
Lumes	Bridge	86.0	—	186.0
	Bridge and Port (de Lumes)	87.0	—	185.0
	Railway bridge	87.0	—	185.0
Dom-le-Mesnil*	Bridge (de Nouvion)	93.0	—	179.0
	Lock (No. 40 de Dom-le-Mesnil) ...	94.0	19	178.0
Vrigne-Meuse	*Junction with Canal des Ardennes (at K.o)*	96.0	—	176.0
Donchery	Lock (No. 39 de Donchery)	99.0	20	173.0
	Bridge (de Donchery)	100.0	—	172.0
Glaire-Villette	Railway bridge	102.0	—	170.0
	Lock (No. 38 de Villette). Bridge ...	103.0	21	169.0
	Bridge (de Glaire)	104.0	—	168.0
Sedan	Bridge (Pont Neuf de Sedan) ...	106.0	—	166.0
	Lock (No. 37 de Sedan). Port. Bridge ...	107.0	22	165.0
Remilly-Aillicourt	Railway bridge	112.0	—	160.0
	Lock (No. 36 de Remilly-Aillicourt) ...	112.0	23	160.0
	Port (de Bazeilles)	112.0	—	160.0

* See Plan No. 11.

Distance Table

		kilom.	lock	kilom.
	Bridge (d'Aillicourt)	113.0	—	159.0
	Bridge and Port (de Remilly)	115.0	—	157.0
	Bridge (Pont Petit Remilly)	116.0	—	156.0
Mouzon	Ferry (de Villers-devant-Mouzon) ...	119.0	—	153.0
	Port (de Villers)	119.0	—	153.0
	Lock (No. 35 de Mouzon) ...	122.0	24	150.0
	Bridge (La Fourberie). Port. Bridge	123.0	—	149.0
Létanne	Lock (No. 34 d'Alma)	130.0	25	142.0
Pouilly	Port (de Létanne)	134.0	—	138.0
	Lock (No. 33 de Pouilly)	137.0	26	135.0
Inor	Port (d'Inor)	141.0	—	131.0
	Lock (No. 32 d'Inor)	142.0	27	130.0
Martincourt	Bridge and Port (de Martincourt)	143.0	—	129.0
Stenay	Port (de Stenay)	148.0	—	124.0
	Lock (No. 31 de Stenay)	148.0	28	124.0
Mouzay	Lock (No. 30 de Mouzay). Port. Bridge ...	152.0	29	120.0
	Bridge	153.0	—	119.0
	Lock (No. 29 du Sep)	155.0	30	117.0
Dun	Port (de Dun)	161.0	—	111.0
	Lock (No. 28 de Dun)	162.0	31	110.0
Liny-devant-Dun	Lock (No. 27 de Warinvaux) ...	163.0	32	109.0
	Bridge. Lock (No. 26 de Liny-d-Dun) ...	165.0	33	107.0
Vilosnes	Port (de Vilosnes)	171.0	—	101.0
Sivry	Lock (No. 25 de la Planchette) ...	172.0	34	100.0
	Port (de Sivry-s-Meuse). Bridge ...	174.0	—	98.0
	Bridge	176.0	—	96.0
Consenvoye	Bridge	178.0	—	94.0
	Lock (No. 24 de Consenvoye). Port	179.0	35	93.0
Brabant	Lock (No. 23 de Brabant) ...	181.0	36	91.0
Samogneux	Lock (No. 22 de Samogneux) ...	184.0	37	88.0
Champneuville	Bridge	186.0	—	86.0
	Lock (No. 21 de Champ)	188.0	38	84.0
Vacherauville	Bridge	194.0	—	78.0
	Bridge	195.0	—	77.0
	Lock (No. 20 de Bras)	196.0	39	76.0
Belleville	Bridge	199.0	—	73.0
	Bridge	200.0	—	72.0
	Railway bridge	201.0	—	71.0
	Bridge (Galavaude). Port (St-Paul de Verdun)	202.0	—	70.0
	Bridge	203.0	—	69.0
	Two Bridges *(Passage dangerous)*	203.0	—	69.0
	Lock (No. 19 de Verdun)	204.0	40	68.0
	Tunnel (de Verdun) (45 m.). *(Dangerous)*	204.0	—	68.0
	Port and Bridge	205.0	—	67.0

Distance Table

			kilom.	*lock*	*kilom.*
Belleray	Lock (No. 18 de Belleray)...	... ...	... 207.0	41	65.0
Haudainville	Bridge	... 209.0	—	63.0
	Lock (No. 17 d'Haudainville)	...	... 210.0	42	62.0
Dieue	Bridge	... 213.0	—	59.0
	Bridge. Lock (No. 16 de Dieue-Aval)	... 214.0	43	58.0
	Lock (No. 15 de Dieue). Port ...	... 216.0	44	56.0
Génicourt	Bridge	... 219.0	—	53.0
	Bridge	... 220.0	—	52.0
Ambly	Port (de Génicourt). Bridge ...	... 221.0	—	51.0
	Bridge and Port (d'Ambly) ...	... 222.0	—	50.0
	Lock (No. 14 d'Ambly)	... 222.0	45	50.0
Troyon	Bridge. Lock (No. 13 de Troyon)	... 225.0	46	47.0
	Port (de Troyon)	... 227.0	—	45.0
Lacroix	Bridge and Port (de Lacroix) ...	... 230.0	—	42.0
	Lock (No. 12 de Lacroix)	... 231.0	47	41.0
Rouvrois	Lock (No. 11 de Rouvrois) ...	... 234.0	48	38.0
Maizey	Port and Bridge (de Maizey) ...	... 236.0	—	36.0
Saint-Mihiel	Bridge	... 240.0	—	32.0
	Lock (No. 10 de St-Mihiel). Port	... 241.0	49	31.0
Koeur-la-Petite	Lock (No. 9 de Koeur-la-Petite) ...	... 247.0	50	25.0
	Lock (No. 8 de Han)	... 247.0	51	25.0
Han	Railway bridge	... 248.0	—	24.0
	Tunnel (des Koeurs) (50 m.) ...	... 249.0	52	23.0
Sampigny	Port and Bridge (de Sampigny) ...	... 252.0	—	20.0
Vadonville	Lock (No. 7 de Vadonville) ...	... 254.0	33	18.0
Lérouville	Port (de Lérouville). Bridge ...	... 256.0	—	16.0
	Two Railway bridges	... 257.0	—	15.0
Commercy	Lock (No. 6 de Commercy) ...	... 260.0	54	12.0
	Bridge and Port (de Commercy) ...	... 262.0	—	10.0
	Lateral barrage ('des Allemands'). *(Passage dangerous)*	... 263.0	—	9.0
Euville	Lock (No. 5 d'Euville)	... 266.0	55	6.0
Vertuzey	Bridge and Port (de Vertuzey) ...	... 268.0	—	4.0
Sorcy	Bridge. Railway bridge. Bridge ...	... 270.0	—	2.0
	Lock (No. 4 de Sorcy). Port ...	... 270.0	56	2.0
	Lock (No. 3 de Sorcy)	... 271.0	57	1.0
	Lock (No. 2 de Sorcy)	... 271.0	58	1.0
Troussey	Lock (No. 1 called 'de Troussey) ...	... 272.0	59	0.0
	Junction with Canal de la Marne au Rhin (at K.111)	... 272.0	—	0.0

Southern Section

General   This section, which joins la Moselle to la Saône, leaves the Canal de la Marne au Rhin at Toul and finally joins the River Saône at Corre. In the first part between Toul and Epinal the canal runs laterally to la Moselle, except between Chaudenay-sur-Moselle and Pont-St-Vincent, over which length it is the rectified river bed; for the remainder of the distance, the canal is an entirely man-made waterway. It contains a summit level (at a height of nearly 1,200 feet above sea level) which lies between the locks of Golby and Girancourt and is no less than 10 kilometres in length. The descent towards la Saône has in its length several places where the width of the passage is much restricted; the narrowest of these places is at the *pont-canal de Châtel (K.69)*, which is only 6 m. 00 wide. The main canal has two branches:

(a) **Branch de Nancy** (Messein to Laneuville).

(b) **Branch d'Epinal** (Golbey to Epinal).

Length	The length of the canal from Toul to Corre, where the junction is made with la Saône, is 147 kilometres.
Locks	There are 99 locks in this section in which 53 fall towards la Moselle and 46 towards la Saône. The first lock (No. 53) has a length of 39 m. 60 with a width of 5 m. 13; the following locks up to and including Lock No. 48 (commune de Pont-St-Vincent) have a useful length of 49 m. 00 with a width of 6 m. 00. From thence to Lock No. 34 (commune de Bainville-aux-Miroirs) the locks have a length of 41 m. 30 with a width of 5 m. 20. The remaining locks, 79 more, have a length of 38 m. 50 with a width of 5 m. 20.
Depth	The normal depth of water is 2 m. 20 throughout.
Bridges	All the fixed bridges have a clear headroom of 3 m. 70 above the normal water level.
Tow-path	There is a tow-path throughout and towing is effected by means of diesel tractors.

Distance Table		*kilom.*	*lock*	*kilom.*
Toul	*Junction with Canal de la Marne au Rhin (at K.131)*. Bridge (called 'de la Vacherie') Railway bridge. Port (de la porte Moselle).	0.0	—	147.0
	Lock (No. 53). Port (de Vauban) ...	1.0	I	146.0
	Bridge (de Valcourt)	3.0	—	144.0
Chaudeney-s-Moselle	Railway bridge	4.0	—	143.0
Pierre-la-Treiche	Lock (No. 52)	6.0	2	141.0
	Port (de l'Arot)	7.0	—	140.0
	Lock (No. 51)	10.0	3	137.0
Sexey-aux-Forges	Lock (No. 50)	15.0	4	132.0
	Port and Bridge (de Maron)	18.0	—	129.0

Distance Table

		kilom.	lock	kilom.
	Port (de Sexey-aux-Forges)	19.0	—	128.0
	Lock (No. 49)	20.0	5	127.0
Pont-St-Vincent	Bridge and Port (de Pont-St-Vincent) ...	23.0	—	124.0
	Lock (No. 48)	24.0	6	123.0
Messein	Lock (No. 47)	25.0	7	122.0
	Bridge	26.0	—	121.0
	Port (de Messein)	27.0	—	120.0
Méréville	Lock (No. 46). *Junction with branch to Nancy*	28.0	8	119.0
Richardménil	Bridge	30.0	—	117.0
Flavigny	Lock (No. 45). Port (de Flavigny) ...	31.0	9	116.0
	Lock (No. 44). Lock (No. 43). Pont-canal	33.0	11	114.0
	Bridge	34.0	—	113.0
Benney	Bridge	36.0	—	111.0
Tonnoy	Bridge	38.0	—	109.0
Benney	Lock (No. 42)	39.0	12	108.0
Crévéchamps	Lock (No. 41)	40.0	13	107.0
Neuviller	Lock (No. 40)	43.0	14	104.0
	Port (de Neuviller)	45.0	—	102.0
Roville-devant Bayon	Lock (No. 39). Port (de Bayon)	46.0	15	101.0
	Lock (No. 38)	47.0	16	100.0
	Bridge. Lock (No. 37)	49.0	17	98.0
Bainville-aux-Miroirs	Port (de Bainville-aux-Miroirs)	50.0	—	97.0
	Lock (No. 36)	51.0	18	96.0
	Turning basin	52.0	—	95.0
Gripport	Lock (No. 35)	53.0	19	94.0
	Bridge	54.0	—	93.0
	Lock (No. 34)	55.0	20	92.0
Socourt	Port (de Socourt). Lock (No. 33) ...	56.0	21	91.0
Charmes	Lock (No. 32 de la Plaine de Charmes) ...	58.0	22	89.0
	Lock (No. 31 de Charmes)	59.0	23	88.0
	Port and Bridge (Grand Pont de Charmes)	60.0	—	87.0
	Lock (No. 30 des Moulins de Charmes)...	61.0	24	86.0
Vincey	Lock (No. 29 de Vincey)	63.0	25	84.0
Portieux	Port and Bridge (de Vincey)	65.0	—	82.0
	Railway bridge. *(Skew. Narrow passage 13 m.)*	65.0	—	82.0
	Lock (No. 28 de Portieux)	65.0	26	82.0
	Lock (No. 27 des Fouys)	67.0	27	80.0
Chatel	Lock (No. 26 de l'Avière). Pont-canal. *(Narrow passage 6 m.)*	69.0	28	78.0
Nomexy	Lock (No. 25 de Nomexy). Port	70.0	29	77.0
	Lock (No. 24 de la Heronnière)	72.0	30	75.0
Igney	Lock (No. 23 de Vaxoncourt)	73.0	31	74.0
	Lock (No. 22 d'Igney). Port	74.0	32	73.0

Distance Table

		kilom.	lock	kilom.
Thaon	Lock (No. 21 de la Plaine de Thaon) ...	76.0	33	71.0
	Lock (No. 20 de Thaon). Skew bridge ...	77.0	34	70.0
	Bridge. *(Narrow passage 7 m.)*	78.0	—	69.0
	Lock (No. 19 de l'Usine de Thaon) ...	78.0	35	69.0
Chavelot	Lock (No. 18 de Chavelot)	80.0	36	67.0
	Lock (No. 17 de la prairie Gérard) ...	81.0	37	66.0
	Lock (No. 16)	82.0	38	65.0
Golbey	Lock (No. 15 de la Côte-Olie) ...	83.0	39	64.0
	Junction with the branch to Epinal ...	83.0	—	64.0
	Lock (No. 14 de la montée de Golbey) ...	83.0	40	64.0
	Lock (No. 13 de la montée de Golbey) ...	83.0	41	64.0
	Lock (No. 12 de la montée de Golbey) ...	83.0	42	64.0
	Lock (No. 11 de la montée de Golbey) ...	83.0	43	64.0
	Lock (No. 10 de la montée de Golbey) ...	84.0	44	63.0
	Lock (No. 9 de la montée de Golbey) ...	84.0	45	63.0
	Lock (No. 8 de la montée de Golbey) ...	84.0	46	62.0
	Lock (No. 7 de la montée de Golbey) ...	85.0	47	62.0
	Lock (No. 6 de la montée de Golbey) ...	85.0	48	62.0
	Lock (No. 5 de la montée de Golbey) ...	85.0	49	62.0
	Lock (No. 4 de la montée de Golbey) ...	85.0	50	62.0
	Lock (No. 3 de la montée de Golbey) ...	85.0	51	62.0
	Lock (No. 2 de la montée de Golbey) ...	86.0	52	61.0
	Lock (No. 1 de Bois-l'Abbé). Beginning of summit level	86.0	53	61.0
Uxegeney	Railway bridge *(skew)* and Bridge (de Nois l'Abbé). *(Narrow passage 7 m.)*	87.0	—	60.0
Forges	Port (des Forges)	88.0	—	59.0
	Bridge (des Forges). *(Narrow passage 7 m.)*	89.0	—	58.0
Sanchey	Bridge (de Sanchey). *(Narrow passage)* ...	91.0	—	56.0
Chaumousey	Bridge (under canal)	92.0	—	55.0
	Two bridges (under canal)	93.0	—	54.0
	Two bridges (under canal)	94.0	—	53.0
	Port (de Chaumousey)	94.0	—	53.0
Girancourt	Bridge (de la gare de Girancourt). *(Narrow passage)*	96.0	—	51.0
	Lock (No. 1 de Trusey). End of summit level. Port (de Girancourt)	97.0	54	50.0
	Lock (No. 2 de Girancourt)	97.0	55	50.0
	Lock (No. 3 de Barbonfoing)	99.0	56	48.0
	Lock (No. 4 de Launois)	99.0	57	48.0
	Lock (No. 5 du Void de Girancourt) ...	100.0	58	47.0
	Lock (No. 6 de la descente du Void) ...	101.0	59	46.0
	Lock (No. 7 de la descente du Void) ...	102.0	60	45.0
Uzemain	Lock (No. 8 de la descente du Void) ...	102.0	61	45.0
	Lock (No. 9 de la descente du Void) ...	103.0	62	44.0

Distance Table

		kilom.	lock	kilom.
	Lock (No. 10 de la descente du Void) ...	103.0	63	44.0
	Lock (No. 11 de la descente du Void) ...	103.0	64	44.0
	Lock (No. 12 de Brennecôte)	104.0	65	43.0
	Lock (No. 13 de Thielouze)	104.0	66	43.0
	Bridge (de Thielouze). *(Narrow passage)*	104.0	—	43.0
	Port and Lock (No. 14 de Thielouze) ...	105.0	67	42.0
	Lock (No. 15 des Thillots)	106.0	68	41.0
	Lock (No. 16 de Méloménil)	106.0	69	41.0
	Lock (No. 17 de Reblangotte)	107.0	70	40.0
Charmois-l'Orgueilleux	Lock (No. 18 d'Uzemain). Port (de la Forge d'Uzemain)	108.0	71	39.0
	Lock (No. 19 de Charmois-l'Orgueilleux)	109.0	72	38.0
	Lock (No. 20 du Coney)	110.0	73	37.0
	Port (du Pont tremblant)	111.0	—	36.0
	Lock (No. 21 du Pont tremblant) ...	111.0	74	36.0
Harsault	Lock (No. 22 de Thunimont)	112.0	75	35.0
	Lock (No. 23 de l'Usine de Thunimont)...	112.0	76	35.0
	Swing bridge. *(Narrow passage)*	113.0	—	34.0
	Lock (No. 24 d'Harsault)	114.0	77	33.0
	Lock (No. 25 de la Colosse)	115.0	78	32.0
Hautmougey	Lock (No. 26 de la Forge Quenot) ...	116.0	79	31.0
	Lock (No. 27 de la Basse-di-Pommier) ...	117.0	80	30.0
	Lock (No. 28 de la Basse Jean-Melin) ...	118.0	81	29.0
Bains	Bridge (du Coney). *(Narrow passage)* ...	119.0	—	28.0
	Port (de Bains). Bridge (du Coney) ...	119.0	—	28.0
	Lock (No. 29 du Pont du Coney) ...	119.0	82	28.0
Fontenoy-le-Château	Lock (No. 30 de Montroche)	120.0	83	27.0
	Lock (No. 31 de la Manufacture de Bains)	121.0	84	26.0
	Lock (No. 32 de Grurupt)	122.0	85	25.0
	Le Grurupt. Port (du Moulin-aux-Bois) ...	122.0	—	25.0
	Port (de la Pipée). Lock (No. 33 de la Pipée)	123.0	86	24.0
	Lock (No. 34 de Fontenoy-le-Château) ...	124.0	87	23.0
	Port (de Fontenoy-le-Château)	124.0	—	23.0
	Bridge. *(Narrow passage)*	125.0	—	22.0
	Lock (No. 35 de Fontenoy-le-Château) ...	125.0	88	22.0
	Bridge. *(Narrow passage)*	126.0	—	21.0
Montmotier	Lock (No. 36 de Montmotier)	127.0	89	20.0
	Lock (No. 37 du Gros-Moulin)	129.0	90	18.0
Ambiévillers	Lock (No. 38 d'Ambiévillers)	130.0	91	17.0
	Swing bridge and Port (de Freland) ...	132.0	—	15.0
Pont-au-Bois	Footbridge	133.0	—	14.0
	Bridge and Port (de Pont-du-Bois) ...	134.0	—	13.0
	Lock (No. 39 du Pont-du-Bois) ...	134.0	92	13.0
Selles	Lock (No. 40 du Bois de Selles). Port ...	136.0	93	11.0

Distance Table

		kilom.	lock	kilom.
	Lock (No. 41 des Carrières de Selles) ...	136.0	94	11.0
	Swing bridge. *(Narrow passage)*	137.0	—	10.0
	Lock (No. 42 du village de Selles)	138.0	95	9.0
Passavant	Bridge	140.0	—	7.0
	Port (de Passavant)	141.0	—	6.0
	Lock (No. 43 de la Basse-Vaivre) ...	142.0	96	5.0
	Lock (No. 44 de Demangevelle)	143.0	97	4.0
Corre	Lock (No. 45 de Vougécourt) ...	145.0	98	2.0
	Two bridges	146.0	—	1.0
	Lock (No. 46 de Corre)	147.0	99	0.0
	Junction with la Saône (canalised) (at K.0)	147.0	—	0.0

Branch de Nancy

General The Branch de Nancy makes a link between the Southern Section of the Canal de l'Est (at K.28 Richardménil commune) and the Canal de la Marne au Rhin (at K.168 Laneuveville-devant-Nancy). It contains a summit level.

Length The length of the branch is 10 kilometres.

Locks There are 18 locks. Five of these fall towards la Moselle and the remaining 13 towards la Meurthe. They all have a length of 41 m. 30 with a width of 5 m. 20.

Depth The depth is maintained at 2 m. 20, the same as in the main canal.

Bridges The bridges have a clear headroom of 3 m. 70.

Tow-path There is a tow-path throughout.

Distance Table

		kilom.	lock	kilom.
Richardménil	*Junction with Canal de l'Est (South) (at K.28).* Lock (No. 5)	0.0	1	10.0
	Lock (No. 4). Lock (No. 3). Lock (No. 2)	1.0	4	9.0
Ludres	Lock (No. 1). Beginning of summit level...	2.0	5	8.0
Fléville	Bridge	5.0	—	5.0
	Lock No. 1. End of summit level (called 'du Mauvais Lieu')	5.0	6	5.0
	Lock (No. 2). Lock (No. 3). Lock (No. 4)	5.0	9	5.0
	Lock (No. 5)	5.0	10	5.0
	Lock (No. 6). Lock (No. 7). Lock (No. 8)	6.0	13	4.0
	Lock (No. 9)	6.0	14	4.0
	Lock (No. 10)	7.0	15	3.0

Distance Table						*kilom.*	*lock*	*kilom.*
Laneuveville-	Lock (No. 11)	...	...	...	...	8.0	16	2.0
devant-Nancy	Railway bridge	...	...	...	...	10.0	—	0.0
	Lock (No. 12). Lock (No. 13)	...	...	10.0	18	0.0
	Junction with Canal de la Marne au Rhin							
	(at K.168)	...	...	...	...	10.0	—	0.0

Branch d'Epinal

General The Branch d'Epinal leaves the main canal at K.83 and runs to the town of Epinal in a distance of a little over 3 kilometres. The headroom under bridges is 3 m. 70, while the other conditions of navigation are the same as those obtaining in the main canal.

Distance Table					*kilom.*	*lock*	*kilom.*
Golbey	*Junction with Canal de l'Est (at K.83)*	...			0.0	—	3.0
	Bridge. Pont-canal. *(Narrow passage)*	...			0.0	—	3.0
Dogneville	Bridge	...	...	...	1.0	—	2.0
Epinal	Bridge. *(Narrow passage)* ...	...		2.0	—	1.0
	Port (d'Epinal). *End of navigation*	...		3.0	—	0.0

CANAL DE FURNES

General The Canal de Furnes begins at the port of Dunkerque at a point on the marine canal which is called *Canal de Jonction*. It extends beyond the Franco-Belge frontier to join with other canals at Nieuport, but after it has crossed the frontier it is called *le Canal de Nieuport à Dunkerque.**

Length The distance from Dunkerque to the Belgian frontier is 13 kilometres.

Locks The only lock is situated at the beginning of the canal, where it joins with the marine canal. This lock, which has one chamber, is 40 m. 40 in length with a width of 6 m. 00.

Depth The depth of water in the canal is 2 m. 50.

Bridges All the fixed bridges have a clear headroom of at least 3 m. 50 above the normal water level.

Tow-path Towing is by diesel tractors along a tow-path which is continuous throughout.

* See *The Inland Waterways of Belgium*, Imray Laurie Norie and Wilson.

Distance Table

		kilom.	lock	kilom.
Dunkerque	Lock (de Furnes). *Junction with 'Canal de Jonction' (marine)*	0.0	I	13.0
	Footbridge (des Corderies)	0.0	—	13.0
	Bridge (called 'Pont Neuf')	1.0	—	12.0
Tétéghem	Railway bridge (called 'Viaduc de Rosendael')	1.0	—	12.0
	Bridge (du Chapeau Rouge)	2.0	—	11.0
Leffrinckoucke	Bridge (de Leffrinckoucke)	4.0	—	9.0
Zuydcoote	Bridge (de Zuydcoote)	8.0	—	5.0
Bray-Dunes	Swing bridge (de Ghyvelde). (Customs) ...	10.0	—	3.0
	Frontier *(Franco-Belge)*. *Junction with Canal de Nieuport à Dunkerque*	13.0	—	0.0

GARONNE AND GIRONDE

General

This river from its source to the sea is one continuous stream, but from its source to Bec-d'Ambès it is called La Garonne, while from Bec-d'Ambès to Ponte-de-Gave, where it falls into the Atlantic, it is given the name of La Gironde. Its principal tributaries are la Dordogne, on the right bank near Bec-d'Ambès, and la Baïse on the left bank near Saint-Léger-Monplaisir. From Toulouse to Castets its course is fairly closely followed by the *canal latéral à la Garonne*, and little or no navigation uses the river itself. It is, however, classified as navigable over a distance of 270 kilometres, of which 200 are reckoned to la Garonne and 70 for la Gironde. The influence of the tides is felt as far up as Casseuil, where the average rise and fall is about 0 m. 36, with, of course, progressively greater amplitude towards the sea. Improvement works have established a minimum depth of 1 m. 10 at low-water neap tides at Castets and 1 m. 50 at Pont-de-pierre (Bordeaux). The Port of Castets is of importance as it is there that the canal latéral à la Garonne joins with the river. At the present time the river is not much used up-stream of Castets, as nearly all the traffic uses *le canal latéral a la Garonne*. As la Garonne below the Pont de pierre, Bordeaux, is counted as a marine navigation, only the section from Castets to the Pont de pierre will be considered here. It should further be noted that a bore *(le mascaret)* is sometimes built up during low tides in the summer between the upper limit of the Port of Bordeaux and the port de Barsac, but it is very irregular in its appearance.

Length

From Casseuil to le Pont de pierre at Bordeaux is 54 kilometres.

Locks

None.

Depth	Variable and subject to the tides. At Castets, 1 m. 10 at low-water neaps; 1 m. 65 at high water neaps. At Pont de pierre, 1 m. 50 at low water neaps; 4 m. 05 at high water neaps. These are average figures, and local advice must always be obtained.			

Bridges	There are seven bridges over the section considered, including le Pont de pierre. All have a minimum headroom of 6 m. 50 above the highest navigable water level.
Tow-path	No tow-path is maintained nor is towing from the banks possible.

Distance Table

		kilom.	lock	kilom.
Castets	Port (de Castets). *Junction with canal latéral à la Garonne.* Bridge	0.0	—	54.0
Saint-Pardon	Port (de Mondiet)	2.0	—	52.0
Saint-Macaire	Port (de Saint-Macaire)	5.0	—	49.0
Langon	Bridge and Port (de Langon). Railway bridge	8.0	—	46.0
Toulenne	Port (de Toulenne)	8.0	—	46.0
Preignac	Port (de la Garonnelle)	11.0	—	43.0
	Port (de Preignac). Ferry	13.0	—	42.0
Barsac	Port (de Barsac)	14.0	—	40.0
Cadillac	Bridge and Port (de Cadillac)	19.0	—	36.0
Cérons	Port (de Cérons)	20.0	—	34.0
Podensac	Port (de Podensac)	22.0	—	32.0
Rions	Port (de Rions)	22.0	—	32.0
Lestiac	Port (de Lestiac)	26.0	—	28.0
Arbanats	Port (d'Arbanats)	28.0	—	26.0
Langoiran	Bridge and Port (de Langoiran)	31.0	—	23.0
Tabanac	Port (de Portets)	32.0	—	22.0
Baurech	Port (called 'Grand Port' de Baurech) ...	37.0	—	17.0
Cambes	Port (de Cambes)	38.0	—	16.0
	Port (d'Esconac)	40.0	—	14.0
Camblanes	Port (Port Neuf de Camblanes)	44.0	—	10.0
La Tresne	Port (Port de l'Homme)	47.0	—	7.0
Begles	*Upper limit of Port de Bordeaux*	49.0	—	5.0
Bordeaux	Railway bridge	53.0	—	1.0
	Bridge (Pont de pierre). Beginning of Port Maritime de Bordeaux	54.0	—	0.0

CANAL LATÉRAL À LA GARONNE

General	The canal latéral à la Garonne joins with the Canal du Midi at the octagonal basin situated in the City of Toulouse. It ends by falling into la Garonne at Castets-en-Dorthe. It thus forms, with the

Canal du Midi, a through route between the Atlantic coast of France and the Mediterranean north-western shore. It has two branches of some importance:

(a) **Branch to Montauban.**

(b) **Branch to la Baïse from Buzet. (Descente en Baïse).**

There are three other small branches; one of these is an urban canal in Toulouse, by which it is possible to reach the river from the canal*; another enables vessels to join le Tarn from the canal at Moissac; and there is also a feeder canal to the water catchment area of Agen. None of these is likely to be of interest to yachtsmen and will not be further discussed here; of all of them local particulars must be obtained.

Length

The distance by canal from Toulouse to Castets is 193 kilometres.

Locks

There are 53 locks, all of which fall towards Castets. The difference of level from one end of the canal to the other is 128 metres. The locks are of uniform size, having a length of 30 m. 65 with a width of 6 m. 00.

Depth

The normal depth of water is 2 m. 20.

Bridges

All the fixed bridges have a headroom of 3 m. 60 above the normal water level.

Tow-path

Most vessels which use this canal are self-propelled. There is, however, a good tow-path throughout.

Distance Table

		kilom.	lock	kilom
Toulouse†	*Junction with Canal du Midi.* Le Bassin octogonal. Port de l'Embouchure à Toulouse	0.0	—	193.0
	Bridge (Pont de Beziat)	2.0	—	191.0
	Lock (No. 1 de Lalande)	2.0	1	190.0
	Bridge (Pont de Ruppe)	5.0	—	188.0
Fenouillet	Lock (No. 2 de Lacourtensourt)	6.0	2	187.0
	Lock (No. 3 de Fenouillet)	7.0	3	186.0
	Bridge (de Latournelle)	8.0	—	185.0
Lespinasse	Lock (No. 4 de Lespinasse)	11.0	4	182.0
	Lock (No. 5 de Bordeneuve)	13.0	5	180.0
Saint-Jory	Lock (No. 6 de Saint-Jory)	15.0	6	178.0
Castelnau	Bridge (de l'Hers). Pont-canal (de l'Hers)	18.0	—	175.0

* Le canal de Brienne. Blue Line Cruisers (France) Ltd., Braunston, Rugby, England have a 'hire-cruiser' base on this canal (1969).
† See Plan No. 20.

Distance Table

		kilom.	lock	kilom.
	Lock (No. 7 de l'Hers)	18.0	7	175.0
	Lock (No. 8 de Castelnau)	19.0	8	174.0
	Bridge (de Bordeneuve)	21.0	—	172.0
	Lock (No. 9 d'Emballens)	22.0	9	171.0
Saint-Rustice	Bridge (de Saint-Rustice)	23.0	—	170.0
Pompignan	Bridge (de Pompignan)	23.0	—	170.0
Grissolles	Bridge (de Grissolles)	25.0	—	168.0
	Port (de Grissolles). Bridge (de Laroque)...	26.0	—	167.0
	Bridge (de Saint-Jean)	27.0	—	166.0
Canals	Bridge (de Villelongue)	29.0	—	164.0
Dieupentale	Bridge (de Dieupentale). Port	31.0	—	162.0
Bessens	Bridge (de Bessens)	33.0	—	160.0
	Bridge (de Lapeyrière)	34.0	—	159.0
Montbartier	Bridge (de Montbéqui)	35.0	—	158.0
	Bridge (de Montbartier)	36.0	—	157.0
	Bridge (de Tourret)	38.0	—	155.0
Montech	Bridge (de Laforêt)	39.0	—	154.0
	Lock (No. 10 de Lavache)	41.0	10	152.0
	Bridge and Port (de Montech)	42.0	—	151.0
	Branch de Montauban	42.0	—	151.0
	Lock (No. 11 de Montech)	43.0	11	150.0
	Lock (No. 12 des Peyrets)	43.0	12	150.0
	Lock (No. 13 de Pellaborie)	44.0	13	149.0
	Lock (No. 14 d'Escudiés)	44.0	14	149.0
	Lock (No. 15 de Pommiès)	45.0	15	148.0
Escatalens	Bridge (d'Escatalens)	46.0	—	147.0
	Lock (No. 16 d'Escatalens)	47.0	16	146.0
Saint-Porquier	Bridge (de Saint-Porquier)	49.0	—	144.0
	Bridge (de Lavilledieu)	49.0	—	144.0
	Bridge (de Saint-André)	50.0	—	143.0
Castelsarrasin	Lock (No. 17 de Saint-Martin)	51.0	17	142.0
	Bridge (de Danton)	52.0	—	141.0
	Railway bridge. Bridge (de Gaillau) ...	53.0	—	140.0
	Lock (No. 18 de Prades)	55.0	18	138.0
	Bridge (de la Briquetterie)	56.0	—	137.0
	Footbridge. Port and Bridge (de Castelsarrasin)	56.0	—	137.0
	Bridge (de Gandalou)	57.0	—	136.0
	Lock (No. 19 de Castelsarrasin)	57.0	19	136.0
	Bridge (de Saint-Jean-des-Vignes) ...	58.0	—	135.0
	Lock (No. 20 de Saint-Jean-des-Vignes) ...	59.0	20	134.0
	Lock (No. 21 des Verries)	59.0	21	134.0
	Lock (No. 22 d'Artel)	59.0	22	134.0
	Bridge (de Caussade)	50.0	—	133.0
Moissac	Pont-canal (over le Tarn) 356 m. ...	62.0	—	131.0

Distance Table

		kilom.	*lock*	*kilom.*
	Lock (No. 23 de Cacor)	62.0	23	131.0
	Lock (No. 24 de Grégonne)	63.0	24	130.0
	Lock (No. 25 de Moissac) ...	63.0	25	130.0
	Junction with canal going to le Tarn ...	63.0	—	130.0
	Swing bridge (des Marronniers) ...	64.0	—	129.0
	Swing bridge (Saint-Jacques) ...	64.0	—	129.0
	Footbridge. Bridge (de St-Catherine) ...	64.0	—	129.0
	Swing bridge (Saint-Martin)	65.0	—	128.0
	Lock (No. 26 d'Espagnette)	67.0	26	126.0
Boudou	Bridge (de Gardol)	69.0	—	124.0
	Lock (No. 27 de Petit-Bezy)	71.0	27	122.0
Malause	Swing bridge (de Malause)	73.0	—	120.0
	Bridge (de Palor)	74.0	—	119.0
Pommevic	Bridge (du Capitaine)	76.0	—	117.0
	Lock (No. 28 de Braguel)	76.0	28	117.0
	Bridge (de Pommevic)	77.0	—	116.0
	Lock (No. 29 de Pommevic)	78.0	29	115.0
Goudourville	Bridge (de la Gauge)	79.0	—	114.0
Valence-d'Agen	Lock (No. 30 de Valence-d'Agen) ...	80.0	30	113.0
	Bridge (d'Auvillars)	80.0	—	113.0
	Port and Bridge (de Valence-d'Agen) ...	81.0	—	112.0
Golfech	Bridge (de Roux)	82.0	—	111.0
	Railway bridge. Bridge (de Coupet) ...	83.0	—	110.0
	Bridge (de Golfech)	84.0	—	109.0
	Pont-canal (de la Barguelonne)	85.0	—	108.0
	Bridge (de la Barguelonne)	85.0	—	108.0
	Lock (No. 31 de Lamagistère)	86.0	31	107.0
	Port and Bridge (de Lamagistère) ...	87.0	—	107.0
	Bridge (de Saint-Pierre)	88.0	—	105.0
Clermont-Dessous	Bridge (de Laspeyres)	90.0	—	103.0
Saint-Romain	Bridge (de Durou)	91.0	—	102.0
	Lock (No. 32 du Noble)	93.0	32	100.0
	Bridge (de Guillemis)	94.0	—	99.0
St-Jean-de-Thurac	Bridge (de Carrère)	95.0	—	98.0
	Lock (No. 33 de la Saint-Christophe) ...	96.0	33	97.0
Lafox	Bridge (de Sauveterre)	97.0	—	96.0
	Bridge (d'Ostende or de Lafox)	98.0	—	95.0
	Pont-canal (de la Seoune)	99.0	—	94.0
	Bridge (de Lascarbonnières)	99.0	—	94.0
Boé	Bridge (de Saint-Marcel)	100.0	—	93.0
	Bridge (de Pourret)	101.0	—	92.0
	Bridge (de Coupat)	103.0	—	90.0
Bon-Encontre	Bridge (de la Bonde)	104.0	—	89.0
	Railway bridge	105.0	—	88.0
Agen	Bridge (de Cahors)	105.0	—	88.0

Distance Table

		kilom.	*lock*	*kilom.*
	Bridge (de Villeneuve). Port (du Pin) ...	107.0	—	86.0
	Bridge (de Coupian). Port (d'Agen) ...	107.0	—	86.0
	Bridge (de St-Georges)	108.0	—	85.0
	Pont-canal (d'Agen over la Garonne) (539 m.)	109.0	—	84.0
	Lock (No. 34 d'Agen)	109.0	34	84.0
	Lock (No. 35 des Mariannettes)	109.0	35	84.0
	Lock (No. 36 de Chabrières)	110.0	36	83.0
Passage d'Agen	Lock (No. 37 de Rosette)	110.0	37	83.0
	Bridge (de Fressonis)	111.0	—	82.0
	Bridge (de Nodigier)	113.0	—	80.0
Brax	Bridge (de Colomay) and Port	115.0	—	78.0
Sérignac	Bridge (de Plaisance)	116.0	—	77.0
	Bridge (de Chicot)	118.0	—	75.0
	Bridge and Port (de Sérignac)	119.0	—	74.0
Montesquieu	Bridge (de Madone)	121.0	—	72.0
	Bridge (de Frèche)	122.0	—	71.0
Bruch	Bridge (de Lapougniane)	123.0	—	70.0
	Bridge (des Pages)	124.0	—	69.0
	Lock (No. 38 de l'Auvignon). Port ...	125.0	38	68.0
	Bridge (de Saint-Martin)	126.0	—	67.0
Feugarolles	Bridge (de Thomas)	127.0	—	66.0
	Bridge (de Castelviel)	128.0	—	65.0
	Port and Bridge (de Feugarolles) ...	129.0	—	64.0
	Railway bridge. Bridge (de Thouars) ...	130.0	—	63.0
	Pont-canal (over la Baïse)	132.0	—	61.0
Vianne	Lock (No. 39 de la Baïse)	132.0	39	61.0
	Lock (No. 40 de Larderet)	132.0	40	61.0
Buzet	Staircase lock ('Descente en Baïse'), two flights. Bridge (de Buzet)	135.0	—	58.0
	Port (de Buzet)	136.0	—	57.0
	Bridge (de Burrenque)	137.0	—	56.0
Saint-Pierre	Bridge (de Doux)	138.0	—	55.0
Damazan	Bridge and Port (de Damazan) ...	139.0	—	54.0
	Bridge (de Lompian)	141.0	—	52.0
Puch	Lock (No. 41 de Berry)	142.0	41	51.0
	Bridge (de Maurin)	143.0	—	50.0
	Bridge (de Vigneau)	144.0	—	49.0
	Bridge (de Monheurt)	145.0	—	48.0
	Bridge (de Lafallotte)	146.0	—	47.0
Villeton	Lock (No. 42 de la Gaule)	147.0	42	46.0
	Bridge (de Labarthe). Port (de Tonneins)	148.0	—	45.0
	Lock (No. 43 de la Gaulette)	150.0	43	43.0
Calonges	Bridge (de Jeanserre)	151.0	—	42.0
Lagruère	Bridge (de Ladonne)	152.0	—	41.0

Distance Table

		kilom.	*lock*	*kilom.*
	Bridge (de Lagruère)	153.0	—	40.0
Agenais	Bridge and Port (du Mas d'Agenais) ...	155.0	—	38.0
	Lock (No. 44 du Mas d'Agenais) ...	155.0	44	38.0
	Bridge (de Larriveau)	156.0	—	37.0
Caumont	Bridge (de Larroque)	158.0	—	35.0
	Bridge (de Caumont). Port ...	160.0	—	33.0
Fourques	Bridge (de l'église de Fourques) ...	161.0	—	32.0
	Bridge (du bourg de Fourques) ...	162.0	—	31.0
	Port and Bridge (des Sables) ...	164.0	—	29.0
Marmande	Pont-canal (Over l'Avance) ...	165.0	—	28.0
	Lock (No. 45 de l'Avance) ...	165.0	45	28.0
	Railway bridge. Bridge (de Laronquière)	166.0	—	27.0
	Bridge (de Rayne)	167.0	—	26.0
Marcellus	Bridge (de Baradat)	168.0	—	25.0
	Bridge (de Marcellus)	169.0	—	24.0
	Bridge (de Campot)	170.0	—	23.0
Meilhan	Lock (No. 46 des Bernès). Port ...	170.0	46	23.0
	Bridge (de Tersac)	171.0	—	22.0
	Bridge (de Cantis)	172.0	—	21.0
	Lock (No. 47 des Gravières) ...	173.0	47	20.0
	Bridge and Port (de Meilhan) ...	175.0	—	18.0
	Bridge (de Pimayne)	176.0	—	17.0
Hure	Bridge (de Lisos)	177.0	—	16.0
	Bridge (de Hure). Bridge (de Julian) ...	179.0	—	14.0
	Lock (No. 48 de l'Auriole) ...	180.0	48	13.0
Fontet	Bridge (de Tartifume)	181.0	—	12.0
	Bridge (de Berrat). Bridge (de Fontet) ...	182.0	—	11.0
	Lock (No. 49 de Fontet)	183.0	49	10.0
Loupiac	Bridge (de Loupiac)	184.0	—	9.0
Puybarban	Bridge (de Gravilla)	185.0	—	8.0
	Bridge (de Puybarban)	186.0	—	7.0
Bassanne	Lock (No. 50 de Bassanne) ...	187.0	50	6.0
Castillon	Bridge (de Castillon)	188.0	—	5.0
	Bridge (de Noël)	189.0	—	4.0
	Bridge (de Hillon)	190.0	—	3.0
Castets-en-Dorthe	Bridge (de Mazerac)	191.0	—	2.0
	Lock (No. 51 de Mazerac) ...	192.0	51	1.0
	Lock (No. 52 des Gares)	192.0	52	1.0
	Basin (de l'embouchure)	193.0	—	0.0
	Lock (No. 53 de Castets). *Junction with la Garonne*	193.0	53	0.0

Branch to Montauban

Montech	*Junction with canal latéral à la Garonne (at K.42)*...	0.0	—	11.0

Distance Table

		kilom.	lock	kilom.
	Bridge (over the Branch)	0.0	—	11.0
	Bridge (du Rat)	1.0	—	10.0
Lacourt-St-Pierre	Bridge (de Lacourt-St-Pierre)	3.0	—	8.0
	Lock (No. 1 bis de Noalhac). Bridge ...	4.0	1	7.0
	Lock (No. 2 bis de Lamothe)	5.0	2	6.0
	Lock (No. 3 bis de Fisset)	5.0	3	6.0
	Lock (No. 4 bis de Brétoille)	6.0	4	5.0
	Lock (No. 5 bis de Mortarieu)	6.0	5	5.0
	Lock (No. 6 bis de la Terrasse)	6.0	6	5.0
	Lock (No. 7 bis de Rabastens)	7.0	7	4.0
	Lock (No. 8 bis de Verlhaguet)	7.0	8	4.0
Montauban	Lock (No. 9 bis de Bordebasse)	9.0	9	2.0
	Port (de Montauban)	10.0	—	1.0
	Locks (Nos. 10 bis & 11 bis). (Flight of 2)	11.0	11	0.0
	Railway bridge. Bridge (de Montauban)...	11.0	—	0.0
	Junction with le Tarn	11.0	—	0.0

Branch to La Baïse from Buzet

La Descente en Baïse consists of a staircase lock of two lifts, each chamber has a length of 30 m. 65 with a width of 6 m. 00. See also under la Baïse.

CANAUX D'HAZEBROUCK

General

Under the general name of *les canaux d'Hazebrouck* is grouped a system of small canals, four in number, namely:

   (a) **Canal de la Nieppe**

   (b) **Canal d'Hazebrouck**

   (c) **Canal de Prèaven**

   (d) **La Bourre canalisée.**

This network establishes a double connection, in the form of a Y, between the town of Hazebrouck and the River la Lys, the one at Thiennes and the other at Merville. The canalised River la Bourre appears at first sight to be but a continuation of the Canal de Prèaven, but it is in fact a distinct canal.

Length

The Canal de la Nieppe begins at Thiennes and ends at la Motte-au-Bois, where it joins with the Canal d'Hazebrouck; its length is 9 kilometres.

The Canal d'Hazebrouck begins at la Motte-au-Bois and ends in the town of Hazebrouck in a distance of 5 kilometres. However, the *kilométrage* is run through from Thiennes to Hazebrouck.

The Canal de Prèaven begins at the lock at Motte-au-Bois and ends at the lock du Grand Dam, where it joins with the canalised River la Bourre; it has a length of only 2 kilometres.

The canalised River la Bourre has a length of 7 kilometres; it begins at the loc du Grand Dam (where it joins the Canal de Prèaven) and ends at Merville on the River la Lys. The *kilométrage* of the Canal de Prèaven and the River la Bourre are consecutive from the lock at Motte-au-Bois to the junction with la Lys at Merville.

Locks

There are 4 locks in all. The lock at Thiennes (Canal de la Nieppe) has a length of 96 m. 00 with a width of 3 m. 54. The lock de la Motte-au-Bois (Canal de Prèaven) has a length of 38 m. 50 with a width of 3 m. 50; the lock du Grand Dam (also Canal de Prèaven) has a length of 38 m. 50 with a width of 3 m. 50. The lock du Pont de Pierre (la Bourre canalisée) has a length of 38 m. 50 with a width of 5 m. 20. There are no locks on the Canal d'Hazebrouck.

Depth

The depth throughout the system is maintained at 1 m. 30.

Bridges

All the fixed bridges have a headroom of 2 m. 50 above the normal water level.

Tow-path

There is a tow-path throughout the system, but not suitable for mechanical traction.

Canal de la Nieppe

		kilom.	*lock*	*kilom.*
Thiennes	*Junction with la Lys (at K.4)*. Lock (No. 4 de Thiennes)	0.0	1	14.0
	Bridge (Pont Bart). Bridge (Pont Cattoir)...	0.0	—	14.0
Steenbecque	Bridge (de la belle Cyska)	4.0	—	10.0
Morbecque	Lift bridge (du Parc)	6.0	—	8.0
	Footbridge (Passerelle Salomé)	7.0	—	7.0
	Lock (de la Motte-au-Bois)	9.0	—	5.0

Canal d'Hazebrouck

		kilom.	*lock*	*kilom.*
Morbecque	*Junction with Canal de la Nieppe.* Lock (de la Motte-au-Bar)	9.0	—	5.0
	Bridge (du Château)	9.0	—	5.0
	Bridge (de la Motte-au-Bois)	9.0	—	5.0
	Barrage Flamingue	10.0	—	4.0
Hazebrouck	Bridge (Pont Verlinde or Claudorez) ...	12.0	—	2.0
	Railway bridge (des Houillères)	13.0	—	1.0
	Lift bridge (des Meuniers)	13.0	—	1.0
	End of canal	14.0	—	0.0

Distance Table

Canal de Prèaven

		kilom.	lock	kilom.
Morbecque	Junction with Canal de la Nieppe and Canal d'Hazebrouck	0.0	—	9.0
	Lock (No. 3 de la Motte-au-Bois)	0.0	I	9.0
	Swing footbridge	0.0	—	9.0
	Bridge (de Prèaven). Railway bridge ...	1.0	—	8.0
Vieux-Berquin	Lock (No. 1 du Grand Dam). *Junction with la Bourre canalisée*	2.0	2	7.0

La Bourre canalisée

		kilom.	lock	kilom.
Vieux-Berquin	*Junction with Canal de Préaven.* Lock (du Grand Dam)	2.0	—	7.0
Merville	Bridge (de Cappel-Boom)	3.0	—	6.0
	Lift bridge (Pont à Loup)	5.0	—	4.0
	Swing bridge (Ghislain)	8.0	—	1.0
	Lift bridge (de Pierre)	9.0	—	0.0
	Lock (No. 2 du Pont de Pierre)	9.0	I	0.0
	Confluence with la Lys (at K.19)	9.0	—	0.0

HÉRAULT (Maritime)

General

Although this river is classed as navigable from Bessan to the sea there is no navigation between Bessan and Agde except for that part of the river—a length of about 900 metres—which is included in le Canal du Midi as a river crossing. The lock at Agde *(écluse ronde)* has three gates. Coming from the direction of Toulouse the gate on the starboard hand in the lock leads down into l'Hérault maritime; the forward gate leads into the river on the upstream side of the electrical power station barrage. This is the river crossing section mentioned above. L'Hérault maritime is that part of the river which lies between the downstream side of the barrage and the confluence with Mediterranean Sea.

Length

From the lower side of *l'écluse ronde* to the junction with l'Hérault maritime *(la descente dans Hérault)** there is a short junction canal reckoned to be half a kilometre: from that point to the sea is a distance of 5 kilometres.

Locks

None. The short length of the junction canal and *l'écluse ronde* are included in *la descente dans Hérault*.

* See p. 154.

99

Depth	The depth is normally 4 m. 00, but it is necessary to remember that the depths are irregular. Local enquiries are indicated.		
Bridges	There is only one bridge over this section and this has a headroom of 5 m. 70 at the normal state of the river. There is a railway bridge over *la descente dans Hérault* which has a headroom of 4 m. 22.		
Tow-path	None.		

Distance Table

		kilom.	lock	kilom.
Agde	*Junction with la descente dans Hérault (at K.0.5)*	0.0	—	5.0
	Port d'Agde	0.0	—	5.0
	Road bridge (R.N.112)	0.2	—	4.8
	Gas-oil filling station	0.5	—	4.5
	Gas-oil filling station	4.5	—	0.5
	Confluence with la Méditerranée	5.0	—	0.0

CANAL DES HOUILLERES DE LA SARRE

General	This canal, as its name indicates, passes through the mining district of the Sarre valley. It leaves the *Canal de la Marne au Rhin* at K.227, near Gondrexange and runs in a northerly direction to finish by joining the canalised river la Sarre at Sarreguemines.
Length	The length of the canal from its junction with the Canal de la Marne au Rhin to its end at Sarreguemines is 63 kilometres.
Locks	There are 27 locks, all of which have a length of 39 m. 00 with a width of 5 m. 20.
Depth	There is a normal depth of water of 2 m. 20 throughout.
Bridges	Above the normal water level the fixed bridges show a clear headroom of 3 m. 65.
Tow-path	The tow-path which extends throughout the length of the canal is used by electric tractors with overhead power lines.

Distance Table

		kilom.	lock	kilom.
Gondrexange	*Junction with Canal de la Marne au Rhin (at K.227)*	0.0	—	63.0
	Port (du Houillon). Bridge (du Houillon)	2.0	—	61.0

Distance Table

		kilom.	lock	kilom.
Diane-Capelle	Bridge	3.0	—	60.0
	Lock (No. 1)	5.0	1	58.0
Langatte	Pont-canal (du Stock)	6.0	—	57.0
Fribourg	Port and Bridge (d'Albeschaux)	10.0	—	53.0
Bisping	Lock (No. 2)	10.0	2	53.0
	Lock (No. 3)	11.0	3	52.0
	Lock (No. 4)	11.0	4	52.0
	Lock (No. 5)	12.0	5	51.0
	Lock (No. 6)	12.0	6	51.0
	Lock (No. 7)	13.0	7	50.0
	Lock (No. 8) Port (de Vorbusch) ...	13.0	8	50.0
	Lock (No. 9)	14.0	9	49.0
	Lock (No. 10)	15.0	10	48.0
	Lock (No. 11)	16.0	11	47.0
Mittersheim	Lock (No. 12)	17.0	12	46.0
	Railway bridge	18.0	—	45.0
	Lock (No. 13)	19.0	13	44.0
	Port (de Mittersheim). Lock (No. 14) ...	20.0	14	43.0
Vibersviller	Port (du Pont-Vert). Lock (No. 15) ...	22.0	15	41.0
	Port (de Burlach)	23.0	—	40.0
Altviller	Lock (No. 16)	27.0	16	36.0
	Bridge (de Neuweyerhoff)	28.0	—	35.0
Harskirchen	Bridge (Pont Muller)	29.0	—	34.0
	Bridge (Pont Freywald)	32.0	—	31.0
	Lock (No. 17)	32.0	17	31.0
Bissert	Port (de Harskirchen-Bissert).			
	Lock (No. 18)	33.0	18	30.0
Sarralbe	Bridge (du Haras). Railway bridge. Lock (No. 19)	37.0	—	26.0
	Lock (No. 19)	38.0	19	25.0
	Bridge (de Rech). Pont-canal (over l'Albe)	39.0	—	24.0
	Lock (No. 20)	40.0	20	23.0
	Port (de Sarralbe). Footbridge	41.0	—	22.0
Willerwald	Railway bridge. Bridge (de Niederau) ...	42.0	—	21.0
Herbitzheim	Port (de Herbitzheim)	44.0	—	19.0
	Bridge (de Herbitzheim). Lock (No. 21) ...	45.0	21	18.0
Wittring	Railway bridge. Lock (No. 22)	51.0	22	12.0
	Port (de Wittring)	52.0	—	11.0
	Railway bridge (de Dieding)	53.0	—	10.0
Zetting	Railway bridge (de Zetting). Lock (No. 23)	57.0	23	6.0
Sarreinsming	Lock (No. 24)	60.0	24	3.0
Remelfing	Port (de Remelfing). Lock (No. 25) ...	61.0	25	2.0
Sarreguemines	Lock (No. 26)	62.0	26	1.0
	Railway bridge. Lock (No. 27)	63.0	27	0.0
	Junction with la Sarre canalisée	63.0	—	0.0

CANAL D'ILLE-ET-RANCE

General The Canal d'Ille-et-Rance joins the River la Vilaine to the maritime part of la Rance. It begins at Rennes and ends at the lock called *du Châtelier* in the commune of la Vicomté-sur-Rance not far from Dinan. It thus forms a through route between the ports on the West Coast of France and those on the North Coast near St. Malo. La Rance maritime is really more of an inlet of the sea than a river, in fact an estuary subject to tidal influences and for that reason no description of the route below l'Ecluse de Châtelier is made here, for details concerning that navigation should be sought in the *Channel Pilot* or in similar nautical works. But it must be mentioned that there is now a barrage *(l'usine marémotrice)* across the river at a distance of 19 kilometres below *l'écluse du Châtelier.* There is a lock at the barrage near the left bank of the river, but the times of working of the lock are dependent upon the tides. The canal has a summit level about 7 kilometres in length, which is about 200 ft. above sea level. The effects of the tides in the Channel are felt as far up as Pont-Perrin, while the barrages at Châtelier and Léhon are at times submerged by the tidal waters.

Length The length of the canal from Rennes to le Châtelier is 85 kilometres.

Locks The canal contains a summit level as mentioned above and the fall in each direction is regulated by a total of 47 locks. Of these 20 fall towards Rennes and are called *de l'Ocean*, and the other 27 towards the Channel and are called 'de la Manche'. They have a length of 27 m. 10 with a width of 4 m. 70, excepting the marine lock *(écluse du Châtelier)* which has a length of 30 m. 80 with a width of 8 m. 00; this lock is counted as belonging to la Rance maritime. The lock at *l'usine marémotrice* has a length of 65 m. 00 with a width of 12 m. 00.

Depth The depth of the canal from Rennes to le Châtelier is 1 m. 35.

Bridges The lowest of the fixed bridges shows a clear headroom of 2 m. 40 above the normal water level.

Tow-path The vessels using the canal are all self-propelled and in consequence the tow-path has been allowed to fall into disuse.

Distance Table

			kilom.	*lock*	*kilom.*
Rennes	*Junction with la Vilaine (at K.o)* ...	...	0.0	—	85.0
	Lock (No. 1 du Mail). Port (du Mail)	...	0.0	I	85.0
	Bridge (Pont Bagoul). Bridge (Pont Legravérend)	...	0.0	—	85.0

Distance Table

						kilom.	lock	kilom.
	Lock (No. 2 Saint-Martin). Port	...		...		1.0	2	84.0
	Railway bridge (viaduct)		...		...	4.0	—	81.0
Saint-Grégoire	Lock (No. 3 de Saint-Grégoire). Quay			...		5.0	3	80.0
	Lock (No. de la Charbonnière)		...		...	7.0	4	78.0
Betton	Lock (No. 5 du Gacet)	...		...		9.0	5	76.0
	Bridge (de la Rennais)	...		...		10.0	—	75.0
	Lock (No. 6 du Haut-Châlet)		...		...	12.0	6	73.0
	Quay and Bridge (de Betton)		...		...	13.0	—	72.0
	Lock (No. 7 des Brosses). Bridge		...		...	15.0	7	70.0
Chevaigné	Bridge (du Moulin du Pont)		...		...	17.0	—	68.0
	Lock (No. 8 de Grugedaine)		...		...	18.0	8	67.0
	Bridge (de la Motte)		...		...	19.0	—	66.0
	Lock (No. 9 des Cours)	...		...		20.0	9	65.0
Melesse	Bridge. Lock (No. 10 de Fresnay) ...			...		21.0	10	64.0
	Lock (No. 11 de St-Germain-sur-Ille)			...		23.0	11	62.0
	Quay (de St-Germain)		...		...	24.0	—	61.0
	Lock (No. 12 de Bouessay)		...		...	24.0	12	61.0
St-Médard-s-Îlle	Railway viaduct (du Bois Marie) ...			...		25.0	—	60.0
	Railway viaduct (d'Euzé)	...		...		26.0	—	59.0
	Railway viaduct (de St-Médard)		...		...	27.0	—	58.0
	Lock (No. 13 de St-Médard-s-Ille)			...		27.0	13	58.0
	Lock (No. 14 du Dialay) ...			...		28.0	14	57.0
	Railway viaduct (de la Bablais)		...		...	29.0	—	56.0
Montreuil-sur-Îlle	Lock (No. 15 d'Ile)...		...		...	30.0	15	55.0
	Lock (No. 16 de Haute-Roche)		...		...	31.0	16	54.0
	Lock (No. 17 de Lengager). Bridge. Quay					32.0	17	53.0
	Lock (No. 18 de Chanclin)		...		...	32.0	18	53.0
	Lock (No. 19 de Courgalais). Bridge			...		33.0	19	52.0
Guipel	Lock (No. 20 de Villemorin). Beginning of summit level...					34.0	20	51.0
	Bridge (de la Plousière). Quay		...		...	35.0	—	50.0
Bazouges-sous-Hédé	Bridge (de la Guénaudière)...		...		...	40.0	—	45.0
	Lock (No. 21 de la Ségerie). End of summit level					41.0	21	44.0
	Lock (No. 22). Lock (No. 23 de la Pêchetière)					41.0	23	44.0
	Lock (No. 24)				...		41.0	24	44.0
	Lock (No. 25 de la Parfraire)		...		...	42.0	25	43.0
	Lock (No. 26). Lock (No. 27)		...		...	42.0	27	43.0
	Lock (No. 28 de la Madeleine). Bridge			...		42.0	28	43.0
	Lock (No. 29 de la Petite-Medeleine)			...		42.0	29	43.0
	Lock (No. 30 de la Guéhardière) ...			...		43.0	30	42.0
	Lock (No. 31 de la Dialais)		...		...	43.0	31	42.0
Tinténiac	Lock (No. 32 de la Moucherie). Bridge			...		45.0	32	40.0
	Lock (No. 33 de Tinténiac). Quay			...		47.0	33	38.0

Distance Table

		kilom.	lock	kilom.
Québriac	Lock (No. 34 de la Gromillais). Bridge ...	48.0	34	37.0
	Lock (No. 35 du Gué Noëllan)	49.0	35	36.0
	Lock (No. 36 de Pont-Houitte). Bridge ...	50.0	36	35.0
La Chapelle-aux-Fitzméens	Bridge and Quay (de la Chapelle-aux-Fitzméens)	53.0	—	32.0
Saint-Domineuc	Lock (No. 37 de Calaudry). Bridge ...	54.0	37	31.0
	Lock (No. 38 de Couadan) ...	56.0	38	29.0
	Bridge and Quay (de St-Domineuc) ...	57.0	—	28.0
Tréverien	Bridge (de Richeville)	58.0	—	27.0
	Lock (No. 39 du Gacet). Bridge	60.0	39	25.0
	Lock (No. 40 de la Butte Jacquette) ...	60.0	40	25.0
	Quay and Bridge (de Tréverien)	61.0	—	24.0
	Lock (No. 41 des Islots)	62.0	41	23.0
Saint-Judoce	Footbridge (Saint-Judoce)	65.0	—	20.0
Evran	Lock (No. 42 d'Evran). Bridge. Quay ...	66.0	42	19.0
	Lock (No. 43 de la Roche). Bridge ...	67.0	43	18.0
	Bridge (des Planches)	68.0	—	17.0
	Lock (No. 44 du Mottay). Bridge ...	69.0	44	16.0
Calorguen	Bridge (du Grand Boutron)	71.0	—	14.0
	Lock (No. 45 de Boutron)	71.0	45	14.0
Champs-Géraux	Quay (de Vaugré)	73.0	—	12.0
Saint-Carné	Lock (No. 46 du Pont-Perrin). Bridge ...	74.0	46	11.0
Léhon	Quay (de Léhon). Bridge (Vieux pont) ...	76.0	—	9.0
Dinan	Lock (No. 47 de Léhon)	76.0	47	9.0
	Viaduct (de Dinan). Bridge (Vieux pon de Dinan)	78.0	—	7.0
	Quay (de Lanvallay)	78.0	—	7.0
Taden	Quay (de l'Asile du Pêcheur)	79.0	—	6.0
Vicomté-sur-Rance	Quay (de Taden)	82.0	—	3.0
	Quay (de Châtelier). Quay (du Petit-Livet)	83.0	—	2.0
	Quay (de Livet)	84.0	—	1.0
	Marine lock (No. 48 du Châtelier)... ...	85.0	—	0.0
	Bridge. *Junction with la Rance Maritime* ...	85.0	—	0.0

Rance Maritime

	Barrage (Marémotrice). Lock	104.0	—	—
	Saint Malo (Cale de Dinan)	108.0	—	—

ISLE

General   Formerly l'Isle was used by vessels as far up as Perigueux, a distance upstream of about 144 kilometres from its confluence with la Dordogne at Libourne. Of this length only 31 kilometres is now used by the navigation, that is to say only the part lying below

Lock No. 40, at Laubardemont. The river is tidal and in fact is classed as marine.

Length   As mentioned above the total length now used for navigation is 31 kilometres subject to tidal action.

Locks   None.

Depth   There is a depth of 1 m. 00 at low water neap tides rising to 1 m. 60 at high water neap tides.

Bridges   The fixed bridges have a clear headroom of 4 m. 20 above the normal water level, which may fall to about 3 m. 60 under flood conditions.

Tow-path   No tow-path is maintained as all the traffic is by self-propelled craft or by tug-towed trains.

Distance Table		*kilom.*	*lock*	*kilom.*
Sablons-de-Guitres	Bridge. Lock (No. 40 de Laubardemont) ...	0.0	—	31.0
Guitres	Suspension bridge. Railway bridge ...	3.0	—	28.0
St.-Martin-de-Laye	Port (de Pommiers)	5.0	—	26.0
St-Denis-de-Piles	Port (de La Grave). Port (du Fleix) ...	9.0	—	22.0
	Bridge and Port	11.0	—	20.0
Savignac	Suspension bridge. Port (de Savignac) ...	15.0	—	16.0
Galgon	Bridge. Railway bridge	20.0	—	11.0
Saillans	Port (de Larroudey)	23.0	—	8.0
	Port (de Saillans)	24.0	—	7.0
Libourne	Port (de la Conque)	28.0	—	3.0
	Railway bridge. Port (de Libourne). Bridge	30.0	—	1.0
	Confluence with la Dordogne (at K.75) ...	31.0	—	0.0

CANAL DE LENS

General   The Canal de Lens is formed by the canalisation of the River La Souchez. It begins at the bridge at Eleu and continues through the town of Lens to join with the Canal de la Deûle at Courrières. That part of the canal which lies between K.7.5 and K.11.25 (where it joins the Canal de la Deûle) has been conceded to les Houillères du Bassin du Nord (Groupe d'Hénin-Liétard) who collect the dues levied for this part of the passage which is called *le Canal de la Souchez*. The total length of the canal is 11.25 kilometres; it contains one lock with a length of 55 m. 00 and a width of 7 m. 50 situated close to the town of Lens. The depth of the canal is maintained at 2 m. 60 and there is a headroom under bridges of 4 m. 00 at normal water level. A tow-path throughout carries both electric and diesel tractors. Local enquiries should be made as to toll charges and other matters.

CANAL DU LOING

General   The Canal du Loing begins at the village of Buges near to Montargis and ends at Saint-Mammes-sur-Séine. It is a link in one of the important through routes which join the valley of la Seine to the valley of le Rhône. This route, which is called 'le Bourbonnais' comprises the Canal du Loing, the Canal de Briare, the canal latéral à la Loire and the Canal du Centre, and is by some considered to be the most convenient way to the South.

Length   The distance from Buges to Saint-Mammes by the canal is 49 kilometres.

Locks   There are 20 locks, all of which have a uniform length of 39 m. 10 with a width of 5 m. 20. It must be noted, however, that the lock at Fromonville, is only put into service during times of flood.

Depth   A depth of 2 m. 20 is maintained throughout the canal.

Bridges   All the fixed bridges have a headroom of 3 m. 70 above the normal water level.

Tow-path   There is a good tow-path all along the canal and towing is by diesel tractors obligatory for all vessels not self-propelled. Nevertheless, towing by animals is still allowed for those craft which have stables on board; these are usually small barges known as *berrichons*, and nowadays are seldom seen.

Distance Table

		kilom.	lock	kilom.
Chalette	Junction with Canal de Briare *(downstream side of lock) (de Buges) (at K.53)*	0.0	—	49.0
	Railway bridge	0.0	—	49.0
Cépoy	Lock (No. 1 de Cépoy). Bridge	2.0	1	47.0
	Port (de Cépoy)	3.0	—	46.0
Girolles	Lock (No. 2 des Vallées). Bridge	5.0	2	44.0
	Lock (No. 3 de Montabon)	5.0	3	44.0
Nargis	Bridge (de Vaux)	8.0	—	41.0
	Lock (No. 4 de Retourné)	8.0	4	41.0
	Bridge (de Nargis). Lock (No. 5 de Nargis). Port (de Nargis)	10.0	5	39.0
	Lock (No. 6 de Brisebarre)	11.0	6	38.0
	Bridge (de Toury)	12.0	—	37.0
	Port (de Dordives)	14.0	—	35.0
Château-Landon	Bridge (de Dordives)	14.0	—	35.0
	Bridge (de Néronville). Lock (No. 7 de Néronville)	15.0	7	34.0
	Bridge (d'Egreville)	16.0	—	33.0
	Lock (No. 8 d'Egreville). Port	16.0	8	33.0

Distance Table

		kilom.	lock	kilom.
Souppes-sur-Loing	Railway bridge. Bridge (de Souppes) ...	18.0	—	31.0
	Port (de Souppes)	19.0	—	30.0
	Railway bridge	20.0	—	29.0
La Madeleine	Lock (No. 9 de Beaumoulin). Bridge. Port	21.0	9	28.0
	Bridge and Port (de Glandelles) ...	22.0	—	27.0
Bagneaux	Bridge (de Bagneaux)	24.0	—	25.0
	Lock (No. 10 de Bagneaux). Bridge ...	25.0	10	24.0
St-Pierre-lès-Nemours	Lock (No. 11 de Chaintréauville)	27.0	11	22.0
Nemours	Port (des Fontaines). Bridge (des Récollets)	28.0	—	21.0
	Bridge (de Paris). Port (de Nemours) ...	29.0	—	20.0
	Lock (No. 12 des Buttes)	30.0	12	19.0
Montcourt-Fromonville	Lock (No. 13 de Fromonville). (Guard lock)	32.0	13	17.0
	Bridge and Port (de Montcourt)	34.0	—	15.0
Genevraye	Lock (No. 14 des Bordes)	36.0	14	13.0
	Bridge and Port (de la Genevraye)... ...	38.0	—	11.0
	Lock (No. 15 de Berville)	38.0	15	11.0
	Port (de Launay)	39.0	—	10.0
Episy	Port (de la Ville de Paris)	40.0	—	9.0
	Lock (No. 16 d'Episy). Port (d'Episy) ...	41.0	16	8.0
Ecuelles	Lock (No. 17 d'Ecuelles)	44.0	17	5.0
Moret	Lock (No. 18 de Bourgogne)	46.0	18	3.0
	Port (du Pont de Bourgogne)	47.0	—	2.0
	Lock (No. 19 de Moret). Port (St-Roch) ...	47.0	19	2.0
*Saint-Mammès**	Railway bridge	48.0	—	1.0
	Lock (No. 20 de Saint-Mammès)	49.0	20	0.0
	Junction with la Seine (at K.81)	49.0	—	0.0

LOIRE

General

La Loire is classed as navigable from Noirie to the sea, which is a distance of about 825 kilometres. Unfortunately this beautiful river no longer carries any appreciable traffic except over the lower reaches (which are considered as marine) between Nantes and the sea. From Noirie, except for a certain number of gravel and sand lighters operating at various local points, the river is abandoned by shipping over a stretch of no less than 685 kilometres. The whole of this length of river remains in its natural state and normally has but a feeble flow of water which wanders about over a wide bed. The depth in many parts is no more than 25 centimetres; but in times of flood the waters rise rapidly and after a depth of 2 metres has been attained (which is considered as a minor flood) the navigation is rendered extremely difficult owing to the violence of the

* See Plan No. 16.

currents, the prevalence of fog and mist and the formation of ice. On this account no further mention of the upper and middle reaches of the river will be made here with the exception of a length of nearly 2 kilometres at Decize where la Loire forms a link between the *Branch to Decize* (which emanates from the canal latéral à la Loire) and the *Canal du Nivernais*, a channel for that purpose having been cut in the river bed. The only important part of la Loire at present in use by navigation is that extending from the confluence with la Maine downstream to Saint Nazaire. Of that length the part from Bouchemaine (the confluence with la Maine) to the upper limit of the port of Nantes at the confluence with the river Erdre is considered to be a fluvial navigation, the remainder marine. Only the river length will be detailed here and nautical works must be consulted for the marine section.

Length   From Bouchemaine, the confluence with la Maine, to the confluence with l'Erdre is a distance of 85 kilometres.

Locks   None.

Depth   A channel, 100 to 150 metres in width, is maintained by means of training works consisting of groins, embankments and submerged training walls. The channel is marked by buoys, RED on the left bank and BLACK on the right bank; at low water the navigable swatchways are indicated by perches about 4 metres high, set in the sand; those on the left bank have their tops partly broken and hanging down. All the shoals are of sand and are also shifting. It is said that the depth at low water neaps is 1 m. 50, but this is very variable according to the season; at exceptional low water and at certain points it may even drop to 0 m. 35. Further, the depth is very much influenced by tidal action which makes itself felt as far up as the bridge at Champtoceaux. In brief the services of a reliable pilot well acquainted with the river appears to be essential.

Bridges   On this section of the river the fixed bridges are usually high above the water level and leave ample headroom; in no case will there be less than 6 m. 50.

Tow-path   There is no tow-path, all traffic being self-propelled.

Junction channel between Branch to Decize (canal latéral à la Loire) and Canal du Nivernais

Distance Table

			kilom.	lock	kilom.
Decize	Junction with the Branch to Decize...	...	0.0	—	1.7
	Bridge	...	0.5	—	1.2
	Port (de Decize) (in the river) ...	...	1.4	—	0.3
	Junction with the Canal du Nivernais	...	1.7	—	0.0

From the confluence with la Maine to the confluence with l'Erdre

Distance Table			kilom.	lock	kilom.
Bouchemaine	*Confluence with la Maine (at K.134)*	...	0.0	—	85.0
	La Pointe-Bouchemaine	0.0	—	85.0
Savannières	Bridges	5.0	—	80.0
La Poissonnière	Port (des Ponts et Chaussées)	8.0	—	77.0
Chalonnes-s-Loire	Railway bridge	11.0	—	74.0
	Bridges (de Chalonnes-s-Loire)	14.0	—	71.0
Montjean	Bridge (de Montjean)	23.0	—	62.0
Ingrande-s-Loire	Bridge (d'Ingrandes-s-Loire)	28.0	—	57.0
St-Florent-le-Vieil	Bridges (St-Florent-le-Vieil)	37.0	—	48.0
Ancenis	Bridge (d'Ancenis)	49.0	—	36.0
Champtoceaux	Bridge (de Champtoceaux)	58.0	—	27.0
Mauves	Bridge (de Mauves)	67.0	—	18.0
Thouaré	Bridge (de Thouaré)	73.0	—	12.0
Saint-Sebastien	Railway bridge	82.0	—	3.0
	Railway bridge	83.0	—	2.0
Nantes	Upper limit of the Port of Nantes. *Junction with l'Erdre canalisé (Canal de Nantes à Brest)*	85.0	—	0.0
	Confluence de la Sèvre-Nantaise (bras de Purmil)	85.0	—	0.0

CANAL LATÉRAL À LA LOIRE

General

The canal latéral à la Loire begins at the town of Digoin and ends at La Cognardière close to the town of Briare. The canal joins with 4 other canals; the Canal du Centre, the Canal de Roanne à Digoin, the Canal du Nivernais (to which it is linked by the Branch to Decize and by the channel cut in la Loire) and the Canal de Briare. Formerly there was a fifth canal with which it was linked, the Canal de Berry, but that canal has now, most unfortunately for those who like quiet waters, been closed to traffic. Besides the branch to Decize the canal has several others, some of which merely lead down to la Loire and one which joins with the River Allier; none of these would appear to be of interest to yachtsmen. However, the branch which leads to la Loire at Nevers will be detailed here as it forms a good resting place for those who can spare a few days.

There are three *pont-canaux*, they are situated at Digoin, le Guétin and at Briare; these last two are of considerable length (that at Briare is 660 metres) and the passage of vessels is regulated in each direction; their width is 5 m. 14. For this reason enquiries should be made locally before making the passage.

Length	The length of the canal from its junction with the Canal du Centre at Digoin to La Cognardière (junction with the Canal de Briare) is 196 kilometres. One peculiarity is that the official *kilométrage* begins at K.4, the first 4 kilometres having been added to the length of the Canal du Centre; but for ease of reckoning the Distance Table has been adjusted to give the true length between junctions.

Locks	There are 37 locks of uniform length of 38 m. 50 and a width of 5 m. 17, except No. 11 (des Gailloux) K.45 which has a width of 5 m. 14.

Depth	The level of the water is maintained at a depth of 2 m. 20.

Bridges	The lowest fixed bridge over the canal has a headroom of 3 m. 70 above the normal water level.

Tow-path	There is a good tow-path throughout the length of the canal and towing is by diesel tractors.

Branch to Decize*

The branch to Decize, which links the canal latéral à la Loire with the Canal du Nivernais as mentioned above, has a length of 544 metres and forms the Port de Decize. This port is a basin with 2 locks, in size similar to those on the main canal, and the depth of water is 2 m. 20.

Branch to Nevers

This branch which leads to la Loire at a point opposite to the town of Nevers has a length of 2.9 kilometres. There are 3 locks, 2 of which are the same size as those on the main canal; the third lock has a length of only 30 m. 50 but as it is the lock which leads down into the river it is of no interest to yachtsmen; in fact it is very seldom used.

Distance Table

		kilom.	lock	kilom.
Digoin†	Junction with Canal du Centre (at K.112) ...	0.0	—	196.0
	Bridge (de Charolles). Bridge (des Perruts).			
	Pont-canal (de Digoin)	0.0	—	196.0
	Lock (No. 1 de Digoin)	0.0	I	196.0
Chassenard	Port (de Chassenard)	1.0	—	195.0
	Junction with Canal de Roanne à Digoin			
	(at K.55). Bridge (de Chassenard)... ...	2.0	—	194.0
	Port (de La Broche)	2.0	—	194.0

* See also under La Loire.
† See Plan No. 4.

Distance Table

					kilom.	lock	kilom.
Molinet	Bridge (du Donjon)	...	...	...	3.0	—	193.0
	Port (de La Fontaine-St-Martin)	...		...	3.0	—	193.0
	Pont-canal (de la Vouzance)		...	...	5.0	—	191.0
	Bridge (du Péage)	...	...	...	5.0	—	191.0
	Bridge (de la Micaudière)	...		...	6.0	—	190.0
Coulanges	Bridge (de Mortillon)		...	...	8.0	—	188.0
	Lock (No. 2 de Thaleine)	...		...	9.0	2	187.0
	Port and Bridge (de Coulanges)		...	...	10.0	—	186.0
	Bridge (de Vesvres). Pont-canal (de l'Oddes)				12.0	—	184.0
Pierrefitte	Lock (No. 3 de l'Oddes)	...	...	...	12.0	3	184.0
	Bridge (des Oddins)		...	...	14.0	—	182.0
	Bridge and Port (de Pierrefitte)	...		...	15.0	—	181.0
	Bridge (de l'Enfer)		...	...	15.0	—	181.0
	Lock (No. 4 du Theil)	...		...	16.0	4	180.0
	Bridge (du Theil)	...	...	...	17.0	—	179.0
Diou	Lock (No. 5 de Putay)	...	...	...	18.0	5	178.0
	Bridge (de Cluzeau)		...	...	19.0	—	177.0
	Railway bridge	...	...	...	20.0	—	176.0
	Bridge and Port (de Diou)		...	...	21.0	—	175.0
	Bridge (de Saligny)		...	...	21.0	—	175.0
	Bridge (des Prats). Pont-canal (du Roudon)				22.0	—	174.0
	Bridge (du Ternat)	...		...	...	23.0	—	173.0
	Pont-canal (de la Besbre)	...		...	24.0	—	172.0
Dompierre	Lock (No. 6 de la Besbre). Port	...		...	25.0	6	171.0
	Bridge (de Sept-Fons)		...	...	25.0	—	171.0
	Bridge (des Taillis)	...	...		...	27.0	—	169.0
Beaulon	Lock (No. 7 des Bessais). Bridge (de Thiel)				28.0	7	168.0
	Bridge (de Petrot)	...	...		...	32.0	—	164.0
	Lock (No. 8 de Beaulon). Port	...		...	33.0	8	163.0
Garnat	Lock (No. 9 du Close du May)	...		...	35.0	9	161.0
	Port and Bridge (de Garnat)		...	...	36.0	—	160.0
	Bridge (de l'Huilerie)		...	...	38.0	—	158.0
St-Martin-des-Lais	Bridge (de Saint-Martin)	...		...	40.0	—	156.0
	Lock (No. 10 de Rozière)	...		...	41.0	10	155.0
	Bridge (de Rozière)	...	...		...	42.0	—	154.0
Gannay	Bridge (de Boise)	...	...		...	43.0	—	153.0
	Lock (No. 11 des Gailloux)	...		...	45.0	11	151.0
	Bridge (des Viviers)	...		...	46.0	—	150.0
	Port (de Gannay)	...	...		...	48.0	—	148.0
	Lock (No. 12 des Vanneaux)	...		...	48.0	12	148.0
Lamenay	Bridge (de la Rue des Gues)	...		...	50.0	—	146.0
	Bridge (de Nogent)	...		...	53.0	—	143.0
Cossaye	Lock (No. 13 de l'Huilerie)	...		...	54.0	13	142.0
	Port and Bridge (de Cornats)	...		...	55.0	—	141.0
Decize	Lock (No 14 de La Motte)	...		...	56.0	14	140.0

Distance Table

		kilom.	lock	kilom.
	Bridge (de La Motte)	57.0	—	139.0
	Bridge (de la Croix-des-Feuillats)	60.0	—	136.0
	Lock (No. 15 de Saulx)	62.0	15	134.0
	Bridge (de Saulx)	63.0	—	133.0
	Junction with the Branch to Decize... ...	64.0	—	132.0
	Bridge and Port (de Germancy)	64.0	—	132.0
	Bridge (de Châlons)	66.0	—	130.0
Avril-sur-Loire	Bridge (de Beaugy). Port (de Beaugy) ...	69.0	—	127.0
	Bridge (du Réau). Pont-canal (de l'Acolin)	70.0	—	126.0
	Lock (No. 16 de l'Acolin)	70.0	16	126.0
	Bridge (de Forge-Neuve). Pont-canal ...	71.0	—	125.0
	Lock (No. 17 de l'Abron)	71.0	17	125.0
	Bridge (d'Avril)	72.0	—	124.0
Fleury	Bridge (de la Perrière)	74.0	—	122.0
	Port and Bridge (de Fleury)	76.0	—	120.0
	Lock (No. 18 de Fleury)	76.0	18	120.0
	Port and Bridge (de la Motte-Farchat) ...	77.0	—	119.0
Uxeloup	Bridge (de la Vèvre)	79.0	—	117.0
	Bridge and Lock (No. 19 d'Uxeloup) ...	81.0	19	115.0
	Bridge (du Chamond). Port (d'Uxeloup)	82.0	—	114.0
Chevenon	Bridge (des Planches)	84.0	—	112.0
	Lock (No. 20 de Jaugenay)	85.0	20	111.0
	Bridge (de l'Atelier)	87.0	—	109.0
	Bridge (de Chevenon)	89.0	—	107.0
	Bridge (de Crezancy)	90.0	—	106.0
Sermoise	Bridge (de la Forêt de Sermoise)	93.0	—	103.0
	Bridge (du Crot de Savigny)	94.0	—	102.0
	Bridge (de l'Avenue de Sermoise) ...	96.0	—	100.0
	*Junction with the Branch to Nevers** ...	96.0	—	100.0
	Bridge (de Peuilly)	96.0	—	100.0
	Port (de Plagny). Bridge (de Plagny) ...	98.0	—	98.0
Challuy	Bridge (du Pavillon). Railway bridge ...	99.0	—	97.0
	Bridge (des Argouniots)	100.0	—	96.0
Gimouille	Bridge (du Marais)	102.0	—	94.0
	Bridge (du Colombier)	103.0	—	93.0
	Bridge (de Gimouille)	104.0	—	92.0
	Port (de Gimouille)	105.0	—	91.0
	Bridge (de Sampagnes)	105.0	—	91.0
	Pont-canal (du Guétin) (350 m.). *(One-way traffic)*	106.0	—	90.0
	Locks (Nos. 21, 22 du Guétin) (flight of two)	106.0	22	90.0
	Port (du Guétin)	106.0	—	90.0

* See Plan No. 12.

Distance Table

		kilom.	lock	kilom.
Cuffy	Bridge (des Gaillettes)	107.0	—	89.0
	Bridge (du Colombier)	107.0	—	89.0
	Footbridge (de Cuffy)	108.0	—	88.0
	Bridge (de Presle)	109.0	—	87.0
	Lock (No. 24 de Laubray)	111.0	23	85.0
	Bridge (de Laubray)	112.0	—	84.0
Cours-les-Barres	Bridge (des Mahauts). Port	114.0	—	82.0
	Bridge (du Domaine de Crille) ...	115.0	—	81.0
	Bridge (de Cours-les-Barres) ...	115.0	—	81.0
Jouet-sur-l'Abois	Bridge (de Dompierre)	117.0	—	79.0
	Bridge (du Poids de Fer)	120.0	—	76.0
Marseilles-	Port (d'Aubigny)	120.0	—	76.0
lès-Aubigny	Lock (No. 25 d'Aubigny). Pont-aqueduc	121.0	24	75.0
	Lock (No. 26 de l'Abois)	121.0	25	75.0
	Lock (No. 27 de Beffes). Port ...	124.0	26	72.0
Beffes	Lock (No. 27 de Beffes). Port ...	124.0	26	72.0
St-Léger-le-Petit	Bridge (des Radis)	126.0	—	70.0
	Bridge (de Saint-Léger)	127.0	—	69.0
Argenvières	Lock (No. 28 d'Argenvières). Port	129.0	27	67.0
	Port (de la Charnaye)	130.0	—	66.0
	Lock (No. 29 des Rousseaux) ...	131.0	28	65.0
La Chapelle-	Port (de la Chapelle-Montlinard) ...	132.0	—	64.0
Montlinard	Bridge (de la Chapelle-Montlinard) ...	133.0	—	63.0
	Bridge (de Nambault)	134.0	—	62.0
	Bridge (de Charreau)	135.0	—	61.0
	Bridge (de Châtillon)	136.0	—	60.0
Herry	Lock (No. 30 d'Herry)	138.0	29	58.0
	Port (d'Herry)	139.0	—	57.0
	Bridge (de la Sarrée)	140.0	—	56.0
	Lock (No. 31 de la Prée)	141.0	30	55.0
	Bridge (de Champalay)	144.0	—	52.0
Saint-Bouize	Lock (No. 32 de La Grange) ...	146.0	31	50.0
	Grand aqueduc du Moule	147.0	—	49.0
	Port and Bridge (de Saint-Bouize) ...	148.0	—	48.0
Thauvenay	Bridge (des Rousseaux)	150.0	—	46.0
Ménétréol	Lock (No. 33 de Thauvenay). Bridge ...	152.0	32	44.0
Saint-Satur	Port and Bridge (de Saint-Satur) ...	155.0	—	41.0
	Bridge (de la Mivoie)	156.0	—	40.0
Bannay	Bridge (de Beaufroy)	159.0	—	37.0
	Port (de Bannay). Bridge (de l'Ile) ...	160.0	—	36.0
	Lock (No. 34 de Bannay). Railway bridge	161.0	33	35.0
	Bridge (de Bussy)	163.0	—	33.0
Boulleret	Bridge (des Fouchards)	163.0	—	33.0
	Port (des Fouchards)	164.0	—	32.0
	Bridge (de la Giraude)	165.0	—	31.0

Distance Table

		kilom.	lock	kilom.
	Lock (No. 35 de Peseau)	165.0	34	31.0
	Bridge (du Gavereau)	166.0	—	30.0
	Bridge (de Ménetreau)	167.0	—	29.0
Léré	Lock (No. 36 des Houards)	169.0	35	27.0
	Bridge (de Léré). Port (de Léré) ...	171.0	—	25.0
Sury	Bridge (de Sury)	172.0	—	24.0
Belleville	Bridge (de la Rue)	174.0	—	22.0
	Lock (No. 37 de Belleville). Bridge	175.0	36	21.0
Beaulieu	Bridge (de Chennevières)	176.0	—	20.0
	Pont-aqueduc (de Maimbray) ...	178.0	—	18.0
	Lock (No. 38 de Maimbray) ...	178.0	37	18.0
	Bridge (du Plessis)	179.0	—	17.0
	Bridge and Port (de Beaulieu) ...	180.0	—	16.0
	Pont-aqueduc and guard lock (de l'Etang)	182.0	—	14.0
	Bridge (des Gannes)	184.0	—	12.0
Châtillon-sur-Loire	Bridge (de la Folie)	185.0	—	11.0
	Guard lock. Bridge (des Rabuteloires) ...	186.0	—	10.0
	Footbridge (de Mantelot)	187.0	—	9.0
	Port and Bridge (de Châtillon) ...	187.0	—	9.0
	Pont-aqueduc (de Châtillon). Bridge (des Hautes-Rives)	188.0	—	8.0
	Bridge (des Chailloux)	189.0	—	7.0
Saint-Firmin	Port (de Saint-Firmin)	191.0	—	5.0
	Guard lock. Bridge (de Beauregard) ...	191.0	—	5.0
	Pont-canal (de Briare) (663 m.). *(One-way traffic)*	193.0	—	3.0
Briare	Bridge (de St-Firmin). Bridge (de Briare)	193.0	—	3.0
	Railway bridge. Bridge (de Bléneau) ...	194.0	—	2.0
	Bridge (de Vaugereau)	195.0	—	1.0
	Pont-aqueduc (de la Cognardière) ...	195.0	—	1.0
	Guard lock. Footbridge (de la Cognardière)	195.0	—	1.0
	Junction with Canal de Briare (at K.0)			

Branch to Decize

Decize	*Beginning of Branch (at K.64)*	0.0	—	0.5
	Lock (No. 16-II de St-Maurice)	0.1	I	0.4
	Port (de Decize)	0.1	—	0.4
	Lock (No. 16-III de Decize)	0.5	2	0.0
	Junction with navigable channel in la Loire	0.5	—	0.0

Branch to Nevers

Sermoize	*Beginning of Branch (at K.96)*	0.0	—	2.9
	Lock (No. 20-II de Verville)	0.1	I	2.8
	Lock (No. 20-III de Rombois)	0.7	2	2.2

Distance Table			*kilom.*	*lock*	*kilom.*
	Skew bridge (de la Levée de Sermoise) ...		2.2	0	0.7
	Port (de la Jonction de Nevers) ...	...	2.3	—	0.6
Nevers	Lock (No. 20-IV de Nevers)	... ...	2.8	3	0.1
	Junction with la Loire	... ...	2.9	—	0.0

LYS

General	La Lys has its source at Lisbourg in the department of Pas-de-Calais. From thence, it flows through the town of Aire to Gand in Belgium.* Close to the railway bridge in Aire, the Canal de Neuffossé and the Canal d'Aire join the river at opposite points on the left and right banks respectively. Between the railway bridge and the junction with the two canals, the river is called *la Lys municipale*; from the junction, in a downstream direction, it takes the name of *la Lys canalisée*. Farther downstream over a length of 24 kilometres, where it forms the frontier between France and Belgium, it is known as *la Lys mitoyenne*. Along that length the right bank is French and the left bank Belgian. La Lys makes junction with le Canal d'Aire, le Canal de Neuffossé, le Canal de la Deûle, and les Canaux d'Haze-brouck. That part of the river which lies between Armentières and Menin carries a considerable amount of traffic.
Length	From the junction of la Lys with the Canals d'Aire and Neuffossé to the Franco-Belge frontier at the end of *la Lys mitoyenne* is a distance of 66 kilometres.
Locks	There are 7 locks. The first 4 of these have a length of 38 m. 50 with a width of 5 m. 18. The remaining 3 are 38 m. 70 long and the width is 5 m. 19. It is to be noted that Lock No. 7 (de Comines) is under Belgian jurisdiction.
Depth	From Aire to Armentières the depth is 2 m. 20; over the remaining distance the depth is slightly more (2 m. 60).
Bridges	The fixed bridges have at least a headroom of 4 m. 50 (at normal water level) as far as K.24 (Quay d'Estaires). From there the head-room is reduced to 4 m. 40 as far as K.42 (écluse d'Armentières), after which it is again 4 m. 50.
Tow-path	There is a tow-path throughout, diesel tractors being employed.

Distance Table		*kilom.*	*lock*	*kilom.*
Aire	*Junction with the Canals d'Aire (at K.40)*			
	and de Neuffossé (at K.0). Footbridge ...	0.0	—	66.0
	Lock (No. 1 de Fort-Gassion)	0.0	1	66.0

* See *The Inland Waterways of Belgium*, Imray Laurie Norie & Wilson.

Distance Table

				kilom.	lock	kilom.
Thiennes	Quay (de Thiennes). Lift-bridge ...	...		3.0	—	63.0
	Railway bridge (des Houillères) ...	...		4.0	—	62.0
	Junction with Canal de la Nieppe ...	...		4.0	—	62.0
	Ferry and Staithe (d'Houleron) ...	...		5.0	—	61.0
Saint-Venant	Lock (No. 2 de Cense) ...	...	...	6.0	2	60.0
Haverskerque	Footbridge (d'Haverskerque) ...	...		10.0	—	56.0
Saint-Venant	Quay (de Saint-Venant). Bridge ...			12.0	—	54.0
	Lock (No. 3 de St-Venant). Bridge	...		12.0	3	54.0
Saint-Floris	Ferry (de Saint-Floris) ...	...	...	14.0	—	52.0
Merville	Ferry (du Sart) ...	...	...	17.0	—	49.0
	Footbridge (de la Basse-Boulogne)	...		18.0	—	48.0
	Confluence with la Bourre canalisée	...		19.0	—	47.0
	Lock (No. 4 de Merville) ...	...	...	19.0	4	47.0
Estaires	Quay (d'Estaires). Bridge (de la Meuse) ...			25.0	—	41.0
	Bridge (d'Estaires) ...	...	...	26.0	—	40.0
Sailly	Bridge (de Sailly). Staithe (de Sailly)	...		30.0	—	36.0
Steenwerk	Lock (No. 5 de Bac-Saint-Maur). Bridge			32.0	5	34.0
Erquinghem	Bridge and Staithe (d'Erquinghem)	...		37.0	—	29.0
Nieppe	Railway bridge ...	...	...	39.0	—	27.0
Armentières	Bridge (d'Armentières) ...	...	...	40.0	—	26.0
	Bridge (du Bizet). Port (d'Armentières) ...			41.0	—	25.0
	Footbridge (Bayard) ...	...	...	42.0	—	24.0
Houplines	Lock (No. 6 nouvelle écluse d'Armentières) ...	...	...	42.0	6	24.0
	Frontier, *Franco-Belge (beginning of la Lys mitoyenne)* ...	...	...	42.0	—	24.0
	Railway bridge ...	...	...	42.0	—	24.0
Frelinghein	Bridge (de Frelinghein) ...	...	...	46.0	—	20.0
Deulémont	Bridge (called 'Pont-Rouge') ...	...		48.0	—	18.0
	Junction with Canal de la Deûle ...			48.0	—	18.0
Warneton	Bridge (de Warneton) ...	...		51.0	—	15.0
Comines	Quay (de Comines) ...	...	...	56.0	—	10.0
	Lock (No. 7 de Comines). Bridge	...		56.0	7	10.0
	Railway bridge ...	...	...	56.0	—	10.0
Wervicq	Bridge and Staithe (de Wervicq) ...	...		59.0	—	7.0
Bousbecque	Ferry (de Bousbecque) ...	...		62.0	—	4.0
Halluin	Railway bridge ...	...	...	65.0	—	1.0
	End of la Lys mitoyenne ...	...		66.0	—	0.0
	Frontier, *Franco-Belge* ...	...	...	66.0	—	0.0

MARNE

General   La Marne is navigable from Epernay to its confluence with la Seine at Charenton. As, however, that part which lies between Epernay and the lock at Dizy *(écluse de Dizy)* is a cul-de-sac and also is not canalised, it is treated here as a branch and not as lying on the principal line. From *l'écluse de Dizy* (which marks the junction with the canal latéral à la Marne) to the confluence with la Seine at Charenton, the river has been canalised and rectified by numerous cuts and deviations, of which more later. The river has two navigable channels in passing the islands of le Moulin de Bry et des Loups (K.169-170) and both these channels have been declared as 'one-way' *(sens unique)*. The channel by the left bank is reserved to vessels and convoys going downstream; the channel by the right bank is reserved to vessels and convoys travelling upstream. At l'île Fanac (K.173) also the passages are 'one-way'. The passage by the left bank is reserved to vessels going upstream; that by the right bank is reserved to vessels running downstream. Nevertheless, when the waste-weir of the *barrage de Joinville* is drawn on account of the high stage of the river, vessels going upstream are allowed to use the right arm. Overtaking is forbidden in both the channels of les îles du Moulin de Bry et des Loups and also in the right bank channel of l'île Fanac. This is also the rule when making the passage past many of the islands, the limits of the overtaking restriction being shown by notice boards erected on the banks. When the level of the river shows 35 m. 32 on the gauge fixed on the bridge at Joinville, the lock at Saint-Maur functions as a flood outlet and is no longer available to navigation.

Great care must be taken when making the passage between Nogent and Joinville and vice versa during the summer season, at which time the river is crowded with pleasure vessels. The river has been, in part, replaced by canals, or more properly by deviations *(dérivations)* which are comprised as follows:

(a) dérivation de Cumières (K.2)

(b) dérivation de Damery (K.6)

(c) dérivation de Vandières (K.17)

(d) Canal de Meaux à Chalifert (K.133/145)

(e) Canal de Chelles (K.155/164)

(f) Canal Saint-Maur (K.173/174).

The deviations are comparatively short, but *the Canal de Meaux à Chalifert*, which starts at Meaux and rejoins the river at Chalifert, has a length of about 12 kilometres, a depth of 2 m. 20 and is regulated by three locks. There is also a tunnel *(le souterrain de Chalifert)* which is 290 metres in length. The tunnel has no signals authorising the passage, but instructions are given by the lock-keeper either at Lesches or at Chalifert, depending upon the direction in which the vessel is going. His advice should always be obtained. *The Canal de Chelles*, which begins at Vaires-sur-Marne and rejoins the river at Neuilly-sur-Marne, has a length of 9 kilometres, a depth of 2 m. 20 and is regulated by a lock at each end.

Tunnel de Chalifert

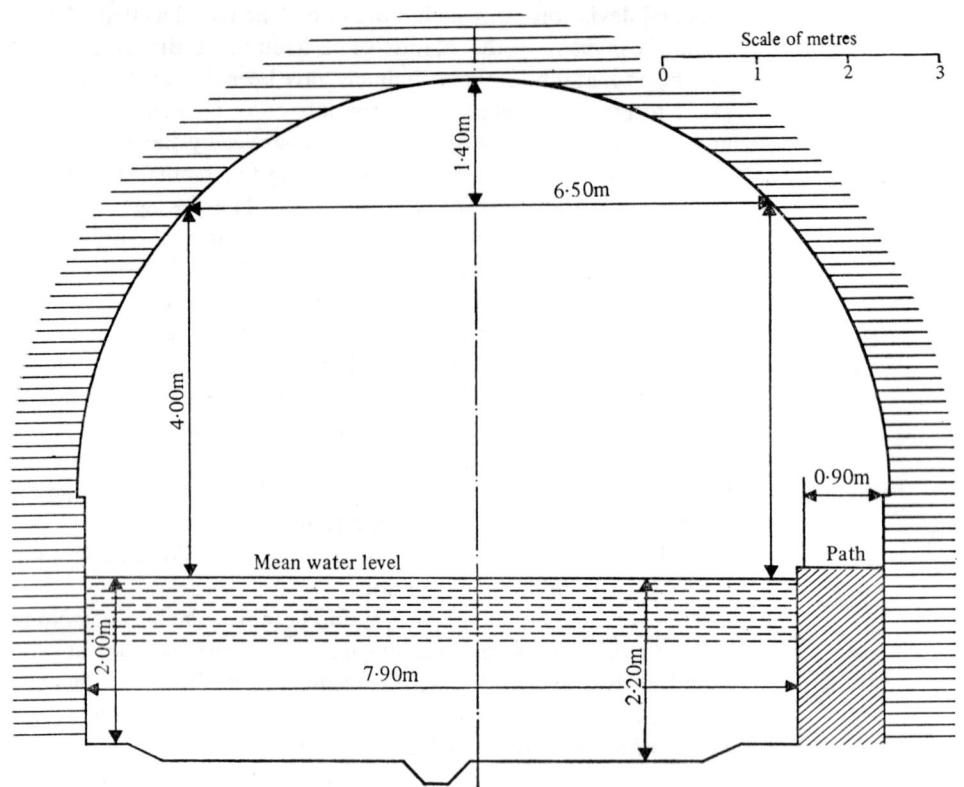

CAUTION. *Live electric wires may be established throughout the length of this tunnel.*

The Canal Saint-Maur runs from Joinville to Maisons-Alfort. It is short, only about a kilometre and a quarter, but the first 600 metres is in tunnel. It ends in a large lock on the downstream side of which there is a depth of 3 m. 20. The passage through the tunnel is made from alternate ends.

The tunnel at Saint-Maur allows passage alternatively, from each end. The direction of the passage is confirmed by traffic lights which conform to international convention.

RED light only — STOP
GREEN light only — PASS
RED and GREEN (horizontally) — PREPARE TO ENTER.

The lights at the upstream end of the tunnel are placed on the right bank 50 metres upstream of the tunnel entrance; the lights at the

Tunnel de St. Maur

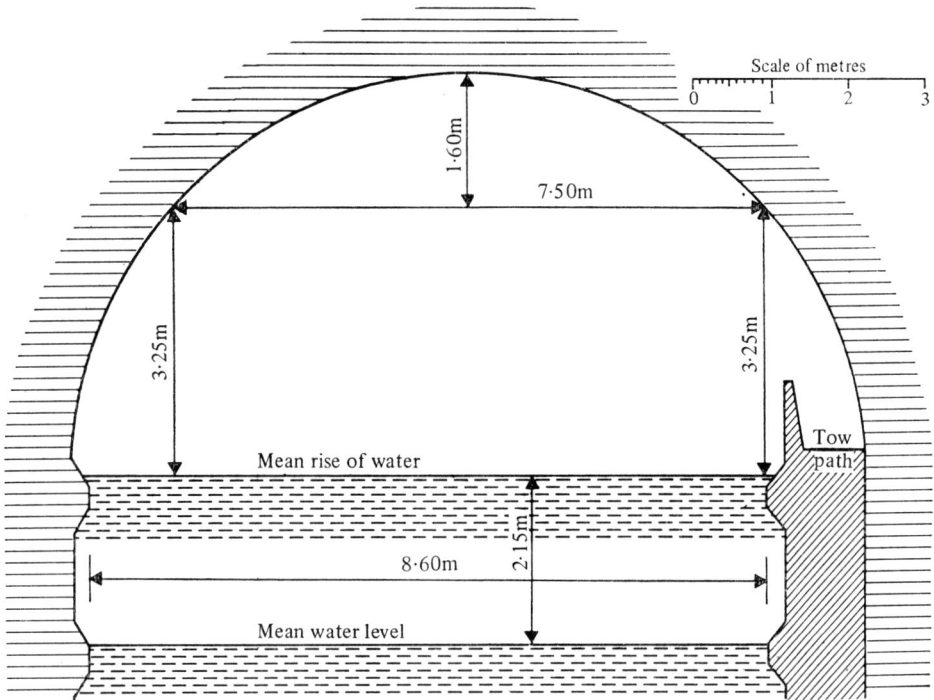

Scale of metres

1·60m

7·50m

3·25m

3·25m

Tow path

Mean rise of water

8·60m

2·15m

Mean water level

CAUTION. Live electric wires may be established throughout the length of this tunnel.

other end of the tunnel are placed on the spandrel of the arch forming the downstream end of the tunnel.

Warning lights situated at the upstream end of l'Ile de Fanac (K.173) inform the masters of vessels going downstream of the lights *likely* to be found, when navigating at normal speed, when he reaches the upstream entrance to the tunnel. Thus:

GREEN light only — 'at normal speed you will find the GREEN light at tunnel entrance'.

RED and GREEN (vertical) — 'prepare to stop at the garage sited at the upstream entrance to tunnel'.

No Permis de Circulation is necessary for the navigation of this river.

Length

The length of the canalised river is 178 kilometres from Ecluse de Dizy to Charenton (the confluence with la Seine). A further 3½ kilometres (here referred to as 'Branch to Epernay') is navigable, but is not canalised.

Locks

There are 18 locks, all of which fall towards la Seine. Of these, 16 have a length of 45 m. 00 with a width of 7 m. 80. The remaining 2, situated at each end of the Canal Saint-Maur, have a length of 125 m. 00 with a width of 12 m. 00.

| | | *Depth* | At normal water level there is a depth of 2 m. 20; this depth is increased to 3 m. 20 from the upstream end of the Canal Saint-Maur to the confluence with la Seine. |

Depth

At normal water level there is a depth of 2 m. 20; this depth is increased to 3 m. 20 from the upstream end of the Canal Saint-Maur to the confluence with la Seine.

Bridges

The ruling bridge is that of Ville-Evrard (at K.163), which has a headroom of 3 m. 80 at a chord of 15 metres. All the rest have a good deal more headroom, but during periods of flood all these figures are much reduced, and local enquiries must always be made at the time of passage.

Tow-path

There is no tow-path.

Distance Table

		kilom.	lock	kilom.
Hautvillers	*Junction with le canal latéral à la Marne (at K.67).* Lock (de Dizy) (not on river)	0.0	0	178.0
Cumières	Bridge (de Cumières). Port (de Cumières)	1.0	—	177.0
	Beginning of deviation (de Cumières) ...	2.0	—	176.0
	Bridge. Lock (No. 1 de Cumières) ...	3.0	1	175.0
	Bridge. End of deviation	3.0	—	175.0
Damery	Port and Bridge (de Damery)	5.0	—	173.0
	Beginning of deviation (de Damery) ...	6.0	—	172.0
	Bridge	6.0	—	172.0
Venteuil	Bridge (called Pont du 'Port aux Vins') ...	7.0	—	171.0
	Lock (No. 2 de Damery). End of deviation	8.0	2	170.0
Reuil	Bridge (de Reuil)	11.0	—	167.0
	Port (de Reuil)	12.0	—	166.0
Leuvrigny	Port (de Port-à-Binson). Port (de Chatillon)	14.0	—	164.0
	Bridge (de Port-à-Binson)	14.0	—	164.0
Vandières	Beginning of deviation (de Vandières) ...	17.0	—	161.0
	Lock (No. 3 de Vandières)	17.0	3	161.0
	End of deviation	17.0	—	161.0
Verneuil	Port (de Verneuil)	22.0	—	156.0
	Bridge (de Try)	22.0	—	156.0
Vincelles	Port (de Vincelles)	24.0	—	154.0
Tréloup	Suspension bridge (de Dormans)	26.0	—	152.0
	Port (de Tréloup)	28.0	—	150.0
Courthiézy	Lock (No. 4 de Courcelles)	30.0	4	148.0
Passy	Bridge (de Passy)	32.0	—	146.0
Barzy	Port (de Rosay)	34.0	—	144.0
	Port (de Marcilly)	35.0	—	143.0
Jaulgonne	Bridge (de Jaulgonne)	37.0	—	141.0
Chartèves	Port (de Chartèves)	41.0	—	137.0
	Bridge (de Mont-Saint-Père)	41.0	—	137.0
	Lock (No. 5 de Mont-Saint-Père) ...	42.0	5	136.0
Château-Thierry	Port (des Filoirs). Bridge (de Château-Thierry)	50.0	—	128.0
	Quay (du Touring Club de France) ...	50.0	—	128.0

Distance Table

			kilom.	lock	kilom.
	Port (de la Pâture au bord de l'eau)	...	50.0	—	128.0
Azy	Lock (No. 6 d'Azy). Bridge (d'Azy)	...	56.0	6	122.0
Nogent-l'Artaud	Bridge (de Nogent-l'Artaud)	... ...	63.0	—	115.0
Charly-s-Marne	Bridge. Lock (No. 7 de Charly) ...		66.0	7	112.0
Nanteuil-s-Marne	Bridge (de Nanteuil-s-Marne)	... ...	74.0	—	104.0
	Railway bridge	...	74.0	—	104.0
Méry-s-Marne	Lock (No. 8 de Méry) ...	...	75.0	8	103.0
Saacy	Port and Bridge (de Saacy)	... ...	76.0	—	102.0
Luzancy	Bridge and Port (de Luzancy)	... ...	80.0	—	98.0
	Railway bridge	...	81.0	—	97.0
	Railway bridge	...	85.0	—	93.0
	Lock (No. 9 de Courtaron)	... ...	87.0	9	91.0
La Ferté-sous-	Port and Bridge (de Ferté-s/s-Jouarre) ...		90.0	—	88.0
Jouarre	Bridge	...	91.0	—	87.0
Ussy-s-Marne	Bridge (d'Ussy)	...	95.0	—	83.0
St-Jean-les-	Bridge and Port (de Saint-Jean) ...		99.0	—	79.0
Deux-Jumeaux	Lock (No. 10 de Saint-Jean)	... ...	100.0	10	78.0
Changis-s-Marne	Railway bridge	...	102.0	—	76.0
Mary-s-Marne	Bridge (de Mary-s-Marne). Railway bridge	110.0	—	68.0
Congis	Lock (No. 11 d'Isles-les-Meldeuses) ...		113.0	11	65.0
	Bridge (de Congis)	...	113.0	—	65.0
Germigny-l'Evêque	Port (de Germigny-l'Evêque)	...	121.0	—	57.0
Trilport+	Railway bridge	...	126.0	—	52.0
	Port and Bridge (de Trilport)	...	126.0	—	52.0
Nanteuil-lès-Meaux	Beginning of Canal de Meaux à Chalifert	133.0	—	45.0
	Lock (No. 12 de Meaux)	...	133.0	12	45.0
	Bridge (des Saints-Pères)		133.0	—	45.0
Mareuil-lès-Meaux	1st Bridge (de Mareuil-lès-Meaux)	...	136.0	—	42.0
	2nd Bridge (de Mareuil-lès-Meaux)	...	137.0	—	41.0
	Bridge (des Roizes)	...	138.0	—	40.0
Condé-Ste-Libiaire	Bridge (de Condé)	...	140.0	—	38.0
	Pont-aqueduc (de Condé) *(narrow passage)*	141.0	—	37.0
Esbly	Pont-aqueduc. 1st Bridge (d'Esbly)	...	141.0	—	37.0
	2nd Bridge and Port (d'Esbly)	...	142.0	—	36.0
	Railway bridge	...	142.0	—	36.0
Coupvray	Bridge (de Coupvray)	...	143.0	—	35.0
	Lock (No. 13 de Lesches)		145.0	13	33.0
Chalifert	Tunnel (de Chalifert) (290 m.) ...		145.0	—	33.0
	Lock (No. 14 de Chalifert) ...		145.0	14	33.0
	End of Canal de Meaux à Chalifert ...		145.0	—	33.0
Lagny	Port (de la Gourdine)	...	151.0	—	27.0
	1st Bridge (de Lagny)	...	151.0	—	27.0
Pomponne	Port. 2nd Bridge (de Lagny) ...		151.0	—	27.0

* S.A.I.N.T. Line Cruiser have a 'hire-cruiser' base at Poincy near Meaux, also on the Canal du Nivernais.

Distance Table

		kilom.	lock	kilom.
Vaires-s-Marne	Beginning of Canal de Chelles	155.0	—	23.0
	Lock (No. 15 de Vaires). Bridge	155.0	15	23.0
	Bridge (de Vaires)	156.0	—	22.0
Chelles	Bridge (de Chelles). Bridge (du Moulin)...	160.0	—	18.0
	Bridge (de Gournay-s-Marne) and Port ...	161.0	—	17.0
Neuilly-s-Marne	Bridge (de Ville-Evrard)	163.0	—	15.0
	Lock (No. 16 de Neuilly-s-Marne). Bridge	164.0	16	14.0
	End of Canal de Chelles	164.0	—	14.0
	Bridge (de Neuilly-s-Marne)	165.0	—	13.0
	Railway viaduct	165.0	—	13.0
Neuilly-Plaisance	Port (de la Maltournée)	166.0	—	12.0
Bry-s-Marne	Footbridge (de Bry)	167.0	—	11.0
	Bridge (de Bry)	168.0	—	10.0
	Upstream end of middle ground (des Iles du Moulin, de Bry et des Loups) ...	169.0	—	9.0
Nogent-s-Marne	Viaduct (de Nogent)	170.0	—	8.0
	Bridge (de Nogent). Downstream end of middle ground. Port (de Nogent) ...	170.0	—	8.0
Joinville	Upstream end of middle ground (de l'Ile Fanac). *Tunnel warning lights*	173.0	—	5.0
	Bridge (de Joinville)	173.0	—	5.0
	Downstream end of middle ground ...	173.0	—	5.0
	Dock at upstream end of tunnel (de Saint-Maur)	173.0	—	5.0
	Gauge (du Pont de Joinville). Beginning of Canal Saint-Maur. Mole	173.0	—	5.0
	Upstream entrance to tunnel (de St-Maur)	173.0	—	5.0
	Downstream entrance to tunnel (de St-Maur)	174.0	—	4.0
	Lock (de Saint-Maur)	174.0	17	4.0
	End of Canal Saint-Maur	174.0	—	4.0
Maisons-Alfort	Footbridge (de Charentonneau)	175.0	—	3.0
	Lock (de Saint-Maurice)	177.0	18	1.0
Charenton	Bridge (de Charenton). Railway bridge ...	177.0	—	1.0
	Footbridge (d'Alfortville)	178.0	—	0.0
	Confluence with la Seine (at K.96) ...	178.0	—	0.0

Branch to Epernay

Hautvillers	Junction with la Marne canalisée	0.0	—	3.6
Epernay	Bridge (d'Epernay)	3.6	—	0.0

CANAL LATÉRAL À LA MARNE

General   The new trace of the canal láteral à la Marne leaves the Canal de la Marne au Rhin on the north-eastern outskirts of Vitry-le-François and joins the ancient part of the lateral canal close to the pont-canal sur le Saulx and l'écluse de Vitry-le-François. The lateral canal finishes at Dizy-Magenta in the commune of Haut-Villers near Epernay, where it joins with the canalised River la Marne. At Condé-sur-Marne this canal makes connection with the Canal de l'Aisne à la Marne.

Length	From the junction near Vitry-le-François to the lock at Dizy, where it joins the canalised Marne, the canal has a length of 67 kilometres.
Locks	There are 15 locks, all of which fall towards Dizy. They have a length of 38 m. 50 with a width of 5 m. 20.
Depth	The normal depth of water is 2 m. 20.
Bridges	The fixed bridges all have a clear headroom of 3 m. 70 above the normal water level.
Tow-path	The tow-path runs throughout, although it changes from side to side.

Distance Table

		kilom.	lock	kilom.
*Vitry-le-François**	*Junction with Canal de la Marne au Rhin (at K.0.9).*	0.0	—	67.0
	Bridge (Route Nationale No. 382) ...	0.4	—	66.6
	Bridge (Route Nationale No. 44) ...	1.4	—	65.6
	Pont-canal (over la Saulx)	2.2	—	64.8
	Lock (No. 0 de Vitry-le-François) ...	2.0	I	65.0
Couvrot	Lock (No. 1 de l'Ermite)	3.6	2	63.4
	Port and Bridge (de Couvrot)	4.0	—	63.0
	Lock (No. 2 de Couvrot)	4.0	3	63.0
	Bridge (de Villers)	5.0	—	62.0
Soulanges	Bridge (de Bayarne)	7.0	—	60.0
	Port (de Soulanges)	8.0	—	59.0
	Lock (No. 3 de Soulanges)	9.0	4	58.0
Ablancourt	Lock (No. 4 d'Ablancourt)	11.0	5	56.0
	Port and Bridge (d'Ablancourt) ...	11.0	—	56.0
La Chaussée-s-Marne	Bridge (du Bois de Marne) ...	13.0	—	54.0
	Port and Bridge (de la Chaussée) ...	14.0	—	53.0
	Lock (No. 5 de la Chaussée-s-Marne) ...	15.0	6	52.0
Omey	Port and Bridge (d'Omey)	16.0	—	51.0
Pogny	Bridge and Port (de Pogny)	17.0	—	50.0
	Port (de Saint-Genest)	18.0	—	49.0
St-Germain-la-Ville	Port (de St-Germain-la-Ville) ...	21.0	—	46.0
	Lock (No. 6 de St-Germain-la-Ville) ...	21.0	7	46.0
	Bridge (de St-Germain-la-Ville) ...	21.0	—	46.0

* See Plan No. 20.

Distance Table

				kilom.	lock	kilom.
Chepy	Port and Bridge (de Chepy)	...	...	23.0	—	44.0
Moncetz	Bridge and Port (de Moncetz)	...	...	25.0	—	42.0
Sarry	Lock (No. 7 de Sarry). Port	...	...	26.0	8	41.0
	Bridge (de Sarry)	...	...	27.0	—	40.0
Chalôns-sur-Marne	Bridge (des Allées de Forêts)	...	...	30.0	—	37.0
	Bridge (Pont-Louis XII). Pont-canal	...		31.0	—	36.0
	Footbridge and Island (du Jard) ...		...	31.0	—	36.0
	Lock (No. 8 de Chalôns-s-Marne). Bridge			32.0	9	35.0
	Entrance to municipal port. Basin		...	32.0	—	33.0
Saint-Martin	Bridge (de Saint-Martin) ...	...	...	34.0	—	33.0
	Railway bridge	...	...	35.0	—	32.0
	Bridge (du Therme-Brouart)	...	...	36.0	—	31.0
Recy	Port and Bridge (de Recy)	...	...	37.0	—	30.0
Juvigny	Lock (No. 9 de Juvigny) ...	...	...	39.0	10	28.0
	Bridge and Port (de Juvigny)	...	...	42.0	—	25.0
Vraux	Bridge and Lock (No. 10 de Vraux)	...		44.0	11	23.0
Aigny	Bridge (d'Aigny)	...	...	46.0	—	21.0
Condé-sur-Marne*	*Junction with Canal de l'Aisne a la Marne*			48.0	—	19.0
	Port and Bridge (de Condé-s-Marne)		...	48.0	—	19.0
Tours-sur-Marne	Port (de Tours-s-Marne) ...	...	...	52.0	—	15.0
	Bridge and Lock (No. 11 de Tours-s-Marne)			53.0	12	14.0
Bisseuil	Bridge (du Bussin)	...	...	55.0	—	12.0
Mareuil-sur-Ay	Lock (No. 12 de Mareuil-s-Ay). Bridge ...			58.0	13	9.0
	Port (de Mareuil-s-Ay) ...	...	...	59.0	—	8.0
	Bridge (des Cheminets) ...	...	...	60.0	—	7.0
Ay	Bridge (des Ruetz). Railway bridge	...		61.0	—	6.0
	Bridge (de Villemoyer). Port (d'Ay)	...		61.0	—	6.0
	Lock (No. 13 d'Ay). Bridge	...	...	62.0	14	5.0
Dizy-Magenta†	Port and Bridge (de Dizy)	...	...	64.0	—	3.0
Hautvillers	Bridge (de Hautvillers) ...	...	...	66.0	—	1.0
	Lock (No. 14 de Dizy) ...	...	...	67.0	15	0.0
	Junction with la Marne canalisée (at K.0)			67.0	—	0.0

CANAL DE LA MARNE AU RHIN

General   The Canal de la Marne au Rhin begins at Vitry-le-François, where it leaves the Canal de la Marne à la Saône and ends in the City of Strasbourg. The Canal de l'Est joins it at Troussey (K.111) and leaves it again at Toul (K.131).

* See Plan No. 3.
† See Plan No. 6.

Tunnel de Mauvages

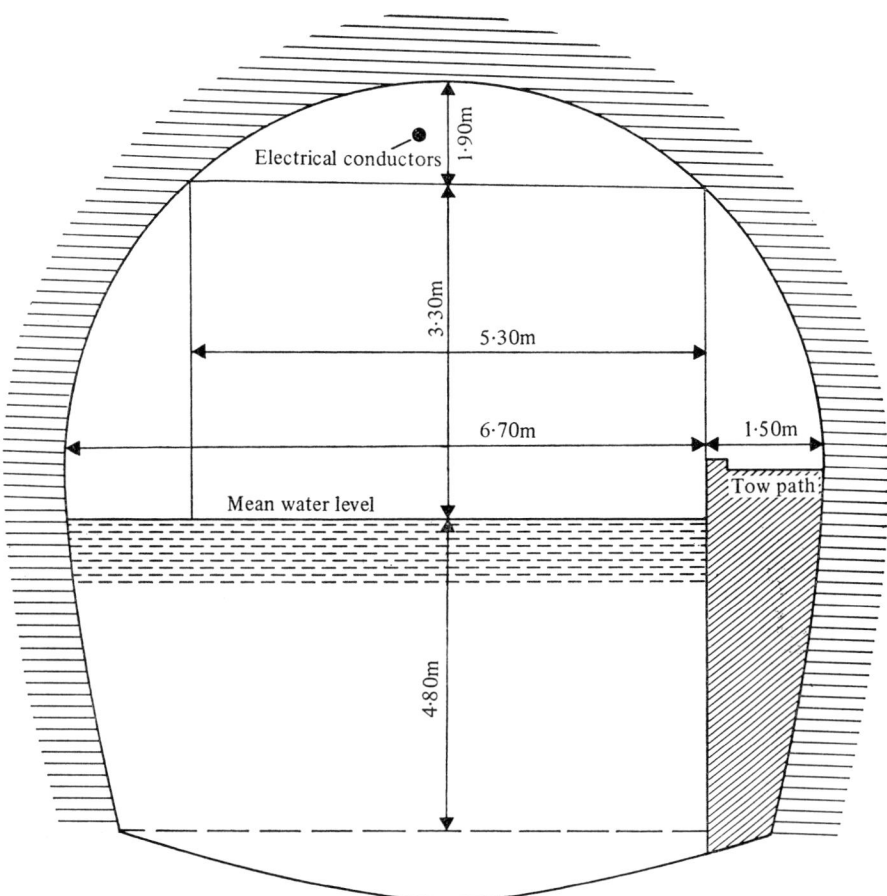

CAUTION. Live electric wires may be established throughout the length of this tunnel.

This canal joins with (*a*) the canalised River Moselle at Frouard (K.154); (*b*) the Canal de l'Est by the Branch to Nancy at Laneuville (K.168); (*c*) the Canal des Houillères de la Sarre at Gondrexange (K.227).

The canal links up the northern and Paris regions with the east and with Germany. Within its length it contains five tunnels. They are: (*a*) de Mauvages (4,877 metres) (K.86); (*b*) de Foug (867 metres) (K.121); (*c*) de Liverdun (388 metres) (K.147); (*d*) de Niderviller (475 metres) (K.247); (*e*) d'Arzviller (2,307 metres) (K.249).

125

Tunnel de Foug

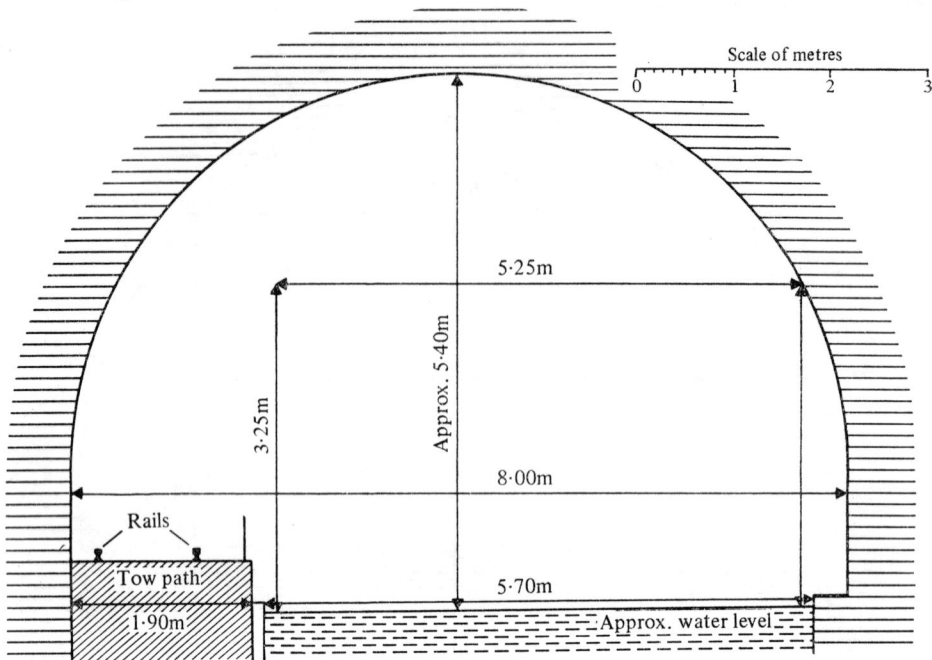

CAUTION. *Live electric wires may be established throughout the length of this tunnel.*

(a) *Tunnel at Mauvages.* All vessels, including those which are self-propelled, are obliged to use the towing service. The trains of vessels leave from:

Demange towards the east — 0600 and 1300 hours.

Mauvages towards the west — 0830 and 1530 hours.

It is to be noted that electric conductors are slung from the keystone of the arch.

(b) *Tunnel at Foug.* All vessels, including those which are self-propelled, are obliged to use the towing service. There are no fixed hours for the departure of the tows, the frequency of which depends upon the disposition of the traffic, but usually at intervals of about $1\frac{1}{2}$ hours. There is no passage by night.

(c) *Tunnel at Liverdun.* Vessels pass through under their own power. The tunnel and its approaches constitute a restricted waterway along which one-way traffic is enforced alternately from each end. This alternate movement is shown on indicator panels displayed one at each end of the passage. The time taken in each direction is in the order of 1 hour, but varies as a function of the traffic and not at any fixed times.

(d) *Tunnels at Niderviller and at Arzviller.* These two tunnels are taken together, because the trains of vessels are made up at the beginning of one tunnel and go through without breaking up to the end of the following tunnel. The use of the towing service is obligatory for all vessels, whether self-propelled or not. The trains depart simultaneously from each end and cross between the tunnels; the times of departure vary with the season of the year, but from 16th March to 15th October they depart at 0630, 1100, 1500 hours.

This canal also contains two summit levels, the one between Demange-aux-Eaux and Mauvages is called *du Mauvages* and the other between Réchicourt-le-Château and Arzviller is called *des Vosges*. The higher of the two summit levels, that at Demange-aux-Eaux, is over 900 feet above sea level.

Tunnels d'Arzviller et de Niderviller

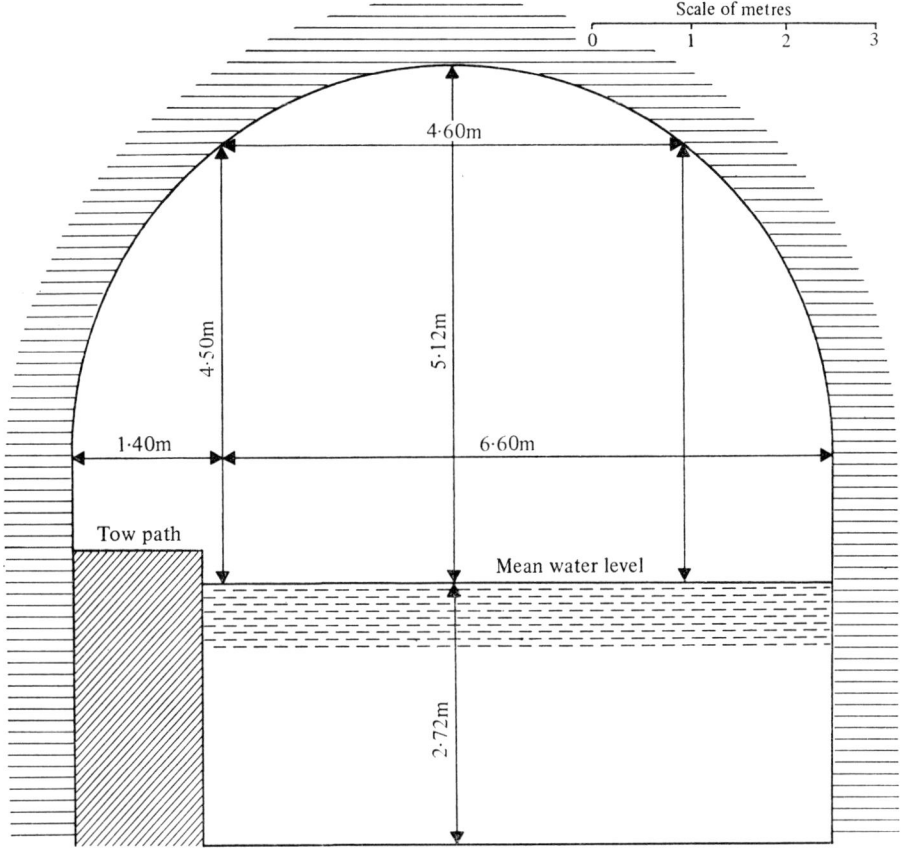

CAUTION. *Live electric wires may be established throughout the length of this tunnel.*

Length   The distance by the canal from Vitry-le-François to Strasbourg is 313 kilometres.

Locks — There are in all 171 locks.* As mentioned above there are two summit-levels. From the first (at Demange) 70 locks fall towards Vitry-le-François and 29 towards Nancy, from the second summit-level (at Réchicourt) 21 locks fall towards Nancy and 51 towards Strasbourg. All the locks have a uniform length of 38 m. 70 with a width of 5 m. 13.

Depth — There is a depth of 2 m. 21 throughout.

Bridges — The fixed bridges have a headroom of 3 m. 70 at normal level.

Tow-path — There is a tow-path throughout. Towing is by electric tractors except between Varangéville and Dombasle where tugs are used.

Distance Table

		kilom.	lock	kilom.
Vitry-le-François†	*Junction with Canal de la Marne à la Saône (at K.o)*	0.0	—	313.0
	Bridge (des Vassues)	0.0	—	313.0
	Junction with canal latéral à la Marne (at K.o).	0.9	—	312.9
Vitry-en-Perthois	Bridge (Pont Saint-Jacques)	1.0	—	312.0
	Lock (No. 70 de St. Etienne). Bridge. Port	3.0	I	310.0
Plichancourt	Lock (No. 69 d'Adecourt). Bridge. Port ...	5.0	2	308.0
	Bridge (de la Caure)	5.0	—	308.0
	Bridge (de Longbois)	6.0	—	307.0
Brusson	Port and Lock (No. 68 de Brusson) ...	7.0	3	306.0
	Bridge (de Brusson). (Pont-canal) ...	7.0	—	306.0
Ponthion	Bridge and Port (de Ponthion)	9.0	—	304.0
	Lock (No. 67 de Ponthion). Bridge ...	10.0	4	303.0
Buisson	Bridge (du Buisson)	12.0	—	301.0
Bignicourt	Bridge (du Pre-le-Doyen)	13.0	—	300.0
	Port (de Bignicourt)	14.0	—	299.0
	Lock (No. 66 de Bignicourt). Bridge ...	14.0	5	299.0
Etrepy	Port and Lock (No. 65 d'Etrepy) ...	16.0	6	297.0
	Bridge and Pont-canal (d'Etrepy) ...	16.0	—	297.0
Pargny-sur-Saulx	Lock (No. 64 de Pargny-s-Saulx). Bridge	18.0	7	295.0
	Port (de Pargny-sur-Saulx)	18.0	—	295.0
	Lock (No. 63 du pont-canal de Pargny)	19.0	8	294.0
	Pont-canal (de Pargny)	19.0	—	294.0
	Bridge (de l'Ajot)	20.0	—	293.0

* During 1969 an Inclined Plane (*le Plan Incliné Transversal d'Arzviller/Saint Louis*), together with appropriate approach canals, was put into service. The Inclined Plane avoids the use of the first seventeen locks which fall towards Strasbourg from the Rechicourt summit-level, thus reducing the number of locks on that side from 51 to 34. The lift has provision for two vessels, but only one caisson is now in action. The installation of the second caisson is in hand and will soon be ready for use. The old route through the 17 locks is being maintained as a safety measure. The *kilométrage* of the canal remains unchanged.

† See Plan No. 21.

Distance Table

		kilom.	*lock*	*kilom.*
Sermaize-les-Bains	Lock (No. 62 de l'Ajot)	21.0	9	292.0
	Lock (No. 61 de la Chaïne). Bridge ...	23.0	10	290.0
	Lock (No. 60 de Sermaize-les-Bains) ...	24.0	11	289.0
	Bridge and Port (de Sermaize)	24.0	—	289.0
	Bridge (de Remennecourt)	24.0	—	289.0
	Railway bridge and Port (de Sermaize) ...	25.0	—	288.0
	Lock (No. 59 de Remennecourt). Bridge	27.0	12	288.0
Contrisson	Lock (No. 58 de Chevol). Bridge ...	27.0	13	286.0
	Port (de Contrisson)	28.0	—	285.0
	Lock (No. 57 de Contrisson)	28.0	14	285.0
	Bridge (de Contrisson). Port (de Braux) ...	28.0	—	285.0
	Lock (No. 56 de Braux). Bridge	29.0	15	284.0
Revigny	Lock (No. 55 de la Haie Herlin)	30.0	16	283.0
	Lock (No. 54 de Damzelle)	30.0	17	283.0
	Lock (No. 53 de Notre-Dame-de-Grâce)	31.0	18	282.0
	Lock (No. 52 de Revigny). Bridge. Port ...	31.0	19	282.0
	Lock (No. 51 du Bois-l'Ecuyer). Bridge ...	32.0	20	281.0
	Lock (No. 50 du Petit-Fraicul)	33.0	21	280.0
Neuville-sur-Ornain	Lock (No. 49 du Grand-Fraicul)	34.0	22	279.0
	Port (de Neuville-sur-Ornain)	35.0	—	278.0
	Lock (No. 48 de Neuville-s-Ornain). Bridge	35.0	23	278.0
	Lock (No. 47 de la Doeuil)	36.0	24	277.0
Mussey	Lock (No. 46 de Mussey). Lift-bridge. Port	38.0	25	275.0
	Lock (No. 45 de Chacolée)	39.0	26	274.0
Varney	Port (de Varney)	40.0	—	273.0
	Lock (No. 44 de Varney). Bridge ...	40.0	27	273.0
	Lock (No. 43 de Rembercourt)	41.0	28	272.0
Fains-les-Sources	Port (de Fains-les-Sources)	43.0	—	270.0
	Lock (No. 42 de Fains-les-Sources). Lift-bridge	43.0	29	270.0
	Railway bridge	44.0	—	269.0
	Lock (No. 41 de Grand-Pré)	44.0	30	269.0
	Lock (No. 40 du pont-canal de Chanteraines)	44.0	31	269.0
	Pont-canal (de Chanteraines)	45.0	—	268.0
Bar-le-Duc	Lock (No. 39 de Bar-le-Duc). Bridge ...	46.0	32	267.0
	Footbridge and Port (de Bar-le-Duc) ...	46.0	—	267.0
	Lift-bridge (de Marbot)	47.0	—	266.0
	Lock (No. 38 de Marbot). Lift-bridge ...	47.0	33	266.0
	Lock (No. 37 de Popey)	48.0	34	265.0
	Railway bridge	49.0	—	264.0
	Bridge (de Dammarie)	49.0	—	264.0
Savonnières-devant-Bar	Lock (No. 36 de Savonnières-d-Bar) ...	49.0	35	264.0

Distance Table

		kilom.	lock	kilom.
Longeville	Lock (No. 35 de Longeville). Bridge ...	50.0	36	263.0
	Pont-canal (de Longeville)	50.0	—	263.0
	Port (de Longeville)	51.0	—	262.0
	Lock (No. 34 de la Grande-Chalaide). Bridge	51.0	37	262.0
	Bridge (de la Petite-Chalaide)	52.0	—	261.0
	Lock (No. 33 de Maheux)	53.0	38	260.0
Tannois	Lock (No. 32 de Tannois). Bridge. Port ...	54.0	39	259.0
	Lock (No. 31 de Silmont). Bridge ...	54.0	40	259.0
	Lock (No. 30 de Guerpont)	55.0	41	258.0
Guerpont	Lock (No. 29 de Bohanne). Bridge ...	56.0	42	257.0
	Lock (No. 28 de Tronville). Bridge ...	56.0	43	257.0
Tronville	Bridge and Ports (de Tronville)	57.0	—	256.0
	Lock (No. 27 de Chessard). Bridge ...	58.0	44	255.0
Velaines	Lock (No. 26 de Nançois-le-Petit) ...	59.0	45	254.0
	Lock (No. 25 de Velaines). Bridge. Port ...	60.0	46	253.0
	Lock (No. 24 de Maulan). Bridge ...	61.0	47	252.0
Ligny-en-Barrois	Lock (No. 23 de Villeroncourt). Bridge ...	62.0	48	251.0
	Port and Lock (No. 22 de Ligny). Bridge	62.0	49	251.0
	Bridge (de la Herval)	63.0	—	250.0
	Lock (No. 21 de Gainval)	64.0	50	249.0
Givrauval	Lock (No. 20 de Grèves)	64.0	51	249.0
	Port and Lock (No. 19 de Givrauval). Bridge	65.0	52	248.0
Longeaux	Lock (No. 18 de Longeaux)	66.0	53	247.0
	Bridge and Port (de Longeaux)	67.0	—	246.0
Menaucourt	Port (de Menaucourt)	67.0	—	246.0
	Bridge (du Patouillat). Railway bridge ...	68.0	—	245.0
	Lock (No. 17 de Menaucourt). Pont-canal	68.0	54	245.0
Naix-aux-Forges	Lock (No. 16 de Nantois). Bridge ...	69.0	55	244.0
	Lock (No. 15 de Naix-aux-Forges). Bridge	70.0	56	243.0
	Port (de Naix-aux-Forges)	70.0	—	243.0
Boviolles	Lock (No. 14 du pont-canal de la Barboure)	71.0	57	242.0
	Pont-canal (de la Barboure)	71.0	—	242.0
Saint-Amand	Port and Bridge (de Saint-Amand) ...	72.0	—	241.0
	Lock (No. 13 de Saint-Amand)	73.0	58	240.0
Tréveray	Lock (No. 12 de Charmasson)	74.0	59	239.0
	Lock (No. 11 de Tréveray). Bridge. Port	75.0	60	238.0
	Lock (No. 10 de Charbonnières)	76.0	61	237.0
	Lock (No. 9 de la Petite-Forge)	77.0	62	236.0
Saint-Joire	Lock (No. 8 de Laneuville-St-Joire) ...	77.0	63	236.0
	Port and Bridge (de Saint-Joire)	78.0	—	235.0
	Lock (No. 7 de Saint-Joire)	79.0	64	234.0
	Lock (No. 6 de Boeval)	80.0	65	233.0

Distance Table

		kilom.	lock	kilom.
	Lock (No. 5 de l'Abbaye d'Evaux) ...	80.0	66	233.0
	Lock (No. 4 de Montfort)	82.0	67	231.0
Demange-aux-Eaux	Lock (No. 3 de Bois-Molu)	83.0	68	230.0
	Lock (No. 2 de Demange-aux-Eaux) ...	83.0	69	230.0
	Lock (No. 1 de Tombois). Bridge. (Beginning of summit level 'de Mauvages') ...	84.0	70	229.0
Mauvages	Tunnel (de Mauvages) (4,877 m.) ...	86.0	—	227.0
	End of tunnel	91.0	—	222.0
	Bridge (de Mauvages)	92.0	—	221.0
	Port (de Mauvages)	93.0	—	220.0
	Lock (No. 1 de Mauvages). End of summit level	94.0	71	219.0
Villeroy	Lock (No. 2 de Villeroy). Bridge	94.0	72	219.0
	Lock (No. 3 de la Chalède)	95.0	73	218.0
	Lock (No. 4 du Grand-Charme). Bridge	95.0	74	218.0
Sauvoy	Lock (No. 5 du Saint-Esprit)	96.0	75	217.0
	Lock (No. 6 de la Corvée)	97.0	76	216.0
	Bridge (de Sauvoy)	97.0	—	216.0
	Port and Lock (No. 7 de Sauvoy) ...	98.0	77	215.0
	Lock (No. 8 des Varonnes). Bridge ...	98.0	78	215.0
Vacon	Lock (No. 9 des Biguiottes)	100.0	79	213.0
	Lock (No. 10 du Haut-Bois). Bridge ...	100.0	80	213.0
	Port and Lock (No. 11 de Vacon). Bridge	101.0	81	212.0
	Lock (No. 12 de Void)	102.0	82	211.0
Void	Port and Lift-bridge (de Void)	103.0	—	210.0
	Railway bridge	104.0	—	209.0
	Bridge (de la Croix-le-Pêcheur)	107.0	—	206.0
Troussey	Bridge (Pont-Naviot)	109.0	—	204.0
	Pont-canal (de Troussey)	110.0	—	203.0
Sorcy and Troussey	*Junction with Canal de l'Est (Northern Branch) (at K.272)*	111.0	—	202.0
Pagny-sur-Meuse	Bridge (de Pagny-s-Meuse)	115.0	—	198.0
	Port (de Pagny-s-Meuse)	116.0	—	197.0
	Railway bridge	117.0	—	195.0
Lay-Saint-Rémy	Port and Bridge (de Lay-St-Rémy) ...	119.0	—	194.0
	Bridge (d'Ugny). Beginning of cut (de Lay-St-Rémy). *One-way traffic (250 m.)* ...	120.0	—	193.0
	Entrance to tunnel (de Foug)	120.0	—	193.0
Foug	Exit from tunnel (de Foug)	121.0	—	—
	Lock (Nos. 14 and 14 bis)*	121.0	83	192.0
	Lock (No. 15). Bridge	122.0	84	191.0
	Lock (No. 16)	123.0	85	190.0
	Lock (No. 17)	123.0	86	190.0

* Twin chambers.

Distance Table

		kilom.	*lock*	*kilom.*
Ecrouves	Lock (No. 18). Bridge	124.0	87	189.0
	Lock (No. 19). Two railway bridges ...	125.0	88	188.0
	Lock (No. 20). Bridge. Port (d'Ecrouves)	126.0	89	187.0
	Lock (No. 21)	126.0	90	187.0
	Lock (No. 22). Bridge. Railway bridge ...	127.0	91	186.0
	Lock (No. 23). Lock (No. 24)	128.0	93	185.0
Toul	Lock (No. 25). Bridge. Port (de la Porte de France)	129.0	94	184.0
	Bridge (du Génie). Lock (No. 26) ...	129.0	95	184.0
	Bridge (de la Caponnière)	130.0	—	183.0
	Port (de Saint-Mansuy). Railway bridge...	130.0	—	183.0
	Lift-bridge (de Saint-Mansuy)	130.0	—	183.0
	Lock (No. 27). Bridge. Port	131.0	96	182.0
	Junction with Canal de l'Est (Southern Branch) (at K.o)	131.0	—	182.0
Condreville	Lock (No. 28). Bridge	134.0	97	179.0
Villey-St-Etienne	Lock (No. 29). Bridge. Railway bridge ...	136.0	98	177.0
	Bridge (de Villey-St-Etienne)	139.0	—	174.0
	Pont-canal (du Terrouin). Port ...	141.0	—	172.0
	Bridge (de Fresnes)	142.0	—	171.0
Liverdun	Bridge (de Vau de Moselle)	144.0	—	169.0
	Bridge (de Sous-Vignal)	146.0	—	167.0
	Waiting Port (de Sous-Vignal) ...	147.0	—	166.0
	Cutting at approach to tunnel (de Liverdun)	147.0	—	166.0
	Tunnel entrance and exit (388 m.) ...	147.0	—	166.0
	Bridge (de la Maladrerie)	148.0	—	165.0
	Port (de Liverdun). Railway bridge ...	148.0	—	165.0
	Entrance and exit to pont-canal	148.0	—	165.0
	Lock (No. 30 and 30 bis de Liverdun)* ...	148.0	99	165.0
Frouard	Two bridges. Port (de Frouard)	153.0	—	160.0
	Junction with la Moselle (canalised) (at K.o)	154.0	—	159.0
	Bridge (de Frouard)	154.0	—	159.0
Champigneulles	Port (de Champigneulles). Bridge ...	157.0	—	156.0
	Railway bridge (skew)	158.0	—	155.0
Maxéville	Bridge (de Maxéville)	160.0	—	153.0
Nancy	Bridge (des Trois-Maisons)	161.0	—	152.0
	Lift bridge (de Malzéville). Port ...	162.0	—	151.0
	Lift bridge (Sainte-Catherine)	163.0	—	150.0
	Bridge (Saint-Georges)	163.0	—	150.0
	Bridge (des Tiercelins)	163.0	—	150.0
	Bridge (de Tomblaine). Railway bridge ...	164 0	—	149.0

* Twin chambers.

Distance Table

		kilom.	lock	kilom.
Jarville	Bridge. Lock (Nos. 26 and 26 bis)* ...	166.0	100	147.0
Laneuville-d-Nancy	Port (de Laneuville-devant-Nancy) ...	168.0	—	145.0
	Junction with Canal de l'Est (Branch de Nancy). (*at K.o*) Bridge	168.0	—	145.0
	Lock (Nos. 25 and 25 bis)* ...	168.0	101	145.0
	Bridge (de la Noue)	169.0	—	144.0
	Lock (Nos. 24 and 24 bis)*. Bridge ...	171.0	102	142.0
	Port (de Saint-Phlin). Pont-canal	172.0	—	141.0
Varangéville	Bridge (called 'de la Station') ...	175.0	—	138.0
	Port (de Varangéville). Footbridge	176.0	—	137.0
	Lock (Nos. 23 and 23 bis)*. Bridge	176.0	103	137.0
Dombasle	Bridge (de Solvay). Bridge ...	178.0	—	135.0
	Lock (No. 22)	179.0	104	134.0
Sommerviller	Bridge (de Sommerviller)	180.0	—	133.0
Crévic	Bridge. Lock (No. 21)	181.0	105	132.0
	Bridge. Lock (No. 20)	182.0	106	131.0
	Bridge. Port (de Crévic)	183.0	—	130.0
Maixe	Bridge and Port (de Maixe) ...	187.0	—	126.0
	Bridge. Lock (No. 19)	187.0	107	126.0
Einville	Bridge. Lock (No. 18)	189.0	108	124.0
	Port (d'Einville)	190.0	—	123.0
	Bridge. Bridge	191.0	—	122.0
Bauzemont	Port (de Bauzement)	194.0	—	119.0
	Bridge. Lock (No. 17)	194.0	109	119.0
	Bridge	195.0	—	118.0
Hénaménil	Port and Bridge (d'Hénaménil) ...	197.0	—	116.0
	Bridge. Lock (No. 16)	198.0	110	115.0
Parroy	Bridge	200.0	—	113.0
	Port and Bridge (de Parroy) ...	201.0	—	112.0
Mouacourt	Bridge. Lock (No. 15)	202.0	111	111.0
	Port (de Mouacourt)	203.0	—	110.0
Xures	Port and Bridge (de Xures) ...	205.0	—	108.0
	Bridge. Lock (No. 14)	206.0	112	107.0
Lagarde	Bridge. Lock (No. 13)	207.0	113	106.0
	Bridge. Port (de Lagarde) ...	209.0	—	104.0
	Bridge. Lock (No. 12)	209.0	114	104.0
	Bridge	211.0	—	102.0
Maizieres-les-Vic	Bridge. Lock (No. 11)	212.0	115	101.0
	Bridge. Lock (No. 10)	215.0	116	98.0
	Port (de Moussey). Bridge ...	215.0	—	98.0
Moussey	Bridge	216.0	—	97.0
	Lock (No. 9)	217.0	117	96.0
Réchicourt-le-Château	Railway bridge. Lock (No. 8). Port	218.0	118	95.0
	Port (Saint-Blaise)	219.0	—	94.0

* Twin chambers.

Distance Table

		kilom.	lock	kilom.
	Bridge. Lock (No. 7)	219.0	119	94.0
	Bridge. (Over lower end of new lock) ..	222.0	—	91.0
	Lock (No. 1). Beginning of summit level (called 'des Vosges'). Bridge	222.0	120	91.0
	Bridge	223.0	—	90.0
Gondrexange	Port (du Lindre). Guard gate	224.0	—	89.0
	Junction with Canal des Houillères de la Sarre (at K.o)	227.0	—	86.0
	Guard gate. Bridge	229.0	—	84.0
	Bridge (des Prés). Railway bridge ...	230.0	—	83.0
	Bridge (d'Hertzing)	231.0	—	82.0
Hertzing	Port (de Héming)	232.0	—	81.0
Héming	Bridge (de Blamont). Port (de Héming) ...	232.0	—	81.0
	Bridge (de Lorquin)	233.0	—	80.0
Xouaxange	Port (de Xouaxange). Cutting (265 m.) ...	235.0	—	78.0
	Bridge (de Xouaxange)	235.0	—	78.0
Imling	Ruined bridge (called 'Haut-pont') ...	237.0	—	76.0
	Footbridge	238.0	—	75.0
Hesse	Pont-canal (de Laforge) (45 m.) ...	238.0	—	75.0
	Bridge (Pont Germain)	239.0	—	74.0
	Port (de Hesse). Bridge (du Village) ...	240.0	—	73.0
	Railway bridge. Bridge (de Charmenack)	240.0	—	73.0
	Cutting (de Hesse). *One-way traffic* (465 m.)	240.0	—	73.0
Buhl	Bridge (de Neuhof)	243.0	—	70.0
Schneckenbusch	Bridge (de Schneckenbusch)	243.0	—	70.0
	Bridge (de Brouderdoff). Bridge (de Buhl)	244.0	—	69.0
Niderviller	Port and Bridge (de Niderviller)	245.0	—	68.0
	Bridge (de Hombesch)	246.0	—	67.0
	Bridge (d'Altmulhe)	247.0	—	66.0
	Port (de Niderviller-Altmulhe). *Grouping point for formation of convoys through tunnels*	247.0	—	66.0
Hommarting	Entrance to tunnel (de Niderviller) ...	248.0	—	65.0
	Exit from tunnel (de Niderviller) ...	248.0	—	65.0
Guntzwiller	Stopping place for crossing of convoys) ...	249.0	—	64.0
Arzviller	Entrance to tunnel (d'Arzviller) ...	249.0	—	64.0
	Exit from tunnel (d'Arzviller)	251.0	—	62.0
	Grouping point for formation of convoys through tunnels	251.0	—	62.0
	*Junction with 'canal d'acces amont'** ...	251.0	—	62.0
	Lock (No. 1). *End of summit level* ...	251.0	121	62.0
	Lock (No. 2). Lock (No. 3)	252.0	123	61.0
	Bridge. Port (d'Arzviller)	252.0	—	61.0

* See footnote p. 128.

Distance Table

		kilom.	lock	kilom.
Henridorff	Lock (No. 4). Lock (No. 5). Lock (No. 6)	252.0	126	61.0
	Lock (No. 7). Lock (No. 8). Lock (No. 9)	253.0	129	60.0
	Lock (No. 10)	253.0	130	60.0
	Lock (No. 11). Lock (No. 12) Lock (No. 13)	254.0	133	59.0
	Lock (No. 14)	254.0	134	59.0
	Lock (No. 15)	255.0	135	58.0
	Inclined Plane (Plan Incliné d'Arzviller/ St. Louis)	255.0	—	58.0
	Lock (No. 16). Lock (No. 17)	255.0	—	58.0
	*Junction of 'canal d'acces aval' with main canal**	256.0	—	57.0
	Lock (No. 18). Railway viaduct. Turning basin	256.0	138	57.0
Lutzelbourg	Lock (No. 19). Bridge	256.0	139	57.0
	Lock (No. 20)	257.0	140	56.0
	Lock (No. 21). Bridge. Port	258.0	141	55.0
	Port (de Lutzelbourg). Lock (No. 22) ...	259.0	142	54.0
	Lock (No. 23)	260.0	143	53.0
	Lock (No. 24). Danne-et-Quatre-Vents ...	261.0	144	52.0
Saverne	Lock (No. 25)	262.0	145	51.0
	Lock (No. 26). Lift bridge	263.0	146	50.0
	Lock (No. 27). Footbridge. Lock (No. 28)	264.0	148	49.0
	Lock (No. 29). Bridge. Railway viaduct ...	266.0	149	47.0
	Footbridge. Bridge. Lock (Nos. 30 and 31)†	268.0	150	45.0
	Bridge. Port (de Saverne). Bridge (de l'Orangerie)	269.0	—	44.0
	Lock (No. 32). Railway bridge	270.0	151	43.0
Monswiller	Lock (No. 33). Bridge	271.0	152	42.0
Steinbourg	Lock (No. 34). Bridge. Lock (No. 35) ...	272.0	154	41.0
	Lock (No. 36). Bridge. Port (de Steinbourg)	273.0	155	40.0
Dettwiller	Port (de Dettwiller). Bridge	277.0	—	36.0
Lupstein	Lock (No. 37)	277.0	156	36.0
	Bridge. Lock (No. 38)	278.0	157	35.0
	Bridge. Lock (No. 39)	279.0	158	34.0
	Bridge	280.0	—	33.0
Ingeheim	Lock (No. 40). Bridge. Bridge	281.0	159	32.0
	Bridge. Lock (No. 41). Bridge	283.0	160	30.0
Hochfelden	Bridge. Port (de Hochfelden)	286.0	—	27.0
Mutzenhouse	Lock (No. 42). Bridge. Port. Bridge ...	288.0	161	25.0
Schwindratzheim	Lock (No. 43)	289.0	162	24.0
Waltenheim	Bridge. Port (de Waltenheim)	290.0	—	23.0
	Lock (No. 44). Bridge	290.0	163	23.0
Wingersheim	Lock (No. 45). Bridge	292.0	164	21.0

* See footnote p. 128.   † Twin chambers.

Distance Table

		kilom.	lock	kilom.
	Lock (No. 46). Bridge	294.0	165	19.0
Brumath	Bridge. Port (de Brumath)	296.0	—	17.0
	Bridge	297.0	—	16.0
Eckwersheim	Bridge. Lock (No. 47)	300.0	166	13.0
Vendenheim	Lock (No. 48). Swing bridge	301.0	167	12.0
	Railway bridge. Bridge. Port	302.0	—	11.0
	Bridge	303.0	—	10.0
Reichstett	Bridge. Lock (No. 49). Bridge	305.0	168	8.0
Souffelweyersheim	Port (de Souffelweyersheim). Lock (No. 50)	306.0	169	7.0
	Bridge. Port (des Tuileries)	307.0	—	6.0
Hoenheim	Railway bridge	307.0	—	6.0
	Bridge	308.0	—	5.0
Bischheim	Port and Bridge (de Bischheim)	309.0	—	4.0
Schiltigheim	Bridge and Port. Lock (No. 51)	310.0	170	3.0
Strasbourg	Lock (No. 52). Bridge. Bridge	311.0	171	2.0
	Bridge	312.0	—	1.0
	Junction with the 'Bassin des Remparts'			
	Port (Autonome de Strasbourg)	313.0	—	0.0

CANAL DE LA MARNE À LA SAÔNE

General

The Canal de la Marne à la Saône provides the shortest route between the *region du Nord* and the valley of la Saône. Beginning at Vitry-le-François, at the junction with the Canal de la Marne au Rhin, it finishes on the River Saône at Heuilley-sur-Saône. Heuilley-s-Saône is only 30 kilometres upstream from Saint-Jean-de-Losne (the terminal point of the Canal de Bourgogne) and slightly less from Saint-Symphorien, where the Canal du Rhône au Rhin branches off from la Saône. Taken with the River Marne and the canal latéral à la Marne, it forms the third of the great arterial waterways joining the City of Paris with the City of Lyon. The canal contains a summit level and two tunnels. The summit level, which is situated near Langres, is at a height of no less than 1,115 feet above sea level. The two tunnels mentioned above are:

(a) de Condes (308 metres) (K.105)

(b) de Balesmes (4,820 metres) (K.155).

(a) Tunnel at Condes. This is a two-way tunnel, and vessels proceed through without grouping or slowing down. There are no special regulations regarding the passage.

(b) Tunnel at Balesmes. This tunnel, which is driven at summit level, offers quite different conditions. It is the normal one-way tunnel and the times of passages are fixed in each direction by schedule. Although the actual length of the tunnel is only 4,820 metres, one-way traffic restrictions are in force for a

distance of 7,300 metres. The times of passing through the length vary with the class of traffic making the passage, but in practice:

From Marne towards Saône	From Saône towards Marne
0000 hours (midnight)	0400 to 1000* hours
1200 to 1600* hours	2000 hours

But enquiries must always be made locally at the time of the proposed passage. The lock-keepers at each end of the summit level will give information.

Tunnel de Balesmes

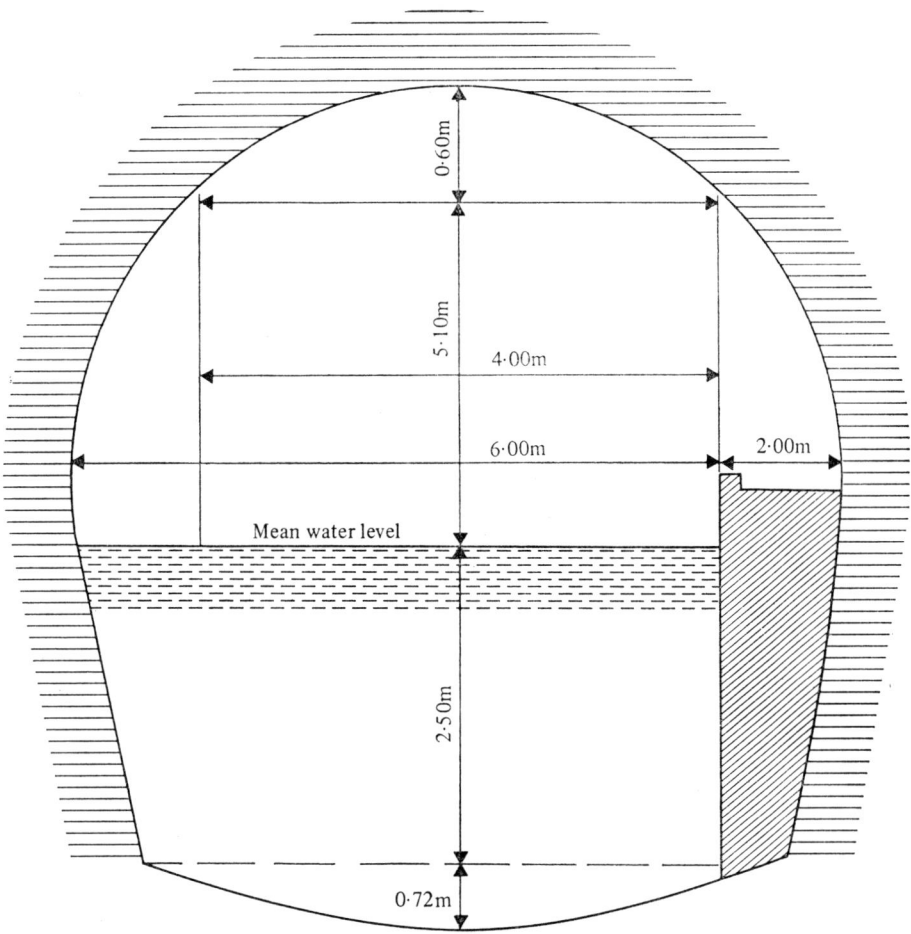

CAUTION. Live electric wires may be established throughout the length of this tunnel.

* In practice the double times of two of the departures arise from the necessity of allowing extra time for the passage depending on the number of vessels comprising the tow ('*rame*'). If the tow is a long one more time is taken in clearing the one-way section with consequent delay in starting the return journey.

Length	The length of the canal from Vitry-le-François to Heuilley-sur-Saône is 224 kilometres.
Locks	There are 114 locks, of which 71 fall towards Vitry-le-François and 43 towards Heuilley. They are of uniform size, 38 m. 30 in length with a width of 5 m. 10.
Depth	The depth of water is maintained at 2 m. 20 throughout the length of the canal.
Bridges	There are many fixed bridges, but they all have a clear headroom of 3 m. 70.
Tow-path	There is a tow-path throughout.

Distance Table

		kilom.	lock	kilom.
*Vitry-le-François**	*Junction with Canal de la Marne au Rhin (at K.0)*	0.0	—	224.0
	Port (de la Citadelle). Bridge (de St-Dizier).			
	Port (du Mont-Vierge). Railway bridge ...	0.0	—	224.0
	Lock (No. 71 de Desert). Port (du Desert)	1.0	1	223.0
Frignicourt	Port and Lock (No. 70 de Frignicourt) ...	2.0	2	222.0
Luxémont	Bridge and Footbridge	5.0	—	219.0
	Port. Bridge. Lock (No. 69 de Luxemnot)	6.0	3	218.0
Goncourt	Bridge and Port (de Goncourt)	7.0	—	217.0
Ecriennes	Bridge. Lock (No. 68 d'Ecriennes) ...	8.0	4	216.0
Matignicourt	Bridge	9.0	—	215.0
Orconte	Footbridge. Lock (No. 67 de Matignicourt)	11.0	5	213.0
	Bridge	12.0	—	212.0
	Port (d'Orconte). Bridge. Lock (No. 66 d'Orconte)	13.0	6	211.0
	Bridge	14.0	—	210.0
	Bridge. Lock (No. 65 des Bruyères) ...	15.0	7	209.0
Perthes	Bridge. Lock (No. 64 de Sapignicourt) ...	18.0	8	206.0
	Bridge. Port (de Perthes)	19.0	—	205.0
	Bridge. Lock (No. 63 de Perthes). Bridge	20.0	9	204.0
Hallignicourt	Bridge. Lock (No. 62 de la Garenne) ...	22.0	10	202.0
	Bridge. Lock (No. 61 d'Hallignicourt) ...	24.0	11	200.0
Saint-Dizier	Bridge. Lock (No. 60)	26.0	12	198.0
	Bridge. Lock (No. 59 de la Noue). Bridge	28.0	13	196.0
	Port (de la Noue)	29.0	—	195.0
	Bridge. Lock (No. 58 de Saint-Dizier) ...	30.0	14	194.0
	Bridge. Bridge	30.0	—	194.0
	Port (de Gigny). Railway bridge	31.0	—	193.0

* See Plan No. 21.

Distance Table

		kilom.	lock	kilom.
Ancerville	Lock (No. 57 de Marnaval). Lift bridge ...	34.0	15	190.0
	Bridge	35.0	—	189.0
	Railway bridge. Lock (No. 56 de Guë).			
	Port (des Hottes). Bridge	36.0	16	188.0
Chamouilley	Bridge. Port (de Chamouilley). Bridge ...	38.0	—	186.0
	Lock (No. 55 de Chamouilley). Railway			
	bridge	39.0	17	185.0
Eurville	Lock (No. 54 d'Eurville)	40.0	18	184.0
Bienville	Port (d'Eurville). Lift bridge	41.0	—	183.0
	Footbridge. Lock (No. 53 de Bienville) ...	42.0	19	182.0
	Lift bridge. *(Usually stands open)*	43.0	—	181.0
	Lift bridge (de Bras)	44.0	—	180.0
Laneuville-à-Bayard	Lock (No. 52 de Bayard)	45.0	20	179.0
	Port (de Bayard). Lift bridge	46.0	—	178.0
Gourzon	Lift bridge	47.0	—	177.0
	Bridge. Lock (No. 51 de Fontaines) ...	48.0	21	176.0
Sommeville	Lift bridge. Port (de Sommeville)	48.0	—	176.0
	Bridge	49.0	—	175.0
Chevillon	Port and Bridge (de Chevillon)	50.0	—	174.0
	Lock (No. 50 de Chevillon). Port	50.0	22	174.0
	Lock (No. 49 de Breuil)	52.0	23	172.0
Curel	Footbridge. Lock (No. 48 de Curel) ...	54.0	24	170.0
	Lift bridge. Port (de Curel)...	54.0	—	170.0
Autigny-le-Petit	Lift bridge	55.0	—	169.0
Autigny-le-Grand	Lift bridge	56.0	—	168.0
	Bridge. Lock (No. 47 d'Autigny-le-Grand)	57.0	25	167.0
Vecqueville	Railway bridge	58.0	—	166.0
Thonnance-lès-	Bridge. Lock (No. 46 de Bussy)	59.0	26	165.0
Joinville	Bridge. Port (de Thonnance)	60.0	—	164.0
Joinville	Lock (No. 45 du Rongeant)	61.0	27	163.0
	Port (de Joinville). Bridge	62.0	—	162.0
	Bridge. Lock (No. 44 de Joinville). Railway			
	bridge	63.0	28	161.0
Saint-Urbain	Footbridge. Bridge	65.0	—	159.0
	Lock (No. 43 de Bonneval)	65.0	29	159.0
	Port (de St-Urbain). Bridge	67.0	—	157.0
	Lock (No. 42 de Saint-Urbain)	67.0	30	157.0
Donjeux	Bridge	70.0	—	154.0
Mussey	Lock (No. 41 de Mussey). Lift bridge ...	70.0	31	154.0
	Port (de Donjeux). Bridge	71.0	—	153.0
	Port (de Rouvroy)	72.0	—	152.0
Rouvroy	Bridge. Lock (No. 40 de Rouvroy) ...	73.0	32	151.0
Gudmont	Bridge	73.0	—	151.0
	Railway bridge	75.0	—	149.0
	Lock (No. 39 de Gudmont). Lift bridge ...	76.0	33	148.0

Distance Table

		kilom.	lock	kilom.
	Port (de Gudmont)	76.0	—	148.0
Villiers-s-Marne	Railway bridge. Bridge	77.0	—	147.0
	Port (de Villiers). Lock (No. 38 de Villiers)	78.0	34	146.0
	Railway bridge	79.0	—	145.0
Provenchères-s-Marne	Bridge. Lock (No. 37 de Provenchères) ...	81.0	35	143.0
	Port (de Provenchères)	81.0	—	143.0
Froncles	Railway bridge	82.0	—	142.0
	Bridge. Lock (No. 36 de Froncles)... ...	84.0	36	140.0
	Port (de Froncles)	84.0	—	140.0
Buxières-lès-Froncles	Bridge and Port (de Buxières)	85.0	—	139.0
	Bridge. Lock (No. 35 de Buxières) ...	86.0	37	138.0
Vouécourt	Bridge	87.0	—	137.0
	Port (de Vouécourt). Bridge	89.0	—	135.0
	Lock (No. 34 de Vouécourt)	89.0	38	135.0
Viéville	Bridge. Lock (No. 33 de Grandvaux) ...	91.0	39	133.0
	Swing bridge. Port (de Viéville)	93.0	—	131.0
	Bridge. Lock (No. 32 de Viéville)	94.0	40	130.0
Roocourt	Bridge. Lock (No. 31 de Roocourt) ...	96.0	41	128.0
Bologne	Railway bridge	96.0	—	128.0
	Port (de Bologne). Bridge	97.0	—	127.0
	Lock (No. 30 de Bologne)	97.0	42	127.0
	Bridge. Port (de la Fenderie)	98.0	—	126.0
Riaucourt	Bridge. Lock (No. 29 de Riaucourt) ...	100.0	43	124.0
Bréthenay	Lock (No. 28 des Mouillerys)	102.0	44	122.0
	Bridge. Lift bridge. Lock (No. 27 de Bréthenay)	104.0	45	120.0
Condes	Port (de Bréthenay). Bridge	105.0	—	119.0
	Lock (No. 26 de Condes)	105.0	46	119.0
	Entrance to tunnel (de Condes) (308 m.) ...	105.0	—	119.0
	Exit from tunnel. Bridge	105.0	—	119.0
	Lift bridge	106.0	—	118.0
Chaumont	Port and Bridge (de Reclancourt)	108.0	—	116.0
	Lock (No. 25 de Reclancourt)	108.0	47	116.0
	Port (de Chaumont). Bridge	109.0	—	115.0
	Lock (No. 24 du Val des Choux)	110.0	48	114.0
Choignes	Bridge. Lock (No. 23 de Choignes) ...	111.0	49	113.0
	Port (de Choignes)	112.0	—	112.0
Chamarandes	Bridge. Lock (No. 22 de Chamarandes) ...	114.0	50	110.0
	Port (de Chamarandes)	114.0	—	110.0
	Footbridge. Lock (No. 21 du Foulon de la Roche)	116.0	51	108.0
Verbiesles	Bridge. Lock (No. 20 du Val des Ecoliers)	117.0	52	107.0
	Bridge	118.0	—	106.0
Luzy	Footbridge. Lift bridge. Port (de Luzy) ...	119.0	—	105.0
	Footbridge. Lock (No. 19 de Luzy) ...	120.0	53	104.0

Distance Table

		kilom.	lock	kilom.
	Lock (No. 18 du Pêcheux). Bridge...	122.0	54	102.0
	Bridge. Lock (No. 17 de Foulain) ...	122.0	55	102.0
Foulain	Port and Bridge (de Foulain) ...	124.0	—	100.0
Poulangy	Port (de Nogent). Bridge ...	125.0	—	99.0
	Lock (No. 16 de la Boichaulle) ...	125.0	56	99.0
	Railway bridge. Lock (No. 15 du Pré-Roche) ...	127.0	57	97.0
Marnay	Bridge. Railway bridge ...	129.0	—	95.0
	Lock (No. 14 de la Pommeraye) ...	129.0	58	95.0
	Bridge. Lock (No. 13 de Marnay) ...	131.0	59	93.0
Vesaignes	Port and Bridge (de Vesaignes) ...	132.0	—	92.0
	Lock (No. 12 de Vesaignes) ...	132.0	60	92.0
Thivet	Bridge. Lock (No. 11 de Thivet) ...	134.0	61	90.0
Rolampont	Bridge. Lock (No. 10 des Prées) ...	136.0	62	88.0
	Ports (de Rolampont). Bridge ...	138.0	—	86.0
	Bridge. Lock (No. 9 de Rolampont) ...	139.0	63	85.0
	Bridge. Lock (No. 8 de Saint-Menge) ...	140.0	63	84.0
Chanoy	Bridge. Lock (No. 7 de Chanoy) ...	142.0	65	82.0
Hûmes	Lock (No. 6 de Pouillot)	143.0	66	81.0
	Bridge. Lock (No. 5 de Hûmes). Port ...	144.0	67	80.0
Jorquenay	Bridge. Swing bridge	145.0	—	79.0
	Bridge. Lock (No. 4 de Jorquenay) ...	146.0	68	78.0
Champigny-lès-Langres	Railway bridge	147.0	—	77.0
	Bridge. Lock (No. 3 du Moulin-Rouge) ...	148.0	69	76.0
	Port (de Langres). Bridge	148.0	—	76.0
Peigney	Bridge. Lock (No. 2 du Moulin-Chapeau)	149.0	70	75.0
	Bridge	150.0	—	74.0
Chatenay-Macheron	Railway bridge	151.0	—	73.0
	Viaduct. Bridge. Lock (No. 1 des Batailles). *Beginning of summit level*	152.0	71	72.0
Corlée	Pont-tunnel	154.0	—	70.0
Balesmes	Entrance to tunnel (de Balesmes) (4,820 m). *One-way traffic*	155.0	—	69.0
Noidant-Chatenoy	Exit from tunnel	160.0	—	64.0
Heuilley-Cotton	Port (de Heuilley-Cotton). Bridge ...	161.0	—	63.0
	Bridge. Lock (No. 1). Bridge. *End of summit level*	162.0	72	62.0
Cohons	Lock (No. 2)	162.0	73	62.0
	Footbridge. Lock (No. 3). Lock (No. 4) ...	163.0	75	61.0
Heuilley-Cotton	Bridge. Lock (No. 5). Lock (No. 6) ...	164.0	77	60.0
Villegusien	Lock (No. 7). Lock (No. 8). Bridge ...	165.0	79	59.0
	Railway bridge	166.0	—	58.0
	Bridge. Port (de Villegusien) ...	167.0	—	57.0
	Bridge. Lock (No. 9 de Villegusien) ...	167.0	80	57.0
	Bridge	167.0	—	57.0

Distance Table

		kilom.	lock	kilom.
Piépape	Lock (No. 10 de Pré-Menier) ...	... 168.0	81	56.0
	Lock (No. 11 du Château). Bridge...	... 168.0	82	56.0
	Footbridge. Lock (No. 12 de Piépape)	... 169.0	83	55.0
	Bridge	... 169.0	—	55.0
Dommarien	Bridge. Lock (No. 13 de Bise l'Asaut)	... 171.0	84	53.0
	Lock (No. 14 de la Croix-Rouge) ...	... 172.0	85	52.0
	Bridge	... 172.0	—	52.0
	Bridge. Lock (No. 15 de Dommarien)	... 173.0	86	51.0
	Bridge and Port (de Dommarien)	... 173.0	—	51.0
Choilley	Footbridge. Lock (No. 16 de Choilley)	... 176.0	87	48.0
	Bridge and Port (de Choilley) ...	... 176.0	—	48.0
	Lock (No. 17 de la Foireuse) ...	... 176.0	88	48.0
	Bridge. Bridge	... 177.0	—	47.0
Dardenay	Lock (No. 18 de Dardenay) ...	... 178.0	89	46.0
	Lock (No. 19 de la Grande-Côte) ...	... 178.0	90	46.0
	Footbridge	... 178.0	—	46.0
Cusey	Lock (No. 20 de Badin). Bridge ...	... 179.0	91	45.0
	Lock (No. 21 de Montrepelle) ...	... 180.0	92	44.0
	Lock (No. 22 de Cusey). Bridge ...	... 180.0	93	44.0
	Bridge. Port (de Cusey)	... 181.0	—	43.0
Percey-le-Petit	Lock (No. 23 du Bech). Bridge ...	... 183.0	94	41.0
	Bridge. Port (de Percey-le-Petit)	... 184.0	—	40.0
Courchamp	Lock (No. 24 de Courchamp) ...	... 185.0	95	39.0
	Bridge and Port (de Courchamp) ...	... 185.0	—	39.0
	Bridge	... 186.0	—	38.0
Saint-Maurice	Lock (No. 25 de la Romagne). Bridge	... 187.0	96	37.0
	Port and Lock (No. 26 de St-Maurice)	... 188.0	97	36.0
	Bridge	... 189.0	—	35.0
	Lock (No. 27 de Lavilleneuve) ...	... 190.0	98	34.0
Lavilleneuve	Bridge and Port (de Lavilleneuve)	... 192.0	—	32.0
Pouilly	Lock (No. 28 de Pouilly). Bridge ...	... 194.0	99	30.0
Saint-Seine	Bridge	... 195.0	—	29.0
	Port (de Saint-Seine)	... 196.0	—	28.0
	Lock (No. 29 de St-Seine). Bridge ...	... 196.0	100	28.0
	Lock (No. 30 de Lalau)	... 197.0	101	27.0
	Lock (No. 31 de Fontaine-Française)	... 198.0	102	26.0
Fontaine-Française	Bridge	... 198.0	—	26.0
	Lock (No. 32 de Fontenelle). Bridge	... 199.0	103	25.0
	Bridge	... 200.0	—	24.0
Licey	Lock (No. 33 de Licey). Bridge ...	... 201.0	104	23.0
	Port (de Licey). Bridge	... 202.0	—	22.0
Dampierre	Port (de Dampierre)	... 203.0	—	21.0
	Bridge. Lock (No. 34 de Dampierre)	... 205.0	105	20.0
	Bridge	... 204.0	—	20.0
Loeuilly	Lock (No. 35 de Beaumont). Bridge	... 205.0	106	19.0

Distance Table

		kilom.	lock	kilom.
Beaumont	Port (de Beaumont)	... 205.0	—	19.0
	Bridge	... 206.0	—	18.0
Blagny	Lock (No. 36 de Blagny). Bridge ...	... 207.0	107	17.0
	Port (de Blagny)	... 208.0	—	16.0
	Lock (No. 37 de la Rochette). Bridge	... 208.0	108	16.0
	Viaduct (Railway)	... 210.0	—	14.0
Oisil	Lock (No. 38 d'Oisilly). Bridge ...	... 210.0	109	14.0
	Bridge. Port (d'Oisilly)	... 211.0	—	13.0
	Bridge. Port Bassot. Port (de la Roye)	... 212.0	—	12.0
Renève	Lock (No. 39 de Renève). Bridge ...	... 214.0	110	10.0
	Port (de Renève)	... 214.0	—	10.0
Cheuge	Lift bridge	... 215.0	—	9.0
	Bridge and Port (de Cheuge) ...	... 216.0	—	8.0
	Lock (No. 40 de Cheuge) ...	... 217.0	111	7.0
Saint-Sauveur	Lock (No. 41 de St-Sauveur) ...	... 219.0	112	5.0
	Bridge and Port (de St-Sauveur) ...	... 219.0	—	5.0
	Bridge	... 220.0	—	4.0
	Bridge	... 221.0	—	3.0
Maxilly-sur-Saône	Port (de Maxilly)	... 222.0	—	2.0
	Lock (No. 42 de Maxilly). Bridge	... 222.0	113	2.0
	Bridge. Lock (No. 43 du chemin de fer)	... 222.0	114	2.0
	Railway bridge	... 223.0	—	1.0
	Footbridge	... 224.0	—	0.0
	Junction with la Saône (at K.125)*	... 224.0	—	0.0

MAYENNE—MAINE

General

La Mayenne is navigable from the town of Mayenne to its confluence with la Loire at la Pointe in the commune de Bouchemaine. Near Angers it is joined by the River la Sarthe and from that point to its confluence with la Loire it takes the name of La Maine. The river is canalised from Mayenne to Montreuil-Belfroy, but retains its natural course from Montreuil-Belfroy to la Pointe. A secondary branch, downstream from Montreuil-Belfroy and close to the bridge at Epinard, joins this river to la Sarthe; this branch is called *la Vieille-Maine* and allows, when passing from one river to the other, a reduction in distance of some five kilometres over the route by the confluence.

Length

From the limit of navigation at Pont Mac-Racken in the town of Mayenne to the confluence with la Loire at La Pointe is a distance of 134 kilometres. The canalised length is 116 kilometres, the remaining 18 kilometres being over its natural bed.

* See plan No. 10.

Locks	Between Pont Mac-Racken and Montreuil-Belfroy there are 45 locks. The first 37 of these have a length of 31 m. 00 with a width of 5 m. 20; the other 8 locks are somewhat longer (33 m. 00) but have the same width.
Depth	The depths vary; from Pont Mac-Racken to K.85 (near Lock No. 37 de Fourmusson) the depth is 1 m. 50. From K.85 to K.122 (the confluence with la Sarthe) the depth is 1 m. 70. The depth then increases to 2 m. 00 and even to 2 m. 60 in the lower reaches of the river.
Bridges	From Pont Mac-Racken to Lock No. 21 (de Laval) all the fixed bridges give a headroom of 3 m. 50 at normal water level; the next section to the beginning of la Maine there is a clearance of 4 m. 40, and slightly more is to be found over the remainder of the waterway.
Tow-path	There is no tow-path, all the traffic being self-propelled.

Distance Table

		kilom.	*lock*	*kilom.*
Mayenne	*Beginning of the navigation.* Bridge (Pont Mac-Racken)	0.0	—	134.0
	Bridge (Notre-Dame)	0.0	—	134.0
	Lock (No. 1 de Mayenne). Port	1.0	1	133.0
Saint-Baudelle	Bridge (de Saint-Baudelle)	3.0	—	131.0
	Lock (No. 2 de Saint-Baudelle)	4.0	2	130.0
Commer	Lock (No. 3 de Grenoux)	8.0	3	126.0
	Lock (No. 4 de la Roche)	10.0	4	124.0
Martigné	Lock (No. 5 de Boussard)	11.0	5	123.0
St-Germain-d'Anxure	Lock (No. 6 de Corçu)	13.0	6	121.0
	Lock (No. 7 de Bas-Hambert). Bridge (de Montgiroux)	14.0	7	120.0
	Lock (No. 8 des Communes)	15.0	8	119.0
Sacé	Lock (No. 9 du Port)	16.0	9	118.0
Andouille	Lock (No. 10 de la Nourrière)	17.0	10	117.0
	Lock (No. 11 de la Verrerie)	18.0	11	116.0
Montflours	Lock (No. 12 de la Richardière)	19.0	12	115.0
	Lock (No. 13 de la Fourmondière) ...	20.0	13	114.0
	Bridge (de Rochefort)	20.0	—	114.0
	Lock (No. 14 de la Fourmondière inférieure)	20.0	14	114.0
	Lock (No. 15 du Moulin-Oger)	21.0	15	113.0
St-Jean-s-Mayenne	Lock (No. 16 d'Ame)	23.0	16	111 0
	Lock (No. 17 de la Maignannerie)	25.0	17	109.0
	Bridge and Port (de Saint-Jean)	26.0	—	108.0
Changé	Lock (No. 18 de Boisseau)	28.0	18	106.0
	Lock (No. 19 de Belle-Poule)	30.0	19	104.0

Distance Table

		kilom.	lock	kilom.
	Bridge (de Changé)	31.0	—	103.0
Laval	Lock (No. 20 de Bootz)	34.0	20	100.0
	Railway viaduct. Bridge (Pont Neuf) ...	34.0	—	100.0
	Port and Lock (No. 21 de Laval)	35.0	21	99.0
	Bridge (Pont Vieux)	35.0	—	99.0
	Lock (No. 22 d'Avesnières). Bridge ...	36.0	22	98.0
Huisserie	Lock (No. 23 de Cumont)	39.0	23	95.0
	Ferry (de Saint-Pierre-le-Potier) ...	39.0	—	95.0
Entrammes	Lock (No. 24 de Bonne)	43.0	24	91.0
	Lock (No. 25 de Port-Rhingeard)	44.0	25	90.0
	Bridge (d'Entrammes)	44.0	—	90.0
Nuille-s-Vicoin	Lock (No. 26 de Perisgand)	46.0	26	88.0
Origné	Lock (No. 27 de Briassé)	50.0	27	84.0
	Lock (No. 28 de la Bénâtre)	52.0	28	82.0
Villiers-Charlemagne	Lock (No. 29 de la Fosse)	54.0	29	80.0
Saint-Sulpice	Bridge and Port (de la Valette)	59.0	—	75.0
	Lock (No. 30 de la Rongère)	60.0	30	74.0
Fromentières	Lock (No. 31 de Neuville)...	63.0	31	71.0
Loigné	Lock (No. 32 de-la-Roche-de-Maine) ...	67.0	32	67.0
Bazouges	Lock (No. 33 de Mirvault)	69.0	33	65.0
Château-Gontier	Bridge (de Château-Gontier)	70.0	—	64.0
	Port (de Château-Gontier)	71.0	—	63.0
Saint-Fort	Lock (No. 34 du Pendu). (Railway viaduct)	72.0	34	62.0
	Lock (No. 35 de la Bavouze)	77.0	35	57.0
Ménil	Lock (No. 36 de Ménil)	79.0	36	55.0
Daon	Lock (No. 37 de Fourmusson)	83.0	37	51.0
	Bridge (de Daon)	84.0	—	50.0
La Jaille-Yvon	Lock (No. 38 de la Jaille-Yvon)	88.0	38	46.0
Chenillé-Changé	Lock (No. 39 de Chenillé-Changé) ...	90.0	39	44.0
Chambellay	Port and Bridge (de Chambellay)	92.0	—	42.0
	Lock (No. 40 de la Roche Chambellay) ...	94.0	40	40.0
Montreuil-s-Maine	Lock (No. 41 de Montreuil-s-Maine) ...	97.0	41	37.0
	Port (de Montreuil-s-Maine)	97.0	—	37.0
Lion-d'Angers	Bridge (de l'Aubinière)	99.0	—	35.0
Grez-Neville	*Confluence with l'Oudon*	101.0	—	33.0
	Lock (No. 42 de Grez-Neville)	103.0	42	31.0
	Port and Bridge (de Grez-Neuville) ...	103.0	—	31.0
Pruillé	Ferry (de Pruillé)	106.0	—	28.0
La Membrolle	Lock (No. 43 de la Roussière). Port ...	107.0	43	27.0
Juigné-Bené	Lock (No. 44 de Sautre)	109.0	44	25.0
	Port (Port Albert)	110.0	—	24.0
	Bridge and Port (de Juigné-Bené)	113.0	—	21.0
Montreuil-Belfroy	Lock (No. 45 de Montreuil-Belfroy) ...	116.0	45	18.0
Cantenay-Epinard	Bridge	118.0	—	16.0
Angers	*Confluence with la Vielle-Maine* ...	119.0	—	15.0

Distance Table

		kilom.	lock	kilom.
	Ferry (du Port de l'Ile)	121.0	—	13.0
	Confluence with la Sarthe (at K.131)			
	(Beginning of la Maine)	122.0	—	12.0
	Railway bridge	123.0	—	11.0
	Port (d'Angers). Quay (Félix-Faure)	124.0	—	10.0
	Bridge (de la Haute-Chaine) ...	124.0	—	10.0
	Quay (Gambetta). Quay (Monge)	125.0	—	9.0
	Bridge (Pont du Centre)	125.0	—	9.0
	Quay (des Carmes and de la Savatte)	125.0	—	9.0
	Bridge (de la Basse-Chaîne) ...	126.0	—	8.0
	Quay (du Roi de Pologne) ...	126.0	—	8.0
Bouchemaine	Railway bridge	129.0	—	5.0
	Railway bridge	132.0	—	2.0
	Bridge	132.0	—	2.0
	Confluence with la Loire (at K.0) ...	134.0	—	0.0

MEUSE

General

La Meuse has been canalised from the lock at Mouzay (about 4 kilometres south of Stenay) to the town of Visé in Belgium. That part of the canalised river which lies on French soil is officially counted as being part of the Northern Branch of the Canal d'Est, and reference should be made to that canal for further particulars.

CANAL DU MIDI

General

The Canal du Midi connects at Toulouse with the canal latéral à la Garonne and also, by a staircase of two locks, with the River Garonne. It runs in an easterly direction until it falls into l'Etang de Thau. The canal contains a tunnel and also a summit level. The summit level (K.51 to K.56) is at Ségala and the Toulouse end of it is close to the obelisk *de Riquet* (la Colonne de Narouze) erected to the memory of de Riquet who planned and cut the canal*. The tunnel, which is further eastward of Le Malpas, has a length of 161 metres and a width of 6 m. 45 at the water level. It is in fact a one-way tunnel, but no special regulations are in force concerning the passage. Its short length together with it being quite straight makes visibility adequate. There are three places on the canal where one-way traffic is enforced, namely over the pont-canal de Cesse (K.167), through the tunnel de Malpas (K.198), and in the immediate neighbourhood of Béziers (from K.202 to K.204). The Canal du Midi has a number of Branches, most of which are short and lead

* In the year 1681.

only from the canal to a point on a nearby river (la Garonne, l'Orb, etc.), so that they are of slight interest to yachtsmen. There are two, however, which are useful to pleasure craft making their way to the Mediterranean: one is called *l'embranchement de la*

Tunnel du Malpas

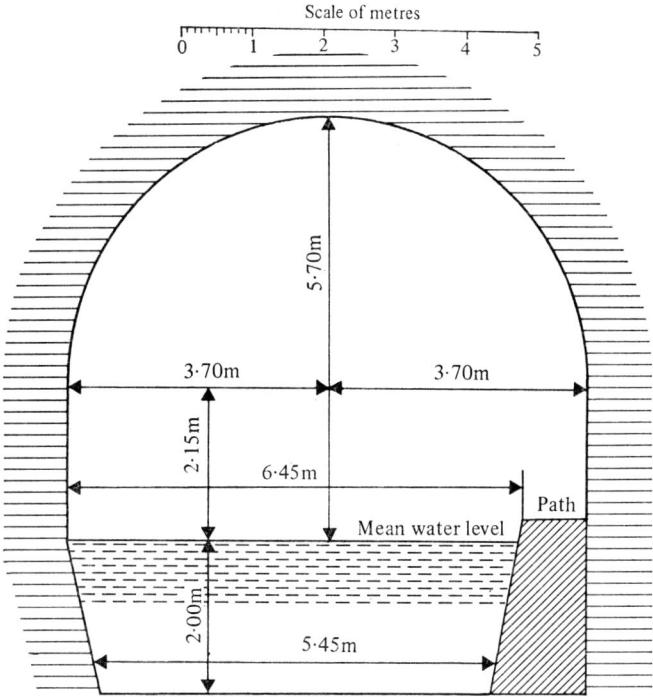

CAUTION. *Live electric wires may be established throughout the length of this tunnel.*

Nouvelle which leads from Sallèles (K.168, close to the pont-canal de Cesse) to the sea port of la Nouvelle. The other branch is Descente dans l'Hérault maritime which, by a short junction canal, leads to Port d'Agde, l'Hérault maritime and finally to la Méditerranée.

Length

The Canal du Midi has a length of 240 kilometres between Toulouse and its entrance to l'Etang de Thau.

Locks

There are in fact 101 locks of which 24 fall towards Toulouse and 77 towards l'Etang de Thau. Many of them are 'staircase' or 'riser' locks, which perhaps accounts for the rather long time required to make the passage. It may be a comfort to know that the flight of 4 locks at Castelnaudary and the flight of 7 locks at Fonserannes are worked electrically. All the locks have a width of 5 m. 50 and the length of each chamber is 30 m. 00.

147

Depth The normal depth of water is 1 m. 80 throughout.

Bridges There are many fixed bridges most of which are near the locks. All have a headroom of 3 m. 50 at the centre line but this may fall away rapidly according to the arch of the structure. This is most notable in the case of *le Pont des Demoiselles, Toulouse*, where about 3 metres from the centre of the arch no more than 1 m. 60 will be found.

Tow-path Most of the traffic using the canal is self-propelled; the tow-path is, however, in good order throughout.

Embranchement de la Nouvelle

General This *embranchement* is really made up of three waterways, *le Canal de Jonction, la traversée de l'Aude*, and *le Canal de la Robine*. The *embranchement* is, at the moment of writing (1969), still open to traffic, but as the *Canal de Jonction* and that part of the *Canal de la Robine* which lies between the River Aude and the lock at Narbonne have been declared as *déclassé* that is, taken out of service, it is quite possible that the passage will become impassable. Therefore those who may think of using this branch should first make enquiries concerning it to l'Ingénieur en Chef, Ponts et Chaussées, Service de la Navigation des Canaux du Midi, 2 port Saint-Etienne, Toulouse.

Length The length of the *Canal de Jonction* is 5 kilometres; the *traversée de l'Aude* a little over half a kilometre, and the *Canal de la Robine* about $31\frac{1}{2}$ kilometres: that is 37 kilometres in all.

Locks The two canals have 8 and 6 locks respectively. Those on *la Jonction* have a length of 29 m. 75 with a width of 5 m. 96; those on *la Robine* have a length of 30 m. 00 with a width of 5 m. 85.

Depth Both canals have a depth of water of 1 m. 80, the same as in the main route; but the depth in the river Aude is variable but normally not less than in the canals.

Bridges There is a clear headroom under all the fixed bridges of 3 m. 10.

Tow-path None.

Descente dans l'Hérault Maritime

General La descente dans l'Hérault maritime begins in l'écluse ronde d'Agde at K.231 of the Canal du Midi. On leaving the lock a junction canal is entered which is 10 m. 00 wide, and, normally has a depth of 1 m. 80. After just over half a kilometre the port d'Agde is reached and there the junction canal joins l'Hérault maritime. There is one railway bridge over the canal which allows a headroom of 4 m. 22. Further information is given under the heading Hérault maritime.

Distance Table		*kilom.*	*lock*	*kilom.*
*Toulouse**	Octagonal Port and Basin. *Junction with canal latéral à la Garonne (at K.o)*. Bridge (Pont Jumeau)	0.0	—	240.0
	Lock (du Bearnais)	1.0	I	239.0
	Staircase locks (des Minimes) (2)	2.0	3	238.0
	Bridge (des Minimes). Footbridge... ...	2.0	—	238.0
	Lock (de Matabiau)	3.0	4	237.0
	Staircase locks (de Bayard) (2)	3.0	6	237.0
	Bridge (Pont Riquet)	3.0	—	237.0
	Bridge (de Constantine). Bridges (de la Colombette) (de Guilheméry)	4.0	—	236.0
	Port (St-Etienne). Bridge (St-Sauveur) ...	5.0	—	235.0
	Port (St-Saveur). Footbridge (des Soupirs)	5.0	—	235.0
	Railway bridge. Bridge (des Demoiselles)...	6.0	—	234.0
Ramonville-St-Agne	Bridge (de Madron)	12.0	—	228.0
Castanet-Tolosan	Staircase locks (de Castanet) (2)	15.0	8	225.0
	Lock (de Vic)	17.0	9	223.0
Deyme	Bridge (de Deyme)	19.0	—	221.0
Donneville	Bridge (de Donneville)	22.0	—	218.0
Montgiscard	Staircase locks (de Montgiscard) (2) ...	24.0	11	216.0
	Bridge and Port (de Montgiscard) ...	24.0	—	216.0
	Bridge (de Baziège)	26.0	—	214.0
Aigues-Vives	Staircase locks (d'Aigues-Vives) (2) ...	28.0	13	212.0
	Staircase locks (du Sanglier) (2) ...	29.0	15	211.0
Montesquieu-Lauragais	Bridge (d'Enserny)	31.0	—	209.0
	Lock (de Négra)	33.0	16	207.0
Viellevigne	Bridge (de Viellevigne)	35.0	—	205.0
Gardouch	Bridge (de Laval)	37.0	—	203.0
	Staircase locks (de Laval) (2) ...	37.0	18	203.0
	Bridge and Lock (de Gardouch). Port ...	38.0	19	202.0
Renneville	Bridge and Lock (de Renneville)	43.0	20	197.0
Avignonet	Staircase locks (d'Encassan). (2). Bridge ...	45.0	22	195.0
	Lock (d'Emborrel)	47.0	23	193.0
	Bridge (de Maraval)	49.0	—	191.0
	Railway bridge	50.0	—	190.0
Montferrand	Lock (called 'de l'Océan'). Beginning of summit level	51.0	24	189.0
Labastide-d'Anjou	Bridge (de Ségala)	53.0	—	187.0

* See Plan No. 20.

Distance Table *kilom.* *lock* *kilom.*

									kilom.	*lock*	*kilom.*
Mas-Stes-Puelles	Lock (called 'de la Mediterranée'). End of summit level	...	...	...	...	56.0	25	184.0
	Staircase locks (du Roc) (2)		...	...	57.0	27	183.0
	Staircase locks (de Laurens) (3)	...	...	58.0	30	182.0
	Lock (de la Domergue)	...	...	...	59.0	31	181.0
	Lock (de Laplanque)	...	...	...	60.0	32	180.0
Castelnaudary	Bridge (Pont Neuf). Port. Bridge (Pont Vieux)	...	...	...	...	64.0	—	176.0
	Bridge (de Saint-Roch)	...	...	...	65.0	—	175.0
	Staircase locks (de Saint-Roch) (4)	...	65.0	36	175.0
	Staircase locks (de Gay) (2)	...	...	67.0	38	173.0
Saint-Martin	Staircase locks (du Vivier) (3)	...	...	68.0	41	172.0
	Lock (de Guilhermin)	...	...	...	69.0	42	171.0
	Lock (de Saint-Sernin). Bridge	...	69.0	43	171.0
	Lock (de Guerre). Bridge	...	...	70.0	44	170.0
	Lock (de la Peyruque). Bridge	...	71.0	45	169.0
	Lock (de la Criminelle)	...	...	72.0	46	168.0
Lasbordes	Lock (de Treboul). Bridge	...	...	73.0	47	167.0
Villepinte	Bridge (de Villepinte)	...	...	75.0	—	165.0
	Lock (de Villepinte)	...	...	...	77.0	48	163.0
Bram	Lock (de Sauzens). Bridge	...	...	79.0	49	161.0
	Lock. Port and Bridge (de Bram)	...	...	80.0	50	160.0
Alzonne	Railway bridge	...	...	...	83.0	—	157.0
Montréal	Bridge (du Diable)	...	...	...	84.0	—	156.0
	Lock (de Béteille)	...	...	...	85.0	51	155.0
Sainte-Eulalie	Bridge (de Sainte-Eulalie)	...	...	89.0	—	151.0
Villesèque	Bridge (de Villesèque)	...	...	91.0	—	149.0
Caux-et-Sauzens	Lock (de Villesèque)	...	...	93.0	52	147.0
	Bridge (de Caux-et-Sauzens)	...	...	94.0	—	146.0
Pezens	Bridge (de Rocles)	...	...	95.0	—	145.0
Carcassonne	Staircase locks (de Lalande) (2)	...	...	98.0	54	142.0
	Lock (d'Herminis). Bridge	...	...	98.0	55	142.0
	Lock (de Ladouce)	...	...	...	99.0	56	141.0
	Railway bridge	...	...	...	103.0	—	137.0
	Bridge (d'Iena). Footbridge	...	...	104.0	—	136.0
	Bridge (Pont de la Paix)	...	...	104.0	—	136.0
	Port and Lock (de Carcassonne)	...	...	105.0	57	135.0
	Railway bridge	...	...	...	105.0	—	135.0
	Lock (de Saint-Jean)	...	...	...	107.0	58	133.0
	Bridge (de Friedland)	...	...	...	108.0	—	132.0
	Pont-canal (de Fresquel)	...	...	108.0	—	132.0
	Staircase locks (de Fresquel) (2). Port	...	108.0	60	132.0
	Lock (de Fresquel)	...	...	...	109.0	61	131.0
Villemoustaussou	Bridge (de Conques)	...	...	109.0	—	131.0
	Bridge (de la Mejeanne)	...	...	110.0	—	130.0

Distance Table

			kilom.	*lock*	*kilom.*
Villedubert	Lock (de l'Evéque). Bridge	... ...	112.0	62	128.0
	Lock (de Villedubert)	... ...	113.0	63	127.0
Trèbes	Bridge (de la Rode)	... ...	116.0	—	124.0
	Pont-canal (d'Orbiel)	... ...	116.0	—	124.0
	Port and Bridge (de Trèbes)	... ...	117.0	—	123.0
	Staircase locks (de Trèbes) (3)	... ...	118.0	66	122.0
	Bridge (de Saint-Julia)	... ...	119.0	—	121.0
	Bridge (de Millepetit)	... ...	121.0	—	119.0
	Bridge (de Millegrand)	... ...	122.0	—	118.0
Marseillette	Bridge (de Marseillette)	... ...	126.0	—	114.0
	Lock (de Marseillette)	... ...	127.0	67	113.0
Blomac	Staircase locks (de Fonfile) (3)	...	130.0	70	110.0
	Staircase locks (de Saint-Martin) (2)	...	131.0	72	109.0
Puichéric	Staircase locks (de l'Aiguille) (2) ...		133.0	74	107.0
	Bridge (d'Aiguille) ...	... ...	133.0	—	107.0
	Bridge (de Rieux) ...	... ...	134.0	—	106.0
	Railway bridge	... ...	135.0	—	105.0
	Staircase locks (de Puichéric) (2) ...		136.0	76	104.0
Redorte	Bridge (Pont vieux de Redorte) ...		139.0	—	101.0
	Bridge (Pont neuf de Redorte). Port	...	140.0	—	100.0
	Bridge (de la Métaireie du Bois) ...		141.0	—	99.0
Azille	Lock (de Jouarres) ...	... ...	142.0	77	98.0
	Bridge (de Jouarres)	... ...	143.0	—	97.0
Homps	Port and Bridge (d'Homps)	...	145.0	—	95.0
	Lock (d'Homps). Bridge ...	...	146.0	78	94.0
Olonzac	Staircase locks (d'Ognon) (2)	...	147.0	80	93.0
	Lock (de Garde d'Ognon). Footbridge ...		147.0	81	93.0
	Bridge (d'Ognon) ...	... ...	147.0	—	93.0
Argens	Staircase locks (de Pechlaurier) (2)	...	149.0	83	91.0
	Bridge (d'Argens) ...	... ...	151.0	—	89.0
	Lock (d'Argens) ...	... ...	152.0	84	88.0
Roubia	Bridge and Port (de Roubia)	...	154.0	—	86.0
Paraza	Port and Bridge (de Paraza)	...	157.0	—	83.0
	Pont-canal (de Répudre) ...		158.0	—	82.0
Ventenac-d'Aude	Port and Bridge (de Ventenac)	...	160.0	—	80.0
Saint-Nazaire	Bridge (de Saint-Nazaire) ...	...	162.0	—	78.0
	Bridge (Pont Neuf). Bridge (Pont Vieux). Port (du Somail) ...	... ...	165.0	—	75.0
Sallèles	Bridge (de Truilhas). *Beginning of one-way traffic section*	...	167.0	—	73.0
	Pont-canal (de Cesse) ...	...	167.0	—	73.0
	Entrance to Canal de Jonction (beginning of Branch de la Nouvelle)		168.0	—	72.0
	End of one-way section ...	...	168.0	—	72.0
	Railway bridge ...	... ...	168.0	—	72.0

Distance Table

		kilom.	lock	kilom.
Ouveillan	Bridge (Pont Neuf d'Argelliers)	171.0	—	69.0
Argelliers	Bridge (Pont Vieux d'Argelliers). Port ...	172.0	—	68.0
Quarante	Port and Bridge (de Sériège)	176.0	—	64.0
	Bridge (de Pigasse)...	178.0	—	62.0
Capestang	Bridge (de Malvies)	180.0	—	60.0
	Bridge and Port (de Capestang). Bridge ...	188.0	—	52.0
	Bridge (de Trézilles)	191.0	—	49.0
Poilhes	Footbridge, Bridge and Port (de Poilhes)	194.0	—	46.0
	Bridge (de Régimont)	196.0	—	44.0
Colombiers	Tunnel (Percée de Malpas) (161 m.) ...	198.0	—	42.0
	Bridge (de Colombiers)	200.0	—	40.0
Béziers	*Beginning of one-way section*	202.0	—	38.0
	1st passing bay	202.75	—	37.25
	2nd passing bay	203.75	—	36.25
	End of one-way section	204.0	—	36.0
	Bridge (de Gourgasse)	204.0	—	36.0
	Bridge (Pont de Narbonne)	205.0	—	35.0
	Staircase locks (de Fonserannes) (7) ...	206.0	91	34.0
	Pont-canal (over l'Orb) (240 m.)	207.0	—	33.0
	Staircase locks (de l'Orb) (2)	208.0	93	32.0
	Port (de Béziers)	208.0	—	32.0
	Staircase locks (de Béziers) (2)	208.0	95	32.0
	Two bridges	208.0	—	32.0
	Bridge, Guard gate and Port (de Sauclière)	208.0	—	32.0
	Footbridge (Saint-Pierre)	209.0	—	31.0
	Lift bridge (Foufa). Bridge (de Capiscol)	210.0	—	30.0
Villeneuve	Lock (d'Ariège)	212.0	96	28.0
	Lock. Bridge (de Villeneuve)	213.0	97	27.0
	Bridge (Pont de Cers)	215.0	—	25.0
	Bridge (Pont de Caylus)	216.0	—	24.0
Portiragnes	Lock and Bridge (de Portiragnes) ...	218.0	98	22.0
	Bridge (de Roucaute)	221.0	—	19.0
Vias	Bridge (du Libron)...	225.0	—	15.0
	Bridge (Pont Vieux de Vias)	226.0	—	14.0
	Bridge (Pont Neuf de Vias)	229.0	—	11.0
	Railway bridge	229.0	—	11.0
Adge	Bridge	229.0	—	11.0
	Port and Bridge (d'Agde)	231.0	—	9.0
	Lock ('écluse ronde') (three-way) ...	231.0	99	9.0
	Origine de la descente dans l'Hérault			
	maritime	231.0	—	9.0
	Junction with l'Hérault	232.0	—	8.0
	Re-entry into Canal du Midi	233.0	—	7.0
	Lock (de Prades)	233.0	100	7.0
	Bridge (de Prades)	233.0	—	7.0

Distance Table		*kilom.*	*lock*	*kilom.*
	Bridge (de Saint-Bauzille)	234.0	—	6.0
	Lock (du Bagnas)	235.0	101	5.0
Marseillan	Bridge (des Onglous)	238.0	—	2.0
	Port (des Onglous)	239.0	—	1.0
	Junction with Etang de Thau	240.0	—	0.0

Embranchement de la Nouvelle Canal de Jonction

Cesse	*Beginning of Canal de Jonction (at K.168 Canal du Midi)*	0.0	—	5.0
	Footbridge. Port. Lock (de Cesse) ...	0.0	1	5.0
	Lock (de Truilhas). Bridge	0.0	2	5.0
	Lock (d'Empare)	1.0	3	4.0
	Lock (d'Argelliers). Bridge	2.0	4	3.0
	Lock (de Saint-Cyr)	2.0	5	3.0
Sallèles	Footbridge and Port (de Salleles) ...	3.0	—	2.0
	Staircase locks (de Sallèles) (2)	3.0	7	2.0
	Bridge (de Sallèles)	3.0	—	2.0
	Lock (de Gailhousty). Bridge	4.0	8	1.0
	End of Canal de Jonction. Descent into River Aude	5.0	—	0.0

Traversée de l'Aude

Sallèles	*End of Canal de Jonction*	0.0	—	0.6
Moussan	Upstream end of navigable channel ...	0.1	—	0.5
	Railway bridge	0.3	—	0.3
	Downstream end of navigable channel ...	0.6	—	0.0
	Entrance to Canal de la Robine	0.6	—	0.0

Canal de la Robine

Moussan	Junction with River Aude	0.0	—	31.0
	Bridge and Lock (de Moussoulens) ...	0.0	1	31.0
	Bridge (Pont Vieux de Moussoulens) ...	0.0	—	31.0
Narbonne	Lock (du Raonel). Bridge	4.0	2	27.0
	Lock and Footbridge (de Gua)	8.0	3	23.0
	Footbridge. Port (de Narbonne)	8.0	—	23.0
	Footbridge. Port	8.0	—	23.0
	Footbridge. Port. Railway bridge ...	9.0	—	22.0
	Bridge (de l'Escoute). Bridge (de la Concorde)	9.0	—	22.0
	Bridge (Pont Voltaire). Lock (de Narbonne)	9.0	4	22.0
	Bridge (des Marchands). Footbridge ...	9.0	—	22.0
	Bridge (Ste-Catherine). 4 Footbridges ...	10.0	—	21.0
	Bridge	10.0	—	21.0
	Footbridge	11.0	—	20.0

Distance Table

		kilom.	lock	kilom.
	Lock, Bridge and Port (de Mandirac) ...	18.0	5	13.0
	Port (de Gruissan)	19.0	—	12.0
La Nouvelle	Lock (de Sainte-Lucie)	28.0	6	3.0
	Port (de Sainte-Lucie)	29.0	—	2.0
	Railway bridge. Footbridge (de La Nouvelle)	31.0	—	0.0
	Junction with the marine channel and Port of La Nouvelle	31.0	—	0.0

Descente dans l'Hérault Maritime

		kilom.	lock	kilom.
Agde	Ecluse ronde. *Origine de descente dans l'Hérault maritime* (at K.231 Canal du Midi)	0.0	(99)	0.5
	Railway bridge	0.3	—	0.2
	Junction with l'Hérault maritime	0.5	—	0.0
	Port d'Agde	0.5	—	0.0

MIGNON

General The canalised part of le Mignon, which is properly known as *Canal du Mignon*, is navigable for shoal draught vessels from Mauzé to its confluence with la Sèvre-Niortaise in the commune of La Ronde (K.34). This canal is also sometimes referred to as *le Canal du Grand Marais*; it is little frequented and what freight is carried is mostly agricultural produce. The conditions found on it are similar to those obtaining on la *Sèvre-Niortaise*.

Length The distance from Mauzé to its confluence with la Sèvre-Niortaise is 17 kilometres.

Locks There are 4 locks which have a length of 31 m. 50 with a width of 5 m. 20.

Depth Between Mauzé and the confluence the normal depth of water is 1 m. 20, but this falls during times of low water to 0 m. 60 near the lock at Chaban.

Bridges The fixed bridges have a minimum headroom of 3 m. 30 above the normal water level.

Tow-path There is a tow-path throughout with a natural earth surface.

Distance Table

		kilom.	lock	kilom.
Mauzé	Port (de Mauzé). *Head of navigation* ...	0.0	—	17.0
Cram-Chaban	Bridge (de Moulin-Neuf)	1.0	—	16.0

Distance Table

					kilom.	lock	kilom.
Prin-Deyrancon	Lock (No. 1 de Chaban) ...	...		...	2.0	I	15.0
	Port (de Chaban) ...	...	...	...	3.0	—	14.0
St-Hilaire-la-Palud	Footbridge ...	...	...	...	4.0	—	13.0
	Lock (No. 2 de Sazay)	...	...	...	5.0	2	12.0
	Port (des Gueux) ...	...	...	...	7.0	—	11.0
	Railway bridge	...	...	...	8.0	—	9.0
Grève-s-le-Mignon	Bridge (de la Grève-s-le-Mignon)		...		8.0	—	9.0
	Lock (No. 3 de la Grève-s-le-Mignon)		...		9.0	3	8.0
La Ronde	Lock (No. 4 de Bazoin) ...	...	...		17.0	4	0.0
	Confluence with la Sèvre-Niortaise (at K.34) ...	...	...	...	17.0	—	0.0

CANAL DE MONS À CONDÉ

General — The Canal de Mons à Condé leaves l'Escaut at Condé and finishes just northward of the town of Mons at its junction with the Canal du Centre*. The greater part of the canal lies on Belgian soil and only a small part of it is in France.

Length — The canal has a length of 25 kilometres, but 20 kilometres is in Belgium, leaving only 5 kilometres on the French side. The official distances are counted as from Mons towards Condé (that is downstream); this method has been retained here, but the zero has been set at the frontier instead of at Mons.

Locks — There are 2 locks on French ground out of a total of 7, the remainder being in Belgium. Both locks have a length of 38 m. 50 with a width of 5 m. 10. The fall is from Mons towards Condé.

Depth — The ruling depth is at the lift bridge de Saint-Aybert (K.0), close to which there is a shoal patch of 2 m. 00; the remainder is somewhat deeper over the French length, namely 2 m. 50.

Bridges — The fixed bridges have a headroom of at least 3 m. 70 above the normal water level.

Tow-path — A tow-path is provided throughout, and towing is by electric trolley tractors and is obligatory for all vessels which are not self-propelled.

Distance Table

					kilom.	lock	kilom.
Belgian Frontier	*Beginning of French section of Canal de Mons à Condé* ...	...	...	...	0.0	—	5.0
Saint-Aybert	Lift bridge (de Saint-Aybert)	...	...		0.0	—	5.0
Thivencelles	Lock (No. 6 de Thivencelles)	...		...	2.0	I	3.0

* See *The Inland Waterways of Belgium*, Imray Laurie Norie & Wilson.

Distance Table

					kilom.	*lock*	*kilom.*
Condé-sur-Escaut	Footbridge (du Marais)	...	...	...	4.0	—	1.0
	Port and Customs Office (de Condé)		...		5.0	—	0.0
	Lock (No. 7 de Goeulzin)		...	...	5.0	2	0.0
	Lift bridge (de Goeulzin) ...		...	...	5.0	—	0.0
	Junction with l'Escaut (at K.46) ...		...	...	5.0	—	0.0

CANAL DE MONTBÉLIARD À LA HAUTE-SAÔNE*

General

The Canal de Montbéliard à la Haute-Saône was projected to form a link between the Canal du Rhône au Rhin at Montbéliard and la Haute-Saône at Conflandey, which lies a few kilometres northward from Port-sur-Saône. This project has not yet been completed and the work is, at present, in abeyance. A short length is, however, open to navigation from Montbéliard and particulars of this part are as follows:

Length

A length of 9.8 kilometres, from the junction with the Canal du Rhône au Rhin (at K.171) to the Port de Botans, which is private, is all that is now used by the inland water transport.

Locks

There are 5 locks in the 9.8 kilometres. The minimum length is 38 m. 00, width 5 m. 20.

Depth

Throughout the 9.8 kilometres the depth is not less than 2 m. 00.

Bridges

The fixed bridges have a headroom of 3 m. 70 above the normal water level.

Distance Table

The approximate distances and numbers of locks over the 9.8 Km. between Allenjoie and Port Privé de Botans are the same as in the Distance Table for Embranchement de Belfort on page 212.

MOSELLE CANALISÉE

General

Prior to the 1939-45 war, the canalised part of the River Moselle extended from Frouard (where it joined le Canal de la Marne au

---

* See *L'Embranchement de Belfort*, pp. 204 and 212.

Rhin) to Metz. In Metz a second section running from Metz to Thionville was in operation under the name of *le Canal des Mines de fer de la Moselle*, the working and revenue of that section having been conceded to a Société of that name, who were empowered to levy tolls and dues. Below Thionville the river was in its natural state, which made the navigation especially difficult, and at times impossible even to those who possessed extensive local knowledge. Within the last few years the lower reaches of the river from Thionville to Coblence have been improved and canalised by a joint venture of the French and German governments. Concurrently, the section between Metz and Thionville was also brought up to the higher standard of the Thionville-Coblence length by the French government, the concession to la Société du Canal des Mines de fer de la Moselle having run out; thus the whole of the canalised river is now under government authority. Only a short length of the river below Thionville lies on French soil, after which it forms the frontier between Luxembourg and Germany; continuing through Germany, it eventually falls into le Rhin at Coblence. The present state of the river between Metz and Coblence is now capable of taking vessels of 1,350 tons and 'pusher-trains' of more than 3,000 tons.

The trace now in use of la Moselle canalisée is located sometimes along the natural bed of the river, at other times along *dérivations* made to ease or cut off severe bends. The process has been carried so far that about two-thirds of the waterway is now on an artificial bed. This has led to the building of a number of 'guard gates' *(portes de garde)* to protect the heads of the deviations during times of flood. When going downstream, la dérivation d'Ars-sur-Moselle (K.39.5) branches off to the left from the main stream and joins it again at K.42.0. This deviation forms the main route for the traffic going towards Thionville and Coblence. Vessels that are bound for Metz keep to the river at the fork (K.39.5) and continue as far as K.40.6; this short length is known as *la rivière de Moselle d'Ancy à Jouy-aux-Arches*. At K.40.6 the route to Metz leaves the river to follow l'Embranchement de Jouy à Metz. Access to the main Frouard-Thionville-Coblence route may be made at two points from l'Embranchement de Jouy à Metz: the first is at K.1.5 (of l'Embranchement) to join the main route at K.42.1; the second is from Metz, on the downstream side of l'écluse de l'Esplanade along a branch (called *bras navigable de la Moselle*) to join with the main route at K.49.2. During periods of flood the navigation presents some difficulty before the guard gates are closed, but notices are shown at all the locks and guard gates giving the height of the water on the lower side of the barrages. Certain police notices, applicable to the situation, are also shown at the locks.

Length   From the junction with le Canal de la Marne au Rhin at Frouard to

157

the German frontier near the lock and barrage d'Apach, the distance is 106 kilometres. This is made up thus:

			kilom.
(a)	l'ancien tronçon de la Moselle canalisée	...	49.24
(b)	l'ancien Canal des Mines de fer ...	... ...	29.10
(c)	Thionville to French-German frontier ...	...	27.50
			———
			105.84

In this book the *kilométrage* is taken from the junction with le Canal de la Marne au Rhin continuously downstream to the Franco-German frontier. But there is another measurement called *le nouveau kilométrage*, which is calculated from the confluence with le Rhin at Coblence upstream towards Metz. This gives the frontier as K.242.22 and l'écluse de Thionville as K.269.72 and l'écluse de Metz-nord as K.297.87.

Locks

There are 17 locks along the main route. From Frouard to Arnaville (K.33) the locks have a length of 39 m. 60 with a width of 6 m. 00. The locks at Novéant (K.35), Ars-s-Moselle (K.41) and de Vaux (K.43) are all being reconstructed to conform with the standard of *grand gabarit*. These locks are expected to be put into service during 1970. The remaining locks downstream are up to the standard with a length of 176 m. 00 and a width of 12 m. 00. A number of the locks are now electrically controlled.

Depth

The normal depth of water from Frouard to K.45 (near the bridge at Moulins-lès-Metz) is 2 m. 60; from that point to the frontier the depth is 2 m. 90 throughout. But as the work of improvement goes on, the depth is being increased accordingly.

Bridges

Similarly, the fixed bridges between Frouard and about Metz have a headroom of 3 m. 70 at normal water level, and over the remaining length the headroom of the fixed bridges under the same conditions is 6 m. 33. As the improvement works go on, the headroom under the bridges will be raised to the standard.

Tow-path

As far as Thionville there is a tow-path.

Distance Table

		kilom.	lock	kilom.
Frouard	*Junction with Canal de la Marne au Rhin* (at K.155)			
	Lock (Nos. 1 and 2 de Frouard)	0.0	1	106.0
Bouxières	Railway bridge. Lock (No. 3 de Clévant)	0.0	2	106.0
	Bridge (de Ban-la-Dame)	1.0	—	105.0
Pompey	Guard gate Beginning of deviation (R.B.)	3.0	—	103.0

Distance Table

		kilom.	lock	kilom.
	Bridge. Port (de Custines)	3.0	—	103.0
	Railway bridge. Bridge	3.0	—	103.0
Marbache	Lock (No. 4 de Custines). End of deviation	4.0	3	102.0
Millery	Guard gate. Deviation (de Millery) (R.B.)	7.0	—	99.0
	Bridge (de Millery)	7.0	—	99.0
Belleville	Bridge (Pont Drouet)	8.0	—	98.0
	Bridge (des Paquis)	9.0	—	97.0
	Port (de Belleville). Bridge (du Grand-Gravier)	9.0	—	97.0
	Lock (No. 5 de Belleville). End of deviation	10.0	4	96.0
Liégeot	Guard gate. Deviation (de Liégeot) (R.B.)	11.0	—	95.0
	Bridge (de Liégeot)	12.0	—	94.0
Dieulouard	Bridge (de la Croix-St-Nicolas)	12.0	—	94.0
	Bridge (de Scarponne). Pont-canal ...	13.0	—	93.0
	Skew bridge (de la Centrale thermique E D F)	15.0	—	91.0
Blénod-lès-Pont-à-Mousson	Lock (No. 6 de Blénod)	16.0	5	90.0
	Bridge (Pont d'Avioux)	18.0	—	88.0
Pont-à-Mousson	Pont-canal	18.0	—	88.0
	Port (de Pont-à-Mousson)	19.0	—	87.0
	Lock (No. 7 de Pont-à-Mousson) ...	19.0	6	87.0
	End of deviation	20.0	—	86.0
	Bridge	20.0	—	86.0
	Guard gate. Beginning of deviation (R.B.)	21.0	—	85.0
	Guard gate	22.0	—	84.0
	Guard gate (de Norroy)	23.0	—	83.0
	Bridge (de Norroy)	24.0	—	82.0
	Pont-canal	25.0	—	81.0
Vandières	Bridge (de Vandières). Bridge (Pont Chécohée)	26.0	—	80.0
	Bridge (de la Haie Mettée)	27.0	—	79.0
Pagny-s-Moselle	Bridge (Pont Navut). Pont-canal. Bridge (Pont Abreuvoir)	29.0	—	77.0
	Lock (No. 8 de Pagny)	31.0	7	75.0
Arnaville	Bridge (d'Arnaville)	32.0	—	74.0
	Pont-canal. Lock (No. 9 d'Arnaville) ...	33.0	8	73.0
Novéant	Bridge. Port (de Novéant)	34.0	—	72.0
	Lock No. 10 (de Novéant). End of deviation. Bridge	35.0	9	71.0

Riviere de Moselle d'Ancy à Jouy-aux-Arches (R.B.)

Ancy-s-Moselle	*Junction with la dérivation d'Ars* (L.B.) ...	39.5	—	66.3
Jouy-aux-Arches	*Junction with Branch de Jouy* (at K.0.0) (R.B.)	40.6	—	—

R.B. = Right Bank.   L.B. = Left Bank.

159

Distance Table

		kilom.	lock	kilom.
Ancy-s-Moselle	Beginning of deviation d'Ars-s-Moselle (L.B.)	39.5	—	66.3
Ars-s-Moselle	Guard gate. Bridge	40.0	—	66.0
Jouy-aux-Arches	Lock (No. 11 d'Ars-sur-Moselle)	41.0	10	65.0
	Two Railway bridges	42.0	—	64.0
	Beginning of deviation de Vaux (R.B.) ...	43.0	—	63.0
Vaux	Lock (No. 12 de Vaux)	43.0	11	63.0
	End of deviation de Vaux	44.0	—	62.0
Moulins-lès-Metz	Bridge	45.0	—	61.0
Montigny	Railway bridge (Pont-Rouge). Bridge (Pont Jaune)	47.0	—	59.0
Ban-St-Martin	Bridge (Pont du Sauvage)	49.0	—	57.0
	Junction with le bras navigable de la Moselle (at K.10.4) (R.B.). Guard gate (de Wadrineau). Barrage (de Wadrineau) in river ...	49.2	—	56.6
	Bridge	50.0	—	56.0
Metz	Lock (No. 1 de Metz-nord). Bridge. (K.297.9)*	51.0	12	55.0
	Railway bridge	52.0	—	54.0
Argancy	Beginning of deviation Argancy-Orne† (R.B.). Guard gate (d'Argancy)	60.0	—	46.0
Hauconcourt	Bridge (d'Amelange)	61.0	—	45.0
	Bridge	63.0	—	43.0
Talange	Lock (No. 2 de Talange)	64.0	13	42.0
	Bridge. Bridge (deck dismantled)	66.0	—	40.0
	Overhead cable	67.0	—	39.0
Mondelange	Bridge	68.0	—	38.0
	Lock (No. 3 de l'Orne)	70.0	14	36.0
Guenange	End of deviation Argancy-Orne*	71.0	—	35.0
	Bridge (auto-route Metz-Thionville) ...	72.0	—	34.0
	Overhead gas main. Bridge	72.0	—	34.0
Bertrange	Overhead gas main	74.0	—	32.0
	Guard gate (d'Uckange)	75.0	—	31.0
Illange	Port (de Thionville-Illange)	76.0	—	30.0
Thionville	Lock (No. 4 de Thionville). (K.269.72)† ...	78.3	15	27.5
	Railway bridge	80.0	—	26.0
	Bridge (des Allies)	80.0	—	26.0
	Railway bridge	81.0	—	25.0
Basse-Yutz	Outfall of *canal des fortifications** ...	81.0	—	25.0
Basse-Ham	Confluence with la Kiesel* (L.B.) ...	85.0	—	21.0
Cattenom	Confluence with la Bibiche* (R.B.) ...	87.0	—	19.0
Konigesmaker	Upstream pierhead at deviation 'de Konigsmaker' (R.B.)	89.0	—	17.0

† Not described.   * Measurement *le nouveau kilométrage.*   R.B. = Right Bank.   L.B. = Left Bank.

Distance Table

		kilom.	lock	kilom.
	Lock (de Koenigsmaker) (K.258.0)† ...	90.0	16	16.0
	Downstream pierhead at end of deviation	90.5	—	15.3
Gavisse	Confluence with la Boler* (L.B.)	94.2	—	11.6
Berg-s-Moselle	Beginning of deviation de Malling (R.B.)	94.9	—	10.9
	End of deviation	95.4	—	10.4
Haute-Contz	Confluence with l'Altbach*	99.6	—	6.2
Contz-les-Bains	Bridge (de Sierck à Contz)	101.3	—	4.5
	Frontier (Grand-Duché du Luxembourg) (L.B.)	104.8	—	1.0
	Lock and barrage (d'Apach). Customs Office	105.6	17	0.2
	French-German Frontier (R.B.)	105.8	—	0.0

MOSELLE CANALISÉE BRANCHES

General

As before mentioned, the main route is duplicated between K.39.50 and K.49.24. The first part of the duplication is not counted as a branch, as it is a short length of the main river which is known as 'la Rivière de Moselle d'Ancy à Jouy-aux-Arches' (K.39.50-K.40.60). The **First Branch** begins at the end of the above short length (K.40.60) under the name of l'Embranchement de Jouy à Metz: it takes off from the right bank of the river and runs north-eastwards to Metz. It contains two locks, both of which are near the downstream end. Immediately below the second lock, the **Second Branch** (called le Bras navigable de la Moselle) makes junction with the end of the first branch. This second branch, which is quite short, leads back to the main route, which it joins at K.49.24. Thus the total length of the duplication is:

				kilom.
(a)	la Rivière de Moselle d'Ancy à Jouy-aux-Arches			1.10‡
(b)	l'Embranchement de Jouy à Metz	...	...	8.68
(c)	le Bras navigable de la Moselle ...	...	...	1.68
				11.46

Throughout the duplication, the depth is 2 m. 20 and the headroom under the fixed bridges not less than 3 m. 70 when the water level is at its normal height. The locks have a length of 39 m. 00 with a width of 6 m. 00.

* Not described.   † Measurement *le nouveau kilométrage*.   R.B. = Right Bank.   L.B. = Left Bank.
‡ See p. 159.

(b)   L'Embranchement de Jouy à Metz

Distance Table		kilom.	lock	kilom.
Jouy-aux-Arches	*Junction with la Rivière de Moselle d'Ancy à Jouy-aux-Arches (at K.1.10)*	0.0	—	8.7
	Guard gate	0.2	—	8.5
	Port (de la Goudronnerie de Jouy-aux-Arches)	1.2	—	7.5
	La Fourche (the divide); left fork leads to main route at K.42.1. Old lock (de la Polka) out of service	1.5	—	7.2
	Bridge (de la Polka)	1.6	—	7.1
	Railway bridge	2.2	—	6.5
Moulins-lès-Metz	Bridge (de Tournebride)	3.5	—	5.2
	Bridge	4.5	—	4.2
Montigny-lès-Metz	Bridge (de la 'Station hydraulique') ...	5.6	—	3.1
	Railway bridge	5.7	—	3.0
	Bridge (de la rue des Couvents) ...	6.9	—	1.8
Metz	Port (du Vieux Canal)	8.0	—	0.7
	Bridge (de la rue Saint-Symphorien) ...	8.1	—	0.6
	Bridge (du chemin du Port)	8.3	—	0.4
	Lock (de la Citadelle)	8.5	1	0.2
	Lock (de l'Esplanade). Bridge	8.6	2	0.1
	End of l'Embranchement. *Junction with le Bras navigable de la Moselle at (K.0.0)* ...	8.7	—	0.0

(c)   Le Bras navigable de la Moselle

Metz	*Junction with l'Embranchement de Jouy à Metz (at K.8.7)*	0.0	—	1.7
Longeville-lès-Metz	Bridge (du Champ de courses)	0.1	—	1.6
	End of bras de Montigny	0.2	—	1.5
	Barrage de Wadrinau (across the river R.B.). *Junction with la Moselle canalisée (at K.49.24)*	1.7	—	0.0

CANAL DE NANTES À BREST

General   The Canal de Nantes à Brest in former times began in the city of Nantes and ended in the town of Châteaulin, where it joined the River Aulne; l'Aulne falls in la Rade de Brest and thus the communication between Nantes and Brest was completed. But now, owing to the construction of a hydro-electric power station, the navigation is cut at Guerlédan (in the commune de Mur de Bretagne, Côtes du Nord) and through traffic is no longer possible. The canal still provides a through waterway between the English Channel and the

Bay of Biscay via the River la Vilaine. There are three possible routes by which to enter the bay from this canal. They are:

(a) by entering la Vilaine maritime through l'écluse des Bellions* at K.88 and so to the sea at Tréhiguier. This is the shortest way.

(b) by joining la Loire at Nantes and so down that river to the sea. This is the most usual route.

(c) by turning north-west, if coming from Rennes, when this canal is reached at Redon and continuing, to make junction with le Canal du Blavet at K.205; thence down le Canal du Blavet to the sea at Hennebont.

The route via la Vilaine maritime is, as mentioned, the shortest, but it must be remembered that downstream of l'écluse des Bellions the river is tidal, so that it is very necessary to pay attention to the state of the tides.

The most usual course is by way of Nantes, for the city provides a convenient base with good facilities for refit or repairs that may be desirable before entering the sea. By far the longest, but also the most interesting, is to turn north-west at Redon and make for the town of Pontivy, where the Canal du Blavet, which leads to the sea at Hennebont, may be entered. But in any case, those amateur voyagers who propose to explore the rivers and canals of Brittany are advised to get a copy of the excellent nautical guide-book (written in English) *The Canals of Brittany.*†

Length	That part of the canal which remains open to navigation has a length of 227 kilometres.
Locks	There are in all 120 locks. Of these, the first 18, between la Loire and the junction with la Vilaine (Commune de St-Nicolas-de-Redon) have a length of 26 m. 50 with a width of 4 m. 70. Lock No. 17 (les Bellions), however, is not on the main route, but leads down into the River Vilaine maritime from the canal, and for this reason it is not counted in the Distance Table. The remaining 102 locks are a little smaller, being 25 m. 70 in length and 4 m. 65 in width.
Depth	The water level is regulated to give a depth of 1 m. 60, but it may fall to 1 m. 30 at the Lock de Quihiex (K.21) during times of exceptional drought.
Bridges	There are a number of fixed bridges. From Nantes to Redon a headroom of not less than 3 m. 90 can be counted upon, but after Redon (K.95) no more than 3 m. 15 should be allowed.

* See p. 272.   † Issued by the Touring Club de France, 178 Piccadilly, London W.1.

		kilom.	lock	kilom.
Tow-path	There is no tow-path along the canal between Nantes and Quiheix, but beyond that point there is a path which can be used. But most of the traffic is by self-propelled vessels.			

Distance Table

		kilom.	lock	kilom.
Nantes	*Junction with la Loire*	0.0	—	227.0
	Lock (No. 1 Saint-Felix). Entrance to tunnel (800 m.)	0.0	1	227.0
	Exit from tunnel. Bridge (St-Mihiel) ...	1.0	—	226.0
	Bridge (du Général de La Motte-Rouge)	2.0	—	225.0
	Bridge (de la Tortière)	3.0	—	224.0
	Port (de la Jonnelière)	5.0	—	222.0
La Chapelle	Railway bridge	5.0	—	222.0
Carquefou	Port (de La Chapelle). La Grimaudière ...	9.0	—	218.0
	Port (le Port Breton)	10.0	—	217.0
Sucé	Port and Bridge (de Sucé)	15.0	—	212.0
Nort-sur-Erdre	Lock (No. 2 de Quiheix)	21.0	2	206.0
	Bridge (de la Blanchetière)	23.0	—	204.0
	Railway bridge	23.0	—	204.0
	Bridge (de Vive-Eve)	25.0	—	202.0
	Lock (No. 3 de la Tindière)	26.0	3	201.0
	Bridge (du Plessis)	27.0	—	200.0
	Bridge (du Rocher). Lock (No. 4 de la Rabinière)	28.0	4	199.0
	Lock (No. 5 de la Maie Pacoret) ...	29.0	5	198.0
	Lock (No. 6 de Cramezeul)	30.0	6	197.0
	Bridge (Pont Rouziou)	30.0	—	197.0
Héric	Lock (No. 7 du Pas-d'Héric). Beginning of summit level	32.0	7	195.0
Saffré	Bridge (des Coudrais)	32.0	—	195.0
	Port (de Coudrais)	33.0	—	194.0
	Bridge (de Saffré)	35.0	—	192.0
Héric	Bridge (de Bout-de-Bois). Port	38.0	—	189.0
	Bridge (de la Remaudais)	39.0	—	188.0
	Lock (No. 8 de la Remaudais). End of summit level	40.0	8	187.0
	Bridge (de la Chevalleraie). Port ...	42.0	—	185.0
	Bridge (du Gué de l'Atelier)	43.0	—	184.0
	Lock (No. 9 de Gué de l'Atelier) ...	43.0	9	184.0
Blain	Lock (No. 10 du Terrier). Bridge ...	45.0	10	182.0
	Lock (No. 11 de Blain)	48.0	11	179.0
	Port (de Blain)	50.0	—	177.0
	Bridge (de la Croix Rouge). Railway bridge	50.0	—	177.0
	Lock (No. 12 de La Paudais)	51.0	12	176.0
	Port and Lock (No. 13) (de Bougard) ...	56.0	13	171.0
	Bridge (de Bougard)	56.0	—	171.0

Distance Table

		kilom.	*lock*	*kilom.*
	Port and Lock (No. 14) (de Barel) ...	59.0	14	168.0
Guenrouet	Bridge (de Barel)	59.0	—	168.0
	Lock (No. 15 de La Touche)	61.0	15	166.0
	Bridge and Port (de Pont-Nozay) ...	63.0	—	164.0
	Lock (No. 16 de Melneuf)	65.0	16	162.0
	Bridge (de Melneuf)	66.0	—	161.0
Plessé	Bridge and Port (de Saint-Clair)	72.0	—	155.0
Fégréac	Bridge (de la Catée)	81.0	—	146.0
	Port and Bridge (de Pont-Miny)	83.0	—	144.0
	Railway bridge and Bridge (de Trouhel)...	85.0	—	142.0
	Bridge (de Saint-Jacques)	88.0	—	139.0
	Lock (No. 17 des Bellions). (Not on main route, leads to la Vilaine maritime) ...	88.0	—	139.0
St-Nicolas-de-Redon	Bridge (Pont du Verger)	90.0	—	137.0
	Bridge (Pont du Tertre)	91.0	—	136.0
	Bridge (de Quinssignac)	92.0	—	135.0
	Bridge (de St-Nicolas-de-Redon)	93.0	—	134.0
	Port (de St-Nicolas-de-Redon)	94.0	—	133.0
	Port (de la Digue)	94.0	—	133.0
	Lock (No. 17 bis Ecluse d'Isac)	94.0	17	133.0
	Lock (No. 18 de Redon). *Crossing of la Vilaine. Junction with La Vilaine (at K.89)*	94.0	18	133.0
	Railway bridge (swing)	95.0	—	132.0
	Suspension bridge (de la Guichaudais) ...	95.0	—	132.0
	Bridge (de Codilo). Railway bridge ...	96.0	—	131.0
	Bridge (de Courée)	97.0	—	130.0
	Bridge (de La Marionnette)	99.0	—	128.0
Bains-sur-Oust	Suspension bridge (de La Potinais) ...	101.0	—	126.0
St-Vincent-d'Oust	Lock (No. 19 de La Maclais)	105.0	19	122.0
	Bridge (de la Prévotaie)	107.0	—	120.0
	Bridge (de Bilaire)	108.0	—	119.0
Fougerets	Lock (No. 20 de Limure)	109.0	20	118.0
	Port (de Pont-d'Oust) *(landing stage)* ...	112.0	—	115.0
	Bridge (de Pont-d'Oust)	112.0	—	115.0
Saint-Gravé	Lock (No. 21 du Gueslin)	116.0	21	111.0
	Bridge (Pont du Gueslin) *(landing stage)*	117.0	—	110.0
Saint-Congard	Lock (No. 22 de Rieux)	120.0	22	107.0
	Landing stage (du Port-d'Oust)	122.0	—	105.0
Saint-Laurent	Lock (No. 23 de Beaumont)	125.0	23	102.0
Missiriac	Lock (No. 24 de Foveno)	129.0	24	98.0
Malestroit	Bridge (Pont Neuf de Malestroit) ...	132.0	—	95.0
	Bridge (Pont Aristide-Briand)	132.0	—	95.0
	Lock (No. 25 de Malestroit)	132.0	25	95.0
Saint-Marcel	Lock (No. 26 de Lanée)	134.0	26	93.0
	Lock (No. 27 de Lanée). Bridge	135.0	27	92.0

Distance Table

		kilom.	lock	kilom.
Roc-Saint-André	Lock (No. 28 de La Ville-aux-Fruglins) ... 139.0		28	88.0
	Bridge (du Roc-Saint-André) 140.0		—	87.0
	Railway bridge (des Hungleux) 141.0		—	86.0
Montertelot	Lock (No. 29 de Montertelot). Bridge.			
	Port 143.0		29	84.0
Ploermel	Railway bridge (des Deux-Rivières) ... 145.0		—	82.0
Guillac	Lock (No. 30 de Blon) 146.0		30	81.0
Saint-Servant	Lock (No. 31 de Guillac) 148.0		31	79.0
	Lock (No. 32 de Carmenai) 152.0		32	75.0
	Bridge (de Saint-Gobrien) 153.0		—	74.0
	Lock (No. 33 de Clan) 154.0		33	73.0
Guégon	Railway bridge 155.0		—	72.0
	Lock (No. 34 de St-Jouan). Bridge ... 155.0		34	72.0
Josselin	Lock (No. 35 de Josselin). Bridge. Port ... 157.0		35	70.0
	Lock (No. 36 de Beaufort) 158.0		36	69.0
	Lock (No. 37 de Caradec). Bridge ... 159.0		37	68.0
Guégon	Lock (No. 38 de Rouvray) 161.0		38	66.0
	Lock (No. 39 de Bocneuf) 163.0		39	64.0
	Bridge (de Bocneuf) 164.0		—	63.0
Lanoué	Lock (No. 40 de Pommeleuc) 165.0		40	62.0
	Lock (No. 41 de La Tertraie). Bridge ... 165.0		41	62.0
Pleugriffet	Lock (No. 42 de La Tertraie). Bridge ... 167.0		42	60.0
	Lock (No. 43 de Cadoret). Bridge ... 169.0		43	58.0
	Lock (No. 44 du Lié) 170.0		44	57.0
Bréhan-Loudéac	Bridge (Pont Perrin) 172.0		—	55.0
	Lock (No. 45 de Griffet). Bridge ... 172.0		45	55.0
Pleugriffet	Lock (No. 46 de La Grenouillère) ... 173.0		46	54.0
	Lock (No. 47 de Trévérend). Bridge ... 174.0		47	53.0
Bréhan-Loudéac	Lock (No. 48 de Penhouët). Bridge ... 175.0		48	52.0
	Lock (No. 49 de Lille). Bridge 176.0		49	51.0
	Lock (No. 50 de Thymadeuc). Bridge ... 178.0		50	49.0
Saint-Samson	Lock (No. 51 de Quengo) 180.0		51	47.0
Rohan	Lock (No. 52 de Rohan). Bridge. Port ... 181.0		52	46.0
	Port (de Rohan). Bridge (Pont Notre-Dame) 181.0		—	46.0
	Bridge (Pont d'Oust) 181.0		—	46.0
Saint-Gouvry	Lock (No. 53 de St-Samson). Bridge ... 183.0		53	44.0
Gueltas	Port. Lock (No. 54 du Guer). Bridge ... 184.0		54	43.0
	Lock (No. 55 de Coëtprat). Bridge ... 185.0		55	42.0
	Lock (No. 56 de Kermelin). Bridge ... 186.0		56	41.0
	Lock (No. 57 de La Sablière) 187.0		57	40.0
	Lock (No. 58 de Kériffe) 187.0		58	40.0
	Lock (No. 59 de Boju). Bridge. Port ... 187.0		59	40.0
	Lock (No. 60 du Parc-Coh) 187.0		60	40.0
	Lock (No. 61 du Goiffre) 188.0		61	39.0

Distance Table

		kilom.	lock	kilom.
	Lock (No. 62 de Goirball)	188.0	62	39.0
	Lock (No. 63 de Guernogas) ...	188.0	63	39.0
	Lock (No. 64 de Branguilly) ...	189.0	64	38.0
	Lock (No. 65 de La Neau-Blanche) ...	189.0	65	38.0
	Lock (No. 66 du Pont-Terre) ...	189.0	66	38.0
	Lock (No. 67 de La Forêt). Bridge ...	189.0	67	38.0
	Lock (No. 68 de Menn-Merle) ...	189.0	68	38.0
	Lock (No. 69 de Toulhouët) ...	189.0	69	38.0
	Lock (No. 70 de La Ville-Perro) ...	190.0	70	37.0
	Lock (No. 71 de Le Gouvly) ...	190.0	71	37.0
	Lock (No. 72). Bridge	190.0	72	37.0
Saint-Gonnery	Lock (No. 73 de Kervezo) ...	190.0	73	37.0
	Lock (No. 74 du Douaran) ...	190.0	74	37.0
	Lock (No. 75 du Grand-Pré) ...	190.0	75	37.0
	Lock (No. 76 d'Hilvern). Bridge ...	191.0	76	36.0
	Lock (No. 77 de la Pépinière) ...	191.0	77	36.0
	Lock (No. 78 de Bel-Air). *Beginning of summit level*	191.0	78	36.0
Saint-Gerand	Bridge (Pont du Brou)	194.0	—	33.0
	Landing stage (de Saint-Gérand) ...	195.0	—	32.0
	End of summit level. Lock (No. 79 de Kéroret). Bridge	196.0	79	31.0
	Lock (No. 80 d'er Houët)	196.0	80	31.0
	Lock (No. 81 de Kérivy)	196.0	81	31.0
	Lock (No. 82 de Parc er Lann) ...	196.0	82	31.0
	Lock (No. 83 de Kerihoué) ...	196.0	83	31.0
	Lock (No. 84 de Parc Lann Bihan) ...	196.0	84	31.0
	Lock (No. 85 de Lann Vras) ...	197.0	85	30.0
	Lock (No. 86 de Parc Buisson) ...	197.0	86	30.0
	Lock (No. 87). Bridge (Pont Le Couëdic)	197.0	87	30.0
	Bridge (de Kergouet)	198.0	—	29.0
	Railway bridge	199.0	—	28.0
Neulliac	Bridge (de Saint-Caradec)	199.0	—	28.0
	Lock (No. 88 de Joli-Coeur) ...	199.0	88	28.0
	Lock (No. 89 de Parc-Lann-Hir) ...	199.0	89	28.0
	Lock (No. 90 de Parc-Lann-Egro) ...	199.0	90	28.0
	Lock (No. 91 de Parc-Bihan) ...	200.0	91	27.0
	Lock (No. 92 de Kerponer) ...	200.0	92	27.0
	Lock (No. 93 de Restériard) ...	200.0	93	27.0
	Lock (No. 94 de Tri-parc-lann-favilette)...	200.0	94	27.0
	Lock (No. 95 de Parc-bras) ...	200.0	95	27.0
	Lock (No. 96 du Ros). Bridge ...	200.0	96	27.0
	Lock (No. 97 de Guerlaunay) ...	200.0	97	27.0
	Lock (No. 98 de Bohumet) ...	201.0	98	26.0
	Lock (No. 99 de Kervégan). Bridge ...	201.0	99	26.0

Distance Table | | *kilom.* | *lock* | *kilom.*

Noyal-Pontivy	Lock (No. 100 de Tren-deur-ros) ... 201.0	100	26.0
	Lock (No. 101 de Kerveno) 202.0	101	25.0
	Lock (No. 102 de Parc-Lann-hoarem) ... 202.0	102	25.0
	Lock (No. 103 de La Haie). Bridge ... 203.0	103	24.0
Pontivy	Lock (No. 104 de La Ville-Neuve) ... 203.0	104	24.0
	Lock (No. 105 de Kerdudaval) 204.0	105	23 0
	Lock (No. 106 de Kervert) 205.0	106	22.0
	Lock (No. 107 du Ponteau). Bridge ... 205.0	107	22.0
	Junction with Canal du Blavet (at K.o).		
	Bridge 205.0	—	22.0
	Bridge 205.0	—	22.0
	Lock (No. 108 de La Cascade) 207.0	108	20.0
Neulliac	Lock (No. 109 de Guernal) 209.0	109	18.0
Cléguérec	Lock (No. 110 de Porzo). Port 212.0	110	15.0
	Bridge (de Lenvos) 213.0	—	14.0
	Lock (No. 111 de Trescleff) 214.0	111	13.0
	Lock (No. 112 d'Auquinian) 216.0	112	11.0
	Lock (No. 113 de Stumo). Bridge ... 218.0	113	9.0
Saint-Aignan	Lock (No. 114 de Boloré). Bridge ... 220.0	114	7.0
Mur-de-Bretagne	Lock (No. 115 de St-Samson) 222.0	115	5.0
	Lock (No. 116 de Poulhibet). Bridge ... 222.0	116	5.0
	Lock (No. 117 de Kergoric). Bridge ... 223.0	117	4.0
	Lock (No. 118 de Quénécan). Bridge ... 224.0	118	3.0
	Lock (No. 119 de Guerlédan). Bridge ... 226.0	119	1.0
	Barrage (de Guerlédan). *End of navigation* 227.0	—	0.0

CANAL DE NEUFFOSSÉ

General

The Canal de Neuffossé begins at the town of Aire and ends at Saint-Omer. It thus joins the River Lys and the Canal d'Aire to the River Aa. At one time the canal passed through the town of Saint-Omer, but a number of years ago that part which passed through the town was by-passed by a new cut between K.14 and K.19, which joined the River Aa at K.2 of that river. The old part of the canal thus by-passed was renamed *Ancien Canal d'Arques à Saint-Omer*. A great deal of work has lately been completed on the whole length of the canal, in order to bring it up to the standard of the other parts of the improved waterway known as *Liaison Dunkerque-Valenciennes*.

Length

The length of the main route is now 19 kilometres; the *Ancien Canal d'Arques à St-Omer* has a length of just over 3 kilometres.

Locks

The canal has now only 2 locks, and these have similar dimensions. Each has a single chamber 144 m. 60 in length with a width of

12 m. 00. The *Ancien Canal* contains 2 locks, l'écluse Carrée and l'écluse St-Bertin, both have single chambers 38 m. 70 in length and 5 m. 19 in width. L'écluse Carrée is a 'feeder lock'.

Depth The depth along the main route is now 3 m. 50 throughout. That along the *Ancien Canal* is unchanged at 2 m. 20.

Bridges All the fixed bridges across the main canal have been raised, to give a headroom of 5 m. 25; along the *Ancien Canal* they remain at 4 m. 50.

Tow-path There is a tow-path throughout.

Distance Table

		kilom.	lock	kilom.
Aire	*Junction with la Lys (at K.0) and Canal d'Aire (at K.40).* Quay (d'Aire)	0.0	—	19.0
	Footbridge (de la Ville d'Hazebrouck) ...	0.0	—	19.0
	Quay (de Garlinghem)	1.0	—	18.0
Wittes	Bridge (de Garlinghem)	2.0	—	17.0
Blaringhem	Bridge (de Blaringhem)	5.0	—	14.0
Wardrecques	Quay (de Wardrecques)	8.0	—	11.0
	Bridge (Pont d'Asquin)	8.0	—	11.0
Campagne	Bridge (de Campagne)	10.0	—	9.0
Arques	Quay (des Fontinettes). Lock (Ecluse des Fontinettes)	13.0	—	6.0
	Quay (d'Arques)	13.0	—	6.0
	Bridge (Pont de Flandres)	14.0	—	5.0
	Junction with 'Ancien Canal d'Arques à Saint-Omer'	14.0	—	5.0
	Lock (Ecluse de Flandres)	14.0	2	5.0
	Railway bridge (de Malhove)	15.0	—	4.0
*Saint-Omer**	Bridge	17.0	—	2.0
	Quay (de St-Omer)	17.0	—	2.0
	Bridge (Pont du Doulague)	18.0	—	1.0
	Junction with l'Aa (at K.2)	19.0	—	0.0

Ancien Canal d'Arques à Saint-Omer

Arques	*Junction with Canal de Neuffossé*	0.0	—	3.0
	Lift bridge (on lock)	0.0	—	3.0
	Lock (Ecluse Carrée)	0.0	1	3.0
Saint-Omer	Lock (Ecluse Saint-Bertin)	2.0	2	1.0
	Port (de St-Omer). Bridge (de la Gare) ...	3.0	—	0.0
	Junction with l'Aa	3.0	—	0.0

* See Plan No. 18.

CANAL DU NIVERNAIS

General

The Canal du Nivernais may be termed a 'link canal', as it forms a cross route between two of the main waterways that join Paris to Lyon, namely le Bourbonnais and la Bourgogne. It begins upstream of the barrage of Decize at Saint-Léger-des-Vignes, where the River Aron flows into la Loire. By a channel cut in the bed of la Loire, it communicates with the canal latéral à la Loire through the spurway called the Branch to Decize*. The Canal du Nivernais ends at Auxerre, where it joins the canalised River Yonne which lies on the Bourgogne route. The canal will only accommodate small vessels between Cercy-la-Tour (K.15) and Champ-Cadoux (K.73), as some of the locks are not up to standard either in length or width. Nevertheless, in spite of the canal being only of the third category, it is well worth a visit, as it runs through a most pleasant part of France. But it is not for those who are in a hurry. Until recently, this waterway was falling into a bad state and much encumbered with weeds, but clearance and repairs are now in hand and it is hoped that this interesting navigation will take on a new lease of life now that Monsieur P. Zivy's S.A.I.N.T. Line hire cruisers have a base at Baye. In a number of places the canal utilises the bed of the river alongside which it is running; l'Aron is so used in three such places, and l'Yonne contributes fifteen more. These sections are termed *râcles*, and when passing along them it is essential to adhere closely to the channel which does not extend to a width of more than 20 metres from the tow-path bank. The canal also contains one summit level, two 'pont-canaux', three tunnels and a river crossing. The summit level is at K.65 to K.70 and is nearly 900 feet above sea level; it is close to Collancelle (which is some 10 kilometres from Corbigny) at the southern end of the Lake of Baye. It is here that three tunnels are encountered, which are:

(1) de la Collancelle (758 m.)
(2) de Mouas (268 m.)
(3) des Breuilles (212 m.).

They have a headroom of 3 m. 75 with a width of 5 m. 60. An obligatory towage service is in force throughout the summit level for all vessels which are not self-propelled and two trips are made each way during the day. Other vessels may pass along under their own power, but only at such times as the official in charge of traffic gives them the 'all clear' to proceed.

At Basseville (K.118) the canal crosses the River Yonne at right-angles and at the same level; as a consequence, in times of flood such vessels experience a strong cross current. However, there is a cable and a winch by means of which the crossing is assisted. The

* See also under La Loire, p. 108.

canal has only one branch—the branch to Vermenton—which leaves the main canal at *la Râcle du Maunoir* (K.154). It serves the Port d'Accolay and the Port de Vermenton.

Length

Between Saint-Leger-des-Vignes and the Pont Paul Bert at Auxerre the distance by canal is 174 kilometres. The branch to Vermenton is 3.9 kilometres in length.

Tunnel de la Collancelle

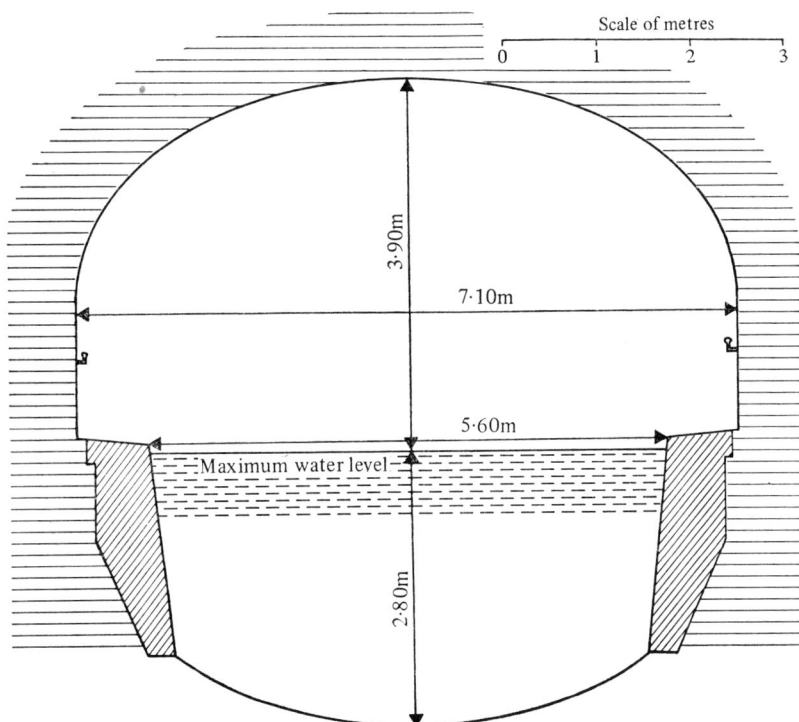

Note: The three tunnels, La Collancelle, Mouas and Les Brevilles all have approximately the same profile.

Locks

There are 114 locks, of which 4 are 'guard' locks; 32 locks and 3 guard locks fall towards la Loire, and the remaining 78 locks and 1 guard lock towards Auxerre (called *vers la Seine*). The first 5 locks from St-Léger have a length of 38 m. 50 with a width of 5 m. 20; of the locks which follow to the summit level and beyond as far as Sardy-lès-Epiry, some are only 30 m. 15 in length with a width of 5 m. 10. From that point to Auxerre the remaining locks are of the larger dimensions (38 m. 50 by 5 m. 20). There are 2 locks on the branch to Vermenton, each 38 m. 50 by 5 m. 20.

Depth

From St. Léger to Port de La Copine (K.3) the canal carries a depth of 2 m. 00, but from thence to Lock No. 15 de Champ Cadoux

171

(K.73) the depth is, normally, not more than 1 m. 60. From Champ Cadoux (Commune de Sardy-lès-Epiry) to the junction with l'Yonne the depth is 2 m. 00. The branch at Vermenton at normal water level has a depth of 2 m. 00.

Bridges

From St. Léger to Port de La Copine (K.3) there is a fixed bridge with a headroom of 3 m. 70 at normal water level. Onwards, the headroom under the fixed bridges at normal water level is 2 m. 70 as far as K.73 (de Champ Cadoux). Beyond that point the fixed bridges have a headroom of 3 m. 10, except the bridge over the upstream end of the Lock No. 21 (l'écluse de Picampoix) under which there is only 2 m. 97. The fixed bridges on the branch to Vermenton have a headroom of 3 m. 35.

Tow-path

There is a good tow-path throughout the length of the canal.

Distance Table

		kilom.	lock	kilom.
St-Léger-des-Vignes	*Junction with la Loire and the canal latéral à la Loire.* Port (de St-Léger-des-Vignes)...	0.0	—	174.0
	Lock (No. 35 de Loire)	0.0	1	174.0
	Port (de St-Thibault). Bridge (de St-Thibault)	1.0	—	173.0
	Port (des Vignots). Lock (No. 34 de Vauzelles). Bridge	1.0	2	173.0
Champvert	Bridge (de la Copine). Railway bridge ...	2.0	—	172.0
	Port (de la Copine). Bridge (du Port) ...	3.0	—	171.0
	Port (de Champvert). Lock (No. 33 de Champvert). Bridge	4.0	3	170.0
	Abutment of footbridge	6.0	—	168.0
	Bridge (de Marcou)	7.0	—	167.0
	Lock (No. 32 de Roche)	8.0	4	166.0
	Port-canal (de Roche) over l'Andarge. Bridge (de Roche)	8.0	—	166.0
Verneuil	Bridge and Port (de St-Gervais)	9.0	—	165.0
Cercy-la-Tour	Bridge (de Vernizy)	12.0	—	162.0
	Bridge (de la Coulangette)	13.0	—	161.0
	Lock (No. 31 de garde de Cercy-la-Tour). Bridge	15.0	5	159.0
	Overflow barrage (de La Canne-Pertuis) ...	15.0	—	159.0
	Râcle (de Cercy-la-Tour). Port (de Cercy-la-Tour)	15.0	—	159.0
	Lock (No. 30 de Cercy-la-Tour). Bridge ...	15.0	6	159.0
	Bridge (de Martigny)	17.0	—	157.0
St-Gratien-Savigny	Lock (No. 29 de Chaumigny). Bridge ...	18.0	7	156.0
	Bridge (de St-Gratien)	20.0	—	154.0

Distance Table

		kilom.	*lock*	*kilom.*
Isenay	Lift bridge (de Tremblay). Port (de Tremblay)	20.0	—	154.0
	Port (d'Isenay). Lock (No. 28 d'Isenay). Bridge	21.0	8	153.0
	Abutments of lift bridge	22.0	—	152.0
	Port (de Moulin d'Isenay). Lock (No. 27 du Moulin d'Isenay). Bridge	23.0	9	151.0
	Bridge (de Baudin)	24.0	—	150.0
	Bridge (des Hâtes de Scia). Port (des Hâtes de Scia)	26.0	—	148.0
	Lock (No. 26 de Sauzay). Bridge	27.0	10	147.0
	... ...	28.0	—	146.0
Limanton	Port (des Sarrots). Lock (No. 25 de garde de Pannecot). Bridge. Port (de Pannecot)	29.0	11	145.0
	Overflow barrage (d'Aron). *Râcle* (de Limanton)	29.0	—	145.0
	Lock (No. 24 d'Anizy)	30.0	12	144.0
	Bridge (d'Anizy)	31.0	—	143.0
	Lock (No. 23 de la Saigne)	32.0	13	142.0
	Port and Bridge (du Magny)	33.0	—	141.0
Brinay	Bridge (de la Prairie)	34.0	—	140.0
Biches	Port (de Bernay). Lock (No. 22 de Bernay). Bridge	36.0	14	138.0
	Port (de Fleury)	37.0	—	137.0
	Mobile barrage (de Fleury sur l'Aron). Aqueduc	38.0	—	136.0
	Lock (No. 21 de Fleury). Lock (No. 20 de Brienne)	38.0	16	136.0
	Port (de Pré Aillon)	39.0	—	135.0
	Lock (No. 19 de Villard). Bridge	40.0	17	134.0
	Bridge and Port (de Romenay). Bridge (du Cray)	41.0	—	133.0
	Lock (No. 18 de Meulot). Bridge	42.0	18	132.0
Alluy	Lock (No. 17 d'Eguilly)	45.0	19	129.0
	Bridge (d'Eguilly)	46.0	—	128.0
	Port and Bridge (de Pont)	47.0	—	127.0
Châtillon-en-Bazois	Lock (No. 16 de garde de Coeuillon). Bridge	49.0	20	125.0
	Overflow barrage (sur l'Aron de Coeullon). *Râcle* (de Chatillon-en-Bazois)	49.0	—	125.0
	Port (de Chatillon-en-Bazois)	50.0	—	124.0
	Lock (No. 15 de Chatillon-en-Bazois) ...	50.0	21	124.0
	Lock (No. 14 de Chatillon-en-Bazois). Bridge	51.0	22	123.0
	Bridge (de Mingot). Lock (No. 13 de			

Distance Table

		kilom.	lock	kilom.
	Mingot). Pont-canal (de Mingot) ...	53.0	23	121.0
	Port (de Mingot). Lock (No. 12 d'Orgue). Bridge	54.0	24	120.0
Mont-et-Marré	... ...	55.0	—	119.0
	Lock (No. 11 d'Orgue). Port (de Mont-et-Marré)	56.0	25	118.0
	Staircase Lock (Nos. 10 and 9 de Mont-et-Marré)	57.0	27	117.0
Achun	Staircase Lock (Nos. 8 and 7 de Chavance). Port	59.0	29	115.0
	Staircase Lock (Nos. 6, 5 and 4 de Chavance). Bridge	59.0	32	115.0
Bazolles	... ...	60.0	—	114.0
	Bridge (de Mougny)	61.0	—	113.0
	Port (de Bazolles). Lock (No. 3 de Bazolles). Bridge Basin. Lock (No. 2 de Bazolles)	64.0	34	111.0
	Lock (No. 1 de Baye). Bridge. *Beginning of summit level*	65.0	35	109.0
	Port (de Baye).* Bridge (des Poujats) ...	66.0	—	108.0
La Collancelle	Tunnel (de La Collancelle). (758 m.) ...	67.0	—	107.0
	Tunnel (de Mouas) (268 m.) ...	68.0	—	106.0
	Tunnel (des Breuilles) (212 m.) ...	68.0	—	106.0
	Bridge (des Breuilles)	69.0	—	105.0
La Collancelle	Bridge (de Port-Brûlé). *End of summit level*	70.0	—	104.0
	Lock (No. 1 de Port-Brûlé). Lock (No. 2 de Crain)	70.0	37	104.0
	Lock (No. 3 de Patureau). Lock (No. 4 de la Roche)	70.0	39	104.0
	Lock (No. 5 de Demain)	70.0	40	104.0
	Lock (No. 6 de la Planche de Belin). Bridge	71.0	41	103.0
	Lock (No. 7 de Gros Bouillon)	71.0	42	103.0
	Lock (No. 8 de Mondain). Lock (No. 9 de Fussy)	71.0	44	103.0
	Port (de Fussy). Lock (No. 10 de Patureau-Volain)	71.0	45	103.0
Sardy-lès Epiry	Lock (No. 11 de Bellevue)	72.0	46	102.0
	Lock (No. 12 de Pré Doven). Lock (No. 13 du Doyen)	72.0	48	102.0
	Lock (No. 14 de Pré Ardent)	72.0	49	102.0
	Lock (No. 15 de Champ Cadoux) ...	73.0	50	101.0
	Lock (No. 16 de Sardy). Bridge. Port ...	73.0	51	101.0
	Lock (No. 17 du Champs du Chêne) ...	74.0	52	100.0
	Lock (No. 18 du Creuzet). Bridge ...	74.0	53	100.0

* S.A.I.N.T. Line Cruisers have a base here.

Distance Table

		kilom.	*lock*	*kilom.*
	Lock (No. 19 de la Petite Corvée)	75.0	54	99.0
	Lock (No. 20 du Bois des Taureaux) ...	75.0	55	99.0
	Lock (No. 21 de Picampoix). Bridge *(head-room 2 m. 97)*	76.0	56	98.0
	Lock (No. 22 de Surpaillis)	76.0	57	98.0
	Lock (No. 23 du Pré Colas). Lock (No. 24 d'Yonne)	77.0	59	97.0
	Bridge. Port (de La Chaise)	77.0	—	97.0
Pazy	Tranchée (de La Chaise). (1300 m.). *One-way traffic*	78.0	—	96.0
	Guard gates (de La Chaise). Pont-aqueduc	78.0	—	96.0
	Bridge (de La Chaise)	78.0	—	96.0
Chaumot	Bridge (d'Eugny). Staircase lock (Nos. 25 and 26 d'Eugny)	79.0	61	95.0
	Lock (No. 27 de Marcy). Port (de Marcy)	80.0	62	94.0
	Lock (No. 28 de Chaumot). Port (de Chitry)	81.0	63	93.0
	Bridge (de Chitry)	81.0	—	93.0
	Port (de Chaumot). Lift bridge (de Germenay)	82.0	—	92.0
Marigny-s-Yonne	Lock (No. 29 de Chitry). Port (de Marigny)	83.0	64	91.0
	Lock (No. 30 de Marigny). Lock (No. 31 du Gravier)	84.0	66	90.0
	Turning basin. Lock (No. 32 des Mortes)...	85.0	67	89.0
	Railway bridge (des Mortes). Lift bridge (de Chazel)	86.0	—	88.0
Dirol	Lock (No. 33 du Mont). Bridge	88.0	68	86.0
	Lock (No. 34 de Dirol). Bridge	89.0	69	85.0
	Lift bridge (de Thoury). Lift bridge (des Marais)	89.0	—	85.0
	Port (de Dirol)	89.0	—	85.0
	One-way traffic for 2 km. (with passing places)	90.0	—	84.0
	Port (de Monceaux-le-Comte). Bridge (de Monceaux)	90.0	—	84.0
St-Didier	Lock (No. 35 de Chatillon)...	92.0	70	82.0
	Lock (No. 36 de Laporte). Lock (No. 37 de Moulin Brûlé)	93.0	72	81.0
	Lift bridge (de St-Didier)	94.0	—	80.0
Tannay	Lift bridge (de Curiot). Port (de Cuzy). Bridge	95.0	—	79.0
	Bridge (de Gravelot)	96.0	—	78.0
	Staircase lock (Nos. 38 and 39 de Tannay). Bridge	98.0	74	76.0
Amazy	Lift bridge (de l'Ane)	99.0	—	75.0

Distance Table

		kilom.	lock	kilom.
Asnois	Bridge (d'Asnois)	100.0	—	74.0
Villiers-s-Yonne	Lock (No. 40 de Brèves). Bridge (de Brèves)	102.0	75	72.0
	Port (de Brèves). Lock (No. 41 de l'Esselier)	102.0	76	72.0
	One-way traffic for 200 metres	103.0	—	71.0
	Lock (No. 42 de Villiers). Bridge (de Villiers)	104.0	77	70.0
	Port (de Villiers-s-Yonne). Swing bridge ...	105.0	—	69.0
	Lock (No. 43 de Cuncy). Bridge	106.0	78	68.0
	Port (de Cuncy). Bridge (de Cuncy) ...	107.0	—	67.0
Chevroches	Port (de la Goulotte)	108.0	—	66.0
	Lock (No. 44 de Chantenot). Bridge ...	109.0	79	65.0
	Bridge and Port (de Chevroches)	110.0	—	64.0
	Lock (No. 45 d'Armes)	110.0	80	64.0
	Port (d'Armes). Port (de la Maladrerie) ...	111.0	—	63.0
	Lock (No. 46 de la Maladrerie)	111.0	81	63.0
	Guard gate (de la Maladrerie). *Connection with l'Yonne (not canalised).* Râcle (de Clamecy)	111.0	—	63.0
Clamecy	Bridge (Pont Picot). Port (de la Rue de Chevroches)	112.0	—	62.0
	Swing bridge on upstream end of Lock (No. 47)	113.0	—	61.0
	Lock (No. 47 de Clamecy). *Descent into l'Yonne (canalised)*	113.0	82	61.0
	Bridge (de Bethléem)	113.0	—	61.0
	Port (St-Roch). Lock (No. 47 *bis* de Clamecy-St-Roch)	114.0	83	60.0
	Ascent to the canal in le bief No. 48 ...	114.0	—	60.0
	Branch to Port of St-Roch. Turning basin	114.0	—	60.0
Surgy	Lock (No. 48 de la Forêt). Bridge	115.0	84	59.0
	Guard gate (de la Forêt). *Connection with le bief No. 49 with l'Yonne (canalised).* Râcle (de Clamecy)	116.0	—	58.0
	Bridge (de Presles)	116.0	—	58.0
	Lock (No. 49 de la Garenne). Bridge (d'Envilliers)	117.0	85	57.0
Pousseaux	Lock (No. 50 de Basseville)	118.0	86	56.0
	Crossing of l'Yonne (at equal level). Movable barrage	118.0	—	56.0
	Lock (No. 51 de garde de Basseville) ...	118.0	87	56.0
	Bridge (de Basseville)	119.0	—	55.0
	One-way traffic for 700 metres	120.0	—	54.0
	Port (de Pousseaux)	120.0	—	54.0
	Bridge and lift bridge (de Pousseaux) ...	121.0	—	53.0

Distance Table   *kilom.*   *lock*   *kilom.*

		kilom.	lock	kilom.
Coulanges-s-Yonne	Port (de Coulanges-s-Yonne)	122.0	—	52.0
	Lock (No. 52 de Coulanges-s-Yonne).			
	Bridge	122.0	88	52.0
Lucy-s-Yonne	Lock (No. 53 de Crain)	123.0	89	51.0
	Guard gate (No. 53 *bis* de Bèze). Bridge ...	124.0	—	50.0
	Lock (No. 54 de Bèze). Bridge	125.0	90	49.0
	Bridge (de Lucy-s-Yonne)	126.0	—	48.0
Lichères-s-Yonne	Lock (No. 55 de Lucy-s-Yonne)	127.0	91	47.0
Châtel-Censoir	Bridge (du Gué Saint-Martin)	127.0	—	47.0
	Railway bridge (de Laplace)	128.0	—	4.60
	Lock (No. 56 de Laplace). Bridge	130.0	92	4.40
	Port (de Châtel-Censoir)	132.0	—	4.20
	Lock (No. 57 de Châtel-Censoir). Bridge ...	132.0	93	4.20
	Bridge (du Gade). Port (du Gade)	133.0	—	4.10
	Lock (No. 58 de Magny). Bridge	134.0	94	4.00
Merry-s-Yonne	Railway bridge (de Terres Rouges) ...	135.0	—	39.0
	Bridge (de Terres Rouges)	136.0	—	38.0
	Lock (No. 59 de Réchimet). *Râcle* (du Saussois). (1160 m.)	136.0	95	38.0
	Guard gate (No. 59 *bis* du Saussois). Bridge	137.0	—	37.0
	Port (du Saussois). Bridge (des Graves) ...	138.0	—	36.0
	Lock (No. 60 de Raverau)	139.0	96	35.0
	Râcle (de Mailly-le-Château) (1400 m.) ...	139.0	—	35.0
Mailly-le-Château	Guard gate (No. 61 de Mailly-le-Château)	140.0	—	34.0
	Railway bridge (de Mailly-le-Château) ...	140.0	—	34.0
	Bridge (de Mailly-le-Château). Port (de Mailly)	141.0	—	33.0
	Railway bridge (du Parc)	142.0	—	32.0
	Lock (No. 62 du Parc. *Râcle* (du Bouchet). (600 m.)	142.0	97	32.0
Mailly-la-Ville	Bridge. Lock (No. 63 de Mailly-la-Ville) ...	145.0	98	29.0
	Râcle (de Mailly-la-Ville). (1350 m.). Bridge	145.0	—	29.0
	Guard gate (No. 64 de Mailly-la-Ville) ...	146.0	—	28.0
Sery	Lock (No. 65 de Sery). Bridge. Bridge (de Sery)	147.0	99	27.0
Prégilbert	Lock (No. 66 de Saint-Maur). *Râcle* (des Dames)	148.0	100	26.0
	Bridge (des Dames)	149.0	—	25.0
	Lock (No. 67 des Dames). Bridge	150.0	101	24.0
	Râcle (de Prégilbert) (880 m.). Bridge (de Prégilbert)	150.0	—	24.0
	Guard gate (No. 68 de Prégilbert)	151.0	—	23.0
Sainte-Pallaye	Bridge (du Parc de Sainte-Pallaye) ...	151.0	—	23.0
	Bridge (des Romains)	151.0	—	23.0

Distance Table

		kilom.	lock	kilom.
	Lock (No. 69 de Sainte-Pallaye)	152.0	102	22.0
	Bridge (de la Croix Minet). Port (de la Croix Minet)	153.0	—	21.0
	Lock (No. 70 de St-Aignan). *Râcle* (du Manoir) (580 m.)	153.0	103	21.0
	Railway bridge (du Maunoir)	153.0	—	21.0
	Junction with the Branch de Vermenton ...	154.0	—	20.0
Bazarnes	Lock (No. 71 du Maunoir)	154.0	104	20.0
Cravant	Port (de Cravant). Bridge (de Cravant) ...	155.0	—	19.0
	Bridge (du Colombier)	156.0	—	18.0
	Lock (No. 72 de Rivottes)...	158.0	105	16.0
Vincelles	Lock (No. 73 de Vincelles). Bridge ...	159.0	106	15.0
	Râcle (de Vincelles) (850 m.)	159.0	—	15.0
	Port (de Vincelles). Port (de Vincelottes) ...	160.0	—	14.0
	Bridge (de Vincelottes)	160.0	—	14.0
	Lock (No. 74 de Vincelottes). *Râcle* (de Bailly) (1600 m.)	161.0	107	13.0
Escolives-St-Camille	Lock (No. 75 de Bailly). *Râcle* (de Bélombre) (1490 m.)	163.0	108	11.0
	Railway bridge (de la Bazine)	163.0	—	11.0
	Lock (No. 76 de Bélombre). Bridge ...	164.0	109	10.0
	Port (de la Cour Barrée)	165.0	—	9.0
Vaux	Lock (No. 77 de Toussac). *Râcle* (de Vaux) (2000 m.)	166.0	110	8.0
	Bridge (de Vaux)	167.0	—	7.0
	Lock (No. 78 de Vaux). *Râcle* (d'Augy) (1700 m.)	168.0	111	6.0
	Lock (No. 79 d'Augy). *Râcle* (de Preuilly) (1210 m.)	170.0	112	4.0
Auxerre	Lock (No. 80 de Preuilly)	172.0	113	2.0
	Râcle (du Batardeau) (1010 m.)	172.0	—	2.0
	Bathing place (de l'Arbre Sec) (Ville d'Auxerre)	172.0	—	1.0
	Railway bridge (du Batardeau)	173.0	—	1.0
	Lock (No. 81 du Batardeau)	173.0	114	1.0
	Bridge (Pont Paul-Bert)	174.0	—	0.0
	Junction with l' Yonne (at K.o)	174.0	—	0.0

Branch to Vermenton

Sainte-Pallaye	*Junction with the main canal (at K.154)* ...	0.0	—	3.9
	Lock (de la Noue). Bridge...	0.7	I	3.2
Accolay	Bridge (du Moulin Jacquot)	2.1	—	1.7
	Bridge (d'Accolay)	2.5	—	1.4
	Port (d'Accolay)	2.7	—	1.2
	Lock (d'Accolay)	2.0	2	1.9

Distance Table	*kilom.*	*lock*	*kilom.*
Guard gate (de Vermenton). Bridge ...	3.8	—	0.1
Port (de Vermenton) (on the River la Cure)	3.9	—	0.0

CANAL DU NORD

General

Excavation for this canal was started in 1908; by 1914 when war was declared three-quarters of the earthwork as well as a number of the locks and bridges had been completed. All this work was completely destroyed. Although several attempts were made to restart the project little was achieved by the summer of 1939 when again war intervened. However, soon after peace was restored the necessity for this waterway became increasingly evident. But it was not until 1957 that the Government was able to allocate funds for the work at an estimated cost of 210 million francs.

The Canal du Nord has its origin at Arleux near Douai and ends at Pont l'Evêque near Noyon. Throughout its length it can take vessels of about 350 tons having a draught of 2 m. 20; it can also be used by 'pusher-trains' of 700 tons consisting of two vessels each of 38 m. 50 placed end to end.

The canal is divided into three sections:

1st: from Arleux on the Canal de la Sensée, to Péronne on the Canal de la Somme

2nd: a borrowed length of the Canal de la Somme near Peronne to a point near Rouy-le-Grand

3rd: from near Rouy-le-Grand on the Canal de la Somme, to Pont l'Evêque on the canal latéral à l'Oise.

The canal contains two tunnels both of which occur at a summit level. The Grand Souterrain de Ruyaulcourt, which is at the summit level of the first section; it has a total length of 4,350 metres. The tunnel is divided into three portions; a length of 1,150 metres of double width (12 m. 30) which lies between two lengths, each of 1,600 metres, of a single width (6 m. 30). Vessels moving in opposite directions enter simultaneously at each end, pass one another in the central portion, and exit simultaneously from each end. A system of traffic lights (red and green) regulate the passage through the one-way lengths and also through the two-way length, so that, by obeying the lights, traffic can freely navigate throughout. The average time taken to pass from end to end of the tunnel has been found to be 1 hr. 30 m. at normal speed. The Souterrain de la Panneterie is at the summit level of the 3rd section; it is 1,100 metres in length, and although its dimensions only provide for one-way working, the length is not sufficiently great to impede normal traffic.

179

Length	The total length of the canal from Arleux to Pont l'Evêque is 95 kilometres.

Locks	There are 19 locks: of these 12 are in the 1st section, 2 in the 2nd section and 5 in the 3rd section. All have a uniform length of 91 m. 60 with a width of 6 m. 00.

Depth	The normal depth of water in the canal is 3 m. 00.

Bridges	All the fixed bridges have a headroom of at least 4 m. 10 above the highest navigable water level.

Distance Table

		kilom.	lock	kilom.
Arleux	Beginning of 1st section. *Junction with Canal de la Sensée (at K.16)*	0.0	—	95.0
	Bridge (d'Arleux)	1.0	—	94.0
Palluel	Lock (No. 1 de Palluel). Bridge	1.0	1	94.0
Oisy-le-Verger	... ...	2.0	—	93.0
	Bridge (d'Oisy-le-Verger)	3.0	—	92.0
Sauchy-Cauchy	... ...	3.0	—	92.0
	Bridge (de Sauchy-Cauchy)	5.0	—	90.0
Baralles	... ...	6.0	—	89.0
Marquion	Turning basin. Quay (de Marquion). Bridge	7.0	—	88.0
	Lock (No. 2 de Marquion)	8.0	2	87.0
Sains-lès-Marquion	Bridge (de Sains-lès-Marquion). Lock (No. 3 de Sains-lès-Marquion)	10.0	3	85.0
Inchy-en-Artois	... ...	10.0	—	85.0
	Bridge (d'Inchy-en-Artois). Quay	11.0	—	84.0
Sains-lès-Marquion	Bridge. Lock (No. 4 de Sains-lès-Marquion)	12.0	4	83.0
Moeuvres	Bridge (de Moeuvres)	13.0	—	82.0
	Lock (No. 5 de Moeuvres). Bridge ...	14.0	5	81.0
Graincourt-lès-Havrincourt	Bridge. Lock (No. 6 de Graincourt-lès-Havrincourt	15.0	6	80.0
	Bridge (de Graincourt-lès-Havrincourt ...	16.0	—	79.0
	Lock (No. 7 de Graincourt-lès-Havrincourt)	17.0	7	78.0
	Beginning of summit level	17.0	—	78.0
Havrincourt	Bridge (called 'chemin-d'Inchy')	17.0	—	78.0
	Railway bridge. Bridge	19.0	—	76.0
Hermies	Turning basin. Bridge	21.0	—	74.0
	Bridge. Quay (private)	22.0	—	73.0
	Bridge	23.0	—	72.0
Ruyaulcourt	... ...	23.0	—	72.0
	Bridge	24.0	—	71.0

Distance Table

		kilom.	*lock*	*kilom.*
	North entrance Tunnel (Soutterain de Ruyaulcourt) (4,350 m.). Traffic lights ...	25.0	—	70.0
Etricourt-Manancourt	South entrance Tunnel (Soutterain de Ruyaulcourt). Traffic lights	29.0	—	66.0
	Bridge	30.0	—	65.0
	Two bridges	31.0	—	64.0
	Bridge	32.0	—	63.0
Moislains	Turning basin	34.0	—	61.0
	Bridge	35.0	—	60.0
	Bridge. Quay (private). Quay (public) ...	37.0	—	58.0
	End of summit level. Lock (No. 8 à Moislains)	37.0	8	58.0
	Turning basin. Lock (No. 9 de Moislains)	38.0	9	57.0
Allaines	Lock (No. 10 d'Allaines)	39.0	10	56.0
	Bridges. Quay (private)	40.0	—	55.0
	Bridge	41.0	—	54.0
Feuillaucourt	Lock (No. 11 de Feuillaucourt) ...	42.0	11	53.0
Cléry-s-Somme	Bridge	42.0	—	53.0
	Lock (No. 12 de Clery-s-Somme) ...	43.0	12	52.0
Biaches	*Junction with Canal de la Somme (at K.37)*	45.0	—	50.0
	Beginning of 2nd section	45.0	—	50.0
Sainte-Radegonde	Turning basin	47.0	—	48.0
Péronne	Port. Bridge	48.0	—	47.0
	Railway bridge. Lock (No. 6 de Péronne)	49.0	13	46.0
Eterpigny	Port (de Pont-les-Brie)	53.0	—	42.0
	Lift bridge	54.0	—	41.0
St.-Christ-Briost	Turning basin. Port	56.0	—	39.0
Epénancourt	Port	59.0	—	36.0
	Bridge. Lock (No. 5 d'Epénancourt) ...	60.0	14	35.0
Pargny	Bridge. Port	61.0	—	34.0
Béthencourt-s-Somme	Turning basin. Port. Bridge	64.0	—	31.0
	Junction with Canal de la Somme (at K.17)	65.0	—	30.0
	Beginning of 3rd section			
Rouy-le-Grand	Bridge	68.0	—	27.0
Nesle	Railway bridge. Bridge	69.0	—	26.0
Languevoisin	Lock (No. 15 de Languevoisin). *Beginning of summit level.* Bridge. Port	70.0	15	25.0
Breuil	Bridge	71.0	—	24.0
Buverchy	Bridge	73.0	—	22.0
Lannoy	Bridge	75.0	—	20.0
Ercheu	Port	75.0	—	20.0
Libermont	Bridge. Tunnel (Souterrain de la Panneterie) north entrance. (1,100 m.)	78.0	—	17.0
	Tunnel (Souterrain de la Panneterie) south entrance	78.0	—	17.0

Distance Table

		kilom.	lock	kilom.
Frétoy-le-Château	Bridge	81.0	—	14.0
Campagne	*End of summit level.* Lock (No. 16 de Campagne)	82.0	16	13.0
	Bridge (de Campagne)	83.0	—	12.0
Catigny	Bridge	84.0	—	11.0
	Bridge	86.0	—	9.0
Surmaize	Bridge (de Surmaize)	87.0	—	8.0
	Lock (No. 17 de Surmaize-Haudival) ...	88.0	17	7.0
Beaurains-lès-Noyon	Bridge (de Beaurains-lès-Noyon)	89.0	—	6.0
	Bridge	91.0	—	4.0
Noyon	Port (de Noyon)	92.0	—	3.0
	Bridge. Lock (No. 18 de Noyon)	93.0	18	2.0
	Bridge	94.0	—	1.0
Pont-L'Evêque	Lock (No. 19 de Pont-l'Evêque)	94.0	19	1.0
	Bridge. Railway bridge	95.0	—	0.0
	Junction with canal latéral à l'Oise (at K.19)	95.0	—	0.0

OISE

General

The navigable part of the River Oise begins at the lock at Janville in the commune de Longueil-Annel and ends at its confluence with la Seine at Conflans-Sainte-Honorine in the commune d'Andresy at the point called *Fin l'Oise*. Since the opening of the canal latéral à l'Oise that part of the river which is situated upstream from Janville has been abandoned by waterborne traffic although above 2 kilometres is still used as a basin to give access to the shipyards which lie along that length. It must be noted that the kilometric posts which are to be found along the river bank are numbered consecutively from the origin of the canal latéral à l'Oise right through to the confluence with la Seine. L'Oise together with the canal latéral à l'Oise, the Canal de Saint-Quentin and the canalised River Escaut form the principal route joining the Paris region with that of the North and with Belgium.

No Permis de Navigation is necessary for the navigation of this river as far up as Compiègne.

Length

The length of the canalised part of l'Oise is 104 kilometres, reckoning from Janville. The number on the P.K. at Janville, however, is 34, which is arrived at as mentioned above. This same numeration has been adhered to here.

Locks

There are 7 locks and 7 barrages. At each barrage there are two locks, the one small (41 m. 00 or 46 m. 00 by 6 m. 00 or 8 m. 00) and one large (125 m. 00 by 12 m. 00). These latter are situated on by-pass channels and are used for trains of barges with their tugs, single self-propelled vessels using the smaller locks. All are electrically operated.

Depth There is a minimum depth of water of 2 m. 50 at the ordinary water level.

Bridges The headroom under the fixed bridges is 6 m. 05 at the ordinary water level, falling to about 4 m. 10 during times of flood.

Tow-path There is a good tow-path throughout.

Distance Table

		kilom.	lock	kilom.
Longueil-Annel	*Junction with canal latéral à l'Oise.* Lock (de Janville). Bridge (de Janville)	34.0	—	104.0
Clairoix	Bridge (de Clairoix)	36.0	—	102.0
	Confluence with l'Aisne (canalised) (at K.57)	38.0	—	100.0
Margny-lès-Compiègne	Railway bridge. Port (de Compiègne) ...	39.0	—	99.0
Compiègne*	Bridge (de Compiègne)	40.0	—	98.0
Venette	Lock (No. 1 de Venette)	41.0	1	97.0
	Port (de Venette)	42.0	—	96.0
Jaux	Port (de Jaux)	46.0	—	92.0
Meux	Suspension bridge (de La Croix-St-Ouen)	49.0	—	89.0
	Port (de Meux)	50.0	—	88.0
Verberie	Railway bridge	53.0	—	85.0
	Lock (No. 2 de Verberie)	54.0	2	84.0
	Port (de Verberie). Bridge (de Verberie) ...	55.0	—	83.0
Houdancourt	Port (d'Houdancourt)	61.0	—	77.0
Pontpoint	Lock (No. 3 de Sarron)	65.0	3	73.0
	Port (de Pontpoint)	66.0	—	72.0
Pont-Ste-Maxence	Bridge (de Pont-Ste-Maxence)	67.0	—	71.0
Rieux	Port (de Rieux)	73.0	—	65.0
Villers-St-Paul	Footbridge (suspension). Port	75.0	—	63.0
Creil	Bridge (de Creil)	79.0	—	59.0
	Port (de Creil) (called 'du Long-Boyau') ...	79.0	—	59.0
St-Leu-d'Esserent	Lock (No. 4 de Creil)	81.0	4	57.0
	Railway bridge (Pont de Laversine) ...	83.0	—	55.0
	Suspension bridge (de Ste-Leu-d'Esserant)	86.0	—	52.0
Gouvieux	Port (de Gouvieux)	88.0	—	50.0
Précy-sur-Oise	Suspension bridge and Port (de Précy) ...	90.0	—	48.0
Boran	Suspension bridge (de Boran)	94.0	—	44.0
Asnières-sur-Oise	Lock (No. 5 de Boran)	95.0	5	43.0
Noisy-sur-Oise	Port (de Noisy)	99.0	—	39.0

* See Plan No. 13.

Distance Table

		kilom.	lock	kilom.
Beaumont	Port (de Beaumont)	103.0	—	35.0
	Bridge (de Persan-Beaumont) ...	103.0	—	35.0
	Railway bridge	104.0	—	34.0
Isle-Adam	Lock (No. 6 de l'Isle-Adam) ...	109.0	6	29.0
	Bridge (de Parmain and de l'Isle-Adam) ...	110.0	—	28.0
Mériel	Road bridge. Railway bridge ...	113.0	—	25.0
Méry	Bridge (de Méry-Auvers)	116.0	—	22.0
St-Ouen-l'Aumone	Railway bridge (Pont de Chaponval) ...	119.0	—	19.0
Pontoise	Bridge (Pont de Pontoise) ...	123.0	—	15.0
	Railway bridge. Port (de Pontoise)	123.0	—	15.0
	Railway bridge. Port (de Pontoise)	123.0	—	15.0
	Lock (No. 7 de Pontoise)	124.0	7	14.0
Cergy	Bridge (de Cergy)	129.0	—	9.0
Jouy-le-Moutier	Port (de Jouy-le-Moutier)	133.0	—	5.0
	Bridge (de Neuville)	134.0	—	4.0
Conflans-Ste-Honorine	Port (de Maurecourt)	137.0	—	1.0
	Railway bridge ('Pont-Eiffel') ...	137.0	—	1.0
	Bridge (de Conflans)	137.0	—	1.0
	Confluence with la Seine (at K.71) ...	138.0	—	0.0

CANAL LATÉRAL À L'OISE

General

The canal latéral à l'Oise begins at Chauny in the commune of the same name, and ends at Janville in the commune of Longueil-Annel. It joins the Canal de Saint-Quentin and the Canal du Nord to the canalised part of the River Oise. At the little town of Abbécourt it makes junction with the Canal de l'Oise à l'Aisne.

The canal latéral à l'Oise carries a considerable volume of traffic, but, thanks to the splendid locks with which this waterway is provided, delay in passing through is not usual. It is one of the train of waterways which puts the Paris region in communication with the North and with Belgium.

Length

The distance from Chauny to Janville by canal is 34 kilometres.

Locks

There are 4 locks entirely worked by electricity. Each lock has two chambers which are separated by a central platform. The chambers have a common length of 39 m. 00, but one chamber has a width of 6 m. 00 while the other has a width of 6 m. 50.

Depth

The depth of the water in the canal is held at 2 m. 60.

Bridges

The fixed bridges all have a minimum headroom of 4 m. 10 clear above the normal water level.

		kilom.	lock	kilom.
Tow-path	There is a good tow-path throughout which is served by a power line for the use of the electric tractors which run on rails.			

Distance Table

		kilom.	lock	kilom.
Chauny	*Junction with Canal de St-Quentin (at K.92).*			
	Port (de Chauny)	0.0	—	*138.0
Abbécourt	*Junction with Canal de l'Oise à l'Aisne* ...	2.0	—	136.0
	Port and Bridge (d'Abbécourt)	3.0	—	135.0
Manicamp	Port (de Manicamp)	5.0	—	133.0
Quierzy	Port and Bridge (de Quierzy). Port ...	6.0	—	132.0
Appilly	Port and Bridge (d'Appilly)	8.0	—	130.0
	Lock (No. 1 'de Saint-Hubert')	8.0	1	130.0
Baboeuf	Port (de Baboeuf)	10.0	—	128.0
	Footbridge (de Pont-à-la-Fosse)	11.0	—	127.0
Salency	Port and Bridge (de Varesnes)	13.0	—	125.0
	Bridge (de Morlincourt)	14.0	—	124.0
	Bridge (de la rue d'Orroire)	15.0	—	123.0
Noyon	Ports (de Noron)	15.0	—	123.0
Sempigny	Port and Bridge (de Sempigny)	17.0	—	121.0
	Lock (No. 2 de Sempigny). Port	18.0	2	120.0
	Pont-l'Evêque. *Junction with 3rd section of Canal du Nord*	19.0	—	119.0
Chiry-Ourscamp	Bridge (de Chiry or du Brûlé)	20.0	—	118 0
	Port (d'Ourscamp). Bridge (d'Ourscamp)	21.0	—	117.0
Pimprez	Bridge (de Pimprez)	24.0	—	114.0
	Deviation *(keep right bank)*	24.0	—	114.0
	Bridge (de la Rouilly)	24.0	—	114.0
Ribécourt	Port and Bridge (de Ribécourt)	26.0	—	112.0
	Railway bridge	26.0	—	112.0
Cambronne	Bridge (de Bellerive)	27.0	—	111.0
	Lock (No. 3 de Bellerive)	28.0	3	110.0
Thourotte	Bridge (de Montmacq)	30.0	—	108.0
	Port (de Thourotte). Bridge (de Thourotte)	31.0	—	107.0
Longueil-Annel†	Bridge (de Longueil)	32.0	—	106.0
	Lock (No. 4 de Janville)	33.0	4	105.0
	Junction with l'Oise (canalised) (at K.34)	34.0	—	104.0

CANAL DE L'OISE À L'AISNE

General   The Canal de l'Oise à l'Aisne begins near the little town of Abbécourt and finishes at Bourg et Comin on the canal latéral à l'Aisne (at K.38). It contains a summit level and also a tunnel. The summit level has a height of about 220 ft. above sea level. The tunnel, which

---

* See l'Oise and note on numbering of kilometre posts.
† See Plan No. 13.

occurs at Braye-en-Laonnois, has a length of 2,365 metres. The width of the tunnel at water level is 6 m. 50 and the headroom is 3 m. 50 above the normal level of the water. Towage is compulsory through this tunnel for vessels that are not self-propelled, and convoys *(rames)* are made up several times during the day which circulate in each direction. The duration of the tow is about 1½ hours but depends somewhat on the circumstances. The hours for navigation also depend upon the season of the year as there is no traffic during the hours of darkness. The times of passage must, therefore, be obtained locally. There are three *pont-canaux* but none of them is of any great length; they are, l'Oise (70 m.) (K.0), l'Ailette (14 m.) (K.3) and l'Aisne (62 m.) (K.47).

Tunnel de Braye en Laonnois

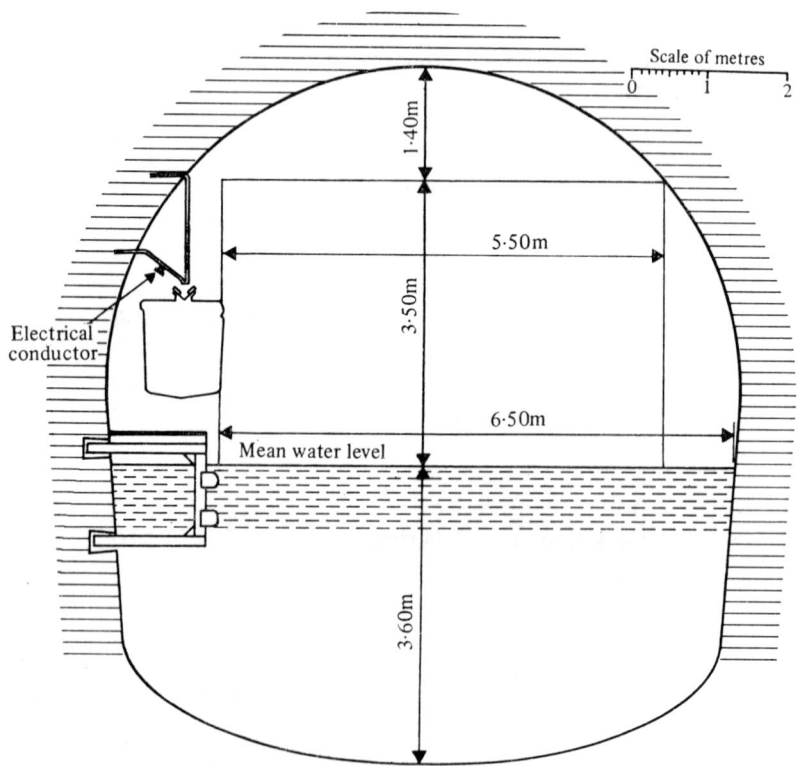

Scale of metres

1·40m

5·50m

3·50m

6·50m

Electrical conductor

Mean water level

3·60m

CAUTION. Live electric wires may be established throughout the length of this tunnel.

Length   From the junction with the canal latéral à l'Oise at Abbécourt to the junction with the canal latéral à l'Aisne at Bourg-et-Comin the canal has a length of 48 kilometres.

Locks   There are 13 locks of which 9 fall towards Abbécourt and 4 towards Bourg-et-Comin. They have a length of 40 m. 50 with a width of 6 m. 00.

		kilom.	lock	kilom.
Depth	Throughout the length of the canal the depth of water at normal water level is 2 m. 60.			
Bridges	The fixed bridges have a headroom of not less than 3 m. 70 above the normal water level.			
Tow-path	There is a tow-path throughout and rails are laid for the use of electric tractors which have an overhead power supply.			

Distance Table

		kilom.	lock	kilom.
Abbécourt	*Junction with canal latéral à l'Oise.* Port.			
	Turning basin	0.0	—	48.0
	Bridge (d'Abbécourt). Lock (No. 1 d'Abbécourt). Pont-canal (d'Oise)* (70 m.) ...	0.0	I	48.0
Bichancourt	Bridge (de Marizelle). Port (de Marizelle)	1.0	—	47.0
	Bridge (du Bac)	2.0	—	46.0
	Pont-canal (l'Ailette) (14 m.)	3.0	—	45.0
Manicamp	Bridge (de Manicamp)	3.0	—	45.0
	Port and Bridge (de St-Paul-aux-Bois) ...	4.0	—	44.0
Trosly-Champs	Bridge and Port (de Trosly-Champs) ...	7.0	—	41.0
Guny	Bridge (de la Quincy)	9.0	—	39.0
	Port and Bridge (de Guny)	10.0	—	38.0
	Bridge (du Tempet). Lock (No. 2 de Guny)	11.0	2	37.0
Pont-St-Mard	Bridge and Port (de Pont-St-Mard) ...	12.0	—	36.0
Crécy-au-Mont	Bridge and Lock (No. 3 de Crécy-au-Mont)	14.0	3	34.0
	Bridge (de Béthancourt)	15.0	—	33.0
	Port (de Crécy-au-Mont)	16.0	—	32.0
Leuilly	Lock (No. 4 de Leuilly)	17.0	4	31.0
	Bridge (de Landricourt)	18.0	—	30.0
Landricourt	Bridge (de Courson). Port (de Leuilly-Courson)	19.0	—	29.0
Vauxaillon	Railway bridge (de Vauxaillon)	21.0	—	27.0
	Lock (No. 5 de Vauxaillon)	22.0	5	26.0
Anizy-la-Château	Port and Bridge (de Vauxaillon) ...	22.0	—	26.0
	Bridge (de Locq)	24.0	—	24.0
Pinon	Bridge and Port (d'Anizy-Pinon)	25 0	—	23.0
	Railway bridge (de Pinon)...	25.0	—	23.0
	Lock (No. 6 de Pinon)	26.0	6	22.0
Chaillevois	Bridge and Lock (No. 7 de Chaillevois) ...	31.0	7	17.0
Chavignon	Port and Bridge (de Chavignon)	33.0	—	15.0
Pargny-Filain	Lock (No. 8 de Chavignon)	33.0	8	15.0
	Bridge (de Pargny-Filain)	34.0	—	14.0
	Lock (No. 9 de Pargny-Filain). Beginning of summit level. Port	35.0	9	13.0

* Width 5 m. 36.

Distance Table

			kilom.	lock	kilom.
Chevregny	Port and Bridge (de Chevregny) ...	...	37.0	—	11.0
	Tunnel (entrance) (called 'Tête Oise')	...	38.0	—	10.0
Braye-en-Laonnois	Tunnel (exit) (called 'Tête Oise') ...	...	40.0	—	8.0
	Bridge (de Braye)	...	40.0	—	8.0
	Bridge (des Epinettes)	...	41.0	—	7.0
	Bridge (du Mont-St-Aubeu) ...	...	41.0	—	7.0
	Port (de Braye)	...	41.0	—	7.0
	End of summit level. Lock (No. 10 du Moulin Brûlé)	...	42.0	10	6.0
Moussy	Lock (No. 11 de Metz)	...	43.0	11	5.0
	Bridge and Port (de Moussy-Soupir)	...	43.0	—	5.0
Soupir	Lock (No. 12 de Moussy-Soupir). Bridge...		43.0	12	5.0
Verneuil-Courtonne	Lock (No. 13 de Verneuil-Courtonne)	...	44.0	13	4.0
	Bridge (de Verneuil)	...	45.0	—	3.0
	Bridge (de Bourg)	...	46.0	—	2.0
*Bourg-et-Comin**	Railway bridge (de Bourg) ...	...	46.0	—	2.0
	Bridge (de Bourg)	...	46.0	—	2.0
	Pont-canal (l'Aisne) (62 m.) ...	...	47.0	—	1.0
	Bridge and Port (de Bourg-et-Comin)	...	48.0	—	0.0
	Junction with canal latéral à l'Aisne (at K.38)...	...	48.0	—	0.0

OUDON

General	The River Oudon is navigable only below the port of Segré (which is situated on the eastern side of that town) as above the port the waterway is obstructed by a low bridge and shoal depth. It makes its confluence with la Mayenne on the right bank of that river at Bec d'Oudon. Nowadays it carries little traffic.
Length	From the Port de Segré to the confluence at Bec d'Oudon is a distance of 18 kilometres.
Locks	There are 3 locks. These each have a length of 33 m. 00 with a width of 5 m. 20.
Depth	The normal depth is 1 m. 70, but this may fall considerably, even to as low as 1 m. 00 during times of drought.
Bridges	The headroom under the fixed bridges is 3 m. 60 measured from the highest navigable water level, normally it is 4 m. 60.
Tow-path	There is a tow-path throughout, but it is of natural earth except at the locks where it has been metalled.

* See Plan No. 1.

Distance Table

		kilom.	lock	kilom.
Segré	Port (de Segré)	0.0	—	18.0
	Lock (No. 1 de Maingue)	1.0	1	17.0
La Chapelle-s-Oudon	Lock (No. 2 de la Chapelle-s-Oudon) ...	4.0	2	14.0
Lion-d'Angers	Bridge (du Port-aux-Anglais)	8.0	—	10.0
St-Martin-du-Bois	Lock (No. 3 de Hindebeaudière)	10.0	3	8.0
Lion-d'Angers	Bridge	15.0	—	3.0
	Port (du Lion-d'Angers)	16.0	—	2.0
	Bec d'Oudon. *Confluence with la Mayenne (at K.103)*	18.0	—	0.0

LE RHIN ET GRAND CANAL D'ALSACE

General*

The River Rhin has its source near Rheinwaldhorn in the Grisons Canton of Switzerland. After passing through Lake Constance it leaves Switzerland in the city of Bâle, thereafter forming the frontier between France and Germany over a distance of nearly 200 kilometres. Leaving the frontier at Lauterbourg it runs at first entirely on German soil; later it enters the Netherlands and finally finishes its course by discharging into the North Sea. The river in the reaches between Bâle and Bingen has Alpine characteristics, that is to say that the lowest water occurs in the winter between November and April and the highest water between May and August. Below Bingen, however, this cycle is modified on account of the great afflux of water that it receives from non-glacial tributaries. The Rhin, owing to the violence of its current, especially when in flood, has always been a difficult and often a dangerous river to navigate. This has led to many proposals for the rectification of its course but hitherto little had been done to give effect to them. In a few places, at the worst bends, deviations were made but the resulting increased speed of the current deepened the river bed and exposed rocky shelves and bars—notably as at d'Istein—thus increasing rather than reducing the difficulty of navigation. One suggestion, mooted before the 1914–18 war, was the provision of a lateral canal along the French bank of the river stretching from Bâle to Strasbourg thus avoiding the more hazardous parts of the passage. Dr. Ch. Béliard published in 1926 a work *Le Grand canal d'Alsace: voie navigable, source d'énergie*, and in fact the first pound of a lateral canal under that title was put into service in 1932. The original intention was the cutting of a canal, fed by the river, having eight pounds between Huningue and Strasbourg, the water of the canal not returning to the river except at the canal's extremity at Strasbourg. The chief object of the canal was to generate electrical energy and, secondly, to provide water for irrigation in the interests of agriculture.

* See Plan No. 14.

The improvement in the conditions for navigation was only a side benefit derived from the major consideration. A concession for this work was given by the French government to l'Electricité de France. Thus, in 1932, the barrage across the Rhin at Kembs and the canal with its hydro-electric station and navigation lock having been completed, the Bief de Kembs was taken into service. By 1956 the succeeding pounds of Ottmarshem, Fressenheim and Vogelgrun were all in service. At that time on account of an agreement reached between the French and German governments, a modification was made to the original plan whereby each of the remaining reaches should have a barrage in the river and a 'feeder and return channel' containing a hydro-electric power station and a navigation lock. Thus each reach *(bief)* consists of a certain length of the river across which, near the upstream end, a barrage has been built. A short distance upstream of the barrage a 'feeder' canal *(une dérivation)* leads to a power station and a navigation lock; these are usually sited towards the downstream end of the feeder canal. Below the power station and lock a 'return channel *(une restitution* or *canal de fuite)* rejoins the river. This is the common arrangement nowadays in 'canalising' a river. The four pounds of le Grand Canal d'Alsace taken together cover a distance of about 53 kilo-metres and lie lateral to the river along the left bank between K.P.173 and K.P.226 *kilométrage du Rhin.* It must be mentioned that the *kilométrage* of the river has been internationally agreed: the zero point of the measurement has been established at the centre of the Rijnbrug at Konstanz. Below are given particulars of the four pounds which make up le Grand Canal d'Alsace:

(1) **Le bief de Kembs**: has a length of 6.5 kilometres. It contains, in addition to the power station, a lock having twin chambers side by side. One is 185 m. 90 in length with a width of 25 m. 00; the other is 95 m. 00 in length with a width of 25 m. 00.

(2) **Le bief d'Ottmarsheim**: has a length of 14.3 kilometres. By the side of the power station there is a lock with twin chambers. Both chambers have a length of 185 m. 00, but the widths differ; one is 23 m. 00 in width, the other is 12 m. 00.

(2) **Le bief de Fessenheim**: has a length of 16.1 kilometres. The dimensions of the works it contains are the same as those in le bief d'Ottmarsheim.

(4) **Le bief de Vogelgrun**: has a length of 15.5 kilometres. The dimensions of the lock are the same as those of the lock in le bief d'Ottmarsheim. This pound, however, discharges into the Rhin at K.P.226.

Downstream of la restitution du Grand Canal d'Alsace with the river (at K.P.226) le Rhin has been subject to rectification by the building of barrages and deviation canals. Between K.P.226 and K.P.295 (Port de Strasbourg) there are four such rectifications, namely, Marckolsheim, Rhinau-Sundhouse, Gerstheim and Strasbourg. Three of these are already in service and that of Strasbourg is expected to be open to navigation in 1970/71. Particulars of these *dérivations* are as under:

(1) **La dérivation de Marckolsheim**: has a length of 8.2 kilometres. The lock has two chambers, side by side; each chamber is 185 m. 00 in length, but one is 25 m. 00 in width, the other only 12 m. 00.

(2) **La dérivation de Rhinau-Sundhouse**: has a length of 12.1 kilometres. The lock has twin chambers each of which is 185 m. 00 in length, but the width of one chamber is 23 m. 00 and of the other 12 m. 00.

(3) **La dérivation de Gerstheim**: has a length of 7.1 kilometres. The lock has twin chambers, but the length of each chamber is 190 m. 00. The width of the chambers is 24 m. 00 and 12 m. 00 respectively.

(4) **La dérivation de Strasbourg***: will have a length of about 7 kilometres. It is expected that the lock will have the same dimensions as the lock in la dérivation de Gerstheim.

The minimum depth is always greater than 3 m. 00 between Huningue and the end of the Grand Canal d'Alsace: on le Rhin canalisé at the normal stage of the river it is 2 m. 70 upstream of Strasbourg, and 2 m. 90 between Strasbourg and Lauterbourg.

All the fixed bridges have a clear headroom of 7 m. 00 above the highest navigable water level.

Ferries operate at Huningue, Rhinau, Gerstheim, Drusenheim and Seltz.

Distance Table		**G.C.A.**	**Rhin G.C.A.**
Commune			*kilométrage*
Huningue	Frontier Franco-Suisse		168.4
	Port de Bâle		169.9
	Water level gauge (de Huningue) ...		170.2
	Ferry (de Huningue)		170.4
	Piles of old railway bridge (Huningue-Weil)		171.3
Village-Neuf	*Junction with le Grand Canal d'Alsace* ...		173.5
	High tension line over Rhin		173.8
	Barrage (de Kembs)		173.9

* Put into service 1970.

Distance Table

		G.C.A.	Rhin	G.C.A.
Bief de Kembs (6.5 km.)				
	Origin of Bief de Kembs	0.0	173.5	51.8
Rosenau	... ...	1.7	175.3	50.1
	Lock (de Kembs)	5.4	179.2	46.4
Kembs	... ...	5.7		46.1
	Power station (de Kembs)	6.0	179.8	45.8
	High tension line (Kembs Laufenbourg) ...	6.1	179.8	45.7
Bief d'Ottmarsheim (14.3 km.)				
	Origin of Bief d'Ottmarsheim	6.5	180.1	45.3
	High tension line	10.8	184.3	41.0
Niffer	*Junction with l'Embranchement de Kembs-Niffer (at K.13.1)*	11.4	—	40.4
Petit-Landau	... ...	13.6	186.9	38.2
Hombourg	... ...	17.5	192.1	34.3
	Turning basin (600 m. × 200 m.) ... ... {	18.0		33.8 }
		18.6		33.2
Ottmarsheim	... ...	19.4	193.3	32.4
	Lock (d'Ottmarsheim)	19.6	193.5	32.2
	Power station (d'Ottmarsheim) ...	20.3	194.5	31.5
Bief de Fessenheim (16.1 km.)				
	Origin of Bief de Fessenheim	20.8	195.0	31.0
	Quai de l'Establissement public. Port de Mulhouse-Ottmarsheim	22.4	196.0	29.4
Bantzenheim	... ...	23.7	197.4	28.1
Chalmpe	... ...	24.7	198.5	27.1
	Quai de l'Establissement public. Port de Mulhouse-Ottmarsheim	24.9	—	26.9
	Loading berth. *Four dolphins*	24.9	198.6	24.9
	Loading berth. *Four dolphins*		198.6	
	Railway bridge (headroom 7 m. 22) ...	25.1	198.7	26.7
	Hydrant (du Génie rural)	26.1	—	25.7
Rumersheim-le-Haut	... ...	29.5	203.3	22.3
	Hydrant (du Génie rural)	31.1		20.7
Blodelsheim	... ...	31.2	205.5	20.6
Fessenheim	... ...	34.6	209.1	17.2
	Lock (de Fessenheim)	36.1	210.5	15.7
	Power station (de Fessenheim)	36.9	211.1	14.9
Bief de Vogelgrun (15.5 km.)				
Balagu	Origin of Bief de Vogelgrun	36.8	211.0	15.7
Nambsheim	... ...	38.5	212.9	13.3
Geiswasser	... ...	41.3	215.8	10.5
Vogelgrun	... ...	47.2	221.7	4.6

Distance Table

		G.C.A.	Rhin	G.C.A.
	Lock (de Vogelgrun)	50.0	224.7	1.8
	Power station (de Vogelgrun)	50.2	224.9	1.6
	Bridge	—	225.0	
	Port rhénan de Colmar-Neuf-Brisach ... ⎰	51.0	225.9	0.8 ⎱
	⎱	51.8	226.7	0.0 ⎰
Biesheim	Restitution du Grand Canal d'Alsace with le Rhin (at K.P.226)	51.8	226.5	0.0

Le Rhin Canalisé

			Rhin	
	*Junction with l'Embranchement de Neuf-Brisach**		226.7	
	Quay (quai 'Cégédur')		228.4	
Kunheim	... ...		229.4	
	Quay (quai 'Beghin')		230.5	
Baltzenheim	... ...		232.9	

		dériv		*dériv*
	Origin of la dérivation de Marckolsheim ...	0.0	234.3	8.2
	Barrage de Marckolsheim		234.8	
Marckolsheim	... ...	2.0	236.3	6.2
	Turning basin	3.9	238.2	4.3
	Lock de Marckolsheim	5.6	239.9	2.6
	Power station de Marckolsheim	6.2	240.5	2.0
	Dolphins	7.1	241.4	1.1
	Dolphins	7.3	241.6	0.9
	Restitution of la dérivation de Marckolsheim	8.2	242.5	0.0
Mackenheim	... ...		243.0	
Boofzheim	... ...		244.6	
Artolsheim	... ...		246.2	
Schoenau	... ...		247.2	

		dériv		*dériv*
	Origin of la dérivation de Rhinau-Sundhouse	0.0	248.2	12.1
	Barrage de Rhinau-Sundhouse		249.2	
	Turning basin	5.9	—	6.2
	Lock de Rhinau-Sundhouse	8.0	256.1	4.1
	Power station de Rhinau-Sundhouse ...	8.3	256.4	3.8
	Restitution of la dérivation de Rhinau-Sundhouse with le Rhin	12.1	260.1	0.0
	Pendulum ferry. Garage de Rhinau ...		261.0	
Daubensand	... ...		265.6	

* See Canal du Rhône au Rhin, p. 210

Distance Table

		dériv	Rhin	dériv
	Origin of la dérivation de Gerstheim ...	0.0	267.5	7.1
	Barrage de Gerstheim		268.6	
	Bridge		270.3	
	Loading berth		270.8	
	Water level gauge de Gerstheim		271.1	
	Wharf		271.5	
	Lock de Gerstheim	5.1	272.2	2.0
	Power station de Gerstheim	5.4	272.5	1.7
Erstein	... ...		273.1	
	Restitution of la dérivation de Gerstheim	7.1	274.1	0.0
Plobsheim	Entrance to loading berths (Graviére Meissenheim)		276.5	
Eschau	... ...		280.0	
Strasbourg	Junction with canal de décharge de l'Ill ...		282.1	
		dériv	Rhin	dériv
	Origin of la dérivation de Strasbourg ...	0.0	283.1	7.4
	Barrage de Strasbourg		284.0	
	Lock de Strasbourg	3.9		3.5
		dériv	Rhin	dériv
	Power station de Strasbourg	4.1		3.3
	Loading berth		288.1	
	Entrance to Basin No. 4 (projected) ...	4.8		2.6
	Entrance to Basin No. 3	5.4		2.0
	Entrance to Basin 'Gaston Haelling' ...	6.0		1.4
	Entrance to Basin 'Auguste Detoeur' ...	6.6		0.8
	Port de Strasbourg (avant-port sud) ...	7.4	291.4	0.0
	High tension line (overhead)		291.4	
	Loading berth		292.6	
	Bridge 'Pont de l'Europe'		293.5	
	Railway bridge		293.7	
	Water level gauge de Strasbourg (Rhénométre)		294.9	
	Port de Strasbourg (avant-port nord) ...		295.6	
	Water level gauge (de la Robertsau) ...		297.6	
	Entrance to Port de Kehl		297.6	
La Wantzenau	... ...		300.7	
	Confluence with 'le Steingiessen'		301.8	
	Water level gauge (de la Wantzenau) ...		302.1	
Gambsheim	Confluence with l'Ill		306.5	
	Water level gauge (de Gambsheim). Military bridge		309.7	
Offendorf	... ...		309.9	
	Wet dock (d'Offendorf)		313.7	
Drusenheim	... ...		315.8	

Distance Table

		Rhin
	Water level gauge de Drusenheim	318.2
	Ferry de Drusenheim-Greffern	318.3
	Haven for small craft (de Drusenheim) ...	319.1
Dalhunden	Wet dock de Dalhunden	319.5
Fort-Louis	... ...	322.3
	Wet dock de Fort-Louis	325.7
	Water level gauge de Fort-Louis	326.9
Neuhaeusel	... ...	330.1
	Confluence with la Moder	332.3
Beinheim	... ...	333.5
	Water level gauge (de Beinheim)	335.1
	Railway bridge, two spans	335.6
Seltz	... ...	337.7
	Wet dock de Beinheim	338.9
	Pendulum ferry de Seltz	340.3
	Water level gauge and Port de Seltz ...	340.4
Munchhausen	Wet dock de Seltz	341.6
	Confluence with la Sauer	343.9
	Water level gauge de Munchhausen ...	344.2
Mothern	... ...	345.1
Lauterbourg	... ...	347.8
	Port de Lauterbourg. Water level gauge ...	349.3
	Mouth of la vielle Lauter	352.1
	Frontier French-German	352.1

RHÔNE

General

Le Rhône is classed as navigable from le Parc (at the Franco-Suisse frontier) to the Mediterranean Sea, into which it falls as a delta made by le Petit Rhône on the right and le Grand Rhône on the left. In reality the river has been abandoned for navigation between the frontier and the confluence with la Saône at Lyon-La Mulatière. By its confluence with la Saône, le Rhône is connected with the waterways of *le Centre, la Région parisienne, le Nord* and *l'Est*. By *le Canal du Rhône à Sète* it is linked with the waterways of *le Midi* and, through them and la Garonne, with the Atlantic Ocean.

From Lyon to Port St-Louis-du-Rhône the river is now being canalised by the building of barrages and the cutting of deviation canals. At present (1969) six barrages have been established across the main stream at each of which a 'feeder canal' (*canal de dérivation*) leads to a hydro-electric power station and a navigation lock. A 'restitution canal' (*canal de fuite*) returns to the river from each lock and power station.

The six deviations now in use are:

Pierre-Bénite ...	...	...	...	K.4.1
Bourg-lès-Valence	...	...	...	K.105.9
Beauchastel ...	...	...	...	K.123.8
Baix-le-Logis-Neuf	...	...	...	K.142.5
Montélimar ...	...	...	...	K.164.0
Donzère-Mondragon ...	...	...	K.187.3

Six other power stations and locks are in course of construction*. The following ports on the river are connected with the S.N.C.F. railway system:

Port Edouard-Herroit; Port de Givors; Port de l'Ardoise; Port du Pontet and Port de l'Oseraie; Port d'Arles-Trinquetaille.

New ports, generally in conjunction with industrial agglomerations, are, under the direction of *les Pouvoirs Public*, being investigated at suitable sites along the banks of the river so as to take advantage of the electric power generated and the improved water transport available.

Because that part of the river which lies downstream of Arles is officially considered to be within the limit of *l'Inscription maritime* it is convenient to divide the river into two sections:

(*a*) Lyon (confluence with la Saône) to Arles.

(*b*) Arles to the Port Saint-Louis-du-Rhône.

Lyon to Arles

Length

From the confluence with la Saône (commune de la Mulatière) to the bridge at Arles-Trinquetaille is 281.8 kilometres, but as the zero of the section is 700 metres above the confluence, the kilométrage at the Arles-Trinquetaille bridge is reckoned as 282.500. The kilométrage is shown on both banks by means of boards erected on posts fixed at every 500 metres: the boards are visible from the channel.

Locks

There are at present 6 locks. See above.

Depth

Variable. The situation now (1969) is that from La Mulatière to Ternay (K.15.3) the depth is 2 m. 60: also between Bourg-lès-Valence (K.98.3) to Mornas (K.200.5) the same depth is assured. These two lengths, aggregating 117 kilometres, represent the canalised sections now in use. Above and below these middle sections (K.98.3—K.200.5) the river is still in its natural state *(courant libre)*. Normally in the natural sections a depth of 2 m. 20 is found, but during times of low water the depth may not be more than 1 m. 50.

* See p. 5. Part I Navigational Notes.

| Bridges | All bridges have a clear headroom of at least 6 m. 30 at highest navigable water level. |

| Beacons | Beacons and buoys mark the right bank of the channel. Along the deviations and restitution channels there are beacons erected along the right banks at intervals of (approximately) 500 metres. Both beacons and buoys carry bands of reflecting material on their upper parts so as to allow navigation to be undertaken during darkness. |

Distance Table

		kilom.	lock	kilom.
Lyon-la-Mulatiere	Confluence with la Saône (at K.375.7) ...	0.7	—	281.8
	Confluence with l'Yzeron (R.D.)	1.4	—	281.1
Pierre-Bénite	... ...	1.9	—	280.6
	Port (Edouard-Herriot) (R.G.)	3.6	—	278.9
	Origin of la dérivation de Pierre-Bénite (R.G.)	4.0	—	278.5
	Lock and power station de Pierre-Bénite ...	4.1	I	278.4
Irigny	... ...	5.0	—	277.0
	Ferry (d'Irigny)	8.0	—	274.0
Vernaison	... ...	9.0	—	273.0
	Bridge (de Vernaison)	10.0	—	272.0
Ternay	... ...	13.0	—	269.0
	Restitution of la dérivation de Pierre-Bénite (R.G.)	15.3	—	267.2
	Railway bridge (viaduc d'Arboras) ...	17.0	—	265.0
Givors	Confluence with le Garon (R.D.)	17.0	—	265.0
	Port and Bridge (de Givors)	18.0	—	264.0
	Port de Chasse	20.0	—	262.0
Seysseul	... ...	22.0	—	260.0
Vienne	... ...	25.0	—	257.0
	Bridge (de Vienne)	28.0	—	254.0
	Footbridge. Port (de Vienne)	29.0	—	253.0
Ampuis	Ferry (d'Ampuis)	34.0	—	248.0
Roches-de-Condrieu	Port and Bridge (de Roches-de-Condrieu)	41.0	—	241.0
St-Alban-du-Rhône	Confluence with la Varèze (R.G.)	46.0	—	236.0
	Bridge (de Chavanay). Confluence with la Valencise (R.D.)	47.0	—	235.0
Serrières	Bridge (de Serrières)	59.0	—	223.0
Peyraud	Confluence with le Dolon (R.G.)	61.0	—	221.0
	Railway bridge (de Peyraud)	62.0	—	220.0
Andance	Bridge (d'Andance). Confluence with le Bancel (R.G.)	69.0	—	213.0
Sarras	Confluence with la Cance (R.D.)	73.0	—	209.0
Saint-Vallier	Confluence with l'Ay (R.D.)	75.0	—	207.0

R.D. = Right Bank.   R.G. = Left Bank.

o

Distance Table

		kilom.	lock	kilom.
	Bridge (de Saint-Vallier)	76.0	—	206.0
Arras-s-Rhône	... ...	80.0	—	202.0
Crozes-l'Hermitage	Small island ('La Table du Roi')	89.0	—	193.0
Tain-l'Hermitage	*Confluence with le Doux (R.D.). Bridge.*			
	Port	90.0	—	192.0
	Bridge (de Tournon)	91.0	—	191.0
La-Roche-de-Glun	Origin of la dérivation de Bourg-lès-Valence (R.G.)	98.3	—	184.2
Bourg-lès-Valence	*Confluence with l'Isère (R.G.)*	104.0	—	178.0
	Lock and power station de Bourg-lès-Valence	105.9	2	176.6
Saint-Péray	Restitution of la dérivation de Bourg-lès-Valence (R.G.)	108.2	—	174.3
	Port (de Valence)	110.0	—	172.0
Portes-lès-Valence	Pier (private; Desmaris frères)	116.0	—	166.0
Charmes-s-Rhône	Origin of la derivation de Beauchastel (R.D.)	119.2	—	163.3
	Bridge (de Charmes-Etoile)	120.0	—	162.0
St-Georges-les-Bains	*Confluence with le Turzon (R.D.)*	122.0	—	160.0
Beauchastel	... ...	123.0	—	159.0
	Lock and power station de Beauchastel ...	123.8	3	158.7
	Bridge	124.0	—	158.0
La Voulte-s-Rhône	*Confluence with l'Eyrieux (R.D.)*	126.0	—	156.0
	Restitution of la dérivation de Beauchastel (R.D.)	126.8	—	155.7
	Bridge (de la Voulte)	128.0	—	154.0
	Railway bridge (de la Voulte) ...	129.0	—	153.0
Loriol-s-Drôme	*Confluence with la Drôme (R.G.)*	132.0	—	150.0
	Port (du Pouzin). Bridge	133.0	—	149.0
	Confluence with l'Ouvéze (R.D.)	134.0	—	148.0
	Origin of la dérivation de Baix-le-Logis-Neuf (R.G.)	135.1	—	147.4
Saulce	Lock and power station du Logis-Neuf ...	142.5	4	140.0
	Bridge	143.0	—	139.0
	Restitution of la dérivation de Baix-le-Logis-Neuf (R.G.)	143.9	—	138.6
Cruas	Port (de Cruas)	145.0	—	137.0
Rochemaure	Origin of la dérivation de Montélimar (R.G.)	152.7	—	129.8
	Bridge (road to Rochemaure)	155.0	—	127.0
Montélimar	Bridge (road to Tiel)	157.0	—	125.0
	Outfall of le Roubion	158.0	—	124.0
	Bridge (de Gournier). Port (de Montélimar)	160.0	—	122.0

R.D. = Right Bank.   R.G. = Left Bank.

Distance Table

		kilom.	lock	kilom.
Châteauneuf-du-Rhône	Lock and power station de Châteauneuf ...	164.0	5	118.5
	Restitution of la dérivation de Montélimar (R.G.)	166.0	—	116.5

Branch to the Port de Lafarge* (port à la restitution de la dérivation de Montélimar)

		kilom.	lock	kilom.
	Junction with the main waterway	166.0	—	116.5
	Quay (de Viviers)	165.5 *bis*	—	117.0
	Confluence with l'Escoutaye (R.D.) ...	165.4 *bis*	—	117.1
	Ferry (private)	163.4 *bis*	—	119.1
	Private port (Ciments Lafarge et du Tiel) (R.D.)	162.0 *bis*	—	120.3
	Bridge (du Viviers)	166.0	—	116.0
Donzère	Bridge (de Donzère)	169.0	—	113.0
	Origin of la dérivation de Donzère à Mondragon (R.G.)	170.2	—	112.3
	Barrage de garde	170.7	—	111.8
	Parking port (de Donzère)	171.0	—	111.0
	Railway bridge. Bridge	174.0	—	108.0
La Garde-Adhémar	Junction with la Berre (R.G.)	175.0	—	107.0
	Bridge	179.0	—	103.0
St-Paul-Trois-Château	Bridge	180.0	—	102.0
Bollène	Bridge	185.0	—	97.0
	Entrance to lock de St-Pierre-de-Bollène ...	187.3	6	95.2
	Power station 'André Blondel'	187.5	—	95.0
	Bridge	192.0	—	90.0
Mondragon	Railway bridge	195.0	—	87.0
	Bridge	196.0	—	86.0
	Bridge	197.0	—	85.0
	Restitution of la dérivation de Donzère à Mondragon (R.G.)	200.5	—	82.0
Mornas	*Confluence with le Lez (R.G.)* ...	201.0	—	81.0
St-Etienne-des-Sorts	Ferry (de St-Etienne-des-Sorts) ...	203.0	—	79.0
Caderousse	... ...	208.0	—	74.0
Laudun	*Confluence with la Ceze (R.D.)* ...	213.0	—	69.0
	Port (de l'Ardoise)	214.0	—	68.0
Roquemaure	Bridge (de Roquemaure). Piles of old bridge	222.0	—	60.0
Villeneuve-lès-Avignon	Confluence with *le brass de Villeneuve* (R.D.)	234.0	—	48.0
Avignon	Ferry (de Cabanne). *Confluence with l'Ouvèze (R.G.)*	234.0	—	48.0
	Port (du Pontet)	236	—	46.0
	Port (d'Avignon). Ferry. Pont de St-Bénézet (ruin)	241.0	—	41.0

* Lies on the main river upstream of the point of restitution.
R.D. = Right Bank.   R.G. = Left Bank.

Distance Table

		kilom.	lock	kilom.
	Bridge (d'Avignon)	242.0	—	40.0
	Railway bridge	244.0	—	38.0
	Confluence with la Durance (R.G.)	248.0	—	34.0
Aramon	Ferry (d'Aramon)	253.0	—	29.0
Vallabregues	*Confluence with le Gardon (R.D.).* Old ferry ramp	262.0	—	20.0
Tarascon	Bridge and Port de Beaucaire (R.D.). Railway bridge	268.0	—	14.0
	Entrance to Canal du Rhône à Sète (R.D.)	268.3	—	14.2
Arles	Island (Ile des Canards). *Origin of le Petit Rhône (R.D.)*	279.0	—	3.0
	Bridge (d'Arles-Trinquetaille). *Limit of l'Inscription maritime*	282.5	—	0.0

Arles to the sea

General

Le Grand Rhône, or le Bas Rhône, unlike the previous sections of the river flows, as a general rule, sedately between its low sandy banks which have become 300 to 500 metres apart. It forms the eastern boundary, as le Petit Rhône forms the western one, of that remarkable triangular shaped island known as La Camargue. This island consists of a vast plain of alluvial soil intersected by numerous salt water lakes *(étangs)* and marshes. Year by year the river, carrying heavy silt, advances seaward and prolongs the delta with uncertain and shifting banks which are locally known as '*theys*'. An area of this tract has been set aside for zoological and botanical research, but most of the rest is now being reclaimed for agriculture.

On the lower reach of le Grand Rhône, about 9 kilometres from the sea, the port of La Tour-Saint-Louis forms the end of the navigation of the river. At Saint-Louis a canal, called the *canal maritime Saint-Louis*, provides a passage for vessels from the river into le Golfe de Fos. This canal, of which full details can be obtained from the appropriate Pilot, contains one lock which has a length of 160 m. 00 with a width of 22 m. 00. The minimum depth of water is 5 m. 50. This lock forms the connection between the canal and the river, the remainder of the canal being free to the sea and having a length of about 3 kilometres. But this is prolonged by a dredged channel of a further 2 kilometres in length extending out into le Golfe de Fos. Below K.283 there are no obstructions to navigation in the river. The one rocky shoal *(le seuil de Terrin)* has now been removed and this allows not only *automoteurs* of 1,350 tons and 'pusher-trains' of 3,000 tons, but also small coasting vessels, which have passed the sea-lock at Port-St-Louis-du-Rhône, to ascend the river to Port d'Arles-Trinquetaille.

R.D. = Right Bank.   R.G. = Left Bank.

Length	From Arles to Port Saint-Louis is 41 kilometres; the distance from Arles to the mouth of the river where it falls into the sea is 48 kilometres*.

Depth The least depth at low water level is 1 m. 50. The normal depth is 2 m. 20.

Bridges There are no bridges between Arles and the sea.

Tow-path None.

Distance Table

		kilom.	*kilom.*	*kilom.*
Arles	Bridge (d'Arles-Trinquetaille). *Limit of l'Inscription maritime*	0.0	282.5	41.0
	Port (d'Arles-Trinquetaille)	0.1	282.6	40.9
	Junction with Canal d'Arles à Bouc (R.G.)	0.5	283.0	40.5
	Slipway and Chantiers de Barriol (R.G.) ...	1.5	284.0	39.5
Port St-Louis-du-Rhône	... ...	29.2	311.7	11.8
	Port (de Barcarin) (private)	34.0	316.5	7.0
	Ferry (de Barcarin)	34.3	316.8	6.7
	Port (de St-Louis-du-Rhône) (R.G.) ...	40.5	323.0	0.5
	Lock and entrance to Bassin du port. *Bassin du port connected with marine canal Saint-Louis*	41.0	323.5	0.0
	Discharge into la Mediterranée		330.0	

CANAL DU RHÔNE AU RHIN

General† The Canal du Rhône au Rhin begins at Saint-Symphorien on la Saône (at K.158) and, by l'embranchement de Kembs-Niffer, joins le Rhin in le bief d'Ottmarsheim of le Grand Canal d'Alsace. It has a summit level and two tunnels. The summit level, which is well over a thousand feet above the sea (340 metres) has a length of about 5 kilometres.

The tunnels do not, however, occur at the summit level but between the summit and la Saône. The first is at Thoraise (K.59) and is 185 metres in length. It is sited at 300 metres upstream of Lock No. 56. As the tunnel is straight and of short length there is no difficulty in seeing right through, but it is necessary to give a good blast of the horn to warn descending vessels that the entrance is engaged because there is a sudden right-hand turn at the upstream

---

* Note: Distances in the centre column are from Lyon.
† See Plan No. 14.
R.D. = Right Bank.   R.G. = Left Bank.

end; the canal at that point is of ample width to allow of all necessary manoeuvres. The width of the tunnel at the water level is 6 m. 00 and the headroom throughout is 4 m. 10. The second tunnel is at Besançon (K.73) and it has a length of 394 metres. It is called *le tunnel de Tarragnoz* or, more rarely *le tunnel de la Citadelle.*

Tunnel de Thoraise

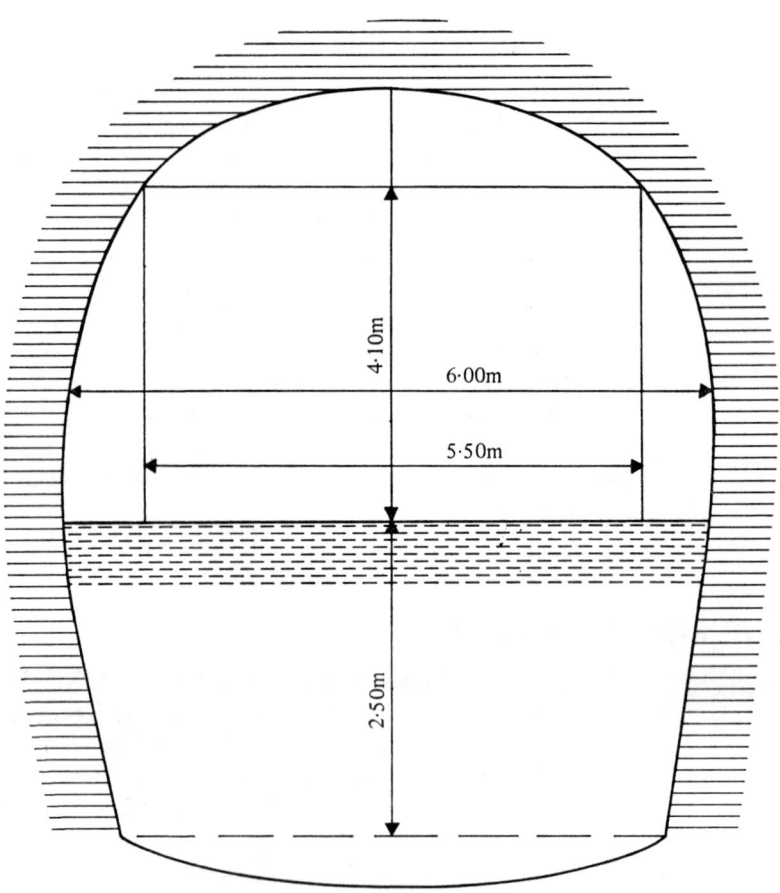

Note: No towpath.

CAUTION. Live electric wires may be established throughout the length of this tunnel.

Immediately at the downstream entrance to the tunnel stands Lock No. 50 and from this lock is worked an illuminated plaque, placed at the upstream entrance to the tunnel, which bears the word

STOP, and thus the passage of the tunnel is controlled. The width of the tunnel at water level is 6 m. 50 and in addition it has a tow-path along one side whereas the Thoraise tunnel is without a tow-path. The depth of water in both tunnels is 2 m. 50.

Tunnel de Tarragnoz

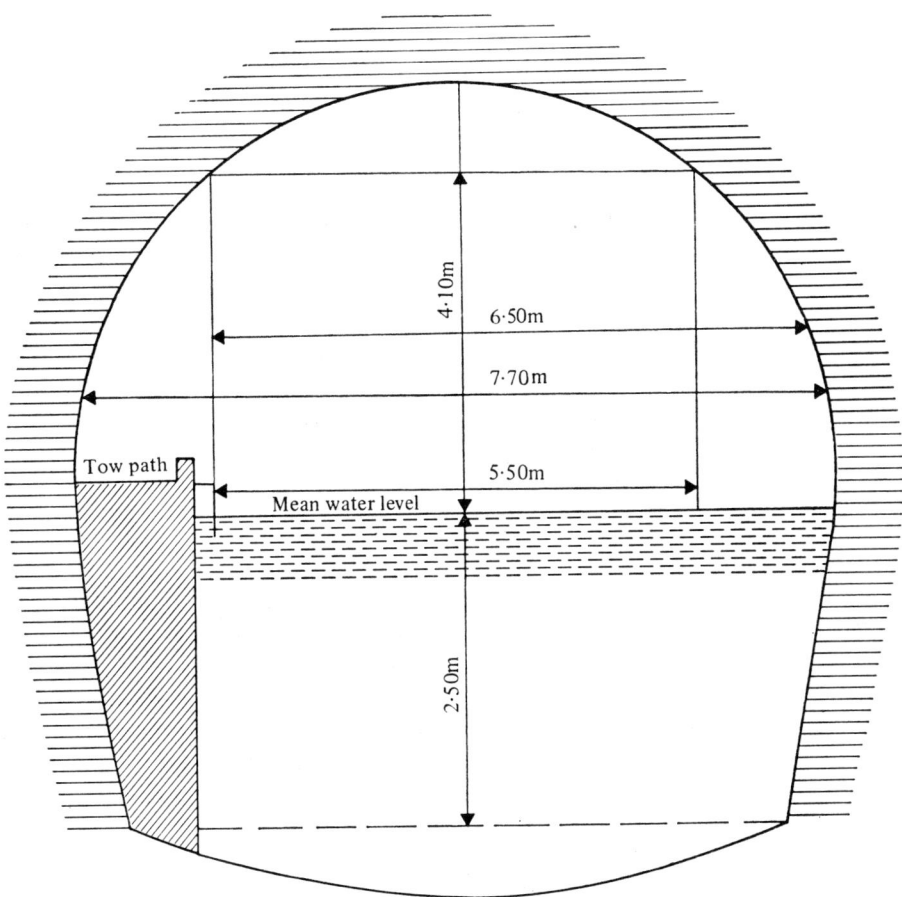

CAUTION. Live electric wires may be established throughout the length of this tunnel.

Owing to the opening in 1932 of the first pound of le Grand Canal d'Alsace and the subsequent construction of three other pounds of that canal, together with three out of four reaches of le Rhin canalisé, that part of le Canal du Rhône au Rhin which lay between Mulhouse and Strasbourg has been greatly modified*. Along the

* See Plan No. 14.

canal from its junction with la Saône to its entry into the new turning-basin at l'Ile Napoléon there has been no significant change; but from that point the canal is closed and no navigation is allowed along it. From the turning-basin a canal, called l'embranchement de Kembs-Niffer, runs eastwards to connect with le Grand Canal d'Alsace in le bief d'Ottmarsheim (at G.C.A. 11.4).† Thus this *embranchement* has actually become the main route to le Rhin. L'embranchement has a length of 13 km. and one lock (85 m. 00 × 12 m. 00): the depth is 2 m. 20 and the least headroom under bridges is 3 m. 70.

There is, however, one section of le Canal du Rhône au Rhin between Mulhouse and Strasbourg which is still in service:

> from K.74.5 to K.77.8—which is part of the connection between le Grand Canal d'Alsace and the Port de Colmar.*

L'Embranchement de Neuf-Brisach. Leaves le Grand Canal d'Alsace at G.C.A. 51.8 and joins le Canal du Rhône au Rhin at K.74.5. It is 6.4 km. in length and has one lock (40 m. 00 × 6 m. 00); the depth is 2 m. 20 and the least headroom under bridges is 3 m. 70. It forms the *first section* connecting le Grand Canal d'Alsace with the Port de Colmar.

The *second section* is the length of le Canal du Rhône au Rhin between K.74.5 and K.77.8, above.

L'Embranchement de Colmar. Leaves les Canal du Rhône au Rhin at K.77.8 (as above) and it is the *final section* joining le Grand Canal d'Alsace with the Port de Colmar. It is 13.0 km. in length and is a 'junction canal' as far as the crossing of l'Ill; beyond that river the section uses la Lauch canalisée. It has one lock (38 m. 85 × 5 m. 20) and a guard-gate where it crosses l'Ill. The depth is 2 m. 30 and the headroom under bridges is 3 m. 70.

L'Embranchement de Belfort. This branch was formerly called 'le Canal de Montbéliard à la Haute-Saône'‡. It leaves the main route at K.171.8 and has an effective length of 9.8 km. to the private port de Botans. From Botans to the port de Belfort is about 5 kilometres, but that part of the branch has been abandoned by the navigation. There are 5 locks from the main canal junction to the port of Botans each 38 m. 70 in length and 5 m. 20 in width. The depth is 2 m. 00 and the headroom under bridges is 3 m. 70.

* See Plan No. 14.
† Kilométrage along Le Grand Canal d'Alsace.
‡ See p. 156.

Length	The length of the canal from Saint-Symphorien to the beginning of l'Embranchement de Kembs-Niffer is 224 kilometres. It is worth mentioning that the kilometre posts are numbered in both directions from the summit level, or rather, from Saint-Symphorien to the summit level is 186 kilometres, and again from the summit to the junction of l'Embranchement de Kembs-Niffer is 38 kilometres.
Locks	There are 118 locks in all, and they are distributed as follows:

79 locks which fall towards la Saône.
39 locks which fall towards le Rhin.

The locks vary in dimensions slightly, but none has a less length than 38 m. 70 or a less width than 5 m. 10. The locks are numbered from the summit downstream in both directions.

Depth	The depth of the canal is maintained at 2 m. 20 throughout.
Bridges	All the bridges have a clear headroom of 3 m. 70 except the bridge at Noyers (K.32) which has only 3 m. 55.
Tow-path	There is a good tow-path throughout.

Distance Table

		kilom.	lock	kilom.
Saint-Symphorien*	*Junction with la Saône (at Section I K.158).*			
	Lock (No. 75 de la Saône)	0.0	1	186.0
	Lock (No. 74 de Laperriere). Bridge ...	0.0	2	186.0
	Lock (No. 73 de la Tuilerie)	1.0	3	185.0
	Bridge (de Samerey)	4.0	—	182.0
Abergement	Lock (No. 72 d'Abergement-la-Ronce) ...	6.0	4	180.0
	Lock (No. 71 de-la-Ronce)...	8.0	5	178.0
Damparis	Lock (No. 70 de Belvoye)	10.0	6	176.0
	Bridge (de Beauregard). Railway bridge ...	11.0	—	175.0
Choisey	Lock (No. 69 de Bon-Repos)	12.0	7	174.0
	Bridge (de Choisey)	14.0	—	172.0
Dôle	Bridge (de St-Ylie)	15.0	—	171.0
	Lock (No. 68 de la Prise-d'Eau)	17.0	8	169.0
	Lock (No. 67 du Jardin Philippe)	18.0	9	168.0
	Bridge (de la Charité). Port (de Prélot) ...	18.0	—	168.0
	Port (de Dôle)	18.0	—	168.0
	Bridge (du Pasquier)	19.0	—	167.0
	Lock (No. 66 de Charles-Quint)	19.0	10	167.0
	Railway bridge	19.0	—	167.0
Brévans	Bridge (de Brévans). Railway bridge ...	21.0	—	165.0
	Lock (No. 65 de Bavernas)	22.0	11	164.0
Rochefort-sur-Nenon	Lock (de garde No. 65 N de Rochefort) ...	25.0	12	161.0
Audelange	Lock (No. 64 d'Audelange)	27.0	13	159.0

* See Plan No. 17.

Distance Table

		kilom.	lock	kilom.
	Bridge (d'Audelange). Guard gate... ...	28.0	—	158.0
Lavans-lès-Dole	Lock (No. 63 de Moulin-Rouge)	29.0	14	157.0
	Bridge (de Lavans)	31.0	—	155.0
Orchamps	Lock (de garde No. 63 N d'Orchamps) ...	33.0	15	153.0
	Bridge (d'Orchamps)	33.0	—	153.0
Labarre	Bridge (de Labarre)	35.0	—	151.0
	Lock (No. 62 du Moulin des Malades) ...	37.0	16	149.0
	Lift bridge (du Moulin des Malades) ...	37.0	—	149.0
Monteplain	Lock (No. 61 de Ranchot)	38.0	17	148.0
	Bridge (de Ranchot). Guard gate	39.0	—	147.0
Dampierre	Lock (No. 60 de Dampierre)	40.0	18	146.0
	Bridge (de Dampierre). Railway bridge ...	41.0	—	145.0
Fraisans	Guard gate. Bridge (de Châteauneuf) ...	42.0	—	144.0
Salans-s-le-Doubs	Bridge (de Salans). Lock (No. 59 de St-Vit)	45.0	19	141.0
Rozet-Fluans	Lock (No. 58 a de Rozet-Fluans). Bridge	48.0	20	138.0
	Lock (No. 58 N de Routelle)	49.0	21	137.0
	Bridge (du Moulin d'Arenthon)	51.0	—	135.0
Osselle	Bridge (d'Osselle)	53.0	—	133.0
	Lock (No. 57 d'Osselle)	53.0	22	133.0
	Bridge (du Portail de Roche)	54.0	—	132.0
	Railway bridge	54.0	—	132.0
	Lock (de garde No. 57 N de Torpes) ...	56.0	23	130.0
Boussière	Bridge (de Torpes/Boussière)	57.0	—	129.0
Thoraise	Lock (No. 56 de Thoraise)	59.0	24	127.0
	Tunnel (de Thoraise) (185 m.)	59.0	—	127.0
	Lock (de garde No. 56 N de Thoraise) ...	60.0	25	126.0
	Bridge (de Montferrand)	60.0	—	126.0
Rancenay	Bridge (de Rancenay)	63.0	—	123.0
	Staircase locks (Nos. 55 and 54 de Rancenay) (2)	63.0	27	123.0
Aveney	Narrows (détroit d'Aveney) (411 m. × 6 m.)	64.0	—	122.0
	Bridge (d'Aveney)	66.0	—	120.0
	Guard gate (No. 54 bis d'Aveney)	66.0	—	120.0
Arguel	Lock (No. 53 de Gouille)	68.0	28	118.0
Besançon	Bridge (de Velotte)	71.0	—	115.0
Velotte	Lock (No. 52 de Velotte)	72.0	29	114.0
Tarragnoz	Lock (No. 51 de Tarragnoz). Basin ...	73.0	30	113.0
	Bridge (de Tarragnoz)	73.0	—	113.0
	Tunnel (de Tarragnoz or 'de la Citadelle') (394 m.)	73.0	—	113.0
	Lock (No. 50 N de Tarragnoz)	73.0	31	113.0
	Bridge and Guard gate. (No. 50 bis de Rivotte). Port	74.0	—	112.0
Besançon	Footbridge (des Prés-de-Vaux)	74.0	—	112.0
	Lock (No. 49 de la Malâte)...	76.0	32	110.0

Distance Table

		kilom.	lock	kilom.
Chalèze	Bridge and Lock (No. 48 de Chalèze) ...	82.0	33	104.0
Roche-lèz-Beaupré	Bridge (de Roche). Guard gate (No. 48 bis)	85.0	—	101.0
	Footbridge (de Grand-Vaire)	88.0	—	98.0
Deluz	Bridge (de Deluz)	90.0	—	96.0
	Staircase locks (Nos. 46 and 47 de Deluz)	90.0	35	96.0
	Guard gate (No. 46 bis de Deluz)	93.0	—	93.0
Aigremont	Lock (No. 45 d'Aigremont)	94.0	36	92.0
	Bridge and Lock (No. 44 de Laissey) ...	96.0	37	90.0
	Bridge (d'Ougney/Douvot)	98.0	—	88.0
Ougney-Douvot	Lock (No. 43 de Douvot)	99.0	38	87.0
	Bridge (d'Ougney)	101.0	—	85.0
	Lock (No. 43 d'Ougney)	101.0	39	85.0
Fourbanne	Lock (No. 41 de Fourbanne)	103.0	40	83.0
	Lock (No. 40 de Baumerousse)	107.0	41	79.0
Baume-lès-Dames	Bridge (de la Grange Villotey)	108.0	—	78.0
	Port (de Baume-lès-Dames)	109.0	—	77.0
	Guard gate (No. 40 bis de Baume-lès-Dames)	109.0	—	77.0
	Lock (No. 39 de Lonot)	111.0	42	75.0
	Lock (No. 38 de la Raie-aux-Chèvres) ...	113.0	43	73.0
Bois-la-Ville	Lock (No. 37 de Grand-Crucifix)	116.0	44	70.0
	Bridge (d'Hyèvre-Magny)	118.0	—	68.0
	Lock (No. 36 d'Hyèvre-Magny)	118.0	45	68.0
Hyèvre-Magny	Lock (No. 35 de l'Ermite)	119.0	46	67.0
	Lock (No. 34)	121.0	47	65.0
Branne	Lock (de garde No. 33 N de Branne) ...	123.0	48	63.0
	Guard gate (No. 33 bis de Branne) ...	125.0	—	61.0
Clerval	Bridge (de Clerval)	126.0	—	60.0
	Lock (No. 32 de Clerval)	127.0	49	59.0
Pompierre	Lock (No. 31 de Pompierre)	130.0	50	56.0
	Lock (No. 30 de la Plaine de Pompierre) ...	132.0	51	54.0
	Railway bridge	133.0	—	53.0
	Bridge (de Rang). Guard gate (No. 30 bis)	134.0	—	52.0
Appenans	Lock (No. 29 d'Appenans)	136.0	52	50.0
	Lock (No. 28 de la Goulisse)	138.0	53	48.0
L'Isle-s-le-Doubs	Lock (No. 27 des Papeteries)	139.0	54	47.0
	Bridge and Port (de l'Isle-s-le-Doubs) ...	140.0	—	46.0
	Lock (No. 26 de l'Isle-s-le-Doubs)... ...	140.0	55	46.0
	Railway bridge	141.0	—	45.0
	Lock (No. 25 de Côteau-Lunans)	142.0	56	44.0
Blussans	Bridge and Lock (No. 24 de Blussans) ...	145.0	57	41.0
	Lock (No. 23 de Colombier-Châtelot) ...	147.0	58	39.0
	Railway bridge	148.0	—	38.0
Saint-Maurice	Bridge (de Saint-Maurice)...	149.0	—	37.0
	Lock (No. 22 de Saint-Maurice)	149.0	59	37.0

Distance Table

		kilom.	lock	kilom.
	Lock (No. 21 de Colombier-Fontaine) ...	151.0	60	35.0
Colombier-Fontaine	Lift bridge (de Colombier-Fontaine) ...	151.0	60	33.0
	Lock (No. 20 de la Raydans)	153.0	61	33.0
Etouvans	Lock (No. 19 de la Plaine de Dampierre)	155.0	62	31.0
	Bridge and Lock (No. 18 de Dampierre)	157.0	63	29.0
	Bridge (de Berche) ...	158.0	—	28.0
Voujeaucourt	Bridge (du Moulin)	159.0	—	27.0
	Lock (de garde No. 18 bis de Voujeau-court	159.0	64	27.0
	Lock (No. 17 de Voujeaucourt) ...	159.0	65	27.0
	Lock (No. 16 de Courcelles-Montbéliard)	162.0	66	24.0
	Lift bridge (de Courcelles)	162.0	—	24.0
	Lock (No. 15 de Côteau-Jouvent) ...	163.0	67	23.0
Montbéliard	Port (de Montbéliard)	164.0	—	22.0
	Lift bridge (de la Petite-Hollande) ...	164.0	—	22.0
	Lock (No. 14 de Montbéliard)	164.0	68	22.0
	Lift bridge (de la Pointerie)	165.0	—	21.0
	Railway bridge	165.0	—	21.0
Exincourt	Lock (No. 13 s/s Exincourt)	166.0	69	20.0
	Port (d'Exincourt)	167.0	—	19.0
	Bridge (du Repos)	168.0	—	18.0
	Lock (No. 12 d'Exincourt)	168.0	70	18.0
Etupes	Lock (No. 11 d'Etupes)	169.0	71	17.0
Fesches-le-Châtel	Lock (No. 10 des Marivées)	171.0	72	15.0
	Lock (No. 9 N d'Allenjoie)	171.0	73	15.0
	Pont-canal (de Fesches)	171.0	—	15.0
	Junction with L'Embranchement de Belfort (at K.0)	171.0	—	15.0
	Bridge (du Moulin-Bois)	172.0	—	14.0
Allenjoie	Bridge (d'Allenjoie)	173.0	—	13.0
	Lock (No. 8 des Fontenelles)	174.0	74	12.0
Bourogne	Lock (No. 7)	176.0	75	10.0
	Port (de Bourogne). Bridge	177.0	—	9.0
	Bridge	177.0	—	9.0
	Railway bridge	178.0	—	8.0
	Port (de Froidefontaine). Quay ...	178.0	—	8.0
Froidefontaine	Lock (No. 6). Swing bridge	179.0	76	7.0
Brébotte	Lock (No. 5). Port (de Brébotte)	181.0	775	.0
	Bridge	181.0	—	5.0
Bretagne	Bridge. Lock (No. 4)	183.0	78	3.0
	Port (de Montreux-Château)	185.0	—	1.0
Montreux-Château	Bridge. Lock (No. 3)	185.0	79	1.0
	Beginning of summit level	185.0	—	1.0
Montreux-Jeune	*Change of kilométrage*	186.0	—	38.0
		or 0.0		or 0.0

Distance Table		*kilom.*	*lock*	*kilom.*
	Turning basin	1.0	—	37.0
Montreux-Vieux	Bridge. Port	2.0	—	36.0
Valdieu	End of summit level. Lock (No. 2). Railway bridge	5.0	1	33.0
	Bridge. Port (de Valdieu). Lock (No. 3). Lock (No. 4)	5.0	3	33.0
	Lock (No. 5)	5.0	4	33.0
	Lock (No. 6). Lock (No. 7). Lock (No. 8)	6.0	7	32.0
Retzwiller	Lock (No. 9). Lock (No. 10)	6.0	9	32.0
	Lock (No. 11). Lock (No 12)	7.0	11	31.0
	Lock (No. 13). Bridge. Port (Gilardoni)...	8.0	12	30.0
Wolfersdorf	Lock (No. 14). Lock (No. 15). Bridge. Port (Gilardoni)	9.0	14	29.0
	Pont-canal. *One-way traffic.* Lock (No. 16)	10.0	15	28.0
	Port (de Wolfersdorf-Dannemarie) ...	10.0	—	28.0
Dannemarie	Turning-basin. Lock (No. 17)	10.0	16	28.0
Gommersdorf	Lock (No. 18). Bridge. Lock (No. 19). Bridge	11.0	18	27.0
	Lock (No. 20). Lock (No. 21). Footbridge	12.0	20	26.0
d'Hagenbach	Lock (No. 22). Turning-basin	13.0	21	25.0
	Port (d'Hagenbach). Lock (No. 23). Bridge	14.0	22	24.0
d'Eglingen	Lock (No. 24)	15.0	23	23.0
	Lock (No. 25). Bridge	16.0	24	22.0
d'Enschingen	Lock (No. 26). Bridge	17.0	25	21.0
Brinighoffen	Lock (No. 27). Bridge	18.0	26	20.0
d'Heidwiller	Bridge. Lock (No. 28)	19.0	27	19.0
	Lock (No. 29). Bridge	20.0	28	18.0
	Lock (No. 30). Bridge	21.0	29	17.0
d'Illfurth	Lock (No. 31)	22.0	30	16.0
	Lock (No. 32). Bridge	23.0	31	15.0
	Lock (No. 33)	24.0	32	14.0
Zillisheim	Lock (No. 34)	25.0	33	13.0
	Bridge	26.0	—	12.0
	Lock (No. 35). Lift bridge	27.0	34	11.0
Brunstatt	Turning basin	28.0	—	10.0
	Lock (No. 36)	29.0	35	9.0
	Bridge. Lock (No. 37)	29.0	36	9.0
	Bridge	30.0	—	8.0
Mulhouse	Lock (No. 38). Bridge	31.0	37	7.0
	Lock (No. 39. Footbridge. Railway bridge	32.0	38	6.0
	Port. Bridge (de Noyers). Bridge (d'Altkirch)	32.0	—	6.0
	Bridge (Jules Ehrmann). Port. Old basin	32.0	—	6.0
	Covered section of canal in front of railway station (de Mulhouse)	33.0	—	5.0

Distance Table

		kilom.	lock	kilom.
	Bridge (des Bonnes Gens). Beginning of Port de Mulhouse. Quay (des Grands Moulins de Strasbourg)	33.0	—	5.0
	Quay (de l'Electricité de France)	34.0	—	4.0
	Lift bridge. Lock (No. 41). Bridge ...	34.0	39	4.0
	Limit of the Port de Mulhouse. Entrance to *le canal de jonction du Nouveau Bassin (R.D.)**	35.0	—	3.0
	Bridge (de Modenheim). Railway bridge	35.0	—	3.0
Illzach	Quay (de la Standard Française des Pétroles)	36.0	—	2.0
	Bridge. Ile Napoléon (R.G.). Turning basin. *Origin of l'Embranchement de Kembs-Niffer (R.G.)*	38.0	—	0.0

The Canal has been taken out of service from K.37.8 to K.74.5

		kilom.	lock	kilom.
	Junction with l'Embranchement de Neuf-Brisach	74.5	—	0.0
Baltzenheim	Lock (No. 63). Bridge	76.4	1	1.9
Artzenheim	*Junction with l'Embranchement de Colmar*	77.8	—	3.3

The Canal is being taken out of service from K.77.8 to K.134.1 (1970)
Which includes the following section to Strasbourg

		kilom.	lock	kilom.
	Junction with le canal du raccordement entre le Canal du Rhône au Rhin et le Rhin canalisé (K.9.7 de la dérivation de Rhinau-Sundhouse)	102.4	—	0.0
	Lock (de guard No. 75). Bridge	103.0	1	1.0
Boofzheim	Lock (No. 76). Port (de Boofzheim) ...	105.0	2	3.0
Obenheim	Lock (No. 77). Bridge	108.0	3	6.0
Gerstheim	Bridge	110.0	—	8.0
	Port (de Gerstheim). Lock (No. 78).	110.0	4	9.0
	Lock (No. 79)	114.0	5	12.0
	Crossing (at one level) of the discharge canal for flood waters of the River Ill ...	115.0	—	13.0
	Lock (de guard No. 80). Bridge. Port d'Erstein)	115.0	6	13.0
Nordhouse	Bridge	117.0	—	15.0
Plobsheim	Pont-canal. Lock (No. 81)	118.0	7	16.0
	Bridge	120.0	—	18.0
	Port (de Plobsheim)	121.0	—	19.0
Eschau	Lock (No. 82)	122.0	8	20.0

R.D. = Right Bank.   R.G. = Left Bank.

Distance Table			*kilom.*	*lock*	*kilom.*
	Bridge. Port (d'Eschau)	123.0	—	21.0
Illkirch-Graffenstaden	Port (d'Illkirch-Graffenstaden)	124.0	—	22.0
	Lock (No. 83). Bridge	125.0	9	23.0
	Bridge	126.0	—	24.0
	Bridge	128.0	—	26.0
	Lock (No. 84). Railway bridge	129.0	10	27.0
Strasbourg	Port (de Strasbourg-Meinau). Lock (No. 85)	131.0	11	29.0
	Railway bridge. *Junction with l'Ill* ...	132.0	—	30.0
	Guard gate (du Heyritz)	132.0	—	30.0
	Basin (de Hôpital). Lock (No. 86) ...	133.0	12	31.0
	Bridge (de l'Hôpital). Two bridges ...	133.0	—	31.0
	Junction with le Bassin Dusuzeau du Port de Strasbourg	134.0	—	32.0

Embranchement de Kembs-Niffer*

		kilom.	*lock*	*kilom.*
Illzach	Ile Napoléon. Beginning of l'embranchement in the turning basin at K.38 du Canal du Rhône au Rhin	0.0	—	13.0
	Railway bridge	0.0	—	13.0
	Quay ('Indénor')	2.0	—	11.0
Hombourg	Bridge (du Bouc)	4.0	—	9.0
Petit-Landau	Bridge	10.0	—	3.0
Niffer	Bridge	12.0	—	1.0
Kembs	Lock. *Junction with le Grand Canal d'Alsace* (at G.C.A. 11.4 of bief d'Ottmarsheim) ...	13.0	1	0.0

Embranchement de Neuf-Brisach

		kilom.	*lock*	*kilom.*
Biesheim	*Junction with l'Embranchement de Neuf-Brisach with le Rhin canalisé (at K.226.7)*	0.0	—	6.4
	Lock (du Rhin)	0.4	1	6.0
	Mouth of le Giessen	1.9	—	4.5
	Bridge (Pont Boulay)	2.1	—	4.3
	Railway bridge	2.2	—	4.2
	Barrage (du Giessen)	2.9	—	3.5
	Bridge (Pont Boebbels)	3.0	—	3.4
Kunheim	Bridge (de Kunheim)	5.2	—	1.2
	Junction with le Canal du Rhône au Rhin (at K.74.5)	6.4	—	0.0

Embranchement de Colmar

		kilom.	*lock*	*kilom.*
Artzenheim	*Junction of l'Embranchement de Colmar with le Canal du Rhône au Rhin (at K.77.8)* ...	0.0	—	13.3
	Bridge	0.4	—	12.9

* See Plan No. 14.

Distance Table

			kilom.	lock	kilom.
Durrenentzen	Bridge	... ...	1.8	—	11.5
Muntzenheim	Bridge	... ...	2.8	—	10.5
	Bridge	... ...	3.7	—	9.6
	Bridge	... ...	4.6	—	8.7
	Bridge	... ...	5.7	—	7.6
Wickersheim	Bridge	... ...	7.0	—	6.3
Bischwihr	Bridge	... ...	7.8	—	5.5
Holtzwihr	Bridge	... ...	8.7	—	4.6
Wihr-en-Plaine	Bridge	... ...	9.5	—	3.8
	Bridge	... ...	10.1	—	3.2
Colmar	Bridge	... ...	11.0	—	2.3
	Lock (de l'Ill) with guard gate	11.1	I	2.2
	Crossing of l'Ill (60 m. long) with barrage on left bank	11.2	—	2.0
	End of la Lauch canalisée with l'Ill ...	11.3	—	2.0
	Port (de la Société Rhin-Rhône)	12.1	—	1.2
	Turning basin	13.0	—	0.3
	End of navigation	13.3	—	0.0

Canal du raccordement entre le Rhin canalisé et le Canal du Rhône au Rhin*

		kilom.	lock	kilom.
Friesenheim	*Junction with le Rhin canalisé (at K.9.7)*	0.0	—	3.8
	Lock (du Rhin)	0.4	I	3.4
	Crossing (at one level) of l'Ischert and canal de drainage E.D.F.	0.5	—	3.3
	Junction with Canal du Rhône au Rhin (at K.102.4)	3.8	—	0.0

Embranchement de Belfort†

		kilom.	lock	kilom.
Allenjoie	*Junction with le Canal du Rhône au Rhin (at K.171)*	0.0	—	15.0
	Bridge (des Jonchets). Bridge (de Brognard)	1.0	—	14.0
Dambenois	Lock (No. 1 de Brognard)	2.0	I	13.0
	Bridge (de Dambenois)	3.0	—	12.0
	Lock (No. 2 de Dambenois)	4.0	2	11.0
Vourvenans	Road bridge	5.0	—	10.0
Trétudans	Turning basin. Port (de Trétudans) ...	5.0	—	10.0
	Lock (No. 3). Lock (No. 4)	6.0	4	9.0
Bermont	Lock (No. 5). Bridge (de Bermont) ...	7.0	5	8.0
Dorans	Bridge (de Dorans)	8.0	—	7.0
Botans	Turning basin. Port (de Botans). Lift bridge	9.0	—	6.0
Andelnans	Bridge	10.0	—	5.0
	Railway bridge	12.0	—	3.0

* This section is being taken out of service (1970).
† See also p. 204.

Distance Table

		kilom.	*lock*	*kilom.*
	Lock (No. 6). Lock (No. 7). Lock (No. 8)	12.0	8	3.0
	Port (de Bavilliers). Lock (No. 9) ...	13.0	9	2.0
	(Actual end of navigation)			
	Lock (No. 10). Lock (No. 11)	13.0	11	2.0
Essert	Port (de Belfort)	15.0	—	0.0

CANAL DU RHÔNE À SÈTE

General

The inland waterway which joins le Rhône to the port of Sète and to the Canal du Midi (via l'Etang de Thau) was first opened to navigation in the year 1820. It leaves le Rhône (at K.267) by a narrow 'cut' which has a length of some 230 metres; at the end of this channel is sited the first lock. When the level of le Rhône permits, this lock stands open; but it is closed as soon as the river rises above 7 m. 60 and is not again reopened until the level of the water has fallen below that figure. The canal is narrow so that to all intents it is a one-way route, but passing places are set at about $1\frac{1}{2}$ kilometres to enable vessels to pass one another. On its way the canal crosses two rivers, Le Vidourle and Le Lez, from which it is isolated; from le Vidourle by means of shutters which are electrically worked, but in the case of le Lez only by a barrage with 'stop' planks. Normally, these works allow the rivers to be crossed without difficulty, but during times of flood the navigation is interrupted. However, it must be pointed out that at the time of writing (1970) a number of very considerable changes are taking place all along this stretch of littoral from Grau-du-Roi in the east to Banyuls near the French-Spanish border in the south-west. A yacht harbour, capable of accommodating 1,000 yachts, has been excavated at la Grand-Motte (which lies about 5 kilometres west of Grau-du-Roi), and Grau-du-Roi itself is being enlarged to hold 1,500 pleasure craft. Similar schemes are projected in respect of a number of places along the coast—namely, at Carnon, Palavas, Cap d'Agde, l'embouchure de l'Aude, Gruissan, Leucate-Barcarès, Grau-St-Ange, St-Cyprien, and Banyuls. It remains to be seen how these developments will affect the canal. Nevertheless, from the point of view of the canal, the removal of le Palier shoal (just upstream of Arles) is more important. This shoal, which entails the dredging of the sand and gravel bed of the river between Beaucaire and the confluence with le Petit Rhône will have the effect of lowering appreciably the water level at Beaucaire, thus putting Lock No. 1 out of action In order to re-establish the through route between Sète and le Rhône a number of suggestions have been put forward and studied, amongst them the rebuilding of the existing lock or the construction of a new lock to the south of the town. The most favoured solution—which has now received official sanction—is to join le Petit Rhône to the existing canal in the region of Saint-Gilles, at which point the river approaches close to the canal. Le Rhône having been brought up to the European Waterway Standard between Lyon and the sea, the necessity for greatly improving the Canal du Rhône à Sète is already receiving serious consideration. Most probably the improvement would eventually have to extend to the Canal du Midi and the canal latéral à la Garonne.

At present there is only one short branch leading off from the main canal—if the marine cut at Aigues-Mortes which connects with the sea at Grau-du-Roi is excepted—and that is le canal de la Peyrade at Sète; but it seems certain that others (such as le Lez canalisé) will be improved or made to link the new Marinas with the main canal. In view of all this development, which is now in hand, local up-to-date enquiries are essential.

Length	The length of the canal measured from Beaucaire (le Rhône) to le Bassin de Thau at Sète is 98 kilometres.
Locks	There are 3 locks: the first at Beaucaire, as mentioned above, and the second at Nourriguier. Both these locks have a length of 80 m. oo with a width of 12 m. oo. The third lock is not really on the main route, but at the head of a marine cut to the sea at Aigues-Mortes, and it was placed there to prevent the sea water from flowing into the canal; it has never been shut and in 1955 the gates were removed.
Depth	The normal depth of water in the canal is 2 m. oo.
Bridges	All the fixed bridges have a minimum headroom of 4 m. 32 above the normal water level.
Tow-path	None. All traffic is self-propelled or in tows.

Distance Table

		kilom.	lock	kilom.
Beaucaire	*Junction with le Rhône* (narrow channel 235 metres). Lock	0.0	I	98.0
	Railway bridge. Bridge. Port (de Beaucaire)	0.0	—	98.0
	Bridge (de la Porte Vieille)	1.0	—	97.0
	Bridge (de la Bagnade)	2.0	—	96.0
	Bridge (de Charenconne)	3 0	—	95.0
	Lock (No. 2 de Nourriguier). Bridge ...	7.0	2	91.0
Bellegarde	Railway bridge	12.0	—	86.0

Distance Table

		kilom.	*lock*	*kilom.*
	Bridge (Pont d'Arles). Port	13.0	—	85.0
	Bridge (de Broussan)	16.0	—	82.0
Fourques	*Private quay*	18.0	—	80.0
Saint-Gilles	Footbridge. Port (de St-Gilles)	23.0	—	75.0
	Bridge and Railway bridge (de St-Gilles)...	24.0	—	74.0
	Bridge (Pont d'Espeyran)	29.0	—	69.0
Beauvoisin	Bridge (de Franquevaux)	35.0	—	63.0
Vauvert	Bridge (de Gallician)	39.0	—	59.0
Cailar	Bridge (Pont des Tourrandons)	43.0	—	55.0
St-Laurent-d'Aigouze	Bridge (Pont du Soulier)	48.0	—	50.0
Aigues-Mortes	Lock (No. 3 de garde)	49.0	3	49.0
	Bridge and Port (d'Aigues-Mortes) ...	50.0	—	48.0
	Swing railway bridge	50.0	—	48.0
	Footbridge. Crossing of la Vidourie ...	55.0	—	43.0
Marsillagues	Junction with Canal de Lunel (not navigable)	55.0	—	43.0
Palavas	Junction with Canal du Grau de Carnon (not navigable). Bridge	70.0	—	28.0
	Railway bridge	75.0	—	23.0
	Crossing of le Lez	75.0	—	23.0
	Bridge and Port (des Quatre-Canaux) ...	75.0	—	23.0
Vic	Footbridge (des Aresquièrs)	86.0	—	12.0
Frontignan	Railway bridge. Port. Lift bridge ...	92.0	—	6.0
	Bridge. Old bridge (de la Peyrade) ...	96.0	—	2.0
Sète	*Junction with Canal de la Peyrade* ...	96.0	—	2.0
	Railway bridge. Bridge	97.0	—	1.0
	Bassin de Thau	98.0	—	0.0

Branch Canal de la Peyrade (Port de Sète)

General   Le Canal de la Peyrade leaves the main route of the Canal du Rhône à Sète at K.96. It allows vessels to reach the Port de Sète without entering le Bassin de Thau, but large vessels cannot conveniently use this canal, owing to two sharp curves near the beginning. The length of the canal is 2 kilometres and there are no locks; the depth of water is 1 m. 50 and the headroom under bridges is 3 m. 72 at normal water level.

Distance Table

		kilom.	*lock*	*kilom.*
La Peyrade	*Junction with Canal du Rhône a Sète (at K.96). Railway bridge*	0.0	—	2.0
Sète	Bridge (Pont de Mascoulet). *Junction with the wet dock 'de La Peyrade' of the Port de Sète*	2.0	—	0.0

CANAL DE ROANNE À DIGOIN

General   The Canal de Roanne à Digoin begins at Roanne and ends close to the town of Digoin, where it joins the canal latéral à la Loire. In reality, it forms the first part of the canal latéral à la Loire, for it is joined to la Loire at Roanne.

Length   From the Port de Roanne to the junction with the canal latéral à la Loire (which is about 1 kilometre from Digoin) the distance is 55 kilometres.

Locks   There are 10 locks, all of a uniform size; they have a length of 39 m. 00 with a width of 5 m. 20. The total fall between Roanne and Digoin is about 37 metres, towards Digoin.

Depth   The normal depth of water is 2 m. 20.

Bridges   There are a number of fixed bridges, but all have a headroom of not less than 3 m. 70 above the normal water level.

Tow-path   Although most of the traffic is by self-propelled vessels, there is a good tow-path throughout, mostly following the right bank.

Distance Table		kilom.	lock	kilom.
Roanne	Port (de Roanne). *Junction with la Loire.*			
	Lock (No. 1) de Roanne	0.0	I	55.0
	Bridge (des Côtes)	1.0	—	54.0
	Port (d'Oudan). Aqueduct over canal ...	2.0	—	53.0
	Bridge (Pont Gardet). Bridge (Pont Matel)	3.0	—	52.0
	Bridge (Pont Vadon)	4.0	—	51.0
Mably	Bridge (Pont d'Aiguilly)	5.0	—	50.0
	Port (de Bonvert)	6.0	—	49.0
	Bridge (de Mably)	7.0	—	48.0
	Bridge (Pont Escroqué)	8.0	—	47.0
	Lock (No. 2 de Cornillon)	9.0	2	46.0
	Bridge (Pont Mathérat)	10.0	—	45.0
Briennon	Bridge (des Justices)	11.0	—	44.0
	Bridge (de Maltaverne)	12.0	—	43.0
	Bridge (de la Rate)	12.0	—	43.0
	Lock (No. 3 de Briennon)	13.0	3	42.0
	Port and Bridge (de Briennon)	14.0	—	41.0
	Bridge (de Boutasson)	16.0	—	39.0
	Pont-canal and Bridge (de la Teyssonne) ...	18.0	—	37.0
	Bridge (Pont Ray)	19.0	—	36.0
Iguerande	Bridge (Pont Valendru)	20.0	—	35.0
	Bridge (Pont Duplan). Port (d'Iguerande)	21.0	—	34.0
Melay	Bridge (Pont Brivet)	22.0	—	33.0

Distance Table

		kilom.	lock	kilom.
	Bridge (Pont Putenat). Bridge (des Gallands)	23.0	—	32.0
	Bridge (des Bagnots)	24.0	—	31.0
	Bridge (des Corretes). Port (de Melay) ...	25.0	—	30.0
	Bridge (de Melay)	26.0	—	29.0
Artaix	Pont-canal (des Brennons)...	26.0	—	29.0
	Bridge (d'Arcelles)	27.0	—	28.0
	Bridge (des Fanges)	28.0	—	27.0
	Port (d'Artaix). Bridges I and II (d'Artaix)	29.0	—	26.0
	Bridge (des Augers). Bridge (Pont Narbot)	30.0	—	25.0
Chambilly	Lock (No. 4 d'Artaix)	31.0	4	24.0
	Lock (No. 5 de Montgrailloux)	32.0	5	23.0
	Lock (No. 6) and Port (de Chambilly) ...	32.0	6	23.0
	Bridge (de la Croix-Valentin)	33.0	—	22.0
	Bridge (des Diens). Bridge (Pont Biscot) ...	34.0	—	21.0
Bourg-le-Comte	Bridge (des Meillerands)	35.0	—	20.0
	Port and Pont-canal (de Bourg-le-Comte)	35.0	—	20.0
	Bridge (Pont Gallay)	36.0	—	19.0
	Bridge and Lock (No. 7). (de Bourg-le-Comte)	36.0	7	19.0
	Bridge (du Bas-du-Riz)	37.0	—	18.0
Avrilly	Bridge (des Bouillets)	38.0	—	17.0
	Bridge (Pont Thynet)	39.0	—	16.0
	Port (d'Avrilly). Bridge (Pont Morgat) ...	40.0	—	15.0
Luneau	Bridge (de Bonant)	42.0	—	13.0
	Bridge (de Lurcy)	44.0	—	11.0
	Bridge (de Giverdon)	46.0	—	9.0
Chassenard	Bridge (de la Beaume), Bridge (de la Croix-Rouge)	48.0	—	7.0
	Bridge (de Séez)	49.0	—	6.0
	Bridge (de Saint-Leger)	50.0	—	5.0
	Bridge (des Blancs)	51.0	—	4.0
	Lock (No. 8 de Chassenard)	52.0	8	3.0
	Lock (No. 9 des Beugnets)	53.0	9	2.0
	Lock (No. 10 des Bretons)	54.0	10	1.0
	Bridge (des Bretons)	55.0	—	0.0
Digoin*	*Junction with canal latéral à Loire (at K.2)*	55.0	—	0.0

CANAL DE ROUBAIX

General   The Canal de Roubaix joins the Canal de la Deûle to l'Escaut after having passed over the Belgian frontier. That part of the canal which lies in Belgium is known as the *Canal de l'Espierres*.

* See Plan No. 4.

Length	From its junction with the Canal de la Deûle at Marquette to the crossing of the Belgian frontier the canal has a length of 20 kilometres; a further length of 8 kilometres brings it to its junction with l'Escaut*.
Locks	There are 12 locks sited upon French soil and the canal contains a summit level. Of the 12 locks 7 fall towards la Deûle and the remaining 5 towards l'Escaut. The locks have a length of 39 m. 40 with a width of 5 m. 18.
Depth	The depth of water is normally 2 m. 00.
Bridges	The fixed bridges have a minimum headroom of 3 m. 68 above the normal water level.
Tow-path	There is a good tow-path throughout.

Distance Table

		kilom.	*lock*	*kilom.*
Marquette	Junction with Canal de la Deûle (la Deûle canalisée) (at K.50). Bridge	0.0	—	20.0
	Lock (No. 1 de Marquette)	0.0	1	20.0
	Bridge (de Marcq-en-Baroeul)	2.0	—	18.0
Marcq-en-Baroeul	Lock (No. 2 de Marcq-en-Baroeul). Staithe	3.0	2	17.0
	Bridge (du Risban)	4.0	—	16.0
	Footbridge (du Collège)	6.0	—	14.0
Wasquehal	Bridge (du Château-Rouge)	6.0	—	14.0
	Bridge and Lock (No. 3 du Trieste) ...	7.0	3	13.0
	Bridge and Lock (No. 4 du Plomeux) ...	8.0	4	12.0
	Lock (No. 5 du Noir Bonnet)	8.0	5	12.0
	Bridge and Lock (No. 6 du Cottigny) ...	8.0	6	12.0
	Lock (No. 7 de la Mazure). Beginning of summit level. Bridge (de la Mazure) Staithe	9.0	7	11.0
	(du Blanc Seau)	10.0	—	10.0
Tourcoing	Footbridge and swing bridge (du Blanc Seau)	10.0	—	10.0
	Footbridge. Bridge (du Fresnoy)	11.0	—	9.0
Roubaix	Bridge (de la République). Quays	12.0	—	8.0
	Railway bridges. Swing bridge (de Fontenoy). Quays	12.0	—	8.0
	Lock (No. 8 de l'Union. End of summit level	12.0	8	8.0
	Quay (de Gand). Quay (d'Anvers)... ...	13.0	—	7.0
	Lift bridge (des Couteaux)	13.0	—	7.0
	Footbridge (du Hutin)	13.0	—	7.0
	Swing bridge (Pont-tournant Daubenton)	14.0	—	6.0

* See *Inland Waterways of Belgium*, Imray Laurie Norie & Wilson.

Distance Table

		kilom.	lock	kilom.
	Footbridge and lift bridge (de la Vigne) ...	14.0	—	6.0
	Lock (No. 9 du Nouveau Monde)... ...	14.0	9	6.0
	Lock (No. 10 du Calvaire)	14.0	10	6.0
	Footbridge and lift bridge (de Wattrelos)...	15.0	—	5.0
	Lock (No. 11 du Galon d'Eau)	15.0	11	5.0
	Footbridge (des Soies)	15.0	—	5.0
	Railway bridge. Bridge (du Sartel)... ...	16.0	—	4.0
	Lock (No. 12 du Sartel)	16.0	12	4.0
Wattrelos	Railway bridge	17.0	—	3.0
	Footbridge (Saint-Marguerite)	17.0	—	3.0
Leers	Lift bridge (de Grimonpont)	18.0	—	2.0
Wattrelos	Customs Office. Staithe (de Grimonpont)	18.0	—	2.0
Wattrelos	Frontier. (Franco/Belge)	20.0	—	0.0

CANAL DE SAINT-QUENTIN

General The Canal de Saint-Quentin begins at the town of Cambrai, where it unites with the canalised river l'Escaut, and ends at Chauny where it joins up with the canal latéral à l'Oise. It thus forms a direct communication between l'Escaut and l'Oise and between le région du Nord and Paris. Near Saint-Simon it joins with the Canal de la Somme; and by its branch to La Fère it connects with la Sambre by the Canal de la Sambre à l'Oise. The Canal de Saint-Quentin besides containing a summit level at an elevation of about 270 ft. above sea level, has two tunnels. The summit level is situated between the locks at le Bosquet and Lesdins (K.24/K.25), and it is along this length that the two tunnels are driven. The first, le Grand Souterrain, is called *de Bony* or *de Macquincourt* and is 5,670 metres in length; the second, called *de Lesdins* or *du Tronquoy* is 1,098 metres in length. The tunnels have a navigable width of 6 m. 75 and a head-room of 3 m. 58. Towage is compulsory for all vessels, whether self-propelled or not, throughout the whole length of the summit level. Tows *(rames)* are made up twice in both directions every 24 hours. The actual times of departure must be ascertained locally, but they are approximately:

Paris towards Belgium (from Lesdins)—12.00 and 22.30 hours.
Belgium towards Paris (from Vendhuile)—13.00 and 22.50 hours.

This service is conducted by a special vessel, electrically operated, which warps itself along a chain laid in the bed of the canal. The time taken to pass through both tunnels is about 8 to 10 hours. There is a halt about halfway in a basin or port to allow the tow from the opposite direction to cross over. Yachts are usually towed from the last barge.

Length	From Cambrai, where the canal joins l'Escaut, to Chauny, where it joins the canal latéral à l'Oise, the distance is 92 kilometres.

Locks	There are 35 locks. Of these 17 fall towards Cambrai and 18 towards Chauny. All these locks are twin locks which consist of two chambers side by side and separated by a central quay. Each chamber has a length of 39 m. 33 with a width of 6 m. 00.

Tunnels des Bony et Lesdins

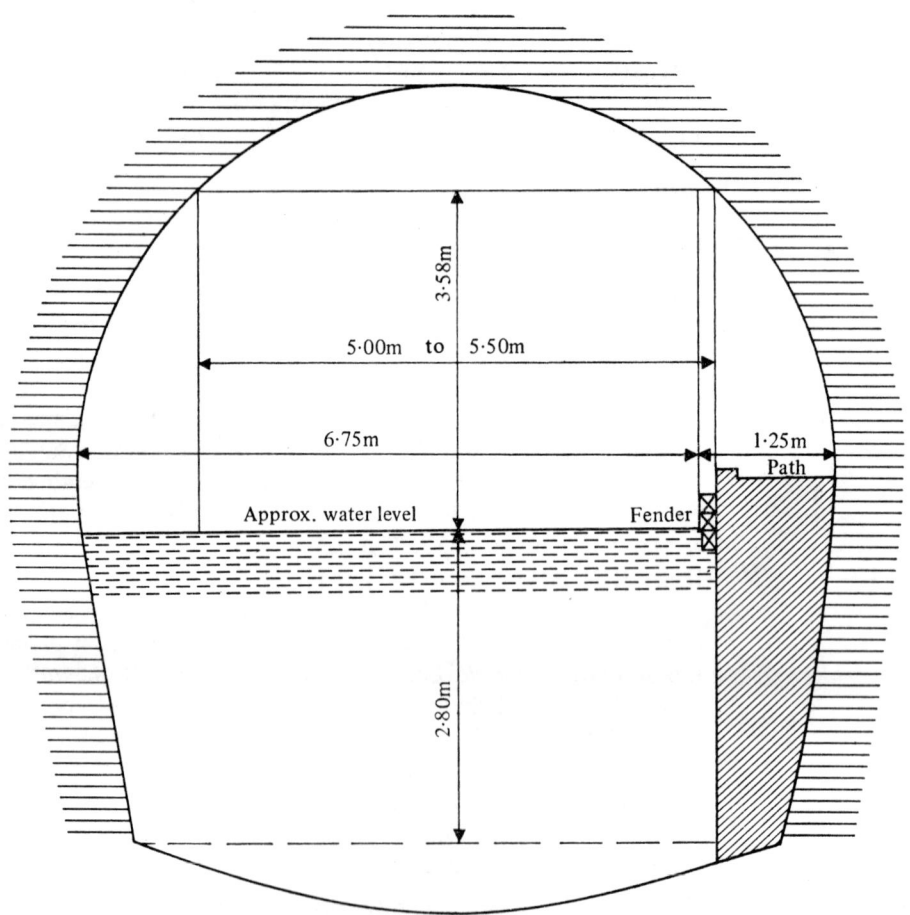

CAUTION. Live electric wires may be established throughout the length of this tunnel.

Depth	The depth of the canal is maintained at 2 m. 80.

Bridges	All fixed bridges have at least a headroom of 3 m. 70, except the bridge at Saint-Quentin which is on a gradient and has one side at 3 m. 58 and the other at 3 m. 83.

| *Tow-path* | There is a service of electric haulage (and this is obligatory for all vessels not mechanically propelled) fed by overhead power lines, which runs along both banks. The banks have bollards planted at intervals of about 50 metres throughout. |

Branch canal to La Fère

General	The branch canal to La Fère leaves the main canal at Fargnier, close to Lock No. 31 at Point 'Y' (K.84.8) and runs to La Fère where it joins with the Canal de la Sambre à l'Oise; actually the junction is made at Beautor, a small place just south of La Fère.
Length	The length of the branch is 3.8 kilometres.
Locks	None.
Depth	The depth varies somewhat being 2 m. 60 from Fargniers to about halfway and thence shallowing to 2 m. 20 for the remainder of the distance, which latter depth is similar to that found in the Canal de la Sambre à l'Oise.
Bridges	The fixed bridges have a headroom of 3 m. 70, as on the main canal.
Tow-path	Throughout.

Distance Table

		kilom.	lock	kilom.
Cambrai	*Junction with l'Escaut (canalised) (at K.0)*	0.0	—	92.0
	Lock (No. 1 de Proville)	2.0	1	90.0
Cantaing-s-Escaut	Bridge. Lock (No. 2 de Cantigneul) ...	3.0	2	89.0
Noyelles-s-Escaut	Lock (No. 3 de Noyelles). Pont-canal ...	4.0	3	88.0
	Bridge	5.0	—	87.0
Marcoing	Lock (No. 4 de Talma). Port. Bridge ...	7.0	4	85.0
	Lock (No. 5 de Marcoing)	7.0	5	85.0
	Railway bridge	8.0	—	84.0
	Lock (No. 6 de Bracheux)	9.0	6	83.0
Masnières	Bridge (de Masnières)	10.0	—	82.0
	Lock (No. 7 de Masnières)	11.0	7	81.0
Crèvecoeur	Lock (No. 8 de Saint-Waast)	12.0	8	80.0
	Quay (de Crèvecoeur)	13.0	—	79.0
	Bridge and Lock (No. 9 de Crèvecoeur) ...	14.0	9	78.0
Rues-des-Vignes	Bridge (de Vinchy)	14.0	—	78.0
	Lock (No. 10 de Vinchy)	15.0	10	77.0
	Lock (No. 11 du Tordoir)	15.0	11	77.0
	Bridge and Lock (No. 12 de Vaucelles) ...	17.0	12	75.0
Bantouzelle	Bridge (de la Grenouillère)	19.0	—	73.0
	Lock (No. 13 de Bantouzelle)	20.0	13	72.0
Banteux	Bridge and Lock (No. 14 de Banteux) ...	20.0	14	72.0
Honnecourt	Bridge and Lock (No. 15 d'Honnecourt) ...	23.0	15	69.0
	Lock (No. 16 de Moulin-Lafosse)	24.0	16	68.0

Distance Table

		kilom.	lock	kilom.
	Lock (No. 17 de Bosquet). Beginning of summit level...	24.0	17	68.0
Vendhuile	Port (de Vendhuile). Bridge	26.0	—	66.0
Bony	Basin (called 'de Macquincourt') for the formation of convoys called 'de la rame Paris'	27.0	—	65.0
	Northern end (called 'Macquincourt') du Grand Souterrain	29.0	—	63.0
	Southern end (called 'de Riqueval') du Grand Souterrain	34.0	—	58.0
	Lay-bys for crossing	35.0	—	57.0
	Bridge	36.0	—	56.0
Bellenglise	Port and Bridge (de Bellenglise)	38.0	—	54.0
	Bridge	39.0	—	53.0
Lehaucourt	Port	40.0	—	52.0
	Bridge and Port	41.0	—	51.0
	Northern end (called 'de Lehaucourt') du Souterrain de Lesdins	41.0	—	51.0
Lesdins	Southern end (called 'du Tronquoy') du Souterrain de Lesdins	43.0	—	49.0
	Basin for the formation of convoys called 'de la rame Belgique'	43.0	—	49.0
	Quay	44.0	—	48.0
	End of summit level	45.0	—	47.0
	Lock (No. 18 de Lesdins). Lock (No. 19) ...	45.0	19	47.0
	Bridge	45.0	—	47.0
Omissy	Lock (No. 20 d'Omissy). Bridge	46.0	20	46.0
	Lock (No. 21 de Moulin-Brûlè). Bridge ...	48.0	21	44.0
Saint-Quentin	Bridge	49.0	—	43.0
	Lock (No. 22 de Saint-Quentin)	50.0	22	42.0
	Bridge. Quay (called 'Quai Gayant') ...	51.0	—	41.0
	Port (de Saint-Quentin). Quay	52.0	—	40.0
	Railway bridge	53.0	—	39.0
	Bridge	54.0	—	38.0
Dallon	Bridge	56.0	—	36.0
Fontaine-lès-Clercs	Quay	58.0	—	34.0
	Lock (No. 23 de Fontaine-lès-Clercs) ...	58.0	23	34.0
	Bridge	58.0	—	34.0
Seraucourt-le-Grand	Bridge	60.0	—	32.0
	Quay. Port. Bridges	61.0	—	31.0
	Lock (No. 24 de Seraucourt-le-Grand) ...	62.0	24	30.0
Artemps	Bridge	64.0	—	28.0
Tugny-et-Pont	Bridge	66.0	—	26.0
Saint-Simon	Lock (No. 25 de Pont-Tugny). Port ...	66.0	25	26.0
	Junction with Canal de la Somme (at K.68)	68.0	—	24.0

Distance Table

		kilom.	lock	kilom.
	Bridge (de Saint-Simon)	69.0	—	23.0
Jussy	Port and Quay (de Jussy). Bridge	74.0	—	18.0
	Railway bridge	76.0	—	16.0
	Lock (No. 26 de Jussy). Quay	77.0	26	15.0
Mennessis	Quay. Lock (No. 27) and Bridge (de Mennessis)	79.0	27	13.0
	Lock (No. 28 de Voyaux)	80.0	28	12.0
Quessy	Bridge (de Quessy). Quay	83.0	—	9.0
Tergnier	Lock (No. 29 de Fargniers)	83.0	29	9.0
	Lock (No. 30 de Fargniers). Bridge ...	84.0	30	8.0
	Quay. Lock (No. 31 de Fargniers)... ...	84.0	31	8.0
	Railway bridge	84.0	—	8.0
	Point 'Y'. *Junction with Branch to La Fère (at K.0.0)*	84.8	—	7.7
	Lock (No. 32 de Tergnier). Bridge... ...	85.0	32	7.0
Condren	Quay	86.0	—	6.0
	Bridge	87.0	—	5.0
Viry	Lock (No. 33 de Viry)	88.0	33	4.0
	Quay. Bridge (de Viry)	89.0	—	3.0
Chauny	Bridge (de Senicourt)	90.0	—	2.0
	Lock (No. 34 de Senicourt)	90.0	34	2.0
	Railway bridge	91.0	—	1.0
	Lock (No. 35 de Chauny). Bridge	92.0	35	0.0
	Junction with canal latéral à l'Oise (at K.0)	92.0	—	0.0

Branch to La Fère

*Fargniers**	*Junction with Canal de St-Quentin at Point 'Y' (K.84.8)*	0.0	—	3.8
	Bridge (de La Frette)	0.8	—	3.0
	Port	2.8	—	1.0
	Bridge (de Beautor)	3.1	—	0.7
	Railway bridge	3.2	—	0.6
	Port (de Beautor)	3.3	—	0.5
	Railway bridge	3.6	—	0.2
	Port (de Beautor)	3.7	—	0.1
Beautor	*Junction with Canal de la Sambre à l'Oise (at K.67)*	3.8	—	0.0

LA SAMBRE

General

The canalised part of la Sambre begins at Landrecies, where it connects with the Canal de la Sambre à l'Oise, and ends in Belgium where it has its confluence with la Meuse at the town of Namur†.

* See Plan No. 9.
† See *Inland Waterways of Belgium*, Imray Laurie Norie & Wilson.

It is thus a link in the system of waterways which connect the rivers la Seine and l'Oise with the basin of la Meuse.

Length

The length of the canalised portion from Landrecies to the Belgian frontier is, according to the kilometre posts, 54.26 kilometres. However, on account of various rectifications made in the course of the river to eliminate bends, the actual distance is now (1962) no more than 52.3 kilometres. This actual distance is the one used in the Distance Table.

Locks

There are nine movable barrages at each one of which there is a lock. The locks have a width of 5 m. 20 with a length of 38 m. 50.

Depth

There is a depth of water of 2 m. 30 at normal water level, but winter floods greatly impede or even stop the navigation.

Bridges

None of the fixed bridges leaves less than 3 m. 28 headroom above the highest navigable water level. Normally the headroom is 3 m. 80.

Tow-path

There is a good tow-path throughout.

Distance Table

Place		kilom.	lock	kilom.
Landrecies	*Junction with the Canal de la Sambre à l'Oise (at K.0)* (upstream side of the lock at Landrecies)	0.0	—	52.0
Locquignol	Lock (No. 1 des Etoquies)	3.0	1	49.0
Maroilles	Bridge (d'Hachette)	6.0	—	46.0
	Lock (No. 2 d'Hachette)	7.0	2	45.0
Sassegnies	Lock (No. 3 de Sassegnies)	10.0	3	42.0
	Lift bridge	12.0	—	40.0
Aulnoye	Railway bridge	14.0	—	38.0
Berlaimont	Railway bridge	15.0	—	37.0
	Bridge (called 'de Montbard')	16.0	—	36.0
	Lock (No. 4 de Berlaimont)	16.0	4	36.0
	Bridge (de Berlaimont). Quay	16.0	—	36.0
Aymeries	Bridge (d'Aymeries)	18.0	—	34.0
Pont-sur-Sambre	Lock (No. 5 de Pont-sur-Sambre)	19.0	5	33.0
Brachant	Bridge (de Pont-sur-Sambre)	20.0	—	32.0
	Bridge (de Brachant)	21.0	—	31.0
Pont-sur-Sambre	Bridge (de Quartes)	24.0	—	28.0
	Lock (No. 6 de Quartes)	24.0	6	28.0
St-Remy-du-Nord	Bridge (de Boussières)	30.0	—	22.0
Hautmont	Railway bridge and footbridge	32.0	—	20.0
	Lock (No. 7 d'Hautmont)	32.0	7	20.0
	Bridge (d'Hautmont)	33.0	—	19.0

Distance Table

						kilom.	*lock*	*kilom.*
Maubeuge	Railway bridge	...	...	...	...	38.0	—	14.0
	Bridge (Pont Rouge)	...	...	...	39.0	—	13.0
	Lock (No. 8 de Maubegue)	...	...		39.0	8	13.0
	Bridge (des Alliés). Quay	...	...	...	39.0	—	13.0
	Railway bridge	...	...	...	...	40.0	—	12.0
Assevant	Bridge (d'Assevant)	...	...	...	43.0	—	9.0
Boussois	Bridge (de Boussois)	...	...	...	45.0	—	7.0
Marpent	Bridge (private)	...	...	...	...	48.0	—	4.0
	Bridge (de Marpent)	...	...	...	49.0	—	3.0
Jeumont	Lock (No. 9 de Marpent)	...	...	...	49.0	9	3.0
	Railway bridge	...	...	...	...	51.0	—	1.0
	Customs Quay (visit)	...	...	...	51.0	—	1.0
	Bridge (de Jeumont)	...	...	...	51.0	—	1.0
	Lift bridge (private)	...	...	...	51.0	—	1.0
	Footbridge (private)	...	...	...	52.0	—	0.0
	Frontier (Franco-Belge)	...	...	...	52.0	—	0.0

CANAL DE LA SAMBRE À L'OISE

General   The Canal de la Sambre à l'Oise begins at Landrecies, where it leaves the canalised river Sambre, and ends at La Fère. A branch canal leaves the Canal de Saint-Quentin at Fargniers and runs to La Fère where it joins with the Canal de la Sambre à l'Oise thus providing a through route between the basin of la Meuse and the basin of la Seine. The Canal de la Sambre à l'Oise contains a summit level which is situated not far from Landrecies between le Bois l'Abbaye and Le Gard: it has an elevation of about 450 ft. above sea level.

Length   The length of the canal is 67 kilometres from Landrecies to La Fère.

Locks   There are 38 locks of a uniform length of 37 m. 60 and a width of 5 m. 15. Three of these locks fall towards Landrecies and 35 towards La Fère.

Depth   The depth of water in the canal is maintained at 2 m. 20 from Landrecies to the gravel-pits (les ballastières) at Vendeuil (K.59). From that point the depth is slightly greater, 2 m. 40, and so to the junction to La Fère.

Bridges   The minimum headroom under the fixed bridges is 3 m. 70.

Tow-path   There is a good tow-path throughout and towing is effected by diesel tractors.

Distance Table

		kilom.	lock	kilom.
Landrecies	*Junction with la Sambre (at K.o)* (canalised).			
	Port. Bridge. Lock (No. 3 de Landrecies)	0.0	I	67.0
Ors	Lock (No. 2 d'Ors)	5.0	2	62.0
Catillon	Swing bridge (de Catillon)	8.0	—	59.0
	Lock (No. 1 de Nois l'Abbaye). *Beginning of summit level*	12.0	3	55.0
Fesmy	Bridge (de Fesmy)	13.0	—	54.0
Oisy	Bridge (d'Oisy)	16.0	—	51.0
Etreux	Railway bridge. Lock (No. 1 du Gard) ...	18.0	4	49.0
	End of summit level...	18.0	—	49.0
	Lock (No. 2 d'Etreux)	19.0	5	48.0
	Lock (No. 3 d'Etreux). Lock (No. 4 d'Etreux)	20.0	7	47.0
	Locks (Nos. 5 and 6 d'Etreux)	21.0	9	46.0
	Port. Swing bridge (d'Etreux)	21.0	—	46.0
	Locks (Nos. 7 and 8 d'Etreux)	22.0	11	45.0
Vénérolles	Lock (No. 9 de Vénérolles)	22.0	12	45.0
	Bridge and Lock (No. 10 de Vénérolles) ...	23.0	13	44.0
	Lock (No. 11 de Vénérolles)	24.0	14	43.0
Hannappes	Swing bridge (d'Hannappes)	25.0	—	42.0
	Lock (No. 12 d'Hannappes)	25.0	15	42.0
	Lock (No. 13 d'Hannappes)	26.0	16	41.0
Tupigny	Lock (No. 14 de Tupigny)...	26.0	17	41.0
	Lock (No. 15 de Tupigny)...	27.0	18	40.0
	Two swing bridges (de Tupigny)	27.0	—	40.0
	Lock (No. 16 de Tupigny)...	28.0	19	39.0
Grand-Verly	Lock (No. 17 de Grand-Verly)	29.0	30	38.0
	Lock (No. 18 de Grand-Verly)	30.0	21	37.0
Vadencourt	Swing bridge (de Vadencourt)	30.0	—	37.0
	Two railway bridges	30.0	—	37.0
	Pont-canal and Lock (No. 19 de Vadencourt)	31.0	22	36.0
	Bridge (Pont de Bohéries)	31.0	—	36.0
Longchamps	Lock (No. 20 de Longchamps)	33.0	23	34.0
Proix	Lock (No. 21 de Noyales)	35.0	24	32.0
Macquigny	Pont-canal (de Macquigny)	37.0	—	30.0
	Lock (No. 22 de Macquigny)	37.0	25	30.0
Hauteville	Lock (No. 23 d'Hautville)	38.0	26	29.0
Bernot	Lock (No. 24 de Bernot)	40.0	27	27.0
Neuvillette	Swing bridge (de Neuvillette)	43.0	—	24.0
Origny-St-Benoite	Lock (No. 25 d'Origny-St-Benoîte) ...	43.0	28	24.0
	Quay and Bridge (d'Origny)	44.0	—	23.0
Thenelles	Lock (No. 26 de Thenelles)	45.0	29	22.0
Ribemont	Lock (No. 27 de Ribemont)	48.0	30	19.0
Sissy	Lock (No. 28 de Sissy)	49.0	31	18.0

Distance Table

		kilom.	lock	kilom.
Chatillon	Pont-canal and Lock (No. 29 de Chatillon)	51.0	32	16.0
Mézières-sur-Oise	Lock (No. 30 de Mézières-sur-Oise) ...	52.0	33	15.0
	Railway bridge	53.0	—	14.0
Berthenicourt	Lock (No. 31 de Berthenicourt)	54.0	34	13.0
Alaincourt	Bridge (d'Alaincourt)	55.0	—	12.0
Hamegicourt	Lock (No. 32 d'Hamegicourt)	56.0	35	11.0
Brissy	Lock (No. 33 de Brissy)	58.0	36	9.0
	Gravel-pits (les ballastières de Vendeuil) ...	59.0	—	8.0
Vendeuil	Bridge (de Vendeuil)	60.0	—	7.0
Travecy	Pont-canal (de Travecy-Montigny) ...	62.0	—	5.0
	Lock (No. 34 de Travecy-Montigny) ...	62.0	37	5.0
	Swing bridge (de Travecy)	63.0	—	4.0
	Pont-canal (de Travecy)	64.0	—	3.0
	Lock (No. 35 de Travecy)	65.0	38	2.0
La Fère*	Bridge	66.0	—	1.0
	Bridge (Pont de La Fère)	67.0	—	0.0
	Junction with Canal de St-Quentin, Branch de La Fère (at K.3)	67.0	—	0.0

LA SAÔNE

General

La Saône rises in the Vosges mountains and after running her course makes confluence with Le Rhône at Lyon-La Mulatière. The river is navigable and canalised from Corre—where it joins the end of le Canal de l'Est (Southern Section)—to Lyon-La Mulatière. It also makes junction with le Canal de la Marne à la Saône at Huilley-s-Saône (K.125); with le Canal du Rhône au Rhin at Saint-Symphorien (K.158); with le Canal de Bourgogne at Saint-Jean-de-Losne (K.162) and with le Canal du Centre at Chalon-s-Saône (K.231). For the purposes of navigation la Saône is divided into two sections, viz.:

(1) Corre to Saint-Symphorien.

(2) Saint-Symphorien to Lyon-La Mulatière.

Corre to Saint-Symphorien

This section joins with the Canal de l'Est at Corre and is joined by the Canal de la Marne à la Saône at Heuilley. The Canal du Rhône au Rhin branches off from it at Saint-Symphorien. That part of the river which lies upstream from Gray is called *la Saône supérieure* while below that town the river is known as *la petite Saône*. The section contains two tunnels. The tunnel at Saint-Albin (at K.48) has a length of 681 metres with a width at the water level of 6 m. 55;

* See Plan No. 9.

227

the height to the keystone is 4 m. 10 and it occurs at a point where the canal is very restricted in width and on a section along which one-way traffic is enforced. The second tunnel, at Seveux-Savoyeux (at K.74) is 643 metres in length, with a width of 6 m. 50, and has a headroom of 3 m. 60. The passage through this tunnel is controlled by traffic lights. The whole of this section of the river has numerous windings, a large number of which have been by-passed (*dérivation*) and along some of these one-way traffic is enforced and passing and overtaking in other parts is also forbidden. Where these restrictions are to be found a note has been made in the Distance Table, notably at La Hang and again at Cubry-lès-Soing. The junction with le Canal de la Marne à la Saône is regulated by traffic lights from the Lock No. 18 d'Heuilley.

Length	The length of this section reckoned from Corre to Saint-Symphorien is 158 kilometres. The total canalised length of this river from Corre to Lyon is 375 kilometres.
Locks	In this section there are 19 locks and 3 guard locks which only come into action at certain stages of the river flood. There are also a number of guard gates not normally used. The first 15 locks (Corre to Gray) have a length of 38 m. 50 with a width of 5 m. 20 while the remaining 4 have a length of 40 m. 00 with a width of 8 m. 00. The locks at Savoyeux, Gray and Heuilley are operated electrically.
Depth	Over the first 64 kilometres, that is to say from Corre to Charentenay, the depth is maintained at 2 m. 10; for the remainder of the section it is somewhat greater being 2 m. 20.
Bridges	The fixed bridges have a minimum headroom of 3 m. 52, this headroom being reckoned at highest navigable water level.
Tow-path	There is a good tow-path throughout and towing is by diesel tractors. However, the greater part of the traffic is by self-propelled vessels.

Distance Table

		kilom.	*lock*	*kilom.*
Corre	Junction with Southern Section of Canal de l'Est (at K.147)	0.0	—	375.0
Ormoy	Guard gate (d'Ormoy)	3.0	—	372.0
	Port and Bridge (d'Ormoy)	4.0	—	371.0
	Bridge (du Devez)	5.0	—	370.0
	Lock (No. 1 d'Ormoy)	5.0	I	370.0
	Bridge (du Denon). Narrow passage ...	6.0	—	369.0
Cendrecourt	Guard gate (de Cendrecourt)	9.0	—	366.0
	Lock (No. 2 de Cendrecourt)	11.0	2	364.0
	Bridge (de Cendrecourt)	12.0	—	363.0

Distance Table

		kilom.	lock	kilom.
Jussey	Railway bridge	13.0	—	362.0
	Narrow passage	14.0	—	361.0
	End of narrow passage (Quarts de Jussey)	15.0	—	360.0
Gevigney	Narrow passage (de la Hang). *Crossing and overtaking forbidden*	17.0	—	358.0
	Bridge (de la Hang)	18.0	—	357.0
	End of narrow passage	18.0	—	357.0
	Bridge (de Montureux-lès-Baulay) ...	20.0	—	355.0
	Lock (No. 3 de Montureux-lès-Baulay) ...	20.0	3	355.0
	Bridge (de Baulay)	23.0	—	352.0
Favernay	Bridge (de Port d'Atelier)	29.0	—	346.0
Conflandey	Bridge and Lock (No. 4 de Conflandey) ...	30.0	4	345.0
	Narrow passage. *Crossing and overtaking forbidden*	30.0	—	345.0
	Suspension bridge (private)	31.0	—	344.0
Chaux-lès-Ports	End of narrow passage	31.0	—	344.0
Port-sur-Saône	Guard gate (de Port-sur-Saône). Bridge ...	37.0	—	338.0
	Port (de la Grenouillère)	38.0	—	337.0
	Bridge (de la Maladière)	38.0	—	337.0
	Lock (No. 5 de Port-sur-Saône)	38.0	5	337.0
Ferrières-lès-Scey	Bridge. Guard gate (de Chemilly)	42.0	—	333.0
	Lock (No. 6 de Chemilly)	42.0	6	333.0
Chassey-lès-Scey	Guard gate (de Scey-sur-Saône)	45.0	—	330.0
	Bridge (de Chassey-lès-Scey)	46.0	—	329.0
	Port and Lock (No. 7 de Scey-sur-Saône)...	46.0	7	329.0
Scey-sur-Saône	Deviation (de St-Aubin). *One-way traffic* ...	47.0	—	328.0
	Bridge. Guard lock (de St-Albin)	47.0	—	328.0
Ovanches	Tunnel (de St-Albin) (681 m.)	48.0	—	327.0
	Bridge and Port (de St-Albin). *End of one-way traffic*	49.0	—	326.0
Rupt-sur-Saône	Lock (No. 8 de Rupt-sur-Saône)	49.0	8	326.0
Chantes	Bridge (de Chantes)	50.0	—	325.0
	Guard gate (de Chantes)	52.0	—	323.0
	Lock (No. 9 de Chantes-Rupt)	52.0	9	323.0
Curbry-lès-Soing	Guard lock (de Curbry-lès-Soing)... ...	55.0	—	320.0
Fédry	Narrow passage. *Crossing and overtaking forbidden*	56.0	—	319.0
	End of narrow passage	57.0	—	318.0
Soing	Island (Ile Barrault) (right bank)	58.0	—	317.0
	Port (de Soing). Guard gate (de Soing) ...	59.0	—	316.0
Vannes	Bridge (de Soing)	60.0	—	315.0
	Lock (No. 10 de Soing)	61.0	10	314.0
Charentenay	Bridge and Guard gate (de Charentenay)...	62.0	—	313.0
Ray-sur-Saône	Lock (No. 11 de Charentenay). Port ...	64.0	11	311.0
Vellexon	Bridge (de Ray-sur-Saône)	65.0	—	310.0

Distance Table

			kilom.	lock	kilom.
Ferrières-lès-Ray	Guard lock (de Ferrières-lès-Ray)	...	67.0	—	308.0
	Bridge (de Ferrières-lès-Ray) ...	...	68.0	—	307.0
Membrey	Guard gate (de Seveux)	...	72.0	—	303.0
Savoyeux	Port and Bridge (de Savoyeux) ...	...	73.0	—	302.0
	Tunnel (de Savoyeux) (643 m.) ...	...	74.0	—	301.0
	Railway bridge. Bridge (de Savoyeux)	...	75.0	—	300.0
	Lock (No. 13 de Savoyeux) ...	...	75.0	12	300.0
Quitteur	Bridge (de Quitteur)	...	80.0	—	295.0
Beaujeu	Guard gate (de Vereux)	...	84.0	—	291.0
	Lock (No. 14 de Vereux)	...	86.0	13	289.0
Montureux-s-Saône	Bridge (de Prantigny)	...	88.0	—	287.0
Rigny	Guard gate (de Rigny)	...	93.0	—	282.0
	Lock (No. 15 de Rigny)	...	94.0	14	281.0
Gray	Lock (No. 16 de Gray). Stone bridge (de Gray). Port	...	99.0	15	276.0
	Bridge (Pont-Neuf de Gray) ...	...	99.0	—	276.0
	Railway bridge	...	101.0	—	274.0
Esmoulin	Port (de Mantoche)	...	106.0	—	269.0
Apremont	Guard gate (de Mantoche). *Narrow passage*		107.0	—	268.0
	Bridge (Pont d'Apremont) ...	...	108.0	—	267.0
	Lock (No. 17 d'Apremont) ...	...	110.0	16	265.0
Essertenne-et-Cecey	Port (de Cecey)	...	111.0	—	264.0
Broye-lès-Pesmes	Ports	...	120.0	—	255.0
*Heuilley-sur-Saône**	Island (Ile de Fley)	...	122.0	—	253.0
	Guard gate (d'Heuilley). *Narrow passage*...		122.0	—	253.0
	Port and Bridge (d'Heuilley) ...	...	123.0	—	252.0
	Junction with Canal de la Marne à la Saône (at K.224). Lock (No. 18 d'Heuilley). Traffic lights	...	125.0	17	250.0
Pontailler	Bridge and Port (de Pontailler) ...		128.0	—	247.0
Lamarche	Port and Bridge (de Lamarche) ...		134.0	—	241.0
Flammerans	Guard gate (de Poncey-lès-Athée)	...	137.0	—	238.0
	Lock (No. 19 de Poncey-lès-Athée). *Narrow passage*	...	138.0	18	237.0
Athée	Port (d'Auxonne)	...	144.0	—	231.0
	Bridge (Pont de France à Auxonne)	...	144.0	—	231.0
Auxonne	Port (d'Auxonne). Railway bridge	...	135.0	—	230.0
	Guard gate (d'Auxonne). *Narrow passage*	145.0	—	230.0
	Lock (No. 20 d'Auxonne) ...	...	147.0	19	228.0
St-Seine-en-Bache	Bridge (des Maillys)	...	154.0	—	221.0
Laperrière	Port (de Mailly-le-Port)	...	155.0	—	220.0
†*Saint-Symphorien*	*Junction with Canal du Rhône au Rhin (at K.0)*	...	158.0	—	217.0

* See Plan No. 10.   † See Plan No. 17.

Saint-Symphorien to Lyon-La Mulatière

General

This section of la Saône is the one that carries the bulk of the commercial freight and practically all the pleasure traffic. It is along this section that the two important routes leading from Paris join la Saône, that is to say le Bourbonnais and la Bourgogne. The Canal de Bourgogne connects with la Saône at St-Jean-de-Losne while the Canal du Centre (the last canal on the Bourbonnais route) enters the river at Chalon-sur-Saône. From Saint-Symphorien to Verdun the river is called la Petite Saône, but below that point until its confluence with le Rhône at Lyon-La Mulatière it is known as la Grande Saône. The river is wide and has but a moderate current at normal level; however in a few places there are strong currents at times, notably at St-Romain-des-Iles and just below Mâcon. The water of the river is nearly always remarkably clear and limpid, the banks are in general low and green and form the sides of delightful pastures. It is true that in some places there are sand banks and submerged training walls, but in the fairway there are no obstructions, and from Chalon-s-Saône to Lyon-La Mulatière the right-hand side of the channel is marked by red and white beacons. The submerged groins and training walls are known locally as *cléonages*.

Length

The length of this section between Saint-Symphorien and Lyon-La Mulatière is 217 kilometres. The official *kilométrage* is taken continuously through from Corre to Lyon-La Mulatière. The total length of the two sections of the river is, as before mentioned, 375 kilometres.

Locks

There are 8 locks in this section. The locks at Chaugey, Lechâtelet, Trugny and Charnay have a length of 39 m. 56 with a width of 8 m. 00, but the chamber width within the gates is 14 m. 00 and can take two vessels abreast. Those at Verdun, Gigny and Thoissey are 150 m. 00 in length with a width of 12 m. 00. The lock at Couzon—which has just lately been improved—now has a length of 185 m. 00 with a width of 12 m. 00. Note that the locks at Port Bernalin, Ile Barbe and La Mulatière have all been taken out of service.

Depth

The normal depth of water in the channel is 2 m. 00. When the state of the river exceeds about two metres above the normal level the barrages at the locks are drawn and the navigation proceeds without using the locks.

Bridges

All the fixed bridges between St-Symphorien and Lyon-La Mulatière have a clear headroom of at least 3 m. 50 above the highest navigable water level. A considerable number of bridges are encountered during the passage through the city.

Tow-path | Traffic is self-propelled or towed by tugs. Within the city limits the use of the tow-path is, in many places, prohibited.

Distance Table

		kilom.	lock	kilom.
Saint-Symphorien*	*Junction with Canal du Rhône au Rhin (at K.o)*	158.0	—	217.0
Saint-Jean-de-Losne	Port and Bridge (de St-Jean-de-Losne) ...	162.0	—	213.0
	Junction with Canal de Bourgogne (at K.242)	162.0	—	213.0
Saint-Usage	Railway bridge (viaduc de St-Usage) ...	163.0	—	212.0
Chaugey	Lock (No. 1 de St-Jean-de-Losne) ...	165.0	I	210.0
Esbarres	Port (de la Chenevasse)	169.0	—	206.0
Bonnencontre	Ile de Pagny (upstream end, left branch navigable)	173.0	—	202.0
Pagny-la-Ville	Ile de Pagny (downstream end)	174.0	—	201.0
	Bridge (de Charrey)	175.0	—	200.0
Lechâtelet	Lock (No. 2 de Lechâtelet)	177.0	2	198.0
Pouilly	Bridge (de Seurre)	188.0	—	187.0
Trugny	Lock (No. 3 de Trugny)	191.0	3	184.0
Labergement	Railway bridge (de Chivres)	192.0	—	183.0
Charnay	Port (de Charnay)	198.0	—	177.0
	Lock (No. 4 de Charnay)	199.0	4	176.0
Ecuelles	Port (d'Ecuelles)	201.0	—	174.0
Bordes	Lock (No. 5 de Verdun)	207.0	5	168.0
Verdun	Confluence with le Doubs (not navigable)	208.0	—	167.0
	Bridge (de Bragny)	208.0	—	167.0
Allerey	Bridge and railway bridge (de Chauvort) ...	210.0	—	165.0
Chalon-sur-Saône†	*Junction with Canal du Centre (at K.o)* ...	230.0	—	143.0
	Bridge (Pont-St-Laurent)	233.0	—	142.0
	Bridge (Pont-Jean-Richard)	234.0	—	141.0
Saint-Rémy	Railway bridge (de Chalon)	234.0	—	141.0
Ouroux	Bridge (d'Ouroux)	245.0	—	130.0
Gigny	Bridge (de Thorey)	250.0	—	125.0
	Lock (No. 6 de Gigny)	252.0	6	123.0
Tournus	Suspension bridge (de Tournus). Port ...	263.0	—	112.0
	Bridge (de Tournus)	264.0	—	111.0
La Truchère	*Confluence with la Seille (at K.o)* ...	268.0	—	107.0
Farges	Port (de Farges)	270.0	—	105.0
Uchizy	Bridge and Port (d'Uchizy)	272.0	—	103.0
Montballet	Bridge (de Fleurville). Port	277.0	—	98.0
Sénozan	... ...	285.0	—	90.0
Vesines	... ...	288.0	—	87.0
Saint-Laurent	Quay (de Breuil)	294.0	—	81.0

* See Plan No. 17.
† See Plan No. 2.

Distance Table

		kilom.	lock	kilom.
Mâcon	Bridge (de Mâcon)	294.0	—	81.0
	Quay (Quai Lamartine)	295.0	—	80.0
	Port (de Mâcon)	296.0	—	79.0
	Railway bridge (viaduc de Mâcon) ...	297.0	—	78.0
Creches	Bridge and Port (d'Arciat)	302.0	—	73.0
St-Romain-des-Iles	Port and Bridge (de St-Romain)	309.0	—	66.0
Thoissey	Bridge and Port (de Thoissey)	311.0	—	64.0
Mogneneins	Lock (No. 7 de Thoissey)	314.0	7	61.0
Belleville-s-Saône	Bridge and Port (de Belleville)	320.0	—	55.0
Montmerle	Ile de Montmerle (upstream end, left branch navigable)	321.0	—	54.0
	Ile de Montmerle (downstream end) ...	323.0	—	52.0
	Bridge (de Montmerle)	323.0	—	52.0
Messimy	Port (Port Rivière)	328.0	—	47.0
Beaureguard	Bridge and Port (de Beaureguard)... ...	333.0	—	42.0
Jassans	Bridge (de Frans)	335.0	—	40.0
	Port (de Villefranche)	335.0	—	40.0
Saint-Bernard	Port (du Colombier). Bridge (Pont St-Bernard)	340.0	—	35.0
Quincieux	Bridge (de Trévoux)	344.0	—	31.0
Reyrieux	Port (Port Bernalin)	345.0	—	30.0
Neuville-s-Saône	Yacht Club du Rhône	352.0	—	23.0
Albigny	Port and Bridge (de Neuville)	354.0	—	21.0
Couzon	Lock (No. 9 de Couzon). Suspension Bridge	358.0	8	17.0
Fontaines-sur-Saône	Bridge (de Fontaines)	360.0	—	15.0
Caluire	Railway bridge and Bridge (de Collonges)	363.0	—	12.0
St-Rambert-l'Ille	Bridge (de l'Ille Barbe)	365.0	—	10.0
Lyon-La Mulatière	Bridge (Pont Masaryk)	368.0	—	7.0
	Bridge (Pont Clemenceau)	368.0	—	7.0
	Bridge (Pont de Serin)	369.0	—	6.0
	Bridge (Pont de l'Homme de la Roche) ...	370.0	—	5.0
	Footbridge (St.Vincent)	370.0	—	5.0
	Bridge (Pont la Feuillée)	370.0	—	5.0
	Bridge (Pont du Change)	371.0	—	4.0
	Bridge (Pont du Palais de Justice) ...	371.0	—	4.0
	Bridge (Pont Tilsitt)	371.0	—	4.0
	Footbridge (Passerelle St-George)... ...	372.0	—	3.0
	Port (Port Maréchal-Joffre)	372.0	—	3.0
	Bridge (Pont Kitchener)	372.0	—	3.0
	Railway bridge (Viaduc de la Quarantine)	372.0	—	3.0
	Port (Port Perrache)	373.0	—	2.0
	Port (Port de l'Arsenal)	373.0	—	2.0
	Port (Port du Gaz)	373.0	—	2.0
	Port (Port Rambaud)	373.0	—	1.0

Distance Table

	kilom.	*lock*	*kilom.*
Railway bridge (de la Mulatière)	374.0	—	0.0
Bridge (de la Mulatière)	375.0	—	0.0
Confluence with le Rhône (at K.0.7) ...	375.0	—	0.0

LA SARTHE

General

La Sarthe is navigable from the barrage of Saint-Gervais, which is upstream of the reach or pound of Le Mans, to its confluence with la Mayenne in the commune of Angers.

Length

The river is navigable for a distance of 131 kilometres; of this length 113 kilometres has been canalised (that is from Saint-Gervais to the lock at Cheffes-sur-Sarthe), but the remaining 18 kilometres have a free run.

Locks

There are 20 locks between Saint-Gervais and Cheffes, the first 16 of which have a length of 30 m. 85 with a width of 5 m. 20; the remaining 4 are somewhat longer, being 33 m. 00 in length but the width is less, namely 5 m. 15.

Depth

For 86 kilometres (as far as Lock No. 17) the depth of water in the canalised river is 1 m. 60; from that point to the lock at Cheffes it is reduced to 1 m. 50. Below Cheffes to the confluence with la Maine and la Mayenne the depth is further reduced to 1 m. 40. During the time of *chômage* and of low water, that is to say generally from mid-August to mid-September, there is but a depth of 1 m. 00 over the sill of the lock at Cheffes, so that intending navigators should make enquiries locally if the passage is to be made during those two months.

Bridges

The bridges show a headroom of not less than 3 m. 90 as far as Lock No. 17; beyond, and to the confluence with La Mayenne, the headroom is 4 m. 40. Both the figures are at normal water level.

Tow-path

There is no regular tow-path, all traffic being for the most part self-propelled though there are occasionally small tugs to be seen.

Distance Table

		kilom.	*lock*	*kilom.*
Le Mans	*Barrage de Saint-Gervais*	0.0	—	131.0
	Bridge (Pont Yssoir). Footbridge (St-Jean).			
	Bridge (Pont Gambetta)	0.0	—	131.0
	Port (du Mans). Bridge (du Greffier) ...	1.0	—	130.0
	Bridge (Pont d'Eichtal). Railway bridge ...	1.0	—	130.0

Distance Table

			kilom.	lock	kilom.
	Lock (No. 1)		2.0	I	129.0
	Railway bridge. Bridge. Bridge (Pont Rouge)		4.0	—	127.0
Allonnes	Lock (No. 2 de Raterie). Bridge		5.0	2	126.0
	Lock (No. 3 de Chahoué)		6.0	3	125.0
Spay	Bridge. Bridge		13.0	—	118.0
	Lock (No. 4 de Spay)		15.0	4	116.0
Fillé	Bridge		16.0	—	115.0
	Bridge		17.0	—	114.0
Roezé	Bridge		20.0	—	111.0
	Lock (No. 5 de Roëzé)		22.0	5	109.0
	Bridge		23.0	—	108.0
La Suze	Bridge and Port (de La Suze)		26.0	—	105.0
	Railway bridge		26.0	—	105.0
	Lock (No. 6 de La Suze)		27.0	6	104.0
Fercé	Bridge		32.0	—	99.0
	Lock (No. 7 de Fercé)		33.0	7	98.0
Noyen	Railway bridge		39.0	—	92.0
	Port and Bridge (de Noyen)		40.0	—	91.0
	Lock (No. 8 de Noyen)		41.0	8	90.0
Malicorne	Bridge		46.0	—	85.0
	Lock (No. 9 de Malicorne)		47.0	9	84.0
Parcé	Lock (No. 10 d'Ignères)		54.0	10	77.0
	Bridge		57.0	—	74.0
	Port and Lock (No. 11 de Parcé) ...		58.0	11	73.0
	Lock (No. 12 de Courtigné)		63.0	12	68.0
	Confluence with la Vègre		64.0	—	67.0
Juigné	Lock (No. 13 de Juigné)		68.0	13	63.0
	Port (de Solesmes). Bridge		69.0	—	62.0
	Lock (No. 14 de Solesmes). Swing bridge...		70.0	14	61.0
Sablé	Port (Port-Etroit). Railway bridge ...		71.0	—	60.0
	Port (de Sablé). Bridge		73.0	—	58.0
	Lock (No. 15 de Sablé)		73.0	15	58.0
Souvigné	Railway bridge		77.0	—	54.0
St-Denis-d'Anjou	Lock (No. 16 de Beffes). Swing bridge ...		81.0	16	50.0
Morannes	Lock (No. 17 de Pendu)		87.0	17	44.0
Chemiré-s-Sarthe	Port (de Morannes). Bridge		90.0	—	41.0
Brissarthe	Lock (No. 18 de Villechien)		93.0	18	38.0
	Port (de Brissarthe)		97.0	—	34.0
Châteauneuf-s-Sarthe	Lock (No. 19 de Châteauneuf)		101.0	19	30.0
	Port (de Châteauneuf). Bridge ...		103.0	—	28.0
Juvardeil	Port (de Juvardeil)		105.0	—	26.0
Cheffes-s-Sarthe	Bridge and Lock (No. 20 de Cheffes) ...		113.0	20	18.0
Ecouflant	*Confluence with la Loire*		121.0	—	10.0
Cantenay-Epinard	*Confluence with la Vielle-Maine* ...		127.0	—	4.0

Distance Table   *kilom.   lock   kilom.*

Angers   *Confluence with la Mayenne and with la*
                  Maine (at K.124) ...   . 131.0   —   0.0

LA SCARPE

General

La Scarpe begins at the Port of Arras and ends at its confluence with l'Escaut at Mortagne. It is canalised throughout its length and for the purposes of navigation it is divided into three sections:

(1) **Arras to Corbehem** (la Scarpe supérieure).
(2) **Corbehem to Lock No. 1 de Fort-de-Scarpe** (la Scarpe moyenne).
(3) **Lock No. 1 de Fort-de-Scarpe to the confluence with l'Escaut** (la Scarpe inférieure).

The system of waterways through and around Douai is complicated by the fact that the second section (the major part of la Scarpe moyenne) is not available to through traffic as navigation is impossible between le Pont des Domincains and le Pont d'Alsace, both of which lie near the centre of the town of Douai. To join up the waterways in the vicinity the following artificial works have been constructed:

(a) A by-pass canal, called *la dérivation de la Scarpe autour de Douai;* which branches off from the left bank at the point where la Scarpe supérieure, la Scarpe moyenne and le canal de la Sensée all meet. This *dérivation* has been much improved as it is part of the amended route *la Liaison Dunkerque-Valenciennes*. *La dérivation* passes round the west of the town and joins with le Canal de la Deûle on the northern outskirts.

(b) About three-quarters of the way along *la dérivation* a link-canal, called *le canal de jonction* leads into la Scarpe moyenne downstream of le Pont d'Alsace.

In brief, if it is desired to reach la Scarpe inférieure from the Scarpe supérieure it is necessary to leave the river at Corbehem (K.23), follow down la dérivation until the *canal de jonction* is reached and then follow along it to rejoin la Scarpe moyenne clear of the navigational obstruction. In a somewhat similar manner if it is desired to gain la Scarpe inférieure from the Canal de la Deûle, it is necessary to go first along *la dérivation* until *le canal de jonction* is reached, thence to la Scarpe moyenne and so, finally, to la Scarpe inférieure*.

Length

La Scarpe supérieure, from Arras to Corbehem, where it makes junction with la Scarpe moyenne and the Canal de la Sensée, has a

* See Plan No. 7.

length of 23 kilometres. The length of *la dérivation* is 8 kilometres; the length of *le canal de jonction* from *la dérivation* to la Scarpe moyenne is 700 metres. From that junction to the lock at Fort-de-Scarpe (where la Scarpe moyenne ends and la Scarpe inférieure begins) is one kilometre. Thus by *la dérivation* and *le jonction* the distance is about one kilometre longer than if it were possible to go through the town. As the official kilometre posts mark the distance as by going through the town it has been thought more convenient to ignore the extra distance caused and to number the Distance Table in accordance with the posts. The length of the Scarpe inférieure from the lock at Fort-de-Scarpe to Montagne (confluence with l'Escaut) is 36 kilometres. Thus the total length of the canalised river, using the by-pass and link canals, is actually 67 kilometres, but is accounted here as 66 only.

Locks

La Scarpe supérieure has 9 locks; 8 of these have a length of 38 m. 50 with a width of 5 m. 18, the last one, the lock at Corbehem, is slightly larger, being 38 m. 70 in length and 5 m. 20 in width.

Only 1¼ kilometres of la Scarpe moyenne is accounted here and this short length contains no lock.

La Scarpe inférieure has 6 locks all with a length of 38 m. 70 and with a width of 5 m. 20. *La dérivation* has two locks each with twin chambers. L'écluse de Courchelettes (dit *écluse sud*) has one chamber 144 m. 60 in length and the other 89 m. 00 in length. Both chambers are 12 m. 00 in width. The chambers of l'écluse de Douai (dit *écluse nord*) are 147 m. 20 and 91 m. 60 in length, their widths being 12 m. 00.

Le canal de jonction has no lock.

Depth

La Scarpe supérieure: from Arras to l'écluse de Biache-St-Vaast the depth is 2 m. 20. From that lock to l'écluse de Brébières-Basse-Tenue the depth is 2 m. 40; thence to the junction with le Canal de la Sensée the depth is 2 m. 50. *Le canal de jonction* has a depth of 2 m. 50, and the same depth is found in la Scarpe moyenne from *le canal de jonction* to l'écluse de Fort-de-Scarpe. La Scarpe inférieure from Fort-de-Scarpe to the confluence with l'Escaut has a depth of 2 m. 40. *La dérivation* is 3 m. 50 throughout.

Bridges

There is a clear headroom of 3 m. 70 under all the fixed bridges measured from the normal water level, except for the two railway bridges over la Scarpe moyenne which are believed to clear only 3 m. 50; but these exceptions should be verified. The bridges over *la dérivation* have a clear headroom of at least 5 m. 25.

Tow-path

The tow-path is continuous throughout.

La Scarpe Supérieure

Distance Table

		kilom.	lock	kilom.
Arras	*Head of navigation*			
Saint-Nicolas	Port. Bridge (Pont de Grès)	0.0	—	66.0
	Lock (No. 28 de St-Nicolas)	0.0	I	66.0
St-Laurent-Blangy	Lock (No. 29 de St-Laurent-Blangy) ...	2.0	2	64.0
	Railway bridge	3.0	—	63.0
Athies	Lock (No. 30 d'Athies)	5.0	3	61.0
Fampoux	Lock (No. 31 de Fampoux)	7.0	4	59.0
	Railway bridge	8.0	—	58.0
Roeux	Bridge and Staithe (de Rouex)	10.0	—	56.0
Biache-St-Vaast	Lock (No. 32 de Biache-St-Vaast) ...	14.0	5	52.0
Vitry-en-Artois	Bridge (de Vitry). Bridge	17.0	—	49.0
	Lock (No. 33 de Vitry)	17.0	6	49.0
Brébières	Lock (No. 34 de Brébières-Haute-Tenue)	20.0	7	46.0
	Lock (No. 35 de Brébières-Basse-Tenue) ...	20.0	8	46.0
Corbehem	Lock (No. 36 de Corbehem). Swing bridge	22.0	9	44.0
	Junction with Canal de la Sensée, and junction with la dérivation de la Scarpe autour de Douai. Beginning of la Scarpe moyenne ...	23.0	—	43.0

Derivation de la Scarpe autour de Douai*

Corbehem	*Junction with Canal de la Sensée; junction with la Scarpe supérieure.* Origin of la Scarpe moyenne	0.0	—	7.9
Courchelettes	Bridge (de Courchelettes)	0.2	—	7.7
	Lock (de Courchelettes) (*écluse sud*) ...	0.3	10	7.6
	Railway bridge	0.7	—	7.2
Lambres	Bridge (Pont d'Arras)	2.0	—	5.9
Douai	Bridge (Pont d'Esquechin)...	4.1	—	3.8
	Lock (de Douai) (*écluse nord*)	4.5	11	3.4
	Bridge (Pont d'Ocre)	4.9	—	3.0
	Origin of canal de jonction	6.2	—	1.7
	Bridge (Pont du Polygone)	6.3	—	1.6
Flers-en-Escrebieux	Bridge (de Flers)	7.1	—	0.8
	Junction with Canal de la Deûle (at K.0) ...	7.9	—	0.0

Canal de Jonction

Douai	*Junction (at K.6.2) with la dérivation de la Scarpe autour de Douai*	0.0	—	0.8
	Bridge (du Boulevard Lahure)	0.1	—	0.7
	Bridge (du Chemin-Vert)	0.7	—	0.1
Douai	*Junction with la Scarpe moyenne (at K.29.0)*	0.8	—	0.0

* See Plan No. 7.

Distance Table

		kilom.	lock	kilom.
La Scarpe moyenne				
Douai	*Junction with the canal de jonction (at K.0.8)*	28.0	—	38.0
	Two railway bridges	28.0	—	38.0
	Junction with Canal de la Deûle (not navigable)	29.0	—	37.0
Douai	*Junction with la Scarpe inférieure (at upstream side of Lock (No. 1 du Fort-de-Scarpe)*	29.0	—	37.0
La Scarpe inférieure				
	Junction with la Scarpe moyenne (at K.29).			
	Lock (No. 1 du Fort-de-Scarpe)	29.0	12	37.0
	Bridge (Pont Rouge)	30.0	—	36.0
Raches	Lift bridge (de Raches)	33.0	—	33.0
Lallaing	Lift bridge (de Lallaing)	36.0	—	30.0
	Lock (No. 2 de Lallaing)	36.0	13	30.0
Flines	Lift bridge (de Germignies)	37.0	—	29.0
Pecquencourt	Footbridge	39.0	—	27.0
Vred	Lift bridge (de Vred)	41.0	—	25.0
Marchiennes-Ville	Lock (No. 3 de Marchiennes). Bridge. Quay	45.0	14	21.0
	Railway bridge	46.0	—	20.0
Alnes-Warlaing	Lock (No. 4 de Warlaing)	49.0	15	17.0
Hasnon	Bridge (d'Hasnon). Railway bridge ...	54.0	—	12.0
St-Amand	Footbridge. Railway bridge	57.0	—	9.0
	Quay (de la ville de St-Amand)	58.0	—	8.0
	Footbridge and lift bridge	58.0	—	8.0
	Footbridge and lift bridge	59.0	—	7.0
	Lock (No. 5 de St-Amand)	59.0	16	7.0
Nivelles	Bridge (de Nivelles)	62.0	—	4.0
Thun	Lock (No. 6 de Thun)	64.0	17	2.0
Mortagne	Lift bridge	65.0	—	1.0
	Confluence with l'Escaut (at K.59)	66.0	—	0.0

LA SEILLE

General   La Seille is navigable for light vessels between Louhans and its confluence with la Saône close to La Truchère. The river is canalised throughout its navigable length.

Length   It is a distance of 39 kilometres from Louhans to the confluence with la Saône.

Locks   There are 4 locks. All these have a length of 30 m. 40 with a width of 5 m. 17.

Depth	The minimum depth is 1 m. 50, but normally there is at least 1 m. 55 and at times even more.			
Bridges	Of the fixed bridges the lowest shows a headroom of 4 m. 70 at normal water level.			
Tow-path	All the craft using this waterway are now self-propelled.			

Distance Table

		kilom.	*lock*	*kilom.*
Louhans	*Head of navigation.* Port	0.0	—	39.0
	Bridge. Railway bridge. New Port... ...	1.0	—	38.0
Branges	Lock (No. 4 de Branges)	4.0	1	35.0
Huilly	Port and Bridge (de Rancy)	16.0	—	23.0
Loisy	Lock (No. 3 de Loisy)	21.0	2	18.0
	Bridge	22.0	—	17.0
Cuisery	Port and Bridge (de Cuisery)	26.0	—	13.0
	Lock (No. 2 de Cuisery)	26.0	3	13.0
Ratenelle	Railway bridge	30.0	—	9.0
	Bridge (de Ratenelle)	31.0	—	8.0
La Truchère	Bridge (de Seille)	36.0	—	3.0
	Lock (No. 1 de La Truchère)	39.0	4	0.0
	Confluence with la Saône (at K.268) ...	39.0	—	0.0

LA SEINE

General   The navigable part of la Seine begins at Marcilly and ends at Le Havre where it falls into the sea. For the purposes of administration the river is divided into five sections, namely:

(1) **Marcilly to Montereau.**

(2) **Montereau to the railway bridge at Argenteuil.**

(3) **Railway bridge at Argenteuil to Cléon** (5 km. downstream from Elbeuf).

(4) **Cléon to le Pont-Jeanne-d'Arc, Rouen.**

(5) **Le Pont-Jeanne-d'Arc to Le Havre.**

There is also another stretch of the river 26 kilometres in length, which lies upstream of Marcilly (Méry to Marcilly) over which navigation is possible but has been abandoned now that traffic proceeds by the *Canal de la Haute-Seine* which runs parallel to the river. Section (5) will not be detailed here as it is considered to be a marine navigation. The appropriate 'Pilot' should be consulted. In this work the river will be divided into four parts:

(1) Marcilly to Montereau.

(2) Montereau to le Pont Marie, Paris.

(3) Le Pont Marie, Paris, to Amfreville-Poses.

(4) Amfreville Poses to Pont Jeanne-d'Arc, Rouen.

As the greater part of the pleasure traffic, for various reasons, does not go further upstream than Montereau, it has been thought best to arrange the Distance Tables so as to leave the first section (Marcilly to Montereau) clear of the others. Thus the first set of distances is between Marcilly and Montereau; the second set is between Montereau and le Pont-Marie, Paris; and the last set of distances is between le Pont-Marie, Paris, and le Pont-Jeanne-d'Arc, Rouen. By this method of reckoning the distance from the centre of Paris to any point on the river between Montereau and Rouen is immediately available.

No Permis de Circulation is necessary for the navigation of this river between Montereau and the sea.

Above Montereau a Permis is required.

1st Section: Marcilly to Montereau (La Petite Seine)

General

This section has been canalised throughout and, in addition, at a number of places the course of the river has been rectified.

Length

The actual distance covered by vessels using this section and taking advantage of the various rectifications is 67 kilometres.

Locks

There are 13 locks. The first 4 of these, up to and including that at Nogent, have a length of 38 m. 90. The next 5 locks, up to and including No. 9 de Jaulnes, have a length of 51 m. 50; the length of the remaining 4 locks is 45 m. 00. All the locks have a uniform width of 7 m. 90.

Depth

The depth varies. Between Marcilly and Nogent there is, normally, a minimum depth of 1 m. 70; from Nogent to Montereau it is somewhat more, being 2 m. 10.

Bridges

From Marcilly to Nogent the headroom under the fixed bridges is 4 m. 30, except under le pont de Parc (K.11) on la dérivation de Conflans à Bernières, which has 3 m. 80. From Nogent to l'écluse de Bray the headroom is 4 m. 55, except under the bridge at l'écluse du Vesoult where it is 3 m. 56. From Bray to Montereau the headroom is 4 m. 03, except under le pont de Marolles (dérivation de Marolles) where during times of flood the headroom is reduced to 3 m. 41; but at such times descending vessels use the river instead of *la dérivation* as soon as le barrage de Marolles is drawn.

Tow path

The tow-path has been allowed to fall into disuse and is no longer practicable, except between Bray and Montereau.

241

Distance Table

		kilom.	lock	kilom.
Marcilly	*Junction with Canal de la Haute-Seine (at K.14)*	0.0	—	67.0
	Port and Bridge (de Marcilly)	0.0	—	67.0
Conflans-s-Seine	Lock (No. 1 de Conflans)	3.0	1	64.0
Crancey	Bridge (de Maugis)	7.0	—	60.0
	Pont-canal (de Crancey). One-way traffic (26 m.)	8.0	—	59.0
	Bridge (des Pâtures)	8.0	—	59.0
Pont-s-Seine	Port (de Pont-s-Seine). Lift bridge ...	10.0	—	57.0
	Bridge (du Parc). Bridge (des Soupirs) ...	11.0	—	56.0
Marnay-s-Seine	Lock (No. 2 de Marnay)	13.0	2	54.0
	Port. Bridge (des Ouitres)	14.0	—	53.0
Nogent-s-Seine	Lock (No. 3 de Bernières)	16.0	3	51.0
	Railway bridge	16.0	—	51.0
	Lock (No. 4 de Nogent-s-Seine)	18.0	4	49.0
	Bridge (Pont St-Edme). Port	19.0	—	48.0
Mériot	Bridge and Lock (No. 5 de Beaulieu) ...	23.0	5	44.0
	Bridge (de Beaulieu)	24.0	—	43.0
Melz-s-Seine	Lock (No. 6 de Melz)	27.0	6	40.0
Courceroy	Bridge (de Courceroy)	29.0	—	38.0
Villiers-s-Seine	Bridge (de Villiers)	30.0	—	37.0
	Lock (No. 7 de Villiers)	31.0	7	36.0
Noyen-s-Seine	Bridge (de Noyen)	34.0	—	33.0
	Lock (No. 8 du Vesoult)	37.0	8	30.0
Jaulnes	Lock (No. 9 de Jaulnes)	43.0	9	24.0
Bray-s-Seine	Bridge and Port (de Bray)	45.0	—	22.0
Mouy-s-Seine	Lock (No. 10 de Bray)	46.0	10	21.0
Bazoches-lès-Bray	Bridge and Lock (No. 11 de Bazoches) ...	49.0	11	18.0
	Bridge (de Dagorneau)	50.0	—	17.0
	Bridge (de Champmorin)	51.0	—	16.0
Balloy	Bridge (de Balloy)	52.0	—	15.0
Gravon	Bridge (de Gravon)	54.0	—	13.0
La Tombe	Lock (No. 12 de La Tombe)	55.0	12	12.0
	Bridge (de la Folie)	56.0	—	11.0
	Bridge (de La Tombe)	57.0	—	10.0
Marolles-s-Seine	Bridge and Lock (No. 13 de Marolles) ...	61.0	13	6.0
	Railway bridge	64.0	—	3.0
Montereau*	*End of La Petite Seine; beginning of La Seine*	67.0	—	0.0

2nd Section: Montereau to Le Pont Marie, Paris

General	The navigation of this section is quite different to that obtaining in the previous one. It consists of tugs with strings of lighters in tow,

* See Plan No. 19.

large motor barges and innumerable commercial craft of all kinds. Frequent quays and ports connected with the railways provide outlets for a constant stream of general and local waterborne freight. Further, this section must be divided into two parts; the first from Montereau to Bas-Vignons (which lies in the vicinity of Corbeil) and the second part which extends from Bas-Vignons to Paris. This second part carries an even greater volume of traffic than the first and is altogether more commercial and urban in character. Large self-propelled oil and petrol tankers which may carry up to 1,500 tons of cargo are frequently met and more tugs with long strings of barges are constantly moving from port to port. The locks, as will be shown later, in this part are all longer and have twin chambers so that tugs and tows can enter at one time; in short, pleasure craft are really a nuisance in such conditions, and every care should be taken not to obstruct those who are using the waterway for their livelihood. Nevertheless, except perhaps in this second part, the beauty of the river above Paris remains largely unspoiled, and it is in the first part of this section that some of the most picturesque river scenery in France is to be found. Near the beginning of this section two important water routes to the South of France leave the river—La Bourgogne route at Montereau, where it continues by the River Yonne; and le Bourbonnais route at Saint-Mammes, where it continues by the Canal du Loing.

Length

The distance from Pont St-Nicolas at Montereau to the Pont-Marie, Paris (or to the Pont de la Tournelle, Paris) is 101 kilometres. It must be mentioned that the official *kilométrage* is taken from *le Pont-Marie* which is situated on *le bras Marie* which is the right-hand channel when facing downstream at the upstream point of *l'Île-St-Louis*. The left-hand channel is *le bras de la Tournelle* when facing downstream from the same position on *l'Île-St-Louis*: the two bridges are opposite to one another and connect the island of St-Louis to the mainland on either side. Thus from the point of view of distance the two bridges form a straight line across the river: formerly the official *kilométrage* was quoted from the Pont de la Tournelle.

Locks

Between le Pont de Montereau and le Pont Marie, Paris, there are 9 locks with barrages *(barrages-éclusés)*. The barrages are set across the river at each lock, are movable, and have a navigable section. At Samois there is an island in mid-stream and the lock and barrage lie between the left bank of the river and the island. Opposite to them and running out from the island to the right bank is the barrage of Héricy. This barrage is movable and has a navigable section; it is, however, only used during times of flood. The first lock downstream from Montereau (de Varennes) is 180 m. 00 in length

243

and 16 m. oo at the gates. The following five locks, up to and including that at Coudray, have a length of 172 m. oo and a width of 11 m. 80 at the gates.

To provide for the increase of traffic which gets progressively greater downstream after passing Corbeil the next lock, which is at Evry-Petit-Bourg, is a twin-chambered lock on the left bank. The large chamber is 180 m. oo in length with a width of 16 m. oo and the older chambers is 172 m. oo in length with a width of 13 m. oo. This latter has a depth of only 2 m. oo at normal water level and is the outer chamber of the two. At Ablon the old lock, which is on the left bank, has a length of 172 m. oo with a width of 13 m. oo; the depth of water over the sill of 2 m. oo at normal water level. The new lock, on the right bank, has a length of 180 m. oo with a width of 16 m. oo. At Port a l'Anglais the old lock, on the left bank, and the new lock on the right bank, both have a length of 180 m. oo with a width of 16 m. oo; but the old lock has only a depth of 2 m. 75 over the sill. All the new locks have a depth of 3 m. oo. The width between the gates of all these locks is 11 m. 80.

Depth	The normal depth of water at Montereau is 2 m. oo and this depth is maintained as far as the Port-Bas-Vignons, which is sited about 3 kilometres upstream of the town of Corbeil. The depth then increases to 3 m. 20 and so continues throughout the remainder of the section. The maximum authorised draught:

Montereau to Bas-Vignon	1 m. 80
Bas-Vignon to Pont National de Paris	2 m. 80

Bridges	Of the numerous fixed bridges none has a less headroom than 5 m. 36 at normal water level, but this is reduced to about 4 m. 36 at highest navigable water level.
Tow-path	There is no tow-path along this section, all vessels using it being either self-propelled or towed.

Distance Table

		kilom.	lock	kilom.
Montereau*	*Confluence with l' Yonne*. Bridge (Pont St-Nicolas). Ports	0.0	—	101.0
La Grande-Paroisse	Railway bridge	3.0	—	98.0
	Lock (No. 1 de Varennes). (R.B.)	4.0	I	97.0
Ecuelles	... ...	9.0	—	92.0
	Bridge (de St-Mammes). Port	14.0	—	87.0
Champagne-s-Seine†	*Junction with Canal du Loing* (L.B.) ...	14.0	—	87.0
	Lock (No. 2 de Champagne). (R.B.) ...	16.0	2	85.0
	Bridge (de Champagne)	17.0	—	84.0

* See Plan No. 19.
† See Plan No. 16.

Distance Table

		kilom.	lock	kilom.
Thomery	... ...	19.0	—	82.0
Samoreau	... ...	23.0	—	78.0
Vulaines	Bridge (de Valvins)	24.0	—	77.0
Samois	Lock (No. 3 de Samois). (L.B.)	26.0	3	75.0
Fontaine-le-Port	Bridge (de Fontaine-le-Port)	30.0	—	71.0
Bois-le-Roi	Lock (No. 4 de la Cave). (L.B.)	34.0	4	67.0
Chartrettes	Bridge (de Chartrettes)	35.0	—	66.0
Vaux-le-Pénil	Railway bridge (du Pet-au-Diable) ...	40.0	—	61.0
Melun	Bridges. Port	42.0	—	59.0
Mée	Railway bridge (du Mée)	44.0	—	57.0
Dammarie-les-Lys	... ...	46.0	—	55.0
Boisettes	... ...	47.0	—	54.0
Boissise-le-Roi	Lock (No. 5 de Vives-Eaux) (L.B.) ...	49.0	5	52.0
	Bridge (de Saint-Assise)	52.0	—	49.0
Saint-Fargeau	... ...	55.0	—	46.0
Seine-Port	... ...	56.0	—	45.0
Coudray	Lock (No. 7 du Coudray) (L.B.)	62.0	6	39.0
Bas-Vignons	Port (private) (river deepens)	64.0	—	37.0
Corbeil	Bridge (de Corbeil). Port	67.0	—	34.0
Evry	Footbridge (d'Evry)	70.0	—	31.0
	Lock (No. 8 d'Evry) (Twin; L.B.)	71.0	7	30.0
Ris-Orangis	Bridge (de Ris-Orangis)	74.0	—	27.0
Chatillon	... ...	78.0	—	23.0
Juvisy	Bridge (de Juvisy-Draveil)	79.0	—	22.0
Athis-Mons	Railway bridge	80.0	—	21.0
Ablon	Lock (No. 9 d'Ablon) (R.B. and L.B.) ...	83.0	9	18.0
Villeneuve-St-Georges	Bridge (de Villeneuve-St-Georges) ...	85.0	—	16.0
Choisy-le-Roi	Railway bridge	88.0	—	13.0
	Bridge (de Choisy)	90.0	—	11.0
Vitry	Suspension bridge (de Vitry)	93.0	—	8.0
Alfortville	Lock (No. 10 de Port-à-l'Anglais) (R.B. and L.B.)	94.0	9	7.0
Ivry	Bridge (Pont-d'Ivry)	96.0	—	5.0
Charenton	*Confluence with la Marne*	96.0	—	5.0
	Bridge (Pont de Conflans)	97.0	—	4.0
Paris	UPSTREAM LIMIT OF LA VILLE DE PARIS	97.6	—	3.0

The passage through the City of Paris

This length of the river leads through the heart of Paris. It is a busy length and carries a great deal of tug and lighter traffic; moreover, the passage is made more difficult by the presence of a number of islands which split the waterway into several branches *(bras)*, some of which are not available to craft travelling in a downstream

R

direction. Thus a stranger, especially if in charge of a pleasure vessel of moderate or large size, is advised to employ a pilot or some reliable person who has a really adequate knowledge of the local rules of the road with regard to which branch to take and where crossing and overtaking is permitted. At the very least, he should have at hand one of the admirable large-scale Cartes de Navigation Fluviale, particulars of which are given elsewhere in this work.* As it is necessary to take a different route when travelling upstream to that which should be followed when running downstream, two Distance Tables are given, one for each direction.

Especially note that the following branches of the river within the City Limits are forbidden to vessels running downstream:

le bras Marie

le bras de la Monnaie

le bras de Grenelle

le bras de Gennevilliers

le bras d'Issy-lès-Moulineaux

le bras de Boulogne

le bras de Clichy et 'Asdnières.

No navigation is allowed in le bras de Neuilly.

Also, in times of flood—that is, when the water level has reached a height of 27 m. 12 at le Pont de la Tournelle—*flood regulations* come into force with regard to the passage and branches to be used.

					kilom.	*lock*	*kilom.*
Distance Table							
Paris	UPSTREAM LIMIT OF LA VILLE DE						
	PARIS			...	97.6	—	3.9
	Bridge (Pont National) ...		...	...	97.9	—	3.6
	Bridge (Pont Tolbiac) ...		...	...	98.6	—	2.9
	Bridge (Pont de Bercy) ...		...	...	99.3	—	2.2
	Viaduct (Viaduc d'Austerlitz) ...		...	100.1	—	1.4
	Bridge (Pont d'Austerlitz) ...		...	100.3	—	1.2

Downstream or upstream

(via las bras de la Tournvelle, Saint-Louis et de la Cité)

Upstream end of l'Île St-Louis; bras Marie						
(R.B.); bras de la Tournelle (L.B.)	...	100.9	—	0.9
Bridge (Pont Sully)	...	101.1	—	0.4
Bridge (Pont de la Tournelle) ...	...	101.5	—	0.0

* See Navigational Notes, page 7. La Carte de la Haute-Seine contains the necessary information.

Upstream only

(via le bras Marie; to the right of l'Île St-Louis)

Upstream end of l'Île St-Louis; bras de la Tournelle (L.B.); bras Marie (R.B.)	...	—		—	0.6
Bridge (Pont Sully)	... ...	—		—	0.5
Bridge (Pont Marie)	... ...	—		—	0.0

3rd Section: Le Pont Marie, Paris to Amfreville—Poses

General   Conditions of traffic are similar to but on a yet heavier scale in this section. The volume of tonnage is greater and there are more tugs with tows and a larger number of big motor barges. To these must be added a considerable number of sea-going coasting vessels of moderate burden, for a draught of over 9 ft. can use the waterway. These coasting vessels and the tugs at times set up an appreciable disturbance by their passage and small craft should be ready to take action necessary to ride the wash. There are a number of islands in this section which divide the waterway into two channels; some, but not all, of these channels are available to traffic and of those that are available some are reserved for the use of vessels going upstream. The route shown in the Distance Table is one that may be used by vessels going either upstream or down, those few places where it is obligatory to take a different course when travelling upstream are clearly shown. Two 'Flood' routes are given (which entail shooting the barrages) although it is presumed that no one would attempt the passage without a pilot or previous experience. This section has been made to end at Amfreville Locks because below them the river is tidal.

Signals*   The navigable branches of the river have signals at the beginning of each bifurcation. The signal at the fork consists of a white rectangular plaque with a red rectangular border; on the white rectangular ground a black arrow shows the direction to be taken. At the passage of each bridge a rectangular plaque, coloured in horizontal stripes of red-white-red, suspended from the centre of a span show that the passage under that span is forbidden. A yellow diamond suspended from the centre of a span denotes that two-way traffic is allowed under it. Where only one-way traffic is allowed two yellow diamonds, hung horizontally side by side from the middle of the span, are displayed. By night a single red light replaces the plaque and a single yellow light replaces the diamond; similarly two yellow lights placed horizontally take the place of the two yellow diamonds. By night the entrances of the locks are indicated by lights; red (closed), red and yellow (about to open), green (open).

* See diagrams, Plan No. 22.

During times of flood when the level of the river has reached a certain height at each barrage, navigation is permitted to pass through the navigable sections of the barrages; a white flag by day and a white light by night indicates the position of the open pass. Underwater shelves and other obstructions are marked by red and white striped buoys. Notices to Mariners are to be seen at the notice boards which are conspicuously displayed at each lock.

Length

From the downstream limit of La Ville de Paris to the locks at Amfreville-Poses the distance is 194 kilometres. As the kilométrage is taken from le Pont Marie, Paris, another 8 kilometres must be added making 202 kilometres from the zero point.

Locks

There are now 7 locks with barrages between Paris and Amfreville-Poses. The locks at Suresnes, Bougival, Méricourt, Notre-Dame-de-la-Garenne and Amfreville-Poses have triple chambers, but at Amfreville only two chambers are at present in use. The new lock at Andresy, which is available by way of *le bras de Plafosse*, forms an alternative to the lock at Carrières-sous-Poissy on *le bras d'Andresy* route, so that in effect there are now only 6 locks to be passed between Paris and Rouen. All locks, except those which are expressly mentioned have a depth of at least 3 m. 50. Summarised the locks are:

Km.			Length	Width	Gate Width	Depth
17	Suresnes	large	160 m. 00	17 m. 00	11 m. 50	4 m. 20
		old	113 m. 00*	11 m. 50	11 m. 50	2 m. 30
		small	51 m. 00*	11 m. 90	11 m. 50	4 m. 20
49	Bougival	large	231 m. 00	17 m. 00	11 m. 95	
		old	113 m. 50	12 m. 00	11 m. 95	2 m. 20
		small	53 m. 00	8 m. 20	8 m. 14	
73	Andresy		116 m. 00	12 m. 00	12 m. 00	
76	Carrières-sous-Poissy		151 m. 25	17 m. 00	11 m. 86	
			53 m. 30	8 m. 20	8 m. 07	
121	Méricourt		167 m. 00	17 m. 00	17 m. 00	
			152 m. 00	17 m. 00	11 m. 60	
			54 m. 00	8 m. 20	7 m. 80	
161	Notre-Dame-de-la-Garenne	old	141 m. 00	17 m. 00	12 m. 00	3 m. 20
		small	41 m. 60	8 m. 20		3 m. 20
		new	160 m. 00	12 m. 00		5 m. 00
202	Amfreville		225 m. 50	16 m. 70	16 m. 94	
			147 m. 00	12 m. 00	11 m. 90	

* The old lock and the small lock can be used as a combined chamber for they are built as a prolongation of each other but separated by an intermediate gate. When this gate is opened the two chambers become one with a length of 170 m. 00. However, the old lock can only offer, at the normal stage of the river, a depth of water over the intermediate sill of 2 m. 30 in place of the 4 m. 20 of the other chambers. The side walls of all three locks are inclined so that the useful width of each chamber is reduced to:
Large lock—17 m. 00; small lock—11 m. 90; old lock—11 m. 50.

Depth	Normally there is a depth of water of 3 m. 20, but it must be noted that this depth is not to be found across the entire width of the river but is confined to a dredged channel. This channel varies in width from 50 to 80 metres and is shown on the chart issued by *l'Institut Geographique National*. The chart is on a scale of 1/10,000 and it is advised, in the interest of safety, that a copy should be obtained.
	If no chart is at hand it may be assumed in general that the channel is in the middle of the river. It is prohibited to anchor in the channel, nor may sailing vessels tack in it.
Bridges	All the fixed bridges have a clear headroom of at least 6 m. 00 above the normal water level.
Tow-path	None.

Distance Table

	kilom.	*lock*	*kilom.*
Bridge (Pont de la Tournelle)	0.0	—	242.4
Upstream end of l'Île de la Cité; bras St-Louis (between islands); bras de la Monnaie (L.B.)	0.2	—	242.2
Bridge (Pont St-Louis)	0.3	—	242.1
Downstream end of l'Île St-Louis; bras Marie (R.B.); bras de la Cité (R.B.); bras St-Louis (between islands)	0.4	—	242.0
Bridge (Pont d'Arcole)	0.5	—	241.9
Bridge (Pont Notre Dame)	0.7	—	241.7
Bridge (Pont au Change)	0.9	—	241.5
Bridge (Pont Neuf)	1.2	—	241.2
Downstream end of l'Île de la Cité; bras de la Cité (R.B.); bras de la Monnaie (L.B.)	1.4	—	241.0

Upstream only

(via le bras Marie; to the right of l'Île St-Louis)

	kilom.	*lock*	*kilom.*
Bridge (Pont Marie)	—	—	242.4
Bridge (Pont Louis-Philippe)	—	—	242.2
Downstream end of l'Île St-Louis; bras St-Louis (between islands); bras de la Cité (R.B.)	—	—	242.0

Upstream only

(via le bras de la Monnaie; to the left of l'Île Saint-Louis)

	kilom.	*lock*	*kilom.*
Upstream end of l'Île de la Cité (R.B.); bras St-Louis (between islands)	—	—	242.2
Bridge (Pont l'Archeveché)	—	—	242.1
Bridge (Pont au Double)	—	—	241.8

R.B. = Right Bank.   L.B. = Left Bank.

Distance Table

		kilom.	lock	kilom.
Bridge (Petit Pont)		—	—	241.7
Bridge (Pont St-Michel)		—	—	241.5
Bridge (Pont Neuf)		—	—	241.1
Downstream end of l'Île de la Cité; bras de la Cité (R.B.)		—	—	241.0

Downstream or upstream

	kilom.	lock	kilom.
Footbridge (Passerelle des Arts)	1.6	—	240.6
Bridge (Pont du Carrousel)	2.0	—	240.4
Bridge (Pont Royal)	2.2	—	240.2
Footbridge (Passerelle de Solférino) ...	2.6	—	239.8
Bridge (Pont de la Concorde)	3.0	—	239.4
Port (des Champs-Elysées). Yacht Station (R.B.)	3.4	—	239.0
Bridge (Pont Alexandre III)	3.5	—	238.9
Bridge (Pont des Invalides). Administration Centrale de l'Office nationale de la Navigation, 2 Boulevard de Latour-Maubourg (L.B.)	3.7	—	238.7
Footbridge (Passerelle Debilly)	4.7	—	237.7
Bridge (Pont d'Iéna)	5.3	—	237.1

(via le bras de Passy; to the right of l'Île des Cygnes)

	kilom.	lock	kilom.
Upstream end of l'Île des Cygnes (R.B.); bras de Grenelle (L.B.)	5.8	—	236.6
Viaduct (Pont-viaduc de Passy)	5.9	—	236.5
Railway Bridge (Pont-rails de Grenelle) ...	6.4	—	236.0
Bridge (Pont de Grenelle)	6.6	—	235.8
Downstream end of l'Île des Cygnes; bras de Grenelle (L.B.)	6.7	—	235.7

Upstream only

(via le bras de Grenelle; to the left of l'Île des Cygnes)

	kilom.	lock	kilom.
Upstream end of l'Île des Cygnes ...	—	—	236.6
Viaduct (Pont-viaduc de Passy)	—	—	236.5
Railway bridge (Pont-rails de Grenelle) ...	—	—	236.1
Bridge (Pont de Grenelle)	—	—	235.7
Downstream end of l'Île des Cygnes ...	—	—	235.7

Downstream or upstream

	kilom.	lock	kilom.
Bridge (Pont Mirabeau)	7.2	—	235.2
Bridge (Pont d'Auteuil)	8.2	—	234.2
DOWNSTREAM LIMIT OF LA VILLE DE PARIS	8.8	—	233.5

R.B. = Right Bank.   L.B. = Left Bank.

Downstream or upstream

(via le bras de Billancourt; to the right of l'Île St-Germain and le bras de Meudon, but to the left of l'Île Séguin)

Upstream end of l'Île St-German ...	...	9.0	—	233.0
Bridge (Pont d'Issy-les-Moulineaux)	...	9.0	—	233.0
Bridge (Pont de Billancourt) ...	...	10.0	—	232.0
Upstream end of l'Île Séguin ...	...	11.0	—	231.0
Downstream end of l'Île St-Germain	...	11.0	—	231.0
Bridge (Pont de l'Usine Renault)	...	11.0	—	231.0
Downstream end of l'Île Séguin ...	...	12.0	—	230.0

Upstream only

(via le bras d'Issy-les-Moulineaux; to the left of l'Île St-Germain)

Upstream end of l'Île St-Germain; bras de Billancourt (R.B.)	—	—	233.0
Bridge (Pont d'Issy)	—	—	233.0
Footbridge (Passerelle des Etablissements militaires)	—	—	232.0
Bridge (Pont de Billancourt)	—	—	232.0
Downstream end of l'Île St-Germain ...	—	—	231.0

Upstream only

(via le bras de Boulogne; to the right of l'Île Séguin)

Upstream end of l'Île Séguin	—	—	231.0
Bridge (Pont de l'Usine Renault)	—	—	231.0
Pier (Estacade Renault No. 11)	—	—	231.0
Downstream end of l'Île Séguin	—	—	230.0

Downstream or upstream

Bridge (Pont de Sèvres)	...	12.0	—	230.0
Bridge (Pont de Saint-Cloud) ...	...	13.0	—	229.0
Footbridge (Passerelle de l'Avre)	...	15.0	—	227.0
Bridge (Pont de Suresnes) ...	...	16.0	—	226.0

R.B. = Right Bank.   L.B. = Left Bank.

Distance Table

		kilom.	lock	kilom.
	Lock (Écluse triple et barrage de Suresnes) (L.B.)	17.0	I	225.0
Puteaux	Upstream end of l'Île de Puteaux	17.0	—	225.0
	Bridge (Pont de Puteaux)	18.0	—	224.0
Neuilly	Bridge (Pont de Neuilly)	19.0	—	223.0
	Downstream end of l'Île de Puteaux ...	20.0	—	222.0
	Upstream end of l'Île de la Grande-Jatte: *navigation forbidden along right bank* ...	20.0	—	222.0
	Bridge (Pont de Courbevoie)	21.0	—	221.0
Levallois-Perret	Bridge (Pont de Levallois)	22.0	—	220.0
	Downstream end of l'Île de la Grande-Jatte	22.0	—	220.0
Clichy	Railway bridge (Pont-rails d'Asnières) ...	23.0	—	219.0
	Bridge (Pont d'Asnières)	23.0	—	219.0

Upstream only

(via le bras d'Asniéres: to the left of l'Île des Ravageurs)

	Upstream end of l'Île Robinson	—	—	219.0
	Upstream end of l'Île des Ravageurs ...	—	—	219.0
	Bridge (Pont de Clichy)	—	—	218.0
	Downstream end of l'Île Robinson ...	—	—	218.0
	Downstream end of l'Île des Ravageurs ...	—	—	218.0

Downstream only

(via le bras central: entre les Îles Robinson et des Ravageurs)

	Upstream end of l'Île Robinson	23.0	—	—
	Upstream end of l'Île des Ravageurs ...	23.0	—	—
	Bridge (Pont de Clichy)	24.0	—	—
	Downstream end of l'Île Robinson ...	24.0	—	—
	Downstream end of l'Île des Ravageurs ...	24.0	—	—

Upstream only

(via le bras de Clichy: to the right of l'Île Robinson. Only for vessels whose destination is le Port public de Clichy)

Downstream or upstream

	Bridge (Pont de Gennevilliers)	25.0	—	217.0
Saint-Ouen	Railway bridge (Pont-rails)	25.0	—	217.0

R.B. = Right Bank.   L.B. = Left Bank.

Distance Table

Downstream or upstream

(via le bras de St-Ouen et St-Denis; to the right of l'Île St-Denis. Le bras de Gennevilliers to the left only for vessels whose destination is along that branch)

		kilom.	lock	kilom.
Île-St-Denis	Upstream end of l'Île St-Denis	25.0	—	217.0
	Bridge (Pont de St-Ouen)	26.0	—	216.0
	Bridge (Pont de l'Île St-Denis)	28.0	—	214.0
	Bridge (Pont d'Epinay)	32.0	—	210.0
	Railway bridge (Pont-rails)	32.0	—	210.0
	Downstream end of l'Île St-Denis ...	33.0	—	209.0
Argenteuil	Railway bridge (Pont-rails d'Argenteuil)...	35.0	—	207.0
	Bridge (Pont d'Argenteuil)	36.0	—	206.0
Colombes	Aqueduct (Pont aqueduc d'Argenteuil) ...	37.0	—	205.0
	Upstream end of l'Île Marante. *Bras du Moulin-Joli* (L.B.) *forbidden to navigation*	37.0	—	205.0
	Downstream end of l'Île Marante. *Bras du Moulin-Joli* (L.B.) *forbidden to navigation*	38.0	—	204.0
Nanterre	Bridge (Pont de Bezons)	39.0	—	203.0

Downstream or upstream

(via le bras de Marly; to the left of l'Île de Chatou as far as the upstream end of l'Île de la Loge, then through the lock to the channel to the right of l'Île de la Loge)

		kilom.	lock	kilom.
Bezons	Upstream end of l'Île de Chatou. *Bras de la Rivière-Neuve to the right for vessels downstream or upstream only during flood times*	40.0	—	202.0
	Railway bridge (Pont-rails de Nanterre) ...	41.0	—	201.0
Rueil	Bridge (Pont de Rueil)	45.0	—	197.0
	Railway bridge (Pont-rails de Rueil) ...	45.0	—	197.0
Bougival	Bridge (Pont de Bougival)	48.0	—	194.0
	Upstream end of old lock. Upstream end of l'Île de la Loge. *Bras de Marly* (L.B.) *not navigable.* Footbridge leading to l'Île de la Loge, protected by four dolphins. Upstream end of large and small locks (Ecluse triple de Bougival)	49.0	2	193.0
	Downstream end of l'Île Gautier. *Downstream end of bras de la Rivière-Neuve for vessels downstream or upstream only during flood times*	49.0	—	193.0

R.B. = Right Bank.   L.B. = Left Bank.

Distance Table

		kilom.	lock	kilom.
Port-Marly	Downstream end of l'Île de la Loge ...	51.0	—	191.0

Downstream or upstream during times of flood

(via le bras de Rivière-Neuve: to the right of l'Île de Chatou)

		kilom.	lock	kilom.
Bezons	Upstream end of l'Île de Chatou. *Bras de Marly to the left for use upstream or downstream in ordinary times*	40.0	—	202.0
	Bridge (Pont-rails de Bezons)	41.0	—	201.0
Carrières	Barrage (de Chatou). Bridge (Pont de Chatou)	45.0	—	197.0
	Railway bridge (Pont-rails de Chatou) ...	46.0	—	196.0
Bougival	Bridge (Pont de Croissy)	48.0	—	194.0
	Downstream end of l'Île Gautier. *Lock (Ecluse triple de Bougival) leads to bras de Marly for use downstream or upstream in ordinary times*	49.0	—	193.0

Downstream only

(via le bras to the right of l'Île Corbière)

		kilom.	lock	kilom.
Pecq	Upstream end of l'Île Corbière	52.0	—	—
	Railway bridge (Pont-rails)	53.0	—	—
	Downstream end of l'Île Corbière ...	53.0	—	—

Upstream only

(via le bras to the left of l'Île Corbière)

		kilom.	lock	kilom.
Pecq	Upstream end of l'Île Corbière	—	—	190.0
	Club-house (Cercle nautique de St-Germain-en-Laye)	—	—	190.0
	Railway bridge (Pont-rails)	—	—	189.0
	Downstream end of l'Île Corbière ...	—	—	189.0

Downstream or upstream

		kilom.	lock	kilom.
Mesnil-le-Roi	Upstream end of l'Île Laborde	56.0	—	186.0
	Bras de Maisons-Laffitte (L.B.), *commercial vessels forbidden*	56.0	—	186.0
Sartrouville	Yacht club (Cercle de la voile Montesson-Sartrouville)	57.0	—	185.0
	Motor yacht club (Paris Motonautique Club)	57.0	—	185.0
	Railway bridge (Pont-rails de Maisons-Lafitte)	58.0	—	184.0

R.B. = Right Bank.   L.B. = Left Bank.

Distance Table

		kilom.	lock	kilom.
	Upstream end of l'Île de la Commune. *Bras Maisons-Laffitte (L.B.)*, *commercial vessels forbidden*	58.0	—	184.0
	Bridge (Pont de Maisons-Laffitte) ...	59.0	—	183.0
La Frette	Sports nautique de la Frette (R.B.) ...	63.0	—	179.0
Herblay	Ferry (Ermery - Herblay)	65.0	—	177.0
	Upstream end of l'Île d'Herblay. *Bras de La Garenne (L.B.)*, *commercial vessels forbidden*	65.0	—	177.0
Conflans-Ste-	Downstream end of l'Île d'Herblay ...	67.0	—	175.0
Honorine	Upstream end of l'Île de Conflans. *Bras Favé (L.B.)*, *unfit for navigation*	68.0	—	174.0
	Downstream end of l'Île de Conflans. *Bras Favé (L.B.)*, *unfit for navigation* ...	70.0	—	172.0
	Bridge (Pont de Conflans)	70.0	—	172.0
Andrésy	*Confluence with l'Oise (R.B.) (at K.138)*...	71.0	—	171.0

Downstream or upstream

(via le bras d'Andrésy and to the right of l'Île de Nancy and l'ile de la dérivation when descending)

		kilom.	lock	kilom.
	Upstream end of l'Île de Nancy. *Bras de Plafosse to the left when descending* ...	72.0	—	170.0
	Downstream end of l'Île de Nancy. *Bras d'Andrésy with barrage de Denouval and old lock to the left*	75.0	—	167.0
Carrières-sous-Poissy	Upstream end of l'île de la dérivation ...	75.0	—	167.0
	Lock (Écluse double de Carrières-sous-Poissy)	76.0	3	166.0
	Downstream end of l'île de la dérivation ...	76.0	—	166.0

Downstream or upstream

(via le bras de Plafosse, to the left of Île de Nancy when descending)

		kilom.	lock	kilom.
	Upstream end of l'Île de Nancy; beginning of bras de Plafosse	72.0	—	170.0
	Lock (Nouveau barrage et écluse d'Andrésy)	73.0	3	169.0
Achères	Downstream end of l'Île de Nancy. *Bras d'Andrésy and barrage de Denouval and old lock on right. Upstream end of l'île de la dérivation*	75.0	—	167.0
Poissy	Downstream end of l'île de la dérivation	76.0	—	166.0
	Upstream end of l'Île de Carrières. *Bras de St-Louis (L.B.)*, *navigation forbidden* ...	76.0	—	166.0

R.B. = Right Bank.   L.B. = Left Bank.

255

Distance Table

		kilom.	lock	kilom.
	Downstream end of l'Île de Carrières. *Bras de St-Louis* (L.B.), *navigation forbidden* ...	77.0	—	165.0
	Bridge (Pont de Poissy)	78.0	—	164.0
	Upstream end of l'Île des Magnaux. *Bras de Mignaux* (L.B.), *not navigable*	78.0	—	164.0

Downstream or upstream

(via le bras de l'Îlot Blanc (R.B.), or by le bras central between l'Îlot Blanc and l'Île des Magnaux)

		kilom.	lock	kilom.
	Upstream end of l'Îlot Blanc.	78.0	—	164.0
	Downstream end of l'Îlot Blanc	79.0	—	163.0
Villennes-sur-Seine	Downstream end of l'Île des Mignaux ...	80.0	—	162.0
	Upstream end of l'Île de Médan. *Bras de Mottes* (R.B.) reserved for downstream traffic: *Bras de Médan* (L.B.) reserved for *upstream* traffic	82.0	—	160.0
Triel	Downstream end of l'Île de Médan ...	83.0	—	159.0
	Upstream end of l'Île Hernière	83.0	—	159.0
	Downstream end of l'Île Hernière. *Bras de Mottes* (R.B.) reserved for *downstream* traffic	84.0	—	158.0
	Bridge (Pont de Triel)	85.0	—	157.0
Vaux	Upstream end of l'Île de Vaux. *Bras de Vaux* (R.B.) *navigation forbidden*	88.0	—	154.0
Mureaux	Downstream end of l'Île de Vaux ...	90.0	—	152.0
Meulan	Upstream end of l'Île du Fort	92.0	—	150.0

Downstream or upstream

(via le chenal en Seine, to the left of l'Île du Fort, l'Île Belle, de Mézy et de Juziers)

		kilom.	lock	kilom.
Meulan	Upstream end of l'Île du Fort	92.0	—	150.0
	Bridge (Pont des Mureaux)	93.0	—	149.0
Juziers	Downstream end of l'Île de Juziers ...	99.0	—	143.0

Downstream only

(via le bras des Fermettes (R.B.))

		kilom.	lock	kilom.
Gargenville	Upstream end of l'Île de Montalet... ...	101.0	—	—
	Bridge (Pont de Rangiport-Épone) ...	101.0	—	—
	Downstream end of l'Île de Montalet ...	102.0	—	—

Upstream only

		kilom.	lock	kilom.
Gargenville	Upstream end of l'Île de Montalet... ...	—	—	141.0

R.B. = Right Bank.   L.B. = Left Bank.

Distance Table

		kilom.	lock	kilom.
	Bridge (Pont de Rangiport-Épone) ...	—	—	141.0
	Downstream end of l'Île de Montalet ...	—	—	140.0

Downstream or upstream

		kilom.	lock	kilom.
Porcheville	Upstream end of l'Île de Porcheville ...	103.0	—	139.0
	Downstream end of l'Île de Porcheville ...	104.0	—	138.0
Mézières	Upstream end of l'Île de l'État. *Bras* (L.B.) *navigation forbidden*	104.0	—	138.0
Porcheville	Upstream end of l'Île de Limay. *Bras de Limay* (R.B.) *only available for a destination within le bras*	106.0	—	136.0
Mantes-la-Jolie	Railway bridge (Pont-rails de Mantes) ...	108.0	—	134.0
	Bridge (Pont de Mantes-Limay)	109.0	—	133.0
	Upstream end of l'Île aux Boeufs	110.0	—	132.0
Follainville	Upstream end of l'Île de Dennemont ...	112.0	—	130.0
	Downstream end of l'Île de Gassicourt ...	112.0	—	130.0
	Downstream end of l'Île de Dennemont. *Bras* (R.B.) *navigation forbidden*	112.0	—	130.0
Rosny	Ferry (bac public de Guernes) ...	117.0	—	125.0
Rolleboise	Upstream end of l'Île de la Sablière ...	120.0	—	122.0
	Downstream end of l'Île de la Sablière ...	121.0	—	121.0
St-Martin-la-Garenne	Lock (Écluse triple de Méricourt) (L.B.) ...	121.0	4	121.0
	Upstream end of l'Île St-Martin	125.0	—	117.0

Downstream only

(via le bras St-Martin (R.B.))

		kilom.	lock	kilom.
St-Martin	Upstream end of l'Île St-Martin	125.0	—	—
Vétheuil	Downstream end of l'Île St-Martin ...	128.0	—	—

Upstream only

(via le bras de Mousseaux (L.B.))

		kilom.	lock	kilom.
St-Martin	Upstream end of l'Île St-Martin	—	—	117.0
Vétheuil	Downstream end of l'Île St-Martin ...	—	—	114.0

Downstream or upstream

		kilom.	lock	kilom.
Moisson	Upstream end of l'Île de Moisson	130.0	—	112.0
	Downstream end of l'Île de Moisson. *Bras* (R.B.) *navigation forbidden*	132.0	—	110.0
Bennecourt	Upstream end of l'Île de Haut. *Bras de Gloton* (R.B.) *navigation forbidden*	138.0	—	104.0

R.B. = Right Bank.   L.B. = Left Bank.

257

Distance Table

		kilom.	lock	kilom.
	Bridge (Pont de Bonnières)...	140.0	—	102.0
	Downstream end of l'Île de Vienne. *Bras de Gloton* (R.B.) *navigation forbidden* ...	141.0	—	101.0
	Upstream end of l'Île de la Flotte. *Bras* (L.B.) *navigation forbidden*	141.0	—	101.0
Giverny	Upstream end of la grande Île de Giverny. *Bras de Giverny* (R.B.) *navigation forbidden*	146.0	—	96.0
Vernon	Downstream end of la grande Île de Giverny. *Bras de Giverny* (R.B.) *navigation forbidden*	148.0	—	94.0
	Bridge (Pont de Vernon)	150.0	—	92.0
	Upstream end of les Îles Réunies	150.0	—	92 0
	Downstream end of les Îles Réunies. *Bras* (R.B.) *navigation forbidden*	152 0	—	90.0
St-Just	Upstream end of l'Île Souveraine. *Bras* (R.B.), *navigation forbidden*	153.0	—	89.0
Pressagny-	Downstream end of l'Île Souveraine ...	154.0	—	88.0
l'Orgueilleux	Upstream end of l'Île Souquet	155.0	—	87.0
	Downstream end of l'Île Souquet ...	156.0	—	86.0
	Upstream end of l'Île Émien. *Bras de Pressagny-l'Orgueilleux* (R.B.), *navigation forbidden*	156.0	—	86.0
	Upstream end of l'Île St-Pierre-la Garenne. Take *new channel* towards R.B. leading to *bras de Port Mort* (to the right of l'Île St-Pierre-la-Garenne). *Le bras du Goulet* (L.B.) *is a dead end*...	157.0	—	85.0

The channel forks:

(a) to the *left* the channel leads to l'écluse Notre-Dame-de-la-Garenne (L.B.)

		kilom.	lock	kilom.
	(b) to the *right* the channel leads to the barrage de Port-Mort, passable during times of flood	160.0	—	82.0
Gaillon	Lock (Écluse triple de Notre-Dame-de-la-Garenne)	161.0	5	81.0
	Barrage de Port-Mort (R.B.)	161.0	—	81.0
Aubevoye	Bridge (Pont de Courcelles)	164.0	—	78.0
Courcelles	Upstream end of l'Île du Roule	165.0	—	77.0
Villers-s-le-Roule	Downstream end of l'île du Roule. *Bras* (R.B.), *navigation forbidden*. Downstream end of island buoyed for 400 metres downstream	167.0	—	75.0

R.B. = Right Bank.　　L.B. = Left Bank.

Distance Table

		kilom.	lock	kilom.
	The channel is buoyed between K1.67.6 and K1.68.2. Keep the buoys on the starboard hand when descending.			
	Upstream end of l'Île d'en-Haut. *Bras* (L.B.), *navigation forbidden*	168.0	—	74.0
Tosny	Upstream end of l'Île Ronde. *Bras* (R.B.) *not navigable*	171.0	—	71.0
	Downstream end of l'Île Ronde. *Bras* (R.B.) *not navigable*	172.0	—	70.0
Les Andelys	Bridge (Pont des Andelys)	173.0	—	69.0
	Harbour for yachts and pleasure craft (R.B.)	174.0	—	68.0
	Upstream end of l'Île Port-Morin. *Bras* (L.B.), *navigation forbidden*	174.0	—	68.0
	Upstream end of l'Île Gringoire. *Bras* (L.B.), *navigation forbidden*	174.0	—	68.0
	Upstream end of l'Île du Chateau. *Bras* (L.B.) *reserved for downstream traffic. Bras* (R.B.) *reserved for upstream traffic* ...	174.0	—	68.0
	Downstream end of l'Île du Chateau ...	175.0	—	67.0
	Upstream end of l'Île Motelle. *Bras* (R.B.) *not navigable*	178.0	—	64.0
La Roquette	Upstream end of l'Île de la Roque ...	178.0	—	64.0
	Downstream end of l'Île Motelle. *Bras* (R.B.) *not navigable*	179.0	—	63.0
	Shoals in mid-stream marked by a dolphin; *keep between dolphin and L.B.*	180.0	—	62.0
		182.0	—	60.0
Muids	Upstream end of l'Île de la Motte. *Bras* (R.B.), *not navigable*	182.0	—	60.0
	Downstream end of l'Île de la Motte ...	183.0	—	59.0
	Upstream end of l'Île aux Bretons. *Bras* (R.B.), *navigation forbidden*	183.0	—	59.0
	Upstream end of l'Île des Grands-Bacs et de la Cage	184.0	—	58.0
	Downstream end of l'Île de la Cage ...	186.0	—	56.0
	Upstream end of l'Île de Lormais ...	186.0	—	56.0
	Downstream end of l'Île de Lormais ...	188.0	—	54.0
St-Pierre-du-Vauvray	Old Bridge (demolished) (de St-Pierre-du-Vauvray)	189.0	—	53.0
	Upstream end of l'Île Héron	189.0	—	53.0
	Downstream end of l'Île Héron	190.0	—	52.0
	Bridge (Pont de St-Pierre-du-Vauvray) ...	191.0	—	51.0

R.B. = Right Bank.   L.B. = Left Bank.

Distance Table

		kilom.	lock	kilom.
	Downstream end of l'Île du Bac. *Bras* (R.B.), *navigation forbidden*	191.0	—	51.0
	Upstream end of l'Île Bunel. *Bras* (R.B.), *navigation forbidden*	191.0	—	51.0
Andé	Downstream end of l'Île Bunel	192.0	—	50.0
	Downstream end of l'Île du Martinet ...	192.0	—	50.0
Porte-Joie	Downstream end of l'Île du Moulin. *Bras* (R.B.), *navigation forbidden*	193.0	—	49.0
	Upstream end of l'Île du Galet. *Bras* (R.B.) *reserved for downstream traffic*	194.0	—	48.0
	Upstream end of l'Île de Port-Pinché. *Bras* (R.B.) *reserved for downstream traffic* ...	194.0	—	48.0
	Downstream end of l'Île de Port-Pinché. *Bras* (R.B.) *reserved for downstream traffic.* *Bras* (L.B.) *reserved for upstream traffic* ...	195.0	—	47.0
Tournedos	Upstream end of l'Île de Pampou. *Bras* (L.B.) *navigation forbidden*	196.0	—	46.0
	Downstream end of l'Île de Pampou. *Bras* (L.B.), *navigation forbidden*	196.0	—	46.0
Poses	Downstream end of l'Île de Tournedos. *Bras* (R.B.), *navigation forbidden*	199.0	—	43.0
	Upstream end of l'Île Dehors. *Bras* (L.B.), *navigation forbidden*	199.0	—	43.0
Poses	Outboard - motor Boat Club (Circle Nautique de Poses)	199.0	—	43.0
	Downstream end of l'Île du Noyer ...	199.0	—	43.0
	Downstream end of l'Île de la Ronde ...	200.0	—	42.0
Amfreville	Upstream end of la Grand Île. Beginning of la dérivation d'Amfreville (leading to the locks)	200.0	—	42.0
	Garage for vessels along R.B.	201.0	—	41.0
	Lock (Écluse triple d'Amfreville) (only two in use)	202.0	6	40.0

4th Section: Amfreville-Poses to Le Pont Jeanne-d'Arc, Rouen

General

The whole of the section is tidal; the traffic is the same as in the preceding section. When mooring by the banks care must be taken to allow for the rise and fall, and precautions taken against grounding on falling water; after having been in locked waters for some time, it is not unusual to forget these obvious matters.

Length

The distance from the locks at Amfreville to le Pont-Jeanne-d'Arc

R.B. = Right Bank.   L.B. = Left Bank.

at Rouen is 40 kilometres, of which the last 17 kilometres form part of the Port of Rouen.

Depth

The normal depth of low-water spring tides is 3 m. 20, but vessels drawing more than 3 m. 00 are not allowed to navigate. It is further to be remarked that the depth of 3 m. 20 cannot be relied upon at low-water exceptional spring tides which occur from time to time.

Bridges

The bridges below Paris have a maximum headroom at normal water level of 6 m. 00, which is reduced to about 3 m. 50 at highest navigable water level.

Tow-path

The old tow-path is no longer in use, is not maintained and is no longer practicable.

Distance Table

		kilom.	lock	kilom.
	Downstream end of lock and barrage (d'Amfreville)	202.0	—	40.0
	Downstream end of lock embankment (Île de la Mouchouette). Barrage de Poses (on le bras de Poses), *navigation forbidden*	202.0	—	40.0
Manoir	Railway bridge (Pont-rails du Manoir) ...	205.0	—	37.0
Pont-de-l'Arche	Bridge (Pont-de-l'Arche)	208.0	—	34.0
	Overflow channel (déversoir de Pont-de-l'Arche) with navigable channel leading to the River Eure	208.0	—	34.0
Freneuse	Upstream end of bras de Freneuse (R.B.), *navigation forbidden*	213.0	—	29.0
	Downstream end of bras de Freneuse (R.B.), *navigation forbidden*	216.0	—	26.0
	Confluence with l'Eure. Downstream end of l'Île Geoffroy	217.0	—	25.0
Elbeuf	Yacht Club (Yachting Club d'Elbeuf) ...	218.0	—	24.0
	Bridge (Pont-route Jean-Jaurès)	219.0	—	23.0
	Suspension bridge (Pont suspendu d'Elbeuf)	219.0	—	23.0
Orival	Railway bridge (Pont-rails d'Orival) ...	221.0	—	21.0
	Upstream end of l'Île Osier. *Bras* (L.B.) *navigation forbidden*	222.0	—	20.0
	Upstream end of l'Île Galet. *Bras* (L.B.) *navigation forbidden*	222.0	—	20.0
	Downstream end of l'Île Osier. *Bras* (L.B.) *navigation forbidden*	222.0	—	20.0
	Upstream end of l'Île du Croc. *Bras* (L.B.) *navigation forbidden*	222.0	—	20.0

R.B. = Right Bank.   L.B. = Left Bank.

Distance Table

		kilom.	lock	kilom.
	Downstream end of l'Île du Croc. *Bras* (L.B.) *navigation forbidden*	223.0	—	19.0
	Upstream end of l'Île Motelle. *Bras* (L.B.) *navigation forbidden*	223.0	—	19.0
	Downstream end of l'Île Motelle. *Bras* (L.B.) *navigation forbidden*	223.0	—	19.0
Cléon	Downstream end of la grande Île d'Orival. *Bras d'Orival* (L.B.) *navigation forbidden* ...	224.0	—	18.0
	UPSTREAM LIMIT OF THE PORT FLUVIAL DE ROUEN	225.0	—	17.0
	(Throughout the Port de Rouen the direction for navigation is 'KEEP to the RIGHT'			
Cléon	Upstream end of l'Île Légarée. *Bras de Bédane* (R.B.) *navigation forbidden* ...	225.0	—	17.0
	Four berthing places along L.B. (called 'des Roches')	226.0	—	16.0
Tourville	Downstream end of l'Île Légarée	227.0	—	15.0
	Bridge (Pont-route d'Oissel)	230.0	—	12.0
Oissel	Viaduct (Viaduc de chemin de fer d'Oissel)	230.0	—	12.0
	Downstream end of l'Île Crocq	231.0	—	11.0
Tourville	Upstream end of l'Île Grard	232.0	—	10.0
	Downstream end of l'Île Grard	232.0	—	10.0
Gouy	Upstream end of l'Île Merdray	233.0	—	9.0
	Downstream end of l'Île Merdray ...	233.0	—	9 0
Belbeuf	Upstream end of l'Île Bas-des-Vases ...	234.0	—	8.0
	Downstream end of l'Île Bas-des-Vases. *Bras* (R.B.) *navigation forbidden*	235.0	—	7.0
St-Etienne	Downstream end of l'Île de la Crapaudière	236.0	—	6.0
Sotteville-lès-Rouen	Pontoon-ferry (d'Amfreville-St-Etienne) ...	238.0	—	4.0
	Upstream end of l'Île du Jonquay	238.0	—	4.0
	Downstream end of l'Île du Jonquay ...	238.0	—	4.0

Basin called Lescure

(a) Right bank: Amfreville and Bonsecours shore

Amfreville-la-Mi-Voie	Upstream end of l'Île du Jonquay ...	238.3	—	4.1
Bonsecours	Pontoon-ferry (de Bonsecours-Sotteville)	240.1	—	2.3
	Upstream end of l'Île Lacroix	240.4	—	2.0
	Railway bridge (Viaduc de chemin de fer d'Eauplet)	240.5	—	1.9

(b) Left bank: Sotteville shore

	Upstream end of l'Île du Jonquay ...	239.8	—	2.6

R.B. = Right Bank.   L.B. = Left Bank.

Distance Table

	kilom.	lock	kilom.
Pontoon-ferry (de Bonsecours-Sotteville)...	240.1	—	2.3
Upstream end of l'Île Lacroix	240.4	—	2.0
Railway bridge (Viaduc de chemin de fer d'Eauplet)	240.5	—	1.9

(a) via the channel called 'Pre-aux-Loups' (between l'Île Lacroix and the right bank)

Only to be used against the current, whether flood or ebb.

Bonsecours

	kilom.	lock	kilom.
Railway bridge (Viaduc de chemin de fer d'Eauplet)	240.5	—	1.9
Bridge (Pont Corneille). Quay (Quai de Paris-aval: 310 m.)...	241.9	—	0.5
Downstream end of l'Île Lacroix	242.0	—	0.4
Bridge (Pont Boieldieu). Quay (Quai de la Bourse: 300 m.)	242.2	—	0.2
Bridge (Pont-Jeanne-d'Arc)	242.4	—	0.0
DOWNSTREAM LIMIT OF THE PORT FLUVIAL DE ROUEN	242.4	—	0.0

(b) via the channel called 'Cours-la-Reine' (between l'Île Lacroix and and left bank)

Sotteville

	kilom.	lock	kilom.
Railway bridge (Viaduc de chemin de fer d'Eauplet)	240.0	—	2.0
Quay (Quai d'Elbeuf: 410 m.)	241.4	—	1.0
Bridge (Pont Corneille). Quay (Quai St-Sever: 300 m.)	241.9	—	0.5
Downstream end of l'Île Lacroix	242.0	—	0.4
Bridge (Pont Boieldieu). Quay (Quai Cavelier-de-la-Salle 220 m.). *Reserved for pleasure craft*	242.2	—	0.2
Bridge (Pont-Jeanne-d'Arc)	242.4	—	0.0
DOWNSTREAM LIMIT OF THE PORT FLUVIAL DE ROUEN	242.4	—	0.0

CANAL DE LA HAUT-SEINE

General

The Canal de la Haute-Seine formerly began at Troyes but since 1957 that part of the canal which lies upstream of the lock at Méry-sur-Seine has been abandoned. Therefore, details are now given only from Méry-sur-Seine downstream towards Marcilly-sur-Seine where the canal joins the river Aube (which is not navigable) at the confluence of that river with la Seine.

R.B. = Right Bank.   L.B. = Left Bank.

Length	From Méry-s-Seine to Marcilly-s-Seine by the canal is a distance of 14½ kilometres, taken here as being 14 kilometres.

Locks	Between Méry-s-Seine and the canal's junction with l'Aube there are 5 locks. The first below Méry has a length of 34 m. 50 with a width of 5 m. 10; the remaining 4 locks all have a length of 39 m. 05 with a width of 5 m. 10. The lock at St-Just is a double staircase lock.

Depth	The normal depth of water is 1 m. 70 throughout.

Bridges	All the fixed bridges have a minimum headroom of 3 m. 70 above the normal water level.

Tow-path	There is a tow-path.

Distance Table		kilom.	lock	kilom.
Méry-sur-Seine	*Downstream side of Lock No. 10 (de Méry)*	0.0	—	14.0
	Bridge (de Méry). Port	0.0	—	14.0
Saint-Oulph	Lock (No. 11 de St-Oulph)	1.0	1	13.0
	Port and Bridge (de St-Oulph)	2.0	—	12.0
Clesles	Bridge	4.0	—	10.0
	Basin and Bridge (de Clesles)	5.0	—	9.0
Saint-Just	Staircase locks (Nos. 12 and 13 de St-Just)	9.0	3	5.0
	Bridge (de St-Just)	9.0	—	5.0
	Lock (No. 14 de St-Just	9.0	4	5.0
	Port and Bridge (de St-Just)	10.0	—	4.0
Saron	Bridge	13.0	—	1.0
Marcilly-sur-Seine	Lock (No. 15 de Marcilly)	14.0	5	0.0
	Junction with l'Aube and la Seine (at Ko.o)	14.0	—	0.0

CANAL DE LA SENSÉE

General	The Canal de la Sensée begins at Etrun on the River Escaut and runs in a westerly direction to the point where la Scarpe supérieure, la Scarpe moyenne and la dérivation de la Scarpe autour de Douai all meet at a short distance to the south of the town of Douai. The Bassin-Rond at Etrun, which was formerly where the Canal de la Sensée joined l'Escaut has now been superseded by a new short canal called 'le canal de jonction Escaut-Sensée*'. The importance of the Canal de la Sensée has been increased of late because it forms a section of the improved route known as *La Liaison Dunkerque-Valenciennes* and also because, about halfway along its course, it receives the northern end of the new Canal du Nord.

* See Plan No. 8.

Length	The length of the canal from its junction with l'Escaut at Etrun to its union with la Scarpe supérieure and la dérivation de la Scarpe autour de Douai is 25 kilometres.
Locks	There is but one lock which is situated at Goeluzin. This lock is 144 m. 00 in length with a width of 12 m. 00.
Depth	There is a depth of water of 3 m. 50 in the canal at the normal water level.
Bridges	The headroom under the bridges is 5 m. 25 at highest navigable water level.
Tow-path	There is a tow-path throughout, in some places on both sides of the canal. The tow-path carries rails along which run electric tractors which tow those vessels which are not self-propelled.

Distance Table

		kilom.	lock	kilom.
Bouchain	Junction with l'Escaut (at K.12)	0.0	—	25.0
	Junction with le canal de jonction Escaut-Sensée*	0.4	—	24.6
	Staithe (d'Estrun)	1.0	—	24.0
Paillencourt	Staithe and Bridge (de Paillencourt) ...	1.0	—	24.0
	Bridge (de Wasnes-au-Bac) (called 'Pont-Rade')	4.0	—	21.0
Hem-Lenglet	Bridge and Staithe (d'Hem-Lenglet) ...	6.0	—	19.0
Fressies	Bridge and Staithe (de Fressies)	8.0	—	17.0
Aubigny-au-Bac	Staithe and Bridge (d'Aubigny-au-Bac) ...	11.0	—	14.0
	Railway bridge	12.0	—	13.0
Oisy-le-Verger	Bridge (de l'Abbaye-du-Verger)	13.0	—	12.0
	Staithe (d'Oisy-le-Verger)	13.0	—	12.0
Arleux	Bridge (d'Arleux)	16.0	—	9.0
	Junction with Canal du Nord			
	Staithe (d'Arleux)	17.0	—	8.0
Goeulzin	Staithe and Bridge (du Moulinet)	19.0	—	6.0
Estrées	Lock (de Goeulzin)...	21.0	I	4.0
Férin	Bridge (de Férin). Staithe (de Férin) ...	22.0	—	3.0
Corbehem†	Bridge (de Corbehem)	24.0	—	1.0
	Junction with la Scarpe supérieure and with la dérivation autour de Douai	25.0	—	0.0

Canal de jonction Escaut-Sensée

Etrun	Beginning of le canal de jonction Escaut-Sensée (at K.0.4 of le Canal de la Sensée) ...	0.0	—	0.7

* See Plan No. 8.   † See Plan No. 7.

Distance Table						*kilom.*	*lock*	*kilom.*
Footbridge	...	...	...	...	...	0.1	—	0.6
End of le canal de jonction (at K.12.9 of the								
River Escaut		...	...	...	...	0.7	—	0.0

SÈVRE-NANTAISE

General

La Sèvre-Nantaise is navigable from the bridge at Monnières to its confluence with la Loire at the city of Nantes. It is divided into two parts by the barrage and lock at Vertou. That part which is situated above the lock has been canalised, while that portion which lies below the lock is subject to tidal influence and is more properly classified as a marine navigation. The river traffic consists of barges and lighters none of which exceeds a burthen of 150 tonnes.

Length

The total distance from the bridge at Monnières to the confluence with la Loire at Nantes is nearly 22 kilometres, of which 15 kilometres has been canalised.

Locks

There is only one lock, situated at Vertou, which has a length of 32 m. 00 with a width of 5 m. 60. At Pont Rousseau barrages have been made under the arches. That under the central arch has a narrow navigable opening 5 m. 60 in width; the opening is marked by two beacons.

Depth

The canalised length of the river above Vertou has a normal depth of water of 2 m. 50, but this may fall to a minimum of 1 m. 50. Below the lock at Vertou, where the river is subject to the tides the depth is as much as 3 m. 00 at high water spring tides, but falls as low as 0 m. 50 at low water neap tides.

Bridges

There are several fixed bridges. Those above Vertou have a head-room of not less than 5 m. 50 above the normal water level; those below the lock have a headroom of 4 m. 00 above the normal high water level.

Tow-path

The tow-path has fallen into disuse; the barges and other commercial craft are nearly all self-propelled and those which are not are towed by small tugs.

Distance Table						*kilom.*	*lock*	*kilom.*
Monnières	*Head of navigation.* Bridge (de Monnières)					0.0	—	22.0
	Port (Port Domino)	...	...	...		0.0	—	22.0
Chateau-Thebaud	Port (de la Bidière)		...	...	...	3.0	—	19.0

Distance Table

		kilom.	lock	kilom.
Haie-Fouassière	Bridge (de la Haie-Fouassière)	5.0	—	17.0
	Port (de la Haie-Fouassière)	6.0	—	16.0
Saint-Fiacre	Bridge (de la Ramée)	9.0	—	13.0
	Confluence with la Petite-Maine *(not navigable)*	11.0	—	11.0
Vertou	Bridge (de Portillon)	12.0	—	10.0
	Port (de Portillon)	13.0	—	9.0
	Bridge and Port (du Chêne)	14.0	—	8.0
	Lock and Barrage (de Vertou)	15.0	I	7.0
	Port (de Beautour)	18.0	—	4.0
Nantes	Bridge (de la Morinière)	19.0	—	3.0
	Bridge (de Pont-Rousseau)	20.0	—	2.0
	Port (de Pont-Rousseau)	21.0	—	1.0
	Confluence with la Loire (at K.85)	22.0	—	0.0

SÈVRE-NIORTAISE

General

La Sèvre-Niortaise is navigable from Niort to its estuary at l'Anse de l'Aiguillon where it falls into the Atlantic Ocean. It is divided into two sections:

(1) Niort to Marans.

(2) Marans to the sea.

The inland waterway part of the river is the first section, while section 2 is classified as a marine navigation and will not be considered here. It is along the first section that the canal de la Vieille Autise and the Canal du Mignon make junction with this river.

Length

The distance from Niort to Marans is 54 kilometres. In many places deviations have been made and the river itself abandoned by the navigation.

Locks

As far as Marans the river is controlled by 8 locks, counting the lock which is at Marans. They all have a length of 31 m. 50 with a width of 5 m. 20. There is 1 lock in the marine section which has a length of 40 m. 00 with a width of 7 m. 00. The distance from Marans to the sea is 18 kilometres.

Depth

From Niort to lock No. 5 (de la Sotterie) the depth is 1 m. 20. Between lock No. 5 and le Pont de la Croix des Maries, 2 m. 20 can be counted upon. From thence to lock No. 8 (du Carreau d'Or) at Marans the depth is 2 m. 50, but this may be reduced to 2 m. 00 during low water.

Bridges

All the fixed bridges have a headroom of not less than 2 m. 20 at the normal water level.

| Tow-path | | There is a tow-path throughout, but the use of animals and men for the work of towing is now nearly given up. Mostly, small tugs or self-propelled vessels are used to carry the agricultural products which form the greater part of the freight transported. |

Distance Table

				kilom.	lock	kilom.
Niort	*Head of navigation.* Port (de Niort)	...		0.0	—	54.0
	Lock (No. 1 de Comporté)	...	...	0.0	1	54.0
St-Liguaire	Lock (No. 2 de la Roussille)	...	...	6.0	2	48.0
	Lock (No. 3 de la Tiffardière)	...	...	7.0	3	47.0
	Bridge (de la Tiffardière). Railway bridge			8.0	—	46.0
Magné	Lift bridge (de Magné)	...	...	10.0	—	44.0
Coulon	Lock (No. 4 de Marais-Pin)	...	...	13.0	4	41.0
	Bridge (de Coulon)	...	...	15.0	—	39.0
	Footbridge ...	...	...	16.0	—	38.0
Sansais	Lock (No. 5 de la Sotterie)	...	...	19.0	5	35.0
	Bridge (Pont d'Irleau)	...	...	21.0	—	33.0
Le Mazeau	Footbridge (de Cabanes de la Sèvre)	...		23.0	—	31.0
Damvix	Lock (No. 6 des Bourdettes)	...	...	28.0	6	26.0
	Bridge (de Damvix)	...	...	30.0	—	24.0
	Junction with Canal de la Vieille-Autise ...			32.0	—	22.0
Maillé	Lock (No. 7 de Bazoin)	...	...	33.0	7	21.0
La Ronde	*Junction with Canal du Mignon*	...	...	34.0	—	20.0
	Bridge (de la Croix des Maries) ...		...	34.0	—	20.0
	Beginning of cut (Contour de Maillé)	...		37.0	—	17.0
	Junction with La Jeune-Autise dans le boucle du Contour de Maillé	...	...	...	—	—	—
	End of cut (Contour de Maillé) ...		...	38.0	—	16.0
Taugon	Bridge (du Sablon) ...	...	...	38.0	—	16.0
	Beginning of cut (Canal du Sablon)	...		41.0	—	13.0
	End of cut (Canal du Sablon)	...	...	42.0	—	12.0
Ille-d'Elle	Beginning of cut (Canal de Pomère)	...		45.0	—	9.0
	Bridge	...	...	...	...	50.0	—	4.0
	End of cut (Canal de Pomère)	...		50.0	—	4.0
Marans	Railway bridge	...	...	...	50.0	—	4.0
	Bridge	...	...	...	...	53.0	—	1.0
	Lock (No. 8 du Carreau-d'Or a Marans)			54.0	8	0.0
	River and Marine Port (de Marans). *Junction with canal maritime de Marans à La Rochelle*	...	...	...	...	54.0	—	0.0

CANAL DE LA SOMME

| General | | The Canal de la Somme begins at Saint-Simon on the Canal de Saint-Quentin and ends at Saint-Valéry-sur-Somme. It thus forms an outlet to the sea from the Canal de Saint-Quentin. Between |

268

St-Simon and Bray-Froissy, in the *Commune de Laneuville,* the canal runs parallel to the River Somme, but for the rest of the distance the canal occupies the river bed with a considerable number of deviations. At Abbeville one of these *dérivations* avoids a large loop in the river, which loop is used as a port and garage. After leaving Abbeville the canal takes the name of *le canal maritime d'Abbeville à Saint-Valéry.* This part of the canal is prolonged by a side drain which forms an overflow berm during times of flood. A section of the canal between K.16.7 and K.36.6 has been 'borrowed' by the Canal du Nord and brought up to the standard *(gabarit)* of that canal and is used jointly by the two canals.

Length	From Saint-Simon to the sea-lock at St-Valéry the distance by canal is 156 kilometres.
Locks	There are 25 locks in all, including the sea-lock at St-Valéry. The summit level is at St-Simon (it is about 65 metres above sea level) and the canal falls continuously towards the sea. The locks vary somewhat in length and width, but none is less in length than 38 m. 50 or is less in width than 6 m. 35.
Depth	From Saint-Simon to the downstream side of lock No. 21 (de Labreilloire) in the Commune de l'Etoile (K.118) the canal has a depth of 1 m. 80. From that point to the Port d'Abbeville there is rather more (2 m. 00). Between Abbeville and St-Valéry there is 3 m. 20 normally, and small coasting vessels ply up as far as Abbeville.
Bridges	There are many fixed bridges; these usually have a headroom of 3 m. 70, but it is to be noted that the *Pont de Beauville* in Amiens has but 3 m. 65. Also, the first bridge downstream from the lock No. 17 (d'Amiens) has even less (3 m. 43) when that pound is full of water.
Tow-path	There is a tow-path throughout and towing is effected by means of diesel tractors.

Distance Table

		kilom.	lock	kilom.
Saint-Simon	*Junction with Canal de Saint-Quentin (at K.68).* Lock (No. 1 de St-Simon)	0.0	I	156.0
	Bridge	1.0	—	155.0
Estouilly	Railway bridge	5.0	—	151.0
Ham	Port. Lock (No. 2 de Ham). Bridge ...	6.0	2	150.0
	Lock (No. 3 de Ham). Bridge	7.0	3	149.0
Eppeville	Footbridge	8.0	—	148.0
Hombleux	Footbridge	10.0	—	146.0

Distance Table				*kilom.*	*lock*	*kilom.*
Voyennes	Lock (No. 4 d'Offroy). Bridge. Port	...		12.0	4	144.0
Port. Bridge	...	...	...	...	14.0	—	142.0
Junction with Canal du Nord (at K.65)	...	16.7	—	139.3
Bethéncourt	Swing bridge	...	...	...	...	17.0	—	139.0
Port ...	...	...	...	...	...	18.0	—	138.0
Pargny	Port. Bridge	...	...	...	...	20.0	—	136.0
Epénancourt	Lock (No. 5 d'Epénancourt). Bridge. Port	22.0	5	134.0
Saint-Christ	Bridge. Port	...	...	...	...	25.0	—	131.0
Eterpigny	Lift bridge. Port (de Pont-les-Brie)	...	28.0	—	128.0
Péronne	Lock (No. 6 de Péronne) ...	...	...	32.0	6	124.0
Railway bridge. Port. Bridge. Port	...	33.0	—	123.0
Biaches	Bridge (de Bazincourt)	...	...	...	36.0	—	120.0
Junction with Canal du Nord (at K.45)	...	36.6	—	119.4
Cléry-s-Somme	Lock (No. 7 de Sormont). Bridge. Port ...	39.0	7	117.0
Feuillères	Port and swing bridge (de Feuillères)	...	41.0	—	115.0
Frise	Port. Lock (No. 8 de Frise). Bridge	...	43.0	8	113.0
Lock (No. 9 de Frise)	...	...	...	44.0	9	112.0
Eclusier	Swing bridge	...	...	...	...	46.0	—	110.0
Cappy	Port and swing bridge	...	...	...	50.0	—	106.0
Lock (No. 10 de Cappy) ...	...	...	51.0	10	105.0
Laneuville	Bridge. Lock (No. 11 de Froissy)	...	52.0	11	104.0
Etineham	Ferry (d'Etinehem)	...	...	...	56.0	—	100.0
Méricourt-s-Somme	Lock (No. 12 de Méricourt-s-Somme).		
Bridge	...	...	...	...	...	58.0	12	98.0
Chipilly	Bridge. Port	...	...	...	...	62.0	—	94.0
Cerisy-Gailly	Bridge	...	...	...	...	...	63.0	—	93.0
Port. Lock (No. 13 de Sailly-Layrette)	...	65.0	13	91.0
Bridge	...	...	...	...	...	65.0	—	91.0
Sailly-le-Sec	Ferry	...	...	...	...	...	67.0	—	89.0
Vaire-sous-Corbie	Bridge (de Vaire-sous-Corbie)	...	...	70.0	—	86.0
Port and Lock (No. 14 de Corbie). Bridge	74.0	14	82.0
Aubigny	Railway bridge	...	...	...	...	77.0	—	79.0
Daours	Bridge. Lock (No. 15 de Daours)	...	79.0	15	77.0
Vecquemont	Railway bridge	...	...	...	...	80.0	—	76.0
Lamotte-Brébière	Lock (No. 16 de Lamotte-Brébière)	...	84.0	16	72.0
Glisy	Railway bridge	...	...	...	...	85.0	—	71.0
Camon	Bridge (Pont de Longeau)	...	...	88.0	—	68.0
Amiens	Bridge (Pont de Camon) ...	...	...	90.0	—	66.0
Bridge (Pont de Beauville). Port ...	...	92.0	—	64.0
Bridges (Pont des Celestins, Pont St-Piere,		
Pont du Maulcreux)	...	...	...	93.0	—	63.0
Lock (No. 17 d'Amiens). Bridge ...	...	94.0	17	62.0
Footbridge (St.-Maurice). Bridge (Pont		
Cagnard)	...	...	...	...	...	94.0	—	62.0
Bridge (Pont Blanc)	...	...	...	95.0	—	61.0

Distance Table | *kilom.* | *lock* | *kilom.*

		kilom.	lock	kilom.
	Railway bridge. Lock (No. 18 de Montières)	97.0	18	59.0
	Bridge	97.0	—	59.0
Dreuil	Bridge (de Dreuil)	99.0	—	57.0
Ailly-s-Somme	Lock (No. 19 d'Ailly-s-Somme). Bridge ...	102.0	19	54.0
Picquigny	Lock (No. 20 de Picquigny). Bridge ...	108.0	20	48.0
Bourdon	Port and Bridge (de Bourdon)	115.0	—	41.0
Flixecourt	Lock (No. 21 de Labreilloire)	117.0	21	39.0
	Two railway bridges	117.0	—	39.0
Condé-Folie	Ferry *(private)*	119.0	—	37.0
	Bridge (de l'Etoile)	120.0	—	36.0
Long	Bridge. Lock (No. 22)	124.0	22	32.0
Fontaine-s-Somme	Bridge	127.0	—	29.0
Pont-Rémy	Tow-path footbridge. Port (de St-Rémy)	130.0	—	26.0
	Bridge. Lock (No. 23)	131.0	23	25.0
Eaucourt	Bridge	133.0	—	23.0
Epagne	Bridge	134.0	—	22.0
	Bridge (Pont d'Epagnette)	136.0	—	20.0
Abbeville	Railway bridge (de Bethune)	139.0	—	17.0
	Bridges (du Boulevard des Prés, de la Portelette, de la Gare)	140.0	—	16.0
	Lock (No. 24). Bridge (Pont d'Hocquet)...	141.0	24	15.0
	Railway bridge (de Boulogne). *Beginning of canal maritime d'Abbeville à St-Valéry-s-Somme*	142.0	—	14.0
	Swing bridge	143.0	—	13.0
Cambron	Swing bridge (de Laviers)	145.0	—	11.0
Saigneville	Swing bridge (de Petit-Port)	148.0	—	8.0
Boismont	Swing bridge (de Boismont)	153.0	—	3.0
	Lift bridge (road bridge)	155.0	—	1.0
St-Valéry-s-Somme	Lock (No. 25). *End of canal maritime. Junction with estuary of la Somme* ...	156.0	25	0.0

ÉTANG DE THAU

General

L'Étang de Thau in the Département de Hérault is so situated as to form a link waterway between the Canal du Midi and the Canal du Rhône à Sète. It starts at Les Onglous, where the Canal du Midi falls into the lake, and ends where the Canal du Rhône á Sète also falls into the lake—or, rather, into the eastern part of l'Étang de Thau, which is known as *l'Étang des Eaux Blanches*. L'Étang de Thau is of a fair depth all over, and at least 2 m. oo may be counted upon at all times. There is no buoyed channel, as a direct line between Les Onglous and the Beacon *(Feu de Roquerols)* which is situated at the entrance to l'Étang des Eaux Blanches is a safe course. The Feu de Roquerols (white occ. light at night) is nearly midway between the Pointe de Barrou on the south and the point of land at Balaruc-les-Bains on the north at the entrance to l'Étang des Eaux Blanches. The Beacon at Les Onglous also shows a white occ. light at night. The traffic consists in the greater part of motor barges, occasionally of a tug with a string of lighters and, exceptionally, of a vessel under sail. The passage across the lake is $17\frac{1}{2}$ kilometres in length.

LA VILAINE

General

The canalized river La Vilaine forms a link in the chain of waterwa y which cut across Brittany from Saint-Malo to the Bay of Biscays The river is navigable from Rennes to below la Roche-Bernard, where it flows into the Atlantic. It is just downstream of le Pont du Boulevard de la Tour d'Auvergne in Rennes that the Canal d'Ille-et-Rance branches off from the river northwards towards St-Malo. That part of the river which lies upstream of le Pont du Boulevard and which formerly led to Cesson-Sévigné has now been abandoned. La Vilaine may be divided into two sections: (1) Rennes to Pont de Saint-Nicolas, Redon. (2) Barrage de Redon to the sea.*

Section (2) is tidal and essentially a marine navigation; nevertheless, a brief account may be useful. The length of the free river between the barrage at Redon and its outfall into the Atlantic, between la Pointe du Moustoir on the right bank and la Pointe du Scal on the left bank, is 47.9 kilometres. The tide is felt as far up as the Redon barrage, where the depth is reckoned to be 3 m. at high-water neaps and 4 m. 50 at high-water springs. The depth increases as the river flows seawards, being at les Bellions about 4 m. at high-water neaps and 6 m. at high-water springs; at La Roche-Bernard it stands at 12 m. and even at 14 m. at high-water spring tides.

At present l'Écluse marine de Redon is not in service*, so that it is necessary to enter la Vilaine maritime via lock No. 17 des Bellions (at K.88) of le Canal de Nantes à Brest. When going seawards this

* A barrage with lock for navigation is now in service on La Vilaine Maritime near Arzal. At the time of going to press (1970), *l'Écluse Marine de Redon* is not in service. The Barrage d'Arzal is across La Vilaine at approx. *Kilomètrage* 131.0 (19 Km. downstream of La Roche-Bernard). The lock is 85 m. long, 13 m. wide with sill depth of −2 m. (Cartes Marines). There is a lift bridge over the lock. It is advisable to obtain local advice from either Le Service de la Navigation, Ponts et Chaussées, Cale de La Barbotière 35, Rennes, or from Dr Thierry at La Roche-Bernard (Soc. Nautique de Vilaine).

lock is best taken at the top of the flood tide, so as to take full advantage of the slack water and the ebb. When arriving at Redon from the direction of Rennes and reaching the Pont de St-Nicolas (mentioned above) the through route joins with the Canal de Nantes à Brest and it is necessary to make a right-angled turn to the left (to port) to enter the next lock (Écluse d'Isac) when making for Nantes, and a right-angled turn to the right (to starboard) when making for Pontivy.

Length	The distance from Rennes to the junction with the Canal de Nantes à Brest at Redon is 89 kilometres.
Locks	There are 12 locks in all. They lie between Rennes and Mâlon (the last lock), all have similar dimensions, namely, 26 m. 60 in length and 4 m. 70 in width.
Depth	The normal depth of water between Rennes and the last lock at Mâlon is 1 m. 60. Below the lock the normal depth is 1 m. 50. These depths may be reduced in times of drought and local enquiries should always be made at the time of proposed passage.
Bridges	All the fixed bridges have a clear headroom of 3 m. 20 above the normal water level.
Tow-path	This is falling into disuse as nearly all the traffic is self-propelled.

Distance Table

		kilom.	lock	kilom.
Rennes	Junction with Canal d'Ille-et-Rance (at K.0).			
	Bridge (Pont du Boulevard de la Tour d'Auvergne). Port. Bridge (de l'Abattoir)...	0.0	—	89.0
	Railway bridge. Lock (No. 2 du Comte) ...	1.0	1	88.0
Rheu	Lock (No. 3 d'Apigné). Bridge	5.0	2	84.0
Chavagne	Bridge (de Chancors)	9.0	—	80.0
Bruz	Lock (No. 4 de Cicé). Lift bridge	10.0	3	79.0
Goven	Bridge (de Mons). Lock (No. 5 de Mons)...	14.0	4	75.0
Guichen	Lock (No. 6 de Pont-Réan)	17.0	5	72.0
	Bridge (de Pont-Réan)	18.0	—	71.0
	Railway bridge	20.0	—	69.0
	Lock (No. 7 du Boël)	21.0	6	68.0
Laillé	Bridge (de Laillé)	23.0	—	66.0
Bourg-des-Comptes	Lock (No. 8 de la Bouëxière)	26.0	7	63.0
	Bridge (de Glanret)...	28.0	—	61.0
	Lock (No. 9 de Gaileiu)	30.0	8	59.0
Saint-Senoux	Lock (No. 10 de la Molière)	33.0	9	56.0
Pléchatel	Bridge (de la Charrière)	35.0	—	54.0
	Railway bridge	37.0	—	52.0

Distance Table

		kilom.	lock	kilom.
St-Malo-de-Phily	Bridge (de Macaire)	39.0	—	50.0
	Lock (No. 11 de Macaire)	40.0	10	49.0
Guipry	Lock (No. 12 de Guipry). Bridge	47.0	11	42.0
	Railway bridge	48.0	—	41.0
	Lock (No. 13 de Mâlon)	51.0	12	38.0
	Bridge (Pont de Saint-Marc)	54.0	—	35.0
Langon	Railway bridge	56.0	—	33.0
St-Anne-s-Vilaine	Bridge (de Port de Roche)...	62.0	—	27.0
Pierric	Railway bridge	67.0	—	22.0
	Bridge (de Beslé)	70.0	—	19.0
La-Chapelle-Ste-Melaine	Bridge (de l'Ilette)	74.0	—	15.0
Avessac	Bridge (de Painfaut)	79.0	—	10.0
Saint-Marie	Bridge (du Grand-Pas)	83.0	—	6.0
Redon	Railway bridge (de Redon)	88.0	—	1.0
	Bridge (Pont de Saint-Nicolas)	89.0	—	0.0
	Junction with Canal de Nantes à Brest *(at K.94)*	89.0	—	0.0

L'YONNE

General

The navigable part of l'Yonne, which has been canalised throughout, begins at Auxerre and ends at the river's confluence with la Seine at Montereau. For over three-quarters of its length it forms a part of the important Bourgogne route between Paris and Lyon, which is one of the three main routes by water (but the one which has the greatest number of locks) between the two cities. The river at its upper end joins with the Canal du Nivernais which canal makes a cross way between the Bourgogne and Bourbonnais routes. In three places the river has been by-passed by *dérivations* or cuts; these cuts are situated at Gurgy, Joigny and at Courlon. The first is about 4 kilometres, the second somewhat less, being about 3 kilometres, while the third and longest is about 5 kilometres.

Length

By river from Auxerre to Montereau is 108 kilometres.

Locks

There are 26 locks; those between Auxerre and Laroche (in the commune de Migennes where the Canal de Bourgogne begins) have a length of 93 m. 00 with a width of 8 m. 30. The remainder which lies between Laroche and Montereau, 17 in number, have a length of 96 m. 00 with a width of 8 m. 30.

Depth

The normal depth of water is 2 m. 00 throughout.

Bridges	From Auxerre to Laroche the bridges have a headroom of 4 m. 40; from thence downstream to Montereau they have slightly greater headroom (4 m. 78), both these figures being at normal water level.

Tow-path	There is a good tow-path throughout and towing is effected by means of diesel tractors.

Distance Table

		kilom.	lock	kilom.
Auxerre	*Junction with Canal du Nivernais (at K.174)*	0.0	—	108.0
	Port. Footbridge. Bridge	0.0	—	108.0
	Lock (No. 1 de la Châinette)	0.0	1	108.0
	Lock (No. 2 de l'Ile Brulée)	2.0	2	106.0
Monéteau	Lock (No. 3 des Dumonts)	4.0	3	104.0
	Lock (No. 4 des Boisseaux)	5.0	4	103.0
	Bridge (de Monéteau)	6.0	—	102.0
	Lock (No. 5 de Monéteau)	7.0	5	101.0
Gurgy	Port. Deviation de Gurgy. Guard gate ...	10.0	—	98.0
	Bridge (des Chaumes)	11.0	—	97.0
	Port (d'Appoigny). Bridge *(Pont Biais)* ...	12.0	—	96.0
	Lock (No. 6 de Néron). Bridge	13.0	6	95.0
	Lock (No. 7 de Raveuse). Bridge	15.0	7	93.0
Chichery	End of deviation de Gurgy...	15.0	—	93.0
Bassou	Lock (No. 8 de Bassou)	16.0	8	92.0
	Suspension bridge (de Bassou)	17.0	—	91.0
Charmoy	Lock (No. 9 de la Gravière)	21.0	9	87.0
Migennes	Bridge (de Charmoy). Railway bridge ...	22.0	—	86.0
	Junction with Canal de Bourgogne (at K.0)	22.0	—	86.0
*Laroche-St-Cydroine**	Port (des Coches)	22.0	—	86.0
Epineau	Lift bridge	23.0	—	85.0
	Lock (No. 1 d'Epineau)	24.0	10	84.0
Champlay	Port (de Champlay)	26.0	—	82.0
Joigny	Lock (No. 2 du Pêchoir)	28.0	11	80.0
	Bridge (de Joigny)	31.0	—	77.0
	Deviation de Joigny. Guard gate	32.0	—	76.0
Saint-Aubin	Lock (No. 3 de Saint-Aubin). Bridge ...	35.0	12	73.0
Cézy	End of deviation de Joigny. Port	35.0	—	73.0
Villecien	Port (de Villecien)	37.0	—	71.0
Villevallier	Lock (No. 4 de Villevallier)	40.0	13	6.0
	Suspension bridge. Port (de Villevallier) ...	41.0	—	67.0
St-Julien-du-Sault	Port (de St-Julien-du-Sault)	42.0	—	66.0
Armeau	Port (d'Armeau)	44.0	—	64.0
	Lock (No. 5 d'Armeau)	44.0	14	64.0
Villeneuve-s-Yonne	Bridge and Port (de Villeneuve)	50.0	—	58.0
	Lock (No. 6 de Villeneuve)	50.0	15	58.0

* See Plan No. 15.

Distance Table

		kilom.	lock	kilom.
Passy	(Port de Passy). Port (de Marsangy) ...	54.0	—	54.0
Etigny	Lock (No. 7 d'Etigny). Port (de Véron) ...	56.0	16	52.0
	Bridge and Port (d'Etigny)...	57.0	—	51.0
Rosoy	Port (de Rosoy)	59.0	—	49.0
	Lock (No. 8 de Rosoy)	60.0	17	48.0
Paron	Port (de Paron)	64.0	—	44.0
	Lock (No. 9 de Saint-Bond) ...	65.0	18	43.0
Sens	Bridge and Port (de la Ville de Sens) ...	66.0	—	42.0
St-Martin-du-Tertre	Port and Lock (No. 10 de St-Martin)	69.0	19	39.0
Courtois	Port (de St-Denis)	70.0	—	38.0
	Port (de Courtois)	71.0	—	37.0
Villenavotte	Port (de Villenavotte)	73.0	—	35.0
Villeperrot	Lock (No. 11 de Villeperrot)	74.0	20	34.0
Gisy	Aqueduct (de la Vanne)	76.0	—	32.0
	Port (de Gisy)	76.0	—	32.0
Pont-sur-Yonne	Port and Bridge (de Pont-s-Yonne) ...	78.0	—	30.0
Michery	Lock (No. 12 de Champfleury) ...	80.0	21	28.0
Courlon	Port. Deviation de Courlon ...	86.0	—	22.0
	Guard gate	87.0	—	21.0
Vinneuf	Bridge (Port Morlaix)	88.0	—	20.0
	Bridge (du Gain)	89.0	—	19.0
	Lock (No. 13 de Venneuf)... ...	90.0	22	18.0
Misy	Lock (No. 14 de Port-Renard) ...	91.0	33	17.0
	End of deviation de Courlon ...	91.0	—	17.0
Villeneuve-la-Guyard	Bridge and Port (de Misy) ...	93.0	—	15.0
Barbey	Lock (No. 15 de Barbey)	96.0	24	12.0
Cannes	Lock (No. 16 de Labrosse) ...	100.0	25	8.0
	Suspension bridge and Port (de Cannes) ...	104.0	—	4.0
	Lock (No. 17 de Cannes) ...	104.0	26	4.0
*Montereau**	Railway bridge	106.0	—	2.0
	Bridge (de Montereau)	107.0	—	1.0
	Confluence with la Seine (at K.67)...	108.0	—	0.0

* See Plan No. 19.

APPENDIX

APPENDIX

CONVERSION TABLES

ENGLISH GALLONS TO LITRES (100 gallons=454.35 litres)

Galls.	0	10	20	30	40	50	60	70	80	90
0	Litres	45.4	90.9	136.3	181.7	227.2	272.6	318.0	363.5	408.9
1	4.5	50.0	95.4	140.8	186.3	231.7	277.1	322.6	368.0	413.4
2	9.1	54.5	99.9	145.4	190.8	236.3	281.7	327.1	372.6	418.0
3	13.6	59.1	104.5	149.9	185.4	240.8	286.2	331.7	377.1	422.5
4	18.2	60.6	109.0	154.4	199.9	245.3	290.8	336.2	381.6	427.1
5	22.7	68.1	113.6	159.0	204.4	249.9	295.3	340.7	386.2	431.6
6	27.3	72.7	118.1	163.6	209.0	254.4	299.9	345.3	390.7	436.2
7	31.8	77.2	122.7	168.1	213.5	259.0	304.4	349.8	395.3	440.7
8	36.3	81.8	127.2	172.6	218.1	263.5	308.9	354.4	399.8	445.2
9	40.9	86.3	131.8	177.2	222.6	268.1	313.5	358.9	404.4	449.8

LITRES TO ENGLISH GALLONS (100 litres=22.01 gallons)

Litres	0	10	20	30	40	50	60	70	80	90
0	Gallons	2.20	4.40	6.60	8.80	11.00	13.20	15.41	17.61	19.81
1	0.22	2.42	4.62	6.82	9.02	11.22	13.42	15.63	17.83	20.03
2	0.44	2.64	4.84	7.04	9.24	11.44	13.65	15.85	18.05	20.25
3	0.66	2.86	5.06	7.26	9.46	11.66	13.87	16.07	18.27	20.47
4	0.88	3.08	5.28	7.48	9.68	11.88	14.09	16.29	18.49	20.69
5	1.10	3.30	5.50	7.70	9.90	12.10	14.31	16.51	18.71	20.91
6	1.32	3.52	5.72	7.92	10.12	12.32	14.53	16.73	18.93	21.13
7	1.54	3.74	5.94	8.14	10.34	12.54	14.75	16.95	19.15	21.35
8	1.76	3.96	6.16	8.36	10.56	12.76	14.97	17.17	19.37	21.57
9	1.98	4.18	6.38	8.58	10.78	12.98	15.19	17.39	19.59	21.79

ENGLISH MILES TO KILOMETRES (100 miles = 160.93 kilometres)

Miles	0	10	20	30	40	50	60	70	80	90
0	Kilometres	16.09	32.19	48.28	64.37	80.47	96.56	112.65	128.75	144.84
1	1.61	17.70	33.80	49.89	65.98	82.08	98.17	114.26	130.36	146.45
2	3.22	19.31	35.41	51.50	67.59	83.69	99.78	115.87	131.97	148.06
3	4.83	20.92	37.01	53.11	69.20	85.29	101.39	117.48	133.58	149.67
4	6.44	22.53	38.62	54.72	70.81	86.90	103.00	119.09	135.18	151.28
5	8.05	24.14	40.23	56.33	72.42	88.51	104.61	120.70	136.79	152.89
6	9.66	25.75	41.84	57.94	74.03	90.12	106.22	122.31	138.40	154.50
7	11.26	27.36	43.45	59.55	75.64	91.73	107.83	123.92	140.01	156.11
8	12.87	28.97	45.06	61.15	77.25	93.34	109.44	125.53	141.62	157.72
9	13.48	30.58	46.67	62.76	78.86	94.95	111.04	127.14	143.23	159.32

KILOMETRES TO ENGLISH MILES (100 kilometres = 62.137 miles)

Kiloms.	0	10	20	30	40	50	60	70	80	90
0	Miles	6.21	12.43	18.64	24.85	31.07	37.28	43.50	49.71	55.92
1	0.62	6.83	13.05	19.26	25.48	31.70	37.90	44.12	50.33	56.54
2	1.24	7.46	13.67	19.88	26.10	32.31	38.52	44.74	50.95	57.17
3	1.86	8.08	14.29	20.50	26.72	32.93	39.15	45.36	51.57	57.79
4	2.48	8.70	14.91	21.13	27.34	33.55	39.77	45.98	52.19	58.41
5	3.11	9.32	15.53	21.75	27.96	34.17	40.39	46.60	52.82	59.03
6	3.73	9.94	16.16	22.37	28.58	34.80	41.01	47.22	53.44	59.65
7	4.35	10.56	16.78	22.99	29.20	35.42	41.63	47.85	54.06	60.27
8	4.97	11.18	17.40	23.61	29.83	36.04	42.25	48.47	54.68	60.89
9	5.59	11.81	18.02	24.23	30.45	36.66	42.87	49.09	55.30	61.52

METRES/MINUTE TO KILOMETRES/HOUR, ENGLISH MILES/HOUR, NAUTICAL MILES/HOUR

Metres/Minute ...	60	70	80	90	100	110	116.66	120	130
Kilometres/Hour ...	3.60	4.20	4.80	5.40	6.00	6.60	7.00	7.20	7.80
Miles/Hour ...	2.24	2.61	2.98	3.35	3.73	4.10	4.34	4.47	4.85
Knots	1.94	2.26	2.59	2.91	3.23	3.56	3.77	3.88	4.20

Metres/Minute ...	140	150	160	170	180	190	200	210	220
Kilometres/Hour ...	8.40	9.00	9.60	10.20	10.80	11.40	12.00	12.60	13.20
Miles/Hour ...	5.22	5.59	5.96	6.34	6.71	7.08	7.46	7.83	8.20
Knots	4.53	4.85	5.17	5.50	5.82	6.14	6.47	6.79	7.11

Metres/Minute ...	230	240	250	260	270	280	290	300	
Kilometres/Hour ...	13.80	14.40	15.00	15.60	16.20	16.80	17.40	18.00	
Miles/Hour ...	8.57	8.95	9.32	9.69	10.07	10.44	10.81	11.18	
Knots	7.44	7.76	8.08	8.41	8.73	9.05	9.38	9.70	

CONVERSION TABLES

ENGLISH FEET TO METRES (100 feet=30.479 metres)

Feet	0	10	20	30	40	50	60	70	80	90
0	Metres	3.05	6.03	9.14	12.19	15.24	18.29	21.33	24.38	27.43
1	0.30	3.35	6.40	9.44	12.50	15.54	18.59	21.64	24.69	27.74
2	0.61	3.66	6.70	9.75	12.80	15.85	18.90	21.94	24.99	28.04
3	0.91	3.96	7.01	10.06	13.11	16.15	19.20	22.25	25.30	28.35
4	1.22	4.28	7.31	10.36	13.41	16.46	19.51	22.55	25.60	28.65
5	1.52	4.57	7.62	10.67	13.72	16.76	19.81	22.86	25.91	28.95
6	1.83	4.88	7.92	10.97	14.02	17.07	20.12	23.16	26.21	29.26
7	2.13	5.18	8.23	11.28	14.32	17.37	20.42	23.47	26.52	29.56
8	2.44	5.49	8.53	11.58	14.63	17.68	20.73	23.77	26.82	29.87
9	2.74	5.79	8.84	11.89	14.93	17.98	21.03	24.08	27.13	30.17

METRES TO ENGLISH FEET (100 metres=328.09 feet)

Metres	0	10	20	30	40	50	60	70	80	90
0	Feet	32.8	65.6	98.4	131.2	164.0	196.8	229.7	262.5	295.3
1	3.3	36.1	68.9	101.7	134.5	167.3	200.1	232.9	265.7	298.6
2	6.6	39.4	72.2	105.0	137.8	170.6	203.4	236.2	269.0	301.8
3	9.8	42.6	75.5	108.3	141.1	173.9	206.7	239.5	272.3	305.1
4	13.1	45.9	78.7	111.5	144.4	177.2	210.0	242.8	275.6	308.4
5	16.4	49.2	82.0	114.8	147.6	180.4	213.3	246.1	278.9	311.7
6	19.7	52.5	85.3	118.1	150.9	183.7	216.5	249.3	282.2	315.0
7	23.0	55.8	88.6	121.4	154.2	187.0	219.8	252.6	285.4	318.2
8	26.2	59.0	91.9	124.7	157.5	190.3	223.1	255.9	288.7	321.5
9	29.5	62.3	95.1	128.0	160.8	193.6	226.4	259.2	292.0	324.8

METRES TO ENGLISH FEET AND INCHES (10 metres=32 feet 9.7 inches)

Metres	1	2	3	4	5
Ft. in.	3 ft. 3.4	6 ft. 6.7	9 ft. 10.1	13 ft. 1.5	16 ft. 4.8

Metres	6	7	8	9	10
Ft. in.	19 ft. 8.2	22 ft. 11.6	26 ft. 3.0	29 ft. 6.3	32 ft. 9.7

ENGLISH INCHES TO METRES AND CENTIMETRES (100 inches = 2 metres 54.0 centimetres)

Inches	0	10	20	30	40	50	60	70	80	90
0	m. cm.	0 m. 25.4	0 m. 50.8	0 m. 76.2	1 m. 1.6	1 m. 27.0	1 m. 52.4	1 m. 77.8	2 m. 3.2	2 m. 28.6
1	0 m. 2.5	0 m. 27.9	0 m. 53.3	0 m. 78.7	1 m. 4.1	1 m. 29.5	1 m. 54.9	1 m. 80.3	2 m. 5.7	2 m. 31.1
2	0 m. 5.1	0 m. 30.5	0 m. 55.9	0 m. 81.3	1 m. 6.7	1 m. 32.1	1 m. 57.5	1 m. 82.9	2 m. 8.3	2 m. 33.7
3	0 m. 7.6	0 m. 33.0	0 m. 58.4	0 m. 83.8	1 m. 9.2	1 m. 34.6	1 m. 60.0	1 m. 85.4	2 m. 10.8	2 m. 36.2
4	0 m. 10.2	0 m. 35.6	0 m. 61.0	0 m. 86.4	1 m. 11.8	1 m. 37.2	1 m. 62.6	1 m. 88.0	2 m. 13.4	2 m. 38.8
5	0 m. 12.7	0 m. 38.1	0 m. 63.5	0 m. 88.9	1 m. 14.3	1 m. 39.7	1 m. 65.1	1 m. 90.5	2 m. 15.9	2 m. 41.3
6	0 m. 15.2	0 m. 40.6	0 m. 66.0	0 m. 91.4	1 m. 16.8	1 m. 42.2	1 m. 67.6	1 m. 93.0	2 m. 18.4	2 m. 43.8
7	0 m. 17.8	0 m. 43.2	0 m. 68.6	0 m. 94.0	1 m. 19.4	1 m. 44.8	1 m. 70.2	1 m. 95.6	2 m. 21.0	2 m. 46.4
8	0 m. 20.3	0 m. 45.7	0 m. 71.1	0 m. 96.5	1 m. 21.9	1 m. 47.3	1 m. 72.7	1 m. 98.1	2 m. 23.5	2 m. 48.9
9	0 m. 22.9	0 m. 48.3	0 m. 73.7	0 m. 99.1	1 m. 24.5	1 m. 49.9	1 m. 75.3	2 m. 1.0	2 m. 26.1	2 m. 51.5

CENTIMETRES TO ENGLISH FEET AND INCHES (100 centimetres = 3 feet 3.37 inches)

Cm.	0	10	20	30	40	50	60	70	80	90
0	ft. ins.	0 ft. 3.9	0 ft. 7.9	0 ft. 11.8	1 ft. 3.7	1 ft. 7.7	1 ft. 11.6	2 ft. 3.6	2 ft. 7.5	2 ft. 11.4
1	0 ft. 0.4	0 ft. 4.3	0 ft. 8.3	1 ft. 0.2	1 ft. 4.1	1 ft. 8.1	2 ft. 0.0	2 ft. 4.0	2 ft. 7.9	2 ft. 11.8
2	0 ft. 0.8	0 ft. 4.7	0 ft. 8.7	1 ft. 0.6	1 ft. 4.5	1 ft. 8.5	2 ft. 0.4	2 ft. 4.4	2 ft. 8.3	3 ft. 0.2
3	0 ft. 1.2	0 ft. 5.1	0 ft. 9.1	1 ft. 1.0	1 ft. 4.9	1 ft. 8.9	2 ft. 0.8	2 ft. 4.7	2 ft. 8.7	3 ft. 0.6
4	0 ft. 1.6	0 ft. 5.5	0 ft. 9.4	1 ft. 1.4	1 ft. 5.3	1 ft. 9.3	2 ft. 1.2	2 ft. 5.1	2 ft. 9.1	3 ft. 1.0
5	0 ft. 2.0	0 ft. 5.9	0 ft. 9.8	1 ft. 1.8	1 ft. 5.7	1 ft. 9.6	2 ft. 1.6	2 ft. 5.5	2 ft. 9.5	3 ft. 1.4
6	0 ft. 2.4	0 ft. 6.3	0 ft. 10.2	1 ft. 2.2	1 ft. 6.1	1 ft. 10.0	2 ft. 2.0	2 ft. 5.9	2 ft. 9.8	3 ft. 1.8
7	0 ft. 2.8	0 ft. 6.7	0 ft. 10.6	1 ft. 2.6	1 ft. 6.5	1 ft. 10.4	2 ft. 2.4	2 ft. 6.3	2 ft. 10.2	3 ft. 2.2
8	0 ft. 3.1	0 ft. 7.1	0 ft. 11.0	1 ft. 3.0	1 ft. 6.9	1 ft. 10.8	2 ft. 2.8	2 ft. 6.7	2 ft. 10.6	3 ft. 2.6
9	0 ft. 3.5	0 ft. 7.5	0 ft. 11.4	1 ft. 3.4	1 ft. 7.3	1 ft. 11.2	2 ft. 3.2	2 ft. 7.1	2 ft. 11.0	3 ft. 2.9

SHORT GLOSSARY

FRENCH—ENGLISH

acajou (m), *mahogany;* okoume, *Gaboon mahogany.*

accoster, *to come alongside.*

affaler, *to lower, to overhaul.*

affluent (m), *confluence, tributary.*

agrèner, *to pump (water from a boat).*

aiguilleter, *to seize.*

aiguillot (m), *pintle (of rudder).*

amarrage (m), *a lashing;* un amarrage en Portugaise, *racking seizing;* faire un amarrage, *to lash, to seize.*

amarrer, *to make fast, to belay.*

amont (en), *upstream;* en amont du pont, *above bridge.*

ancre (f), *anchor;* le bras, *the arm;* les pattes (f), *the flukes;* le jas, *the stock;* la cigale, *the ring;* chasser sur l'ancre, *to drag the anchor.*

anse (f), *cove, small bay.*

arborder, *to hoist (a flag).*

arbre (m), *shaft;* arbre à cames, *camshaft.*

assureur (m), *underwriter.*

aube (f), *paddle wheel.*

aval, *downstream;* en aval du pont, *below bridge.*

avant (m), *the bow (of a vessel).*

bac (m), *a ferry.*

bâche (f), *canvas cover, hood.*

bague (f), *a hank, a grummet.*

balise (f), *a beacon.*

bande (f), *a list, a heel;* avoir de la bande, *to have a list.*

barrage (m), *a weir.*

bas-fonds (m), *shallows, shoals.* (Note: 'bas-fonds' and 'haut-fonds' are used indiscriminately, but a sailor generally uses 'bas-fonds' for a shoal passable for light-draught vessels and 'haut-fonds' for a shoal which is quite impassable.)

bâtiment (m), *a ship, a vessel (either man-of-war or merchantman)*; vaisseau, *man-of-war;* navaire, *merchantman.*

bauquière (f), *the shelf (of a ship).*

ber (m), *a launching cradle.*

berceau (m), *a cradle, engine-bed.*

berge (f), *bank (of a canal).*

bief (m), *a 'pound' or reach of a canal.*

bielle (f), *connecting rod.*

bitord (f), *spun yarn.*

bitte (f), *bollard.*

bosse (f), *painter (of a boat).*

boucle (f), *mooring ring.*

bouée (f), *buoy.*

boujaron (m), *a tot;* un boujaron de rhum, *a tot of rum.*

busc (m), *sill (of a lock).*

cale (f), *slipway, the hold (of ship).*

calaison (f), *draught (of ship).*

calanque (f), *cove, fiord.*

calfatage (m), *caulking.*

calfater, *to caulk.*

caréner, *to careen;* bassin de carénage, *basin for careening.*

carlingue (f), *keelson.*

carreau (m), *sheer strake.*

chaland (m), *a lighter, a barge.*

chatterton (m), *insulation tape.*

chaumard (m), *fairlead.*

chavirer, *to capsize.*

chignole (f), *hand-drill.*

chômage (m), *a closing or shutting down, stoppage. Used when a canal is closed for repairs.*

choquer, *to check, to surge;* choquez les amarres, *check the mooring ropes.*

cigale (f), *anchor ring.*

clayonnage (m), *facines, wicker-work, training mattress.*

clin (m), *clinker;* constuuit a clin, *clinker-built.*

cloison (f), *bulkhead;* cloison étanché, *watertight bulkhead.*

connaissance (des tempts) (f), *the Nautical Almanac.*

contre-étrave (f), *apron (at stem).*

contre-plaqué (m), *plywood.*

cordage (m), *rope.*

cosse (f), *thimble, eyelet.*

cote (f), *height above datum, spot height.*

couple (m), *frame, timber.*

courbe (f), *knee.*

courtier maritime (m), *ship broker.*

crépine (f), *strainer.*

croisement (m), *meeting (two ships).*

dalot (m), *scupper.*
dames (f), *crutches (for oars).*
darse (f), *tidal basin, dock.*
déclinaison (f), *variation (magnetic).*
décommetre, *to unlay (a rope).*
démarrer, *to unmoor.*
démarreur (m), *starter (motor).*
dérive (f), *drift, leeway;* aile de dérive, *leeboard;* quille de dérive, *centre-board.*
désarmer, *to lay up (vessel).*
déversoir (m), *a weir.*
déviation (f), *deviation (compass).*
digue (f), *dike, embankment, training-wall.*
drisse (f), *halliard.*

écueil (m), *a reef, a shelf.*
élingue (f), *sling, strop.*
élinguer, *to sling.*
enter, *to scarf, to joint.*
épi (m), *a training-wall (river).*
épisser, *to splice.*
epissoir (m), *fid, marline-spike.*
épissure (f), *a splice;* une épissure à oeil, *an eye splice.*
épuisette (f), *bailer.*
équiper, *to fit out (a ship).*
erse (f), *strop, becket;* erse en bitord, *selvagee strop.*
éscope (f), *bailer.*
étambot (m), *sternpost.*
étampe (f), *a punch.*
étoupe (f), *oakum.*
étrave (f), *stem.*

fanal (m), *mast-head light.*
faubert (m), *swab.*
faux-bras (m), *tow-rope, warp.*
femelots (m), *gudgeons (rudder).*
feu (m), *a light;* feu-de-position, *riding light;* feux-de-route, *navigation lights.*
fil (m), *wire, twine;* fil de cuivre rouge, *copper wire;* fil de fer, *iron wire;* fil de laiton, *brass wire;* fil de caret, *rope yarn;* fil de voile, *sail twine;* fil de bougie, *ignition wire.*
filer, *to pay out, to veer.*
filière (f), *stocks and dies.*
fleur (d'eau), *awash.*
franc-bord (m), *freeboard;* a franc-bord, *carvel built.*
fond (m), *bottom;* bas-fonds haut-fonds, *shallow water (see note under* bas-fonds); à fond plat, *flat-bottomed.*
fortune (f), *jury;* mat de fortune, *jury mast.*
fraiser, *to ream out, to countersink.*
franchir, *to freshen;* le vent franchit, *the wind freshens.*

gabare (f), *a lighter.*
gabarit (m), *a mould, a gauge.*
galbord (m), *garboard strake.*

garants (m), *the falls of a tackle.*
genoper, *to belay, to seize.*
gicleur (m), *jet;* gicleur bouché, *choked jet (carburettor).*
gisement (m), *a bearing (compass).*
godiller, *to scull (over stern of boat).*
goudron (m), *tar;* goudron à bois, *Stockholm tar;* brai (m), *pitch.*
goupille (f), *a pin;* goupille fendue, *split-pin;* goupille conique, *taper-pin.*
grau (m), *a channel connecting a salt lake to the sea.*
grelin (m), *a warp, a hawser.*
guidon (m), *a burgee, a pennant.*
guipon (m), *a mop.*

habitacle (m), *a binnacle.*
halage (m), *towage;* chemin de halage, *tow-path.*
hausse (f), *rising water (river).*
haut-fonds (m), *shoal.* See note under 'bas-fonds'.
hélice (f), *propeller;* pas de l'hélice, *pitch of propeller.*
hermétic (m), *jointing compound.*
herminette (f), *an adze.*
hiloire (f), *a coaming.*

instructions (f), *sailing directions.*
interrupteur (m), *a switch (electric).*

jas (m), *stock (of an anchor).*

kiosque (m), (de timonerie), *wheelhouse;* kiosque des cartes, *charthouse.*

laiton (m), *brass.*
largeur (f), *beam, breadth of beam.*
larguer, *to let go;* larguez les amarres, *let go the mooring ropes.*
levier (m) (du rupteur), *contact-breaker arm.*
liège (m), *cork.*
ligne (f) (de foi), *lubber's line.*
limander, *to parcel (a rope).*
lisse (f), *a ribband, a stringer, a moulding.*
louvoyer, *to tack (under sail).*
lover, *to coil down.*
lusin (m), *houseline, marline.*

manchon (m), *a collar, a bush.*
mandrin (m), *mandrel (for lathe).*
manille (f), *a shackle.*
mascaret (m), *a bore, a tidal wave.*
mèche (f), *drill, bit, heart (of a rope).*
mélèze (m), *larch.*
minium (m), *red lead.*
montant (m), *a stanchion.*
mouillage (m), *an anchorage.*
mouiller, *to anchor, to moor.*

284

nable (m), *plug-hole (of a boat)*.
noeud (m), *knot, bend, hitch;* noeud d'arret, *figure of* 8; noeud de vache, *granny;* noeud d'anguille, *running bowline;* noeud de chaise, *bow-line;* noeud plat, *reef;* noeud de grapplin, *fisherman's bend;* noeud d'écoute, *sheet bend;* demi-clef, *half-hitch;* deux demi-clefs à capeler, *clove hitch;* noeud de fouet, *rolling hitch;* noeud de bois, *timber hitch;* gueule de loup, *Blackwall hitch.*
nouer, *to hitch.*

oeil (m) (de pie), *eyelet.*
ordre (m) (d'allumage), *firing order (motor).*
organeau (m), *mooring ring.*
orin (m), *buoy rope.*

palan (m), *a tackle;* palan à croc, *luff tackle;* palan à chaine, *a chain block;* palan de dimanche, *handy-billy;* greer un palan, *rig a tackle.*
palier (m), *a bearing (machine);* palier à billes, *ball-bearing;* palier de butée, *thrust bearing.*
papillon (m), *a wing nut.*
pas (m), *pitch (of a screw or propeller).*
passoire (f), *a strainer, a filter.*
patte (f), *a cringle;* patte d'une ancre, *flukes of an anchor;* pattes d'araignée, *oil-grooves.*
paumelle (f), *palm (and needle).*
péniche (f), *lighter, barge, pinnace.*
pin (m), *pine wood;* pitchpin, *pitchpine.*
plat-bord (m), *gunwale.*
plot (m), *contact-point (motor).*
pointeau (m), *centre-punch, needle of carburettor.*
poinçon (m), *a pricker, bradawl.*
pomme (f), *truck (of a mast).*
pompe (f), *pump;* pompe de cale, *bilge-pump;* allumer une pompe, *prime a pump;* la pompe est eventée, *the pump sucks.*
poulie (f), *block, sheave;* poulie simple, *single block;* poulie double, *double block;* poulie coupée, *snatch block.*
pont-canal (m), *a bridge carrying a canal.*
prélart (m), *tarpaulin.*
presse-étoupe (m), *stuffing-box or gland.*

queue (f), *tang (of a file or tool);* queue d'aronde, *dovetail;* queue de rat, *pointing (rope's end), rat-tail file.*

rabattre, *to clench (a nail).*
râblure (f), *a rabbet.*
rabot (m), *a plane (for wood);* passer le rabot sur, *to plane.*
radeau (m), *a raft.*
radouber, *to refit (a vessel);* cale de redoub, *graving slip.*

ras (m), (de marée), *tidal wave, a bore.*
rate (m), *misfire (motor).*
rea (m), *sheave (of a block).*
récif (m), *a reef (of rocks).*
relâche (f), *a port of call;* relâcher à, *to call at.*
relèvement (m), *a bearing (compass);* relèvement croisé, *cross-bearing.*
remorquer, *to tow.*
remorqueur (m), *tugboat;* remorqueur à l'aubes, *paddle-wheel tug;* remorquer à couple, *to tow alongside.*
remous (m), *backwash, eddy.*
rive (f), *bank (of a river).*
rondelle (f), *washer;* rondelle à ressort, *spring washer.*
rose (f) (de vent), *compass rose.*
roulement (m) (à billes), *ball-bearing, ball-race;* roulement de butée, *ball-bearing thrust.*
rupteur (m), *contact-breaker.*

sapin (m), *fir, deal, spruce.*
sas (m), *a lock chamber.*
scaphandrier (m), *a diver.*
semence (f), *tacks, fine nails.*
souder, *to weld, to solder;* souder à l'etain, *soft solder;* souder à l'autogene, *oxyacet, weld.*
surbau (m), *a coaming.*
surlier, *to whip (a rope).*
surlieure (f), *whipping (of a rope).*

taquet (m), *a cleat, a kevel.*
tarière (f), *an auger.*
tirant (m), (d'eau), *draught (of ship).*
tolletière (f), *rowlock.*
tonture (f), *sheer (of a vessel).*
tornon (m), *strand (of a rope).*
touage (m), *warping, tracking (canal).*
touer, *to warp, to track.*
toueur (m), *tow-boat (operated by a chain in the river bed).*
tour (m), *a turn;* un tour mort, *a round turn.*
trait (m), *tow-rope (on river).*
trématage (m), *overtaking (canal).*
treuil (m), *winch.*

vanne (f), *sluice.*
versant (m), *watershed.*
vibord (m), *sheer strake.*
vilebreqin (m), *a brace;* vilebrequin à cliquet, *a ratchet-brace.*
virement (m), *a turning, a turn.*
virure (f), *a strake (of a vessel).*
visser, *to thread, to screw.*
voie (f) (d'eau), *a leak;* faire une voie d'eau, *spring a leak;* aveugler une voie d'eau, *stop a leak.*
vrille (f), *a gimlet.*

ENGLISH—FRENCH

alongside, *bord à bord;* to come along, *accoster.*
anchor (an), *ancre (f);* an anchorage, *mouillage (m).*
anchor (to), *mouiller.*
apron, *contre-étave (f).*
auger, *tarière (f).*
awash, *à fleur d'eau.*

backwash, *remous (m).*
bailer, *épuisette (m),* éscope *(,).*
ball-bearing, *roulement à filles (m);* ball-thrust, *roulement de butée.*
bank (of river), *rive (f);* of a canal, *berge (f).*
barge, *péniche (f), chaland (m).*
basin (tidal), *darse (f).*
bay (small), *anse (f).*
beacon, *balise (f).*
beam (breadth of), *largeur (f).*
bearing (of machine), *palier (m);* ball-bearing, *palier à billes;* thrust bearing, *palier butée.*
bearing (compass), *relèvement (m).*
becket, *erse (f).*
belay (to), *amarrer.*
binnacle (a), *habitacle (m).*
block, *poulie (f);* single block, *poulie simple;* double block, *poulie double;* snatch block, *poulie coupée.*
bollard, *bitte (f).*
bore (river), *mascaret (m), ras de marée (m).*
bottom, *fond (m);* flat-bottomed, *à fond-plat.*
bow, *avant (m);* on the port bow, *par babord avant.*
bowline (knot), *noeud de chaise (m);* running bowline, *noeud d'anguille.*
brace, *vilebrequin (m);* ratchet-brace, *vilebrequin à cliquet.*
bradawl, *poinçon (m).*
brass, *laiton (m).*
bulkhead, *cloison (f);* watertight bulkhead, *cloison étanché.*
buoy, *bouée (f);* mooring-buoy, *bouée de corps mort;* buoy-rope, *orin (m).*
burgee, *guidon (m).*
bush (of machine), *manchon (m).*

capsize (to), *chavirer.*
carburettor (needle), *pointeau (m);* float, *flotteur (m);* jet, *gicleur (m).*
careen (to), *caréner;* careening-basin, *bassin de carénage.*
carvel (built), *a franc-bord (m).*
caulk (to), *calfater;* caulking, *calfatage (m).*
chart-house, *kiosque des cartes (m).*
check (to), *choquer;* to check the mooring ropes, *choquez les amarres.*
cleat (a), *taquet (m).*
clench (a nail), *rabattre.*
clinker, *clin (m);* clinker-built, *construit à clin.*
coil (to), *lover.*

coamings, *hiloire (f), surbau (m).*
collar (machine), *manchon (m).*
compass (a), *compas (m);* compass bearing, *relèvement (m); gisement (m);* cross-bearing, *relèvement croisè;* compass rose, *rose des vents (f).*
confluence (rivers), *affluent (m).*
connecting-rod, *bielle (f).*
contact-breaker, *rupteur (m);* contact-breaker arm, *levier du rupteur;* contact-point, *plot (m).*
cork, *liège (m).*
cotter, *goupille (f).*
countersink (to), *fraiser.*
cardle (for vessel), *berceau (m);* launching cradle, *ber (m).*
cringle, *patte (f).*
crutches (for oars), *dames (f).*
cove (small), *anse (f), calanque (f).*

deviation (compass), *déviation (f).*
dike (a), *digue (f).*
diver (a), *scaphandrier (m).*
dock (no gates), *darse (f).*
dovetail (a), *queue d'aronde (f).*
draught (of vessel), *calaison (f).*
drift, *dérive (f);* leeboard, *aile de dérive;* centre-board, *quille de dérive.*
drill (a), *mèche (f);* hand-drill, *chignole (,).*

eddy (an), *remous (m).*
embankment (an), *digue (f).*
eyelet (canvas), *oeil de pie (m).*

fairlead (a), *chaumard (m).*
fast (to make), *amarrer.*
ferry (a), *bac (m).*
figure of 8 (knot), *noeud d'arret (m).*
fiord (a cove), *calanque (f).*
fir, *sapin (m).*
firing order (motor), *ordre d'allumage (f).*
fisherman's bend, *noeud de grapplin (m).*
fit out (to), *équiper.*
flukes (of anchor), *pattes (f).*
frame (of hull), *couple (m).*
freeboard, *franc-bors (m).*
freshen (to), *franchir;* the wind freshens, *le vent franchit.*

gauge (a), *gabaret (m).*
garboard (strake), *galbord (m).*
gimlet, *vrille (f).*
gland (stuffing), *presse-étoupe (m).*
granny (knot), *noeud de vache (m).*
grummet (a), *bague (f).*
gudgeons (of rudder), *femelots (m).*
gunwale, *plat-bord (m).*

halliard (a), *drisse (f)*.

hank (sail), *bague (f)*.

heart (of rope), *mèche (f)*.

heel (to), *donner à la bande (f)*; to have a list, *avoir de la bande*.

hitch (to), *nouer*.

hitch (rolling), *noeud de fouet (m)*; clove hitch, *deux demi-clefs à capeler*; half-hitch, *demi-clef*; timber hitch, *noeud de bois*; Blackwall hitch, *guele de loup*.

hoist (to), *arborder*.

houseline, *lusin (m)*.

insulation tape, *chatterton (m)*.

jet (carburettor), *gicleur (m)*; choked jet, *gicleur bouché*.

jointing (compound), *hermétic (m)*.

jury, *fortune (f)*; jury mast, *mat de fortune*.

keelson, *carlingue (f)*.

knee, *courbe (f)*.

knot, *noeud (m)*; figure of 8, *noeud d'arret*; granny, *noeud de vache*; bow-line, *noeud de chaise*; running bow-line, *noeud d'anguille*; reef, *noeud de plat*; fisherman's bend, *noeud de grapplin*; sheet bend, *noeud d'éoute*.

larch, *mélèze (m)*.

lashing (a), *amarrage (m)*.

lay up (to), *désarmer*.

leak (a), *voie d'eau*; spring a leak, *faire une voie d'eau*; stop a leak, *aveugler une voie d'eau*.

leeway, *dérive (f)*; leeboard, *aile de dérive*; centre-board, *quille de dérive*.

let go (to), *larguer*; to let go the mooring ropes, *larguez les amarres*.

lights (navigation), *feux de route*; riding-light, *feu de position*; masthead, *fanal (m)*.

lighter, *péniche (f)*, *chaland (m)*, *gabare (f)*.

lock, *écluse (f)*; lock sill, *busc (m)*; lock chamber, *sas (m)*.

lower (to), *affaler*.

lubber's line, *ligne de foi*.

mahogany, *acajou (m)*; Gaboon, *okoume (m)*.

mandrel (for lathe), *mandrin (m)*.

marline, *lusin (m)*.

meeting (in a river), *croisment (m)*.

misfire (motor), *rate (m)*.

moor (to), *mouiller*; a mooring, *amarrage (m)*; mooring ring, *boucle (f)*; mooring buoy, *bouée de corps mort*.

mop (a), *guipon (m)*.

mould (a), *gabarit (m)*; moulding, *lisse (f)*.

nails (fine), *semence (f)*.

Nautical Almanac, *connaissance des temps (f)*.

nut (wing), *papillon (m)*.

oakum, *étoupe (f)*.

oil-grooves, *pattes d'araignée (f)*.

overtaking (on river), *trématage*.

paddle-wheel, *aube (f)*.

painter (of boat), *bosse (f)*.

palm (sewing), *paumelle (f)*.

parcel (to), *limander*.

pay out (a rope), *filer*.

pennant (a), *guidon (m)*.

pin (machine), *goupille (f)*; split-pin, *goupille fendue*.

pine, *pin (m)*; pitch-pine, *pitch-pin (m)*.

pintle (of rudder), *aiguillot (m)*.

pitch (tar), *brai (m)*.

pitch (of a screw), *pas (m)*.

plane (for wood), *rabot (m)*.

plug-hole (of boat), *nable (m)*.

plywood, *contre-plaqué (m)*.

pointing (rope's end), *queue de rat (f)*.

port (of call), *relâche (f)*; to call at, *relâcher à*.

'pound' (of canal), *bief (m)*.

pricker (a), *poincon (m)*.

propeller, *hélice (f)*; pitch of a propeller, *pas de l'hélice*.

pump (a), *pompe (f)*; bilge-pump, *pompe de cale*; to prime a pump, *allumer une pompe*; the pump sucks, *la pompe est evantée*.

punch (tool), *etampe (f)*.

rabbet (a), *râblure (f)*.

raft (a), *radeau (m)*.

reach (of a canal), *bief (m)*.

ream (to ream a hole), *fraiser*.

red lead, *minium (m)*.

reef (of rocks), *récif (m), écueil (m)*.

reef-knot, *noeud de plat (m)*.

refit (to), *radouber*; graving-slip, *cale de redoub*.

ribband (a), *lisse (f)*.

rising water (river), *hausse (f)*.

rope, *cordage (m)*; hemp rope, *cordage en chanvre*.

rope-yard, *fil de caret*.

rowlocks, *tolletières (f)*.

sailing directions, *instructions (f)*.

scarf (to), *enter*.

screw (to) (thread), *visser*.

scull (to) (over stern), *godiller*.

scupper (a), *dalot (m)*.

seize (to), *aiguiller*, *genoper*.

seizing (a), *amarrage (m)*; racking-seizing, *amarrage en Portuguese*.

shackle (a), *manille (f)*.

shaft (machine), *arbre (m);* crankshaft, *vilebrequin (m);* cam-shaft, *arbre à cames.*

sheave, *poulie (f), rea (m).*

sheer (of a vessel), *tonture (f);* sheer-strake, *carreau (m), vibord (m).*

sheet-bend, *noeud d'écoute (m).*

shelf (of a ship), *bauquière (f).*

shelf (a reef), *écueil (m).*

ship (a), *bâtiment (m);* man-of-war, *vaisseau (m);* merchantman, *navaire (m).*

ship-broker, *courtier maritime (m).*

shoals, *haut-fonds (m), bas-fonds (m).* (See note under 'bas-fonds'.)

sill (of a lock), *busc (m).*

sling (to), *élinguer.*

sling (a), *élingue (f).*

slipway, *cale (f).*

sluice (a), *vanne (f).*

solder (to), *souder;* soft-solder, *souder à l'etain.*

splice (to), *épisser;* eye-splice, *épissure à oeil.*

spun-yarn, *bitford (m).*

stanchion (a), *montant (m).*

starter (motor), *démarreur (m).*

stem (of ship), *étrave (f).*

stern-post, *étambot (m).*

stock (of anchor), *jas (m).*

stock (and die), *filière (f).*

strainer (a), *crépine (f), passoire (f).*

strake (a), *virure (f);* garboard-strake, *galbord (m)*

strand (of a rope), *tournon (m).*

stringer (a), *lisse (f).*

strop (a), *erse (f), élingue (f);* selvagee strop, *erse en bitord.*

stuffing-box, *presse-étoupe (f).*

swab (a), *faubert (m).*

switch (electrical). *interrupteur (m).*

tack (to), *louvoyer.*

tacks (fine nails), *semence (f).*

tackle, *palan (m);* falls of a tackle, *garants (m);* luff tackle, *palan à croc;* handy-billy, *palan de dimanche;* chain-block, *palan à chaine;* to rig a tackle, *greer un palan.*

tang (of a file), *queue (f).*

tar (coal), *goudron (m);* Stockholm tar, *goudron à bois;* pitch, *brai (m).*

tarpaulin, *prelart (m), bâche goudronnée (f).*

thimble (a), *cosse (f).*

tidal wave (river), *mascaret (m), ras de marée (m).*

timber (frame of ship), *couple (m).*

timber-hitch, *noeud de bois (m).*

tot (a), *boujaron (m);* a tot of rum, *un boujaron du rhum.*

tow (to) (by boat), *remorquer.*

towage, *halage (m);* tow-path, *chemin de halage;* tow-rope, *faux-bras (m);* tow-rope (on river), *trait (m).*

training-wall (river), *digue (f), épine (f);* facines, wickerwork, *clayonnage (m).*

truck (of a mast), *pomme (f).*

tug-boat, *remorqueur (m);* paddle-wheel tug-boat, *remorqueur à l'aubes;* to tow alongside, *remorqueur à couple.*

turn (a) (of a rope), *tour;* a round turn, *un tour mort.*

turn (a) (or turning), *viremont (m).*

twine, *fil (m);* sail twine, *fil à voile.*

underwriter, *assureur (m).*

unlay (to), *décommetre.*

upstream, *amont;* above bridge, *en amont du pont.*

variation (of compass), *déclinaison (f).*

veer (to), *filer.*

vessel (ship), *bâtiment (m);* man-of-war, *vaisseau (m);* merchantman, *navaire (m).*

wall (training in river), *digue (f), épine (f),* facines, wickerwork, *clayonnage (m).*

warp (to), *touer;* warping, *touage (m).*

warp (a), *faux-bras (m), grelin (m).*

washer (a), *rondelle (f).*

watershed (the), *versant (m), ligne de partage (f).*

weir (a), *barrage (m), déversoir (m).*

weld (to), *souder à l'autogene (oxyacet).*

wheel-house, *kiosque de timonerie (f).*

whip (to) (a rope), *surlier.*

whipping (a), *serliure (f).*

winch (a), *treuil (m).*

wire (metal), *fil (m);* iron wire, *fil de fer;* brass wire, *fil de laiton;* copper wire, *de cuivre rouge;* ignition wire, *fil de bougie.*

yarn (rope), *fil de caret (f).*

PLANS

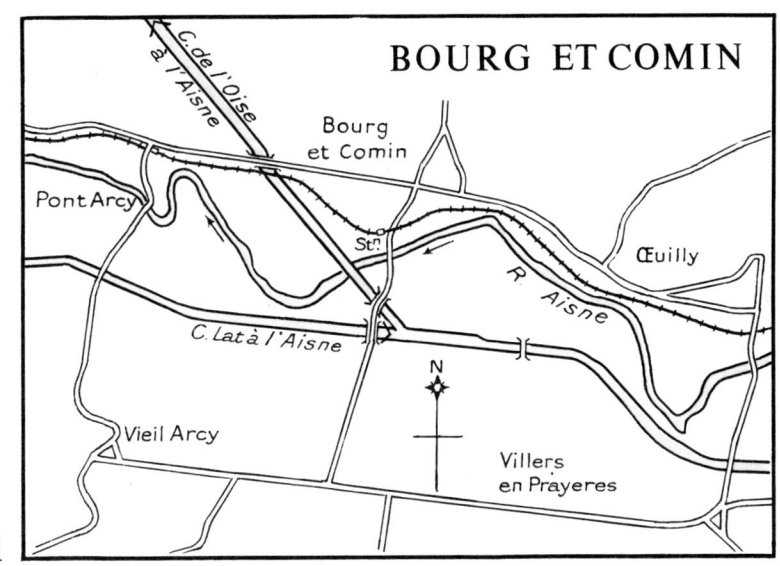

BOURG ET COMIN

C. de l'Oise à l'Aisne

Bourg et Comin

Pont Arcy

Stn.

Œuilly

R. Aisne

C. Lat à l'Aisne

N

Vieil Arcy

Villers en Prayeres

1

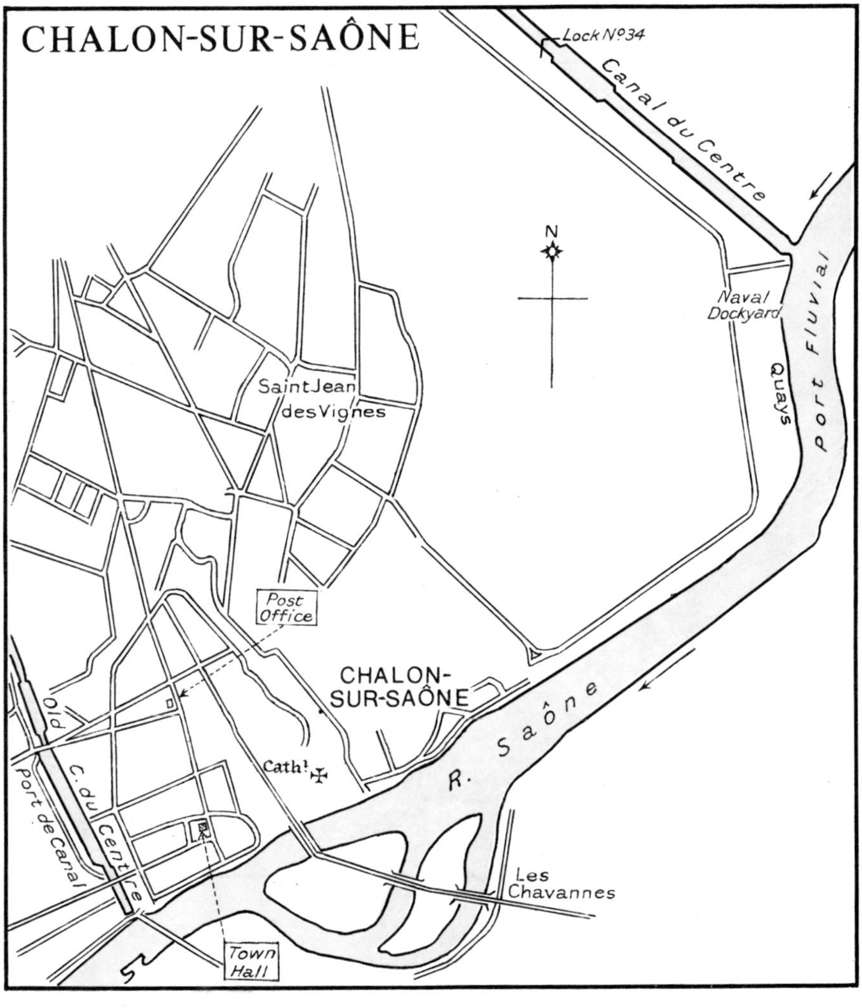

CHALON-SUR-SAÔNE

Lock Nº 34

Canal du Centre

Naval Dockyard

N

Port Fluvial

Saint Jean des Vignes

Quays

Post Office

CHALON-SUR-SAÔNE

R. Saône

Cathl.

Old Port de Canal

C. du Centre

Les Chavannes

Town Hall

2

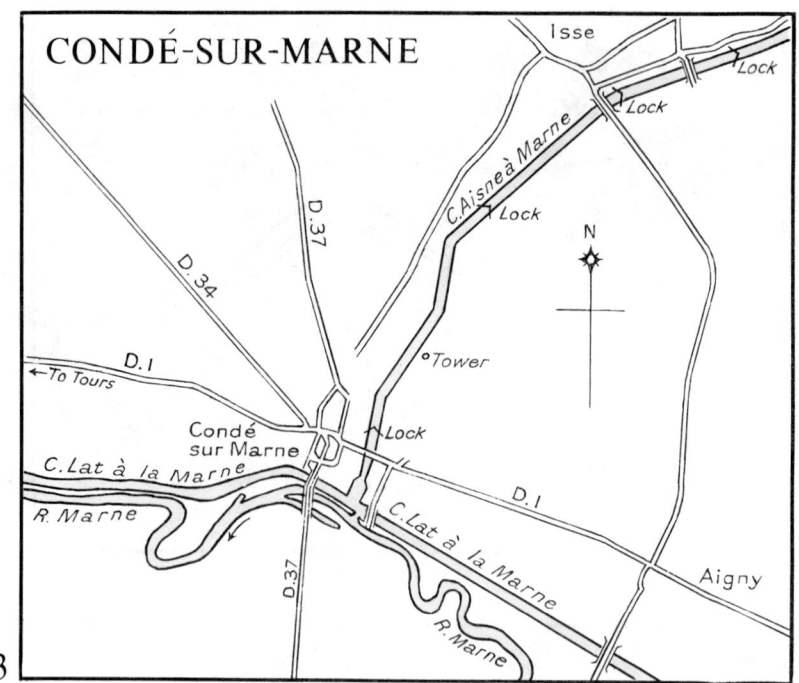

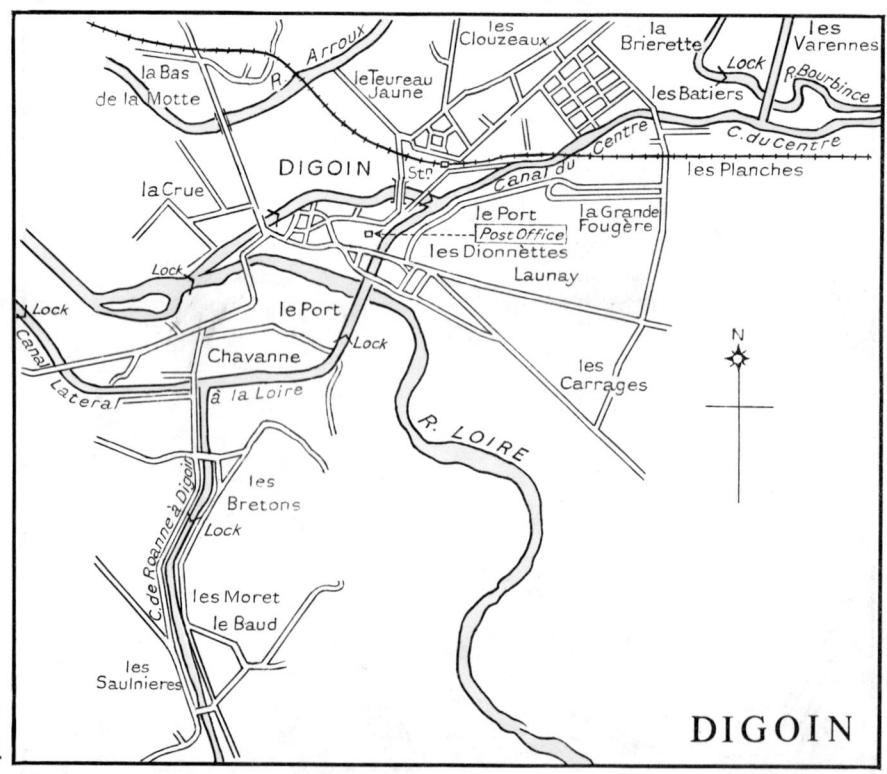

DIJON

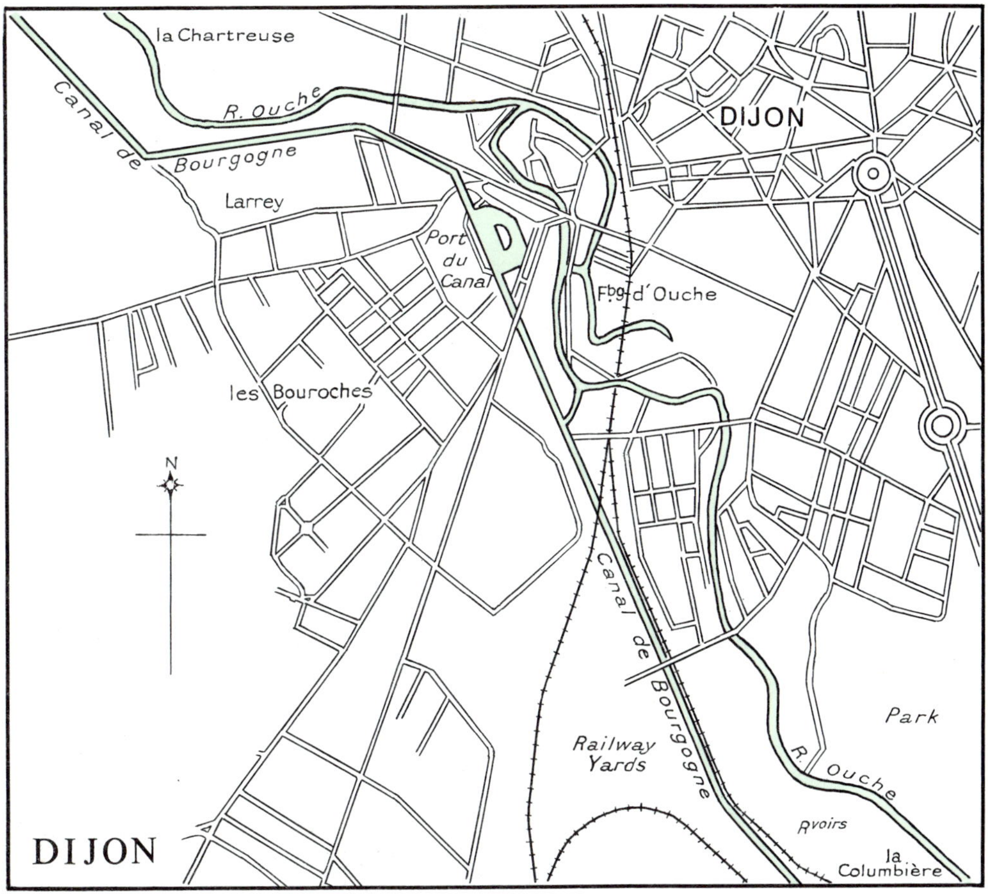

la Chartreuse

Canal de Bourgogne

R. Ouche

DIJON

Larrey

Port du Canal

Fbg d'Ouche

les Bouroches

N

Park

Railway Yards

Canal de Bourgogne

R. Ouche

Rvoirs

la Columbière

5

DIJON

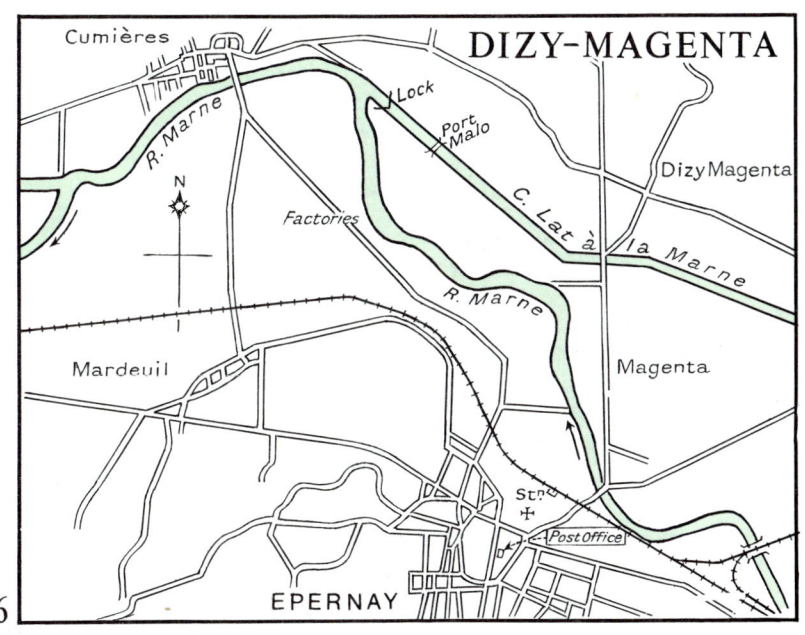

DIZY-MAGENTA

Cumières

R. Marne

Lock

Port Malo

Dizy Magenta

N

Factories

C. Lat à la Marne

R. Marne

Mardeuil

Magenta

St⁺

Post Office

6

EPERNAY

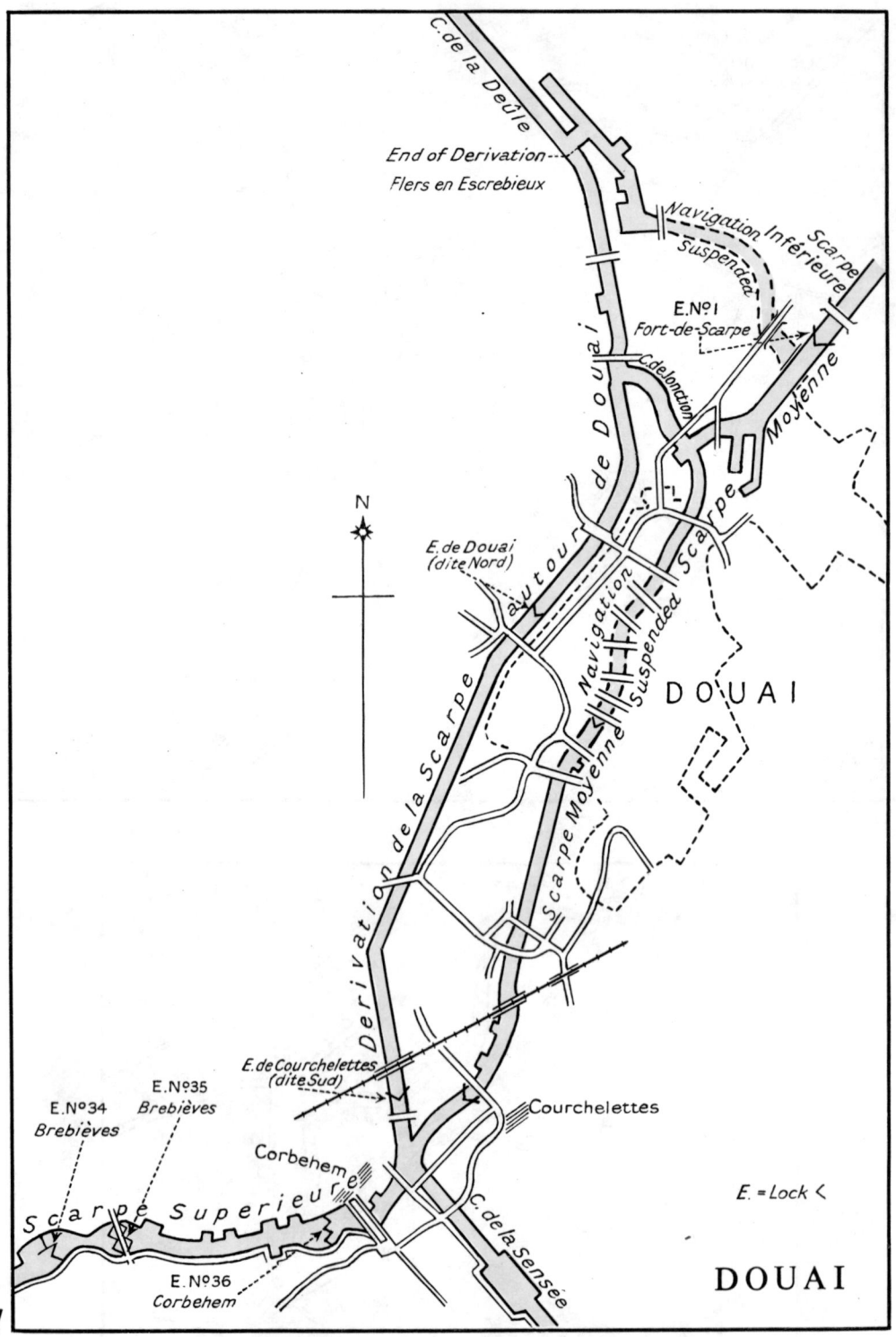

C. de la Deûle

End of Derivation-
Flers en Escrebieux

Navigation Inférieure
Suspendée

Scarpe

E.Nº1
Fort-de-Scarpe

C. de Jonction

Scarpe Moyenne

autour de Douai

E. de Douai
(dite Nord)

Navigation Moyenne Suspended

DOUAI

Scarpe Moyenne

Derivation de la Scarpe

E. de Courchelettes
(dite Sud)

Courchelettes

E. Nº34
Brebièves

E. Nº35
Brebièves

Corbeheme

Scarpe Superieure

E. = Lock <

E. Nº36
Corbehem

C. de la Sensée

DOUAI

7

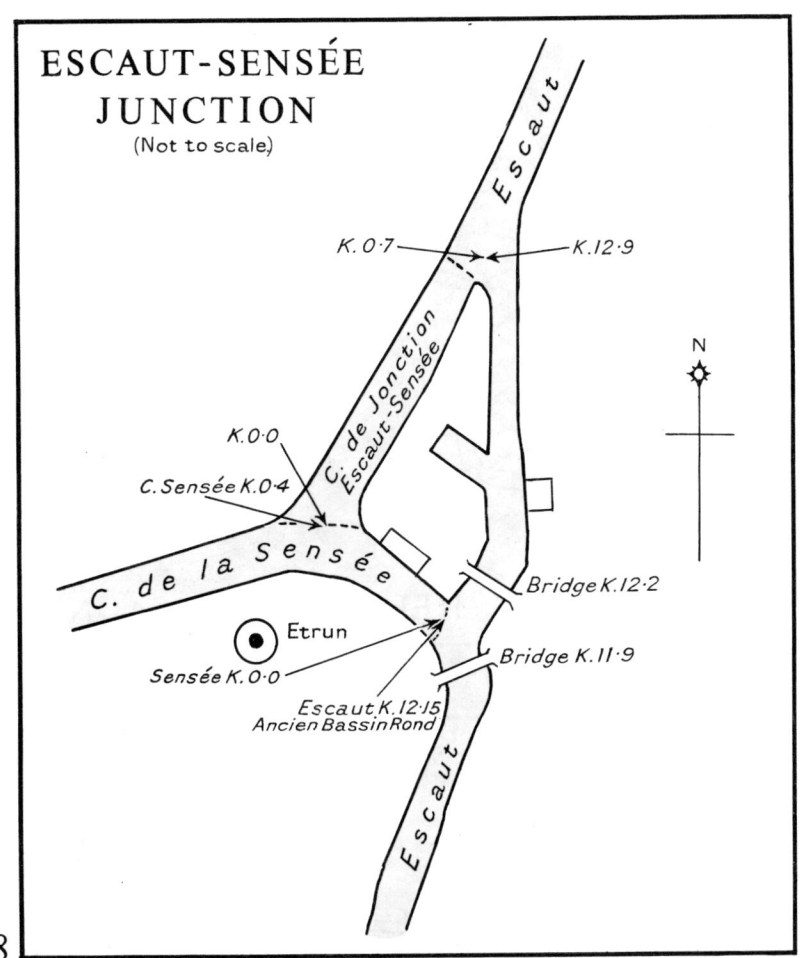

ESCAUT-SENSÉE
JUNCTION
(Not to scale)

Escaut

K.0·7   K.12·9

C. de Jonction
Escaut-Sensée

N

K.0·0

C. Sensée K.0·4

C. de la Sensée

Bridge K.12·2

Etrun

Bridge K.11·9

Sensée K.0·0

Escaut K.12·15
Ancien Bassin Rond

Escaut

8

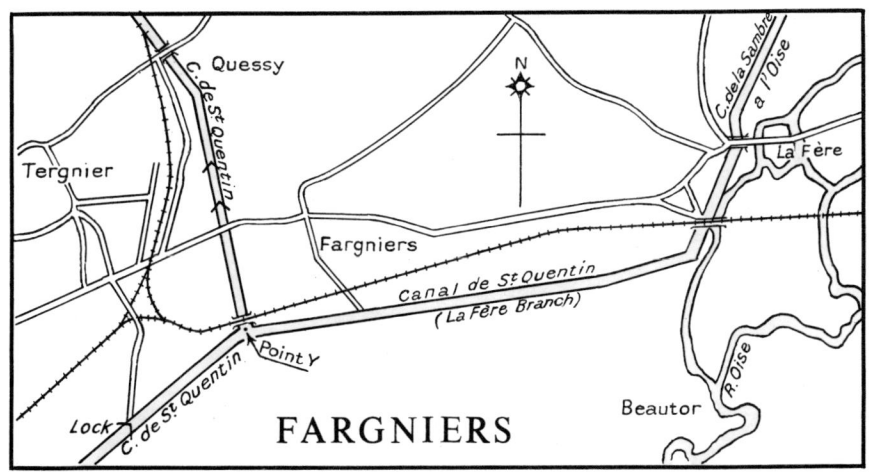

Quessy

C. de St Quentin

Tergnier

Fargniers

Canal de St Quentin
(La Fère Branch)

Point Y

Lock

C. de St Quentin

FARGNIERS

N

C. de la Sambre
a l'Oise

La Fère

Beautor

R. Oise

9

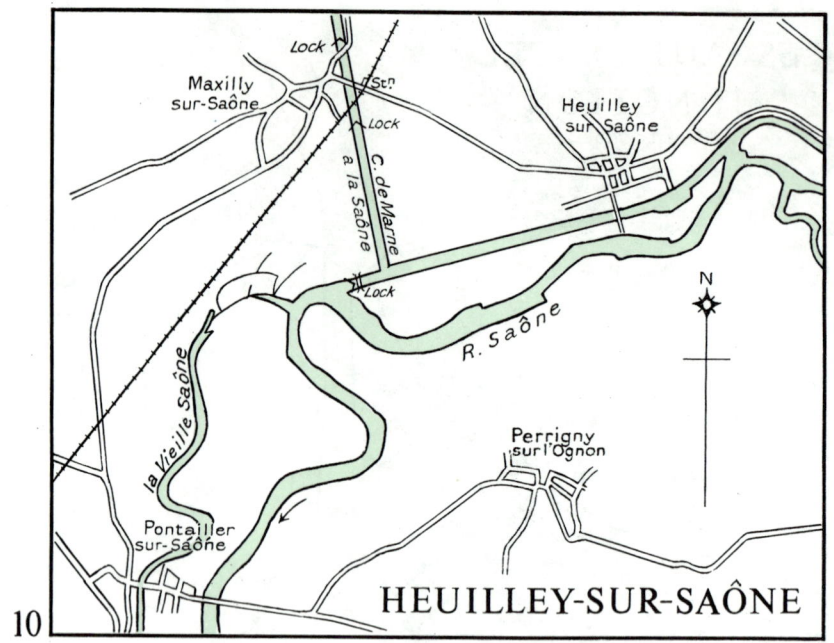

10 **HEUILLEY-SUR-SAÔNE**

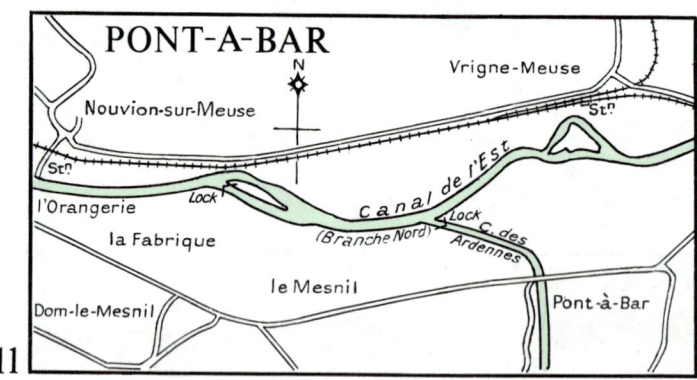

11 **PONT-A-BAR**

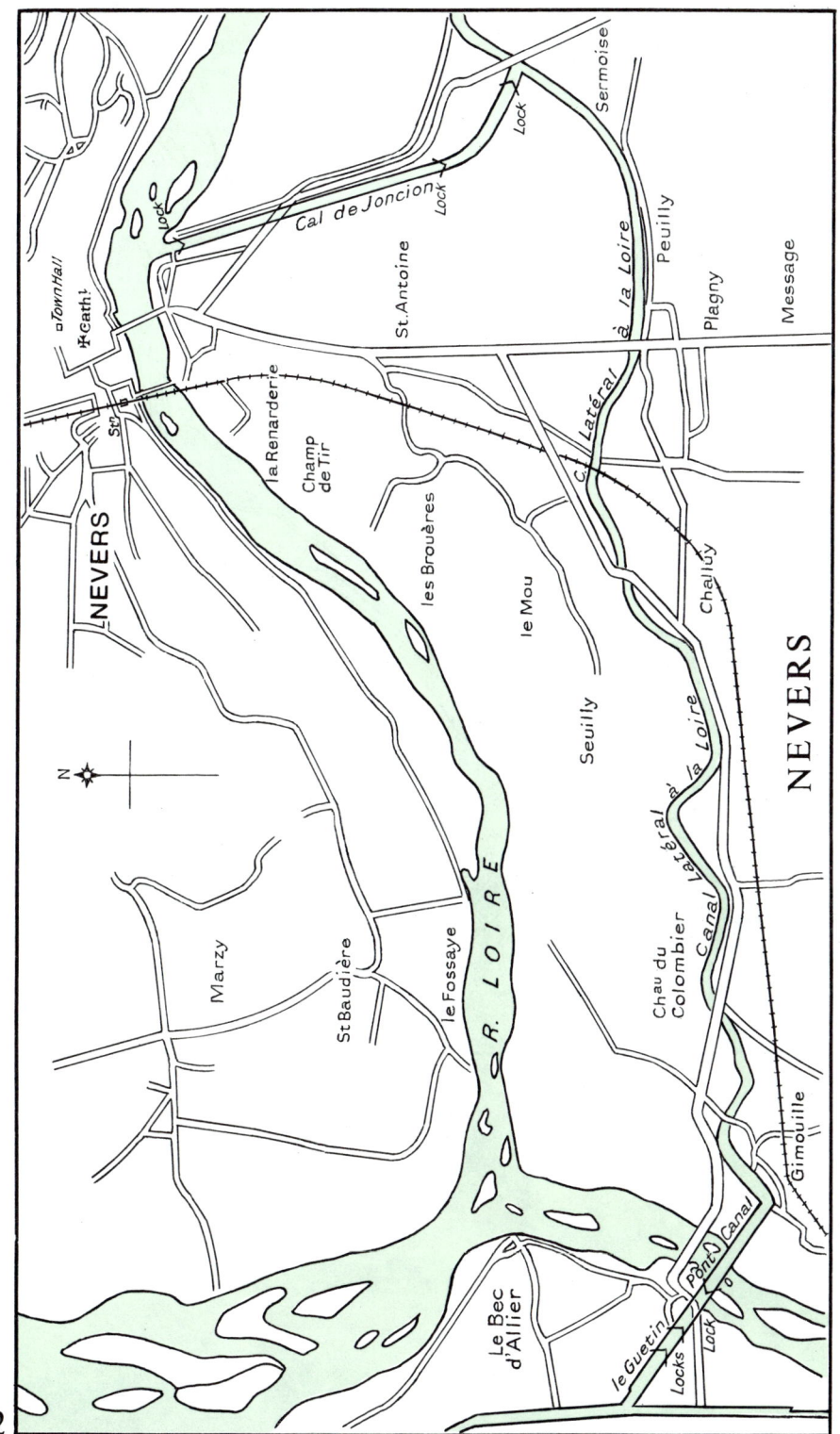

NEVERS

NEVERS

R. LOIRE

Le Bec d'Allier

le Guetin

Locks

Lock

Lock

Pont-Canal

Gimouille

Canal latéral à la Loire

Chau du Colombier

Canal latéral à la Loire

Seuilly

le Mou

Challuy

les Brouères

Champ de Tir

la Renarderie

St.

le Fossaye

St Baudière

Marzy

St.Antoine

Cal de Joncion

Lock

Lock

Sermoise

Peuilly

Plagny

Message

Cath.

Town Hall

N

12

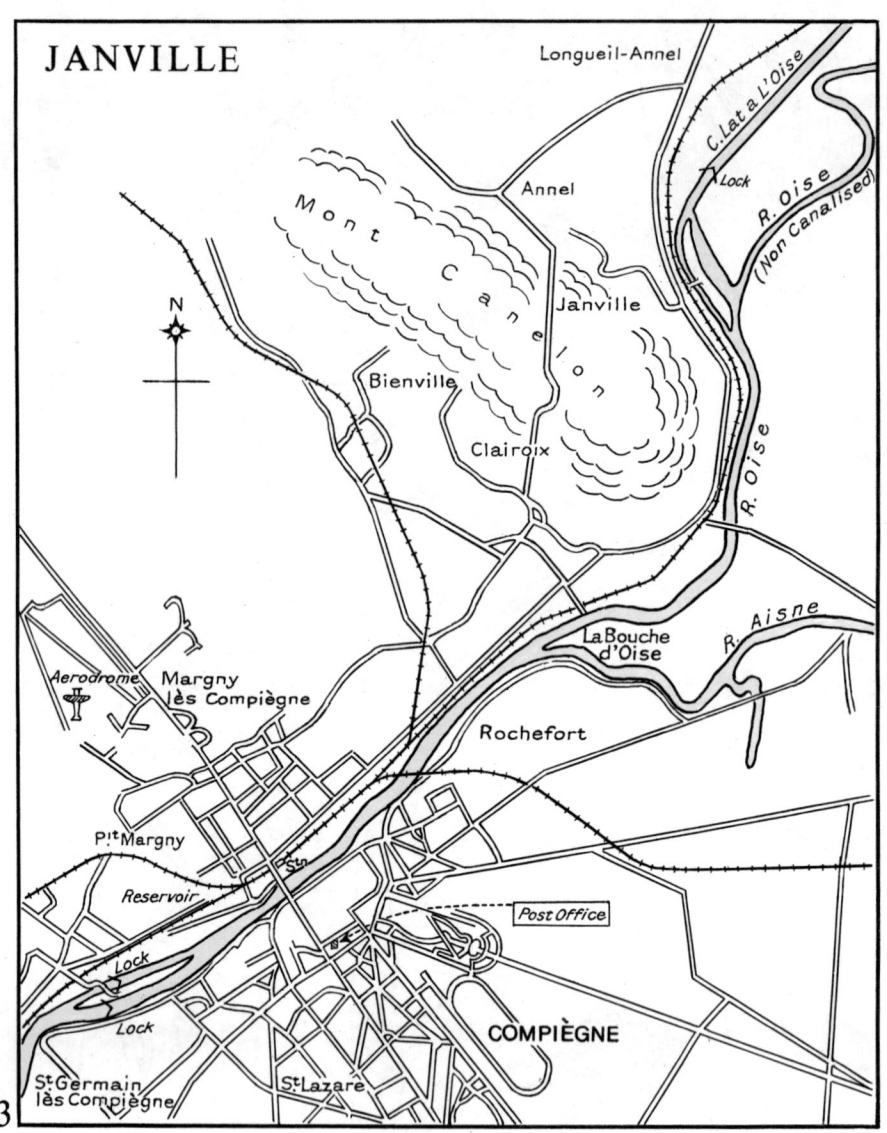

JANVILLE

Longueil-Annel

C. Lat à L'Oise

Lock

R. Oise
(Non Canalised)

Annel

Mont Canelon

N

Janville

Bienville

R. Oise

Clairoix

R. Aisne

La Bouche
d'Oise

Aerodrome Margny
lès Compiègne

Rochefort

P.te Margny

Stn

Reservoir

Post Office

Lock

Lock

COMPIÈGNE

St Germain
lès Compiègne

St Lazare

13

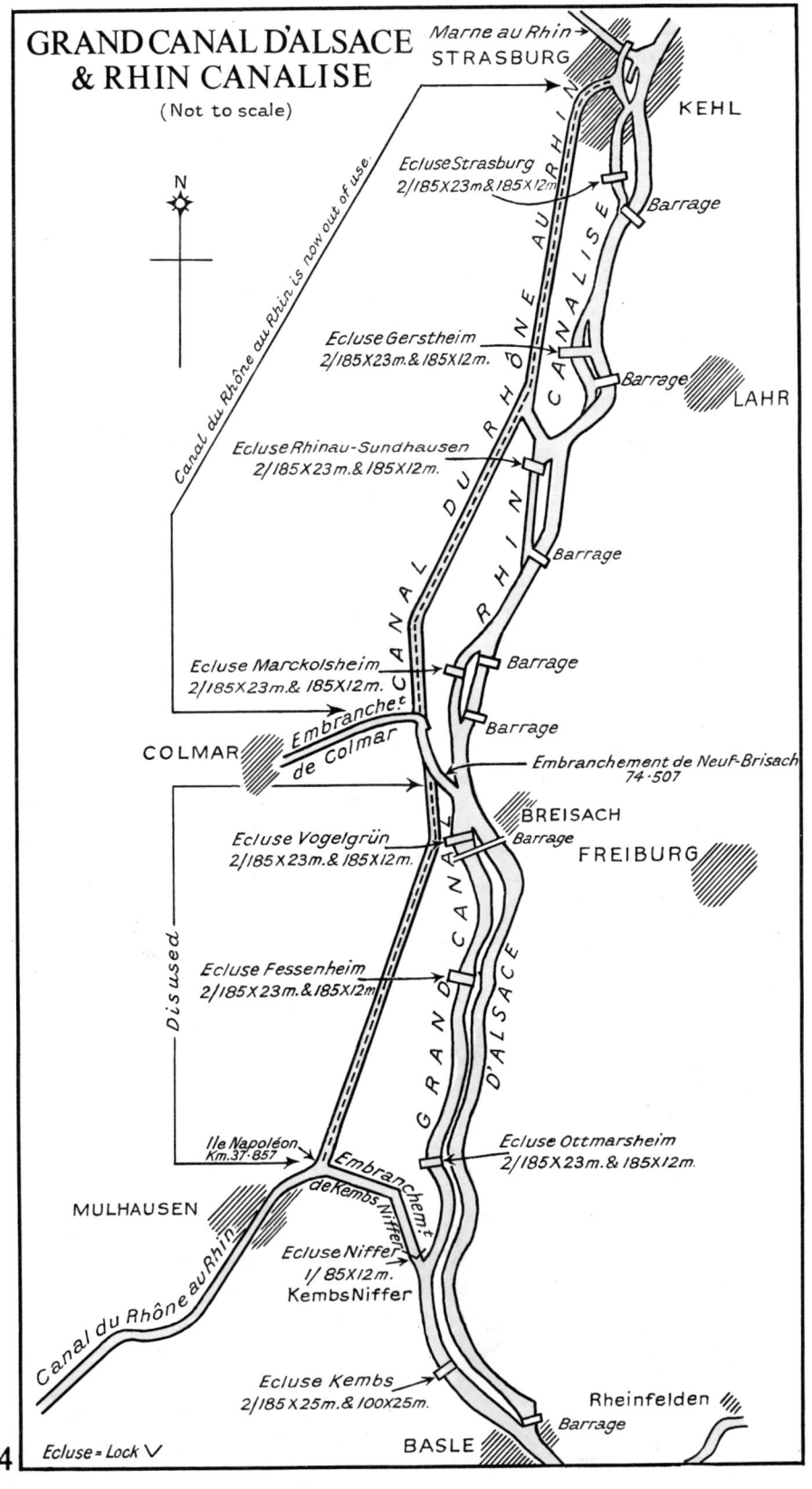

GRAND CANAL D'ALSACE
& RHIN CANALISE
(Not to scale)

N

Marne au Rhin →
STRASBURG

KEHL

Canal du Rhône au Rhin is now out of use

Ecluse Strasburg
2/185 x 23m & 185 x 12m.

Barrage

Ecluse Gerstheim
2/185 x 23m. & 185 x 12m.

Barrage

LAHR

Ecluse Rhinau-Sundhausen
2/185 x 23 m. & 185 x 12 m.

Barrage

Ecluse Marckolsheim
2/185 x 23m.& 185 x 12m.

Barrage

COLMAR Embranche.t de Colmar

Barrage

Embranchement de Neuf-Brisach
74·507

BREISACH

Ecluse Vogelgrün
2/185 x 23m.& 185 x 12m.

Barrage

FREIBURG

Disused

Ecluse Fessenheim
2/185 x 23m.& 185 x 12m

Ecluse Ottmarsheim
2/185 x 23 m. & 185 x 12m.

Ile Napoléon
Km.37·857

Embranchem.t de Kembs Niffer

MULHAUSEN

Ecluse Niffer
1/ 85 x 12 m.
Kembs Niffer

Canal du Rhône au Rhin

Ecluse Kembs
2/185 x 25m.& 100 x 25m.

Rheinfelden

Barrage

BASLE

14 Ecluse = Lock ∨

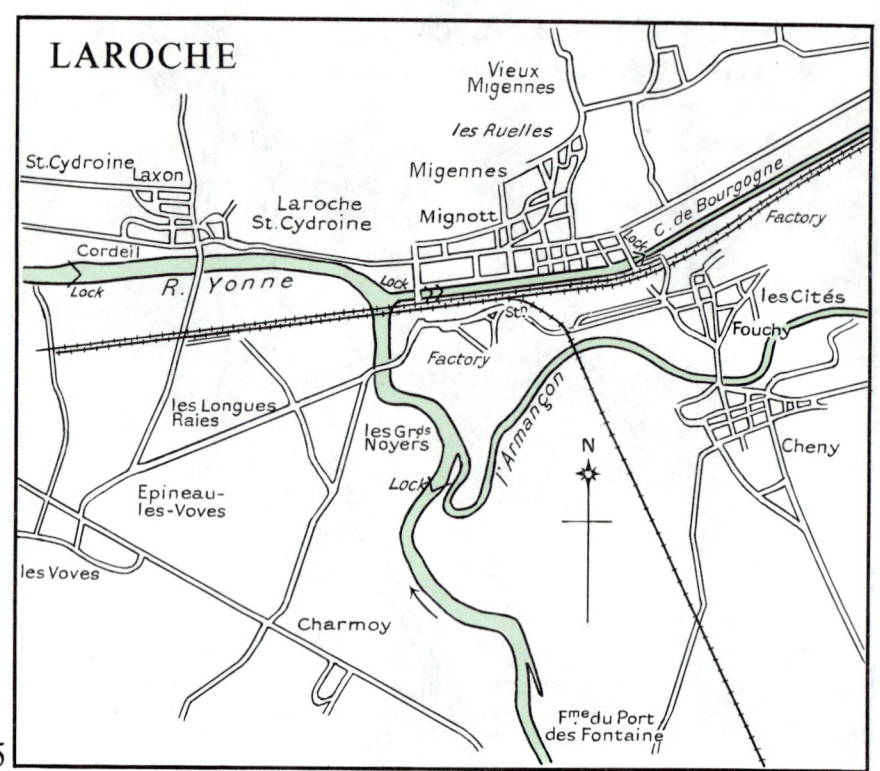

LAROCHE

Vieux Migennes

les Ruelles

St.Cydroine
Laxon

Migennes

Laroche
St.Cydroine

Mignott

C. de Bourgogne

Factory

Cordeil

Lock

R. Yonne

Lock

St?

les Cités

Fouchy

Factory

les Longues
Raies

les Grds
Noyers

l'Armançon

N

Cheny

Lock

Epineau-
les-Voves

les Voves

Charmoy

Fme du Port
des Fontaine

15

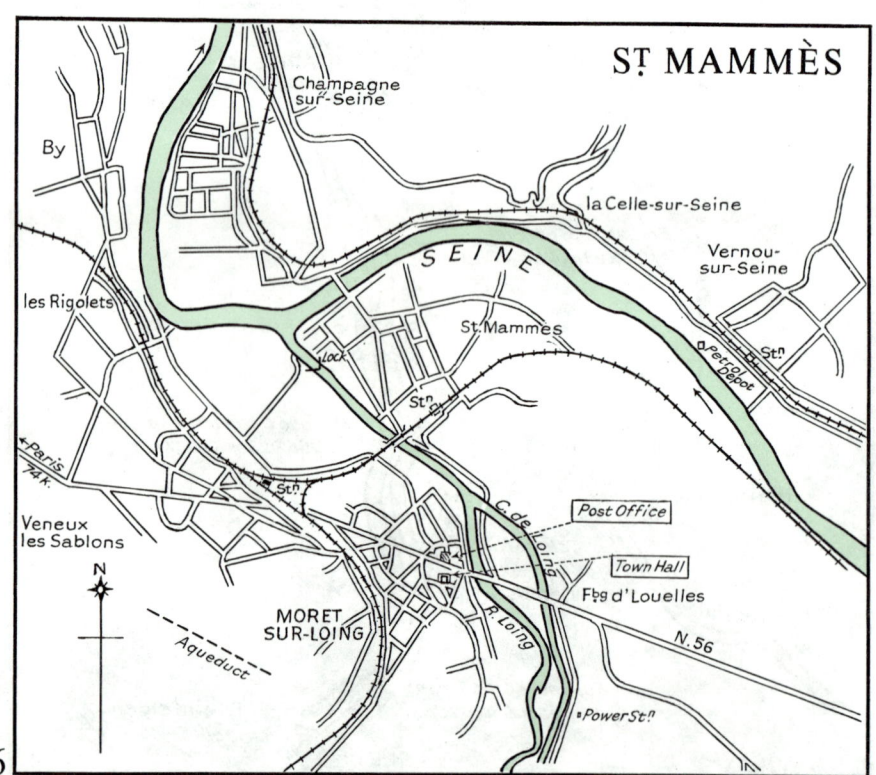

ST MAMMÈS

Champagne
sur-Seine

By

la Celle-sur-Seine

Vernou-
sur-Seine

les Rigolets

SEINE

St?

St. Mammes

Petit Dépôt

St?

←Paris
74 k.

Lock

St?

Post Office

C. de Loing

St?

Veneux
les Sablons

N

Town Hall

Fbg d'Louelles

MORET
SUR-LOING

R. Loing

N. 56

Aqueduct

Power St?

16

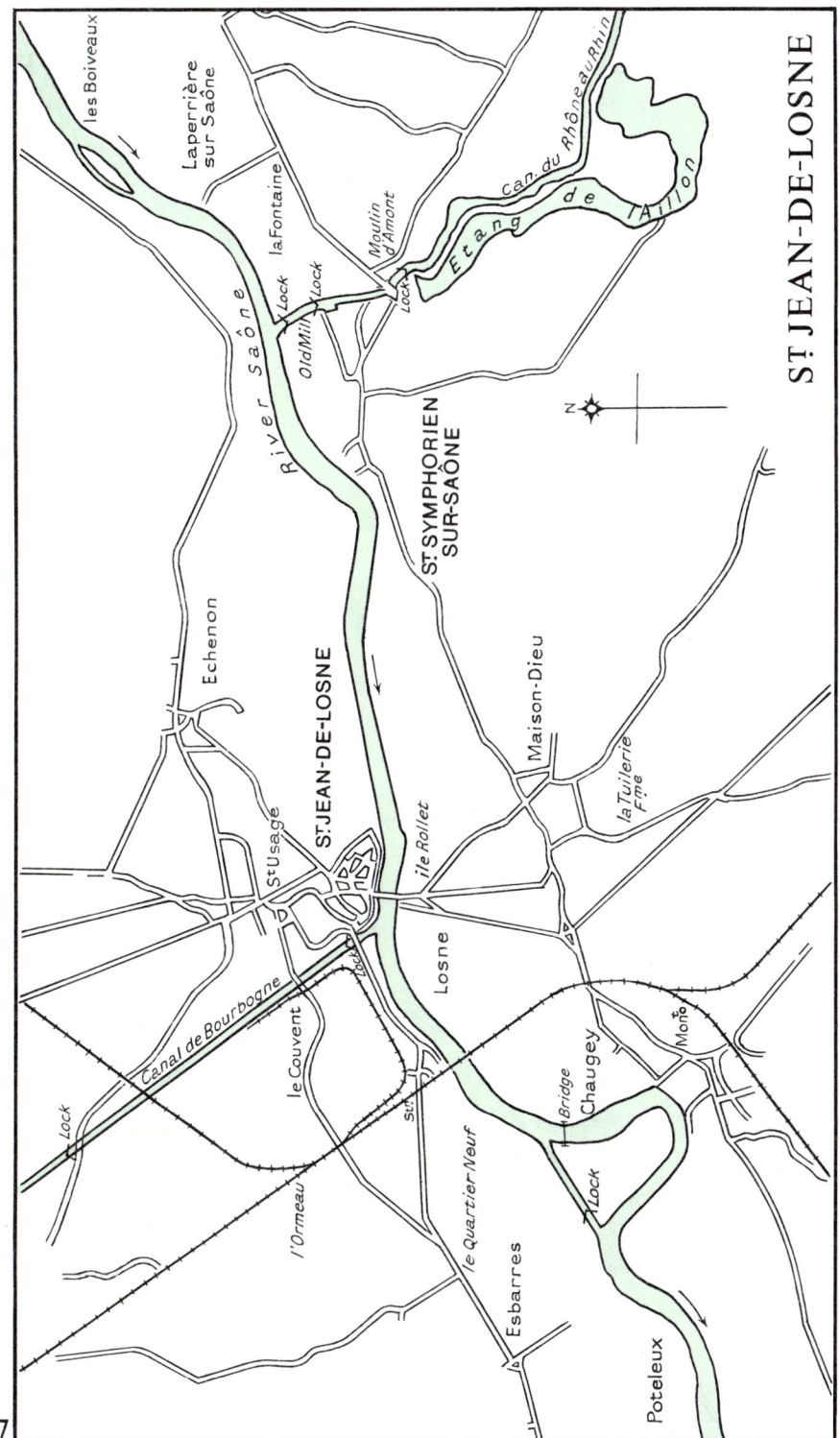

ST JEAN-DE-LOSNE

les Boiveaux

Laperrière
sur Saône

River Saône

laFontaine
Lock

Old Mill Lock

Moulin
d'Amont
Lock

Can. du Rhône au Rhin

Etang de l'Aillon

ST SYMPHORIEN
SUR-SAÔNE

N

Echenon

ST JEAN-DE-LOSNE

St Usage

ile Rollet

Maison-Dieu

la Tuilerie
Fme

Losne

Canal de Bourbogne

le Couvent

Lock

Lock

Bridge

Chaugey

Mono

l'Ormeau

le Quartier Neuf

Esbarres

Lock

Poteleux

17

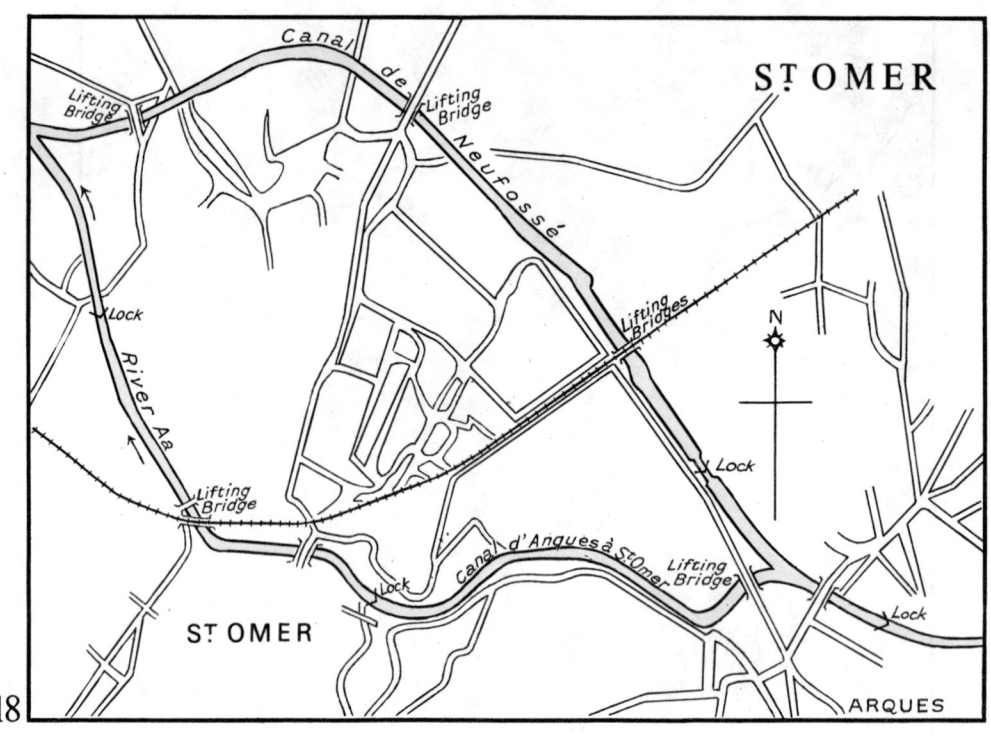

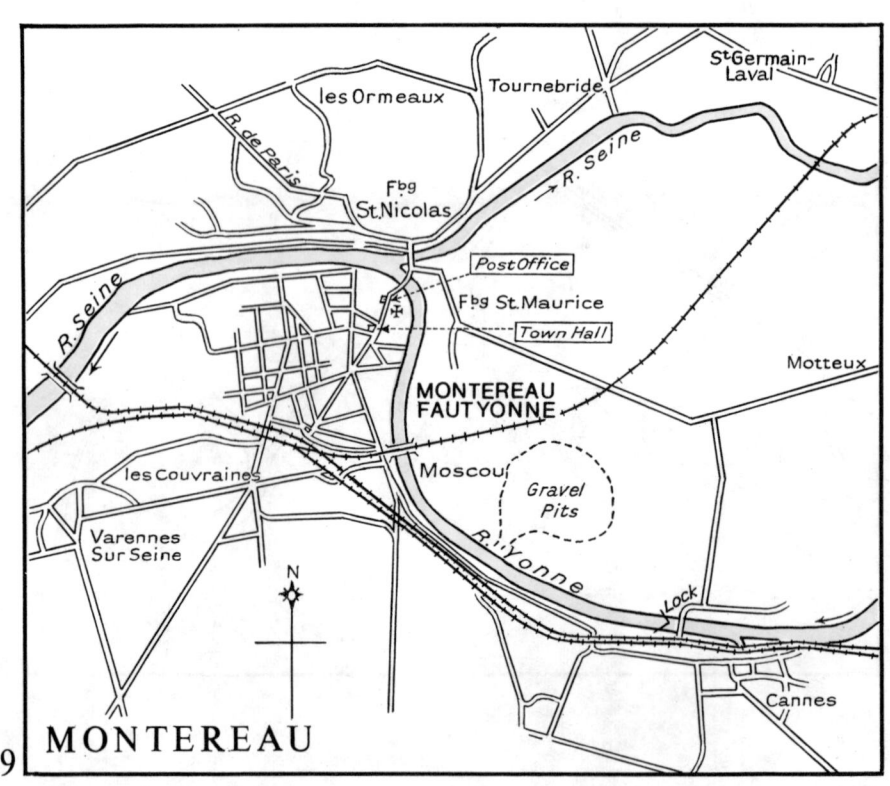

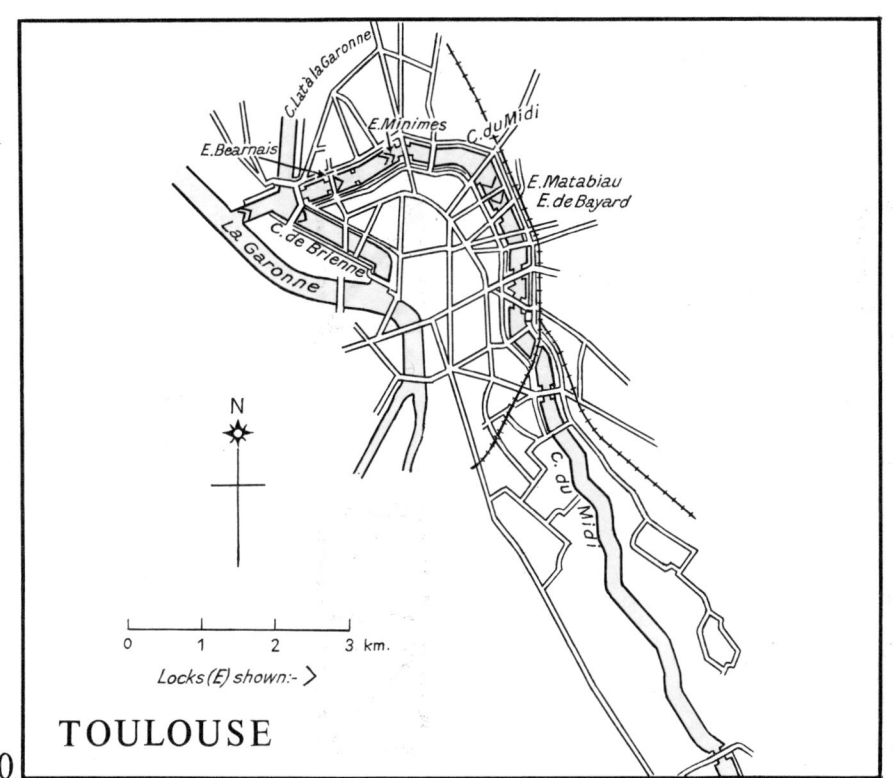

C.Lat à la Garonne

E.Minimes

C.du Midi

E.Bearnais

E.Matabiau
E.de Bayard

La Garonne

C. de Brienne

N

C. du Midi

0   1   2   3 km.

Locks (E) shown:- ⟩

TOULOUSE

20

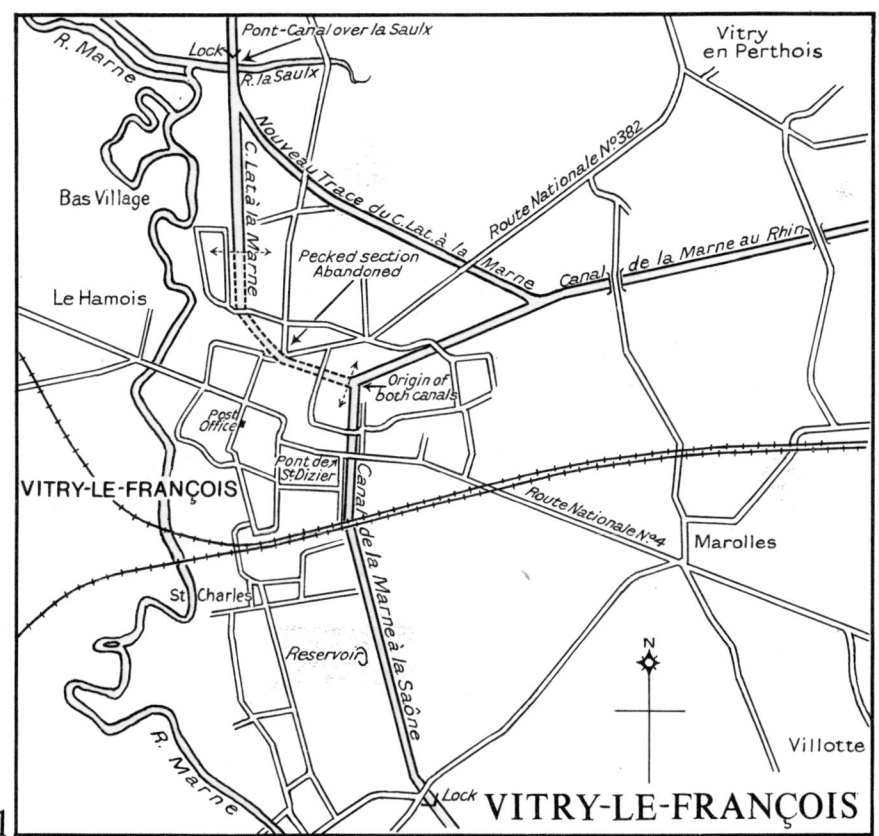

R. Marne

Pont-Canal over la Saulx

Lock

R. la Saulx

Vitry
en Perthois

Nouveau Tracé du C. Lat. à la Marne

Route Nationale No 382

C. Lat à la Marne

Bas Village

Pecked section
Abandoned

Canal de la Marne au Rhin

Le Hamois

Origin of
both canals

Post
Office

VITRY-LE-FRANÇOIS

Pont de
St-Dizier

Canal de la Marne à la Saône

Route Nationale No 4

Marolles

St Charles

Reservoir

N

Villotte

R. Marne

Lock

VITRY-LE-FRANÇOIS

21

INTERNATIONAL TRAFFIC SIGNS ON RIVERS
(In France only in force on la Basse-Seine)

SIGNALS ON RIVER BANKS

 Keep to right
(left if signal is reversed.)

 No overtaking

 No crossing and overtaking

 End of overtaking prohibition

 Maximum speed limit

 Special care required

 Give sound signal

 Anchoring or "driving" with anchor forbidden

 Left hand of channel

 Right hand of channel

SIGNALS AT BRIDGES AND BARRAGES

By Day	By Night

 Passage forbidden

 Passage forbidden

Two-way navigable channel

Two-way navigable channel

 One-way navigable channel

 One-way navigable channel

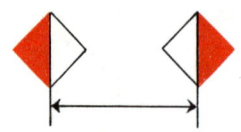 Pass within these limits

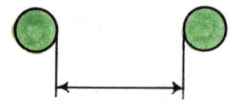 Pass within these limits

NOTICE BOARDS SHOWING NAVIGABLE CHANNELS

 Left bank

 Right bank

Note *Those channels not provided with signals may be used by navigators at their own risk and peril. A similar warning is given to those branches not open to commercial navigation.*

INDEX

'j' *preceding a name means* 'junction with'. s=sur; lat.=latéral; St(e)=Saint(e).